Penance in Medieval Euro

Penance has traditionally been viewed exclusively as the domain of church history but penance and confession also had important social functions in medieval society. In this book, Rob Meens comprehensively reassesses the evidence from Late Antiquity to the thirteenth century, employing a broad range of sources, including letters, documentation of saints' lives, visions, liturgical texts, monastic rules and conciliar legislation from across Europe. Recent discoveries have unearthed fascinating new evidence, established new relationships between key texts and given more attention to the manuscripts in which penitential books are found. Many of these discoveries and new approaches are revealed here for the first time to a general audience. Providing a full and up-to-date overview of penitential literature during the period, Meens sets the rituals of penance and confession in their social contexts, offering the first introduction to this fundamental feature of medieval religion and society for more than fifty years.

ROB MEENS is Lecturer in Medieval History at the University of Utrecht. He has published extensively in the field of medieval religious culture with a particular emphasis on penance and his publications include *The Bobbio Missal: Liturgy and Religious Culture in Merovingian Gaul* (co-edited with Y. Hen, 2004) and *Texts and Identities in the Early Middle Ages* (with R. Corradini, 2006). He is general editor of the series *Paenitentialia Franciae, Italiae et Hispaniae Saeculi VIII–XI* of Corpus Christianorum.

Penance in Medieval Europe, 600–1200

Rob Meens

CAMBRIDGE
UNIVERSITY PRESS

CAMBRIDGE
UNIVERSITY PRESS

University Printing House, Cambridge CB2 8BS, United Kingdom

Cambridge University Press is part of the University of Cambridge.

It furthers the University's mission by disseminating knowledge in the pursuit of education, learning and research at the highest international levels of excellence.

www.cambridge.org
Information on this title: www.cambridge.org/9780521693110

First published 2014

Printed in the United Kingdom by Clays, St Ives plc

A catalogue record for this publication is available from the British Library

Library of Congress Cataloguing in Publication data
Meens, Rob, 1959–
Penance in medieval Europe, 600–1200 / Rob Meens.
    pages   cm
Includes bibliographical references and index.
ISBN 978-0-521-87212-6 (Hardback) – ISBN 978-0-521-69311-0 (Paperback)
1. Penance–History–Europe.   2. Europe–Church history–600–1500.
I. Title.
BV840.M44 2014
264′.020860940902–dc23   2014007618

ISBN 978-0-521-87212-6 Hardback
ISBN 978-0-521-69311-0 Paperback

For Maria

Contents

List of figures   *page* viii
Acknowledgments   ix

1   Introduction   1

2   The late antique legacy   12

3   A new beginning? Penitential practice in the insular world   37

4   Insular texts on the move: penance in Francia and England   70

5   Penance and the Carolingian Reforms   101

6   New penitential territories: the tenth and eleventh centuries   140

7   The twelfth century   190

    Conclusion   214

    Appendix 1   *The manuscripts of Theodore's penitential*   226
    Appendix 2   *The manuscripts of the* Excarpsus Cummeani   229
    Appendix 3   *The manuscripts of the Bede and Egbert penitentials*   231
    Appendix 4   *The manuscripts of Halitgar's penitential*   234
    Sources   238
    Bibliography   247
    General index   272
    Manuscript index   279

Figures

The author and publishers acknowledge the following sources of copyright material and are grateful for the permissions granted. While every effort has been made, it has not always been possible to identify the sources of all material used, or to trace all copyright holders. If any omissions are brought to our notice, we will be happy to include the appropriate acknowledgments on reprinting.

1 Ms. St Petersburg, National Library, Cod. lat. Oct. v.1.5,
   f. 10v: St Peter drives away the demons (*Visio Baronti*).
   Reproduced by kind permission of the Russian
   National Library.   *page* 86
2 Ms. Vienna, Österreichische Nationalbibliothek, Ms. lat.
   2195: the beginning of Theodore's penitential.
   Reproduced by permission of Österreichische
   Nationalbibliothek.   92
3 *P. Egberti*, Vat. Pal. lat. 554, f. 5r: the beginning of the Egbert
   penitential. Reproduced by permission of the Vatican
   Apostolic Library.   98
4 Ms. El Escorial, Real Biblioteca, Ms.d.I. 2 (Codex Vigilanus),
   f. 428r: illustration containing representations of Visigothic
   kings and a queen, with beneath them the scribe Vigilanus
   accompanied by a socius and a disciple.   166
5 Ms. Vatican Library, Vat. lat. 1339, f. 12r, depiction
   of canonical authorities. In the middle is the Irish author
   Cummean. Reproduced by permission of the Vatican
   Apostolic Library.   178

Acknowledgments

My interest in medieval penance goes back a long way. During this long period of studying medieval penance I received a lot of enthusiastic support from many friends, teachers, colleagues and students, too many to mention them all here. Yet, there are some that I really need to thank for their always generous support. My journey into medieval penitential landscapes started under the stimulating guidance of Mayke de Jong, who has always remained a trustworthy guide and spiritual mentor. The year I spent at the university of Bonn in 1986–7 was in many ways a formative period during which the late Raymund Kottje proved to be a generous and learned host. This was also the time that I came to know Ludger Körntgen (now in Mainz), who has remained a close colleague and friend until today.

At the History Department of Utrecht University, I have always received generous support from my fellow historians as well as my colleagues in medieval studies. I shall name only Wolfert van Egmond, Bram van den Hoven, Marco Mostert, Giselle de Nie, Janneke Raaijmakers, Carine van Rhijn, Els Rose and Henk Teunis for their interest and support, but many others gave support as well. Between 2002 and 2006 the Dutch Organization of Scientific Research (NWO) generously funded a five-year programme for the study of penitential texts, a project that has contributed substantially to the present book. Adriaan Gaastra, Marjolein Saan, Carine van Rhijn and Gerda Heydemann (Vienna) actively contributed to this project. Over the years I also profited a lot from the meetings of the research group 'Texts and Identities', founded in 1997 by Mayke de Jong, Rosamond McKitterick, Walter Pohl and Ian Wood, which has now almost grown into a venerable institution with its annual contributions to the International Medieval Congress in Leeds. The benevolent sphere, perfectly suited for frank intellectual discourse, created by these founding fathers and mothers (later joined by Regine Le Jan and her students), was always a stimulus for further thinking and research. It is wonderful to see that this research group is still thriving and that so many talented young students are participating in it. I hope they profit from it as much as I did.

Over the years many have contributed to the genesis of this book by sharing their thoughts with me, by sending their publications or by providing access to unpublished material. I hope that those not mentioned will understand that I cannot refer to them all here. Among those who contributed in this way to the genesis of this study are Arnold Angenendt, Martin Brett, Peter Brown, Wendy Davies, Albrecht Diem, Roy Flechner, Michael Glatthaar, Joe Goering, Sarah Hamilton, Wilfried Hartmann, Yitzhak Hen, Atria Larson, Paul Meyvaert, the late Hubert Mordek, Jinty Nelson, Roger Reynolds, Jason Taliadoros and Anton Weiler. For reading the manuscript or parts thereof, I want to thank Julia Helmus, Mayke de Jong, Ludger Körntgen and Kevin Uhalde. Their comments and criticism were extremely helpful as were those made by the anonymous reader for Cambridge University Press. They have given me much to think about, but as always it is I who remain responsible for any remaining faults or errors. I hope they are not too numerous.

Being married to a husband writing a book surely can be a kind of penance in itself. For being able to cope with such a husband and for creating a warm home for me and our three children, Anna, Mark and Tom, over all those years, I cannot thank my wife Maria enough. She alone knows how much I owe to her. For that reason, I dedicate this book to her.

1   Introduction

In the late seventh century an anonymous compiler of a penitential handbook included the following phrase: 'If someone [is] a magician and is able to provoke storms, he should do penance for seven years, three on bread and water.'[1] This short sentence can be an entrance into a world in which farmers fear for their crops because of heavy hail and thunderstorms and try to protect them by supernatural means. Some people, in the sources of the period referred to as *tempestarii*, a term that one could translate as 'stormmakers', apparently played on these fears and offered protection against such meteorological disasters in return for material rewards. A treatise composed by the ninth-century bishop of Lyon, Agobard, arguing against such beliefs, provides a useful background to this penitential canon.[2] Agobard describes a belief in magical ships travelling through the sky coming from a land called Magonia and communicating with *tempestarii* as to where to land their ship, provoking a heavy storm and robbing the land of its crops by taking these aboard the ship. Farmers gave the *tempestarii* a material reward, which they called the *canonicum*, so Agobard informs us, and used this fact as an excuse not to pay the tithe that they owed the church. Thanks to Agobard's treatise the terse formulation of the penitential text cited above reveals a broader context, yet there still remain unsolved riddles. One of these concerns the question who these *tempestarii* were. Were they pagan priests competing with Christian clerics, as has recently been maintained?[3] Or are we dealing with independent village sorcerers, who were

---

[1] *Paenitentiale Bobbiense*, c. 18, ed. R. Kottje, in *Paenitentialia minora Franciae et Italiae saeculi VIII–IX*, CC SL 156 (Turnhout 1994), p. 69.

[2] Agobard, *Liber contra insulsam vulgi opinionem de grandine et tonitruis*, ed. L. van Acker, Corpus Christianorum CM 52 (Turnhout 1981), pp. 3–15; the text is partly translated in P. Dutton (ed.), *Carolingian Civilization. A Reader* (Peterborough, Ontario 1993), pp. 189–91.

[3] P. Dutton, 'Thunder and hail over the Carolingian countryside', in Dutton, *Charlemagne's Mustache and Other Cultural Clusters of a Dark Age* (New York 2004), pp. 169–88, at pp. 174–5.

nominally Christian, yet dabbled in sorcery and witchcraft?[4] One could even argue that Agobard was combatting Christian priests or monks offering liturgical protection against thunderstorms.[5] The small number of source materials from this period makes it hard to provide definite answers to basic questions. Penitential texts do provide essential information regarding these ways to ward off bad weather, but it is hard to reach any definitive solutions. As we shall see, such uncertainty also characterizes the debate about medieval penance, particularly in the earlier period before *c.* 1200.

The debate about the role of penance and confession in the Middle Ages is closely linked to the debate about the nature of medieval religion. Historians have read the evidence for this period as indicating that many people were in fact only nominally Christian, and that their basic world view remained basically pagan for many centuries. The traditional forms of religion and the basic categories with which to interpret the world remained stable for many centuries and coloured the ways in which Christianity was interpreted and practised during the Middle Ages.[6] A related view holds that Christianity as a Mediterranean religion changed profoundly in the period after 400 because of the influence of converted Germanic peoples. As a result Christianity became a religion of formalistic ritual supervised by kings of a sacral nature and dominated by an aristocratic ethical code.[7] Both of these views regard medieval religion in the period up to the twelfth century as deeply influenced by pre-Christian, pagan attitudes towards the supernatural.

Lately, historians tend to see things differently, arguing that paganism for the early Middle Ages is merely a literary construct employed by ecclesiastical authors for their own purposes.[8] That medieval forms

[4] M. Blöcker, 'Wetterzauber: Zu einem Glaubenskomplex des frühen Mittelalters', *Francia* 9 (1981), pp. 117–31, at p. 125.
[5] R. Meens, 'Thunder over Lyon. Agobard, the tempestarii and Christianity', in C. Steel, J. Marenbon and W. Verbeke (eds.), *Paganism in the Middle Ages*, Mediaevalia Lovaniensia Studia 42 (Leuven 2013), pp. 157–66.
[6] As ingenuously argued by A. Gurevich, *Medieval Popular Culture. Problems of Belief and Perception* (Cambridge 1988); the same basic stance is found in J. Delumeau, *Le catholicisme entre Luther et Voltaire* (Paris 1979), who held that the later Middle Ages were only nominally Christian.
[7] J. C. Russell, *The Germanization of Early Medieval Christianity. A Sociohistorical Approach to Religious Transformation* (Oxford / New York 1994); C. Cusack, *Conversion among the Germanic Peoples* (London / New York 1998).
[8] The basic study arguing literary dependence is D. Harmening, *Superstitio. Ueberlieferungs- und theoriegeschichtliche Untersuchungen zur kirchlich-theologischen Aberglaubensliteratur des Mittelalters* (Berlin 1979); see also Y. Hen, *Culture and Religion in Merovingian Gaul A.D. 481–751* (Leiden / New York / Cologne 1995); J. Palmer, 'Defining paganism

of Christianity differed from what went on before and after is obvious, and it is surely problematic to interpret all change as the result of non-Christian influences. Nor does it seem helpful to speak about the archaization or rearchaization of Christianity, from an intrinsically ethical religion towards a purely formalistic one.[9] While ritual and ethical aspects may receive more or less emphasis in particular circumstances, human life is always characterized by a combination of moral and ritual commitments. As it is extremely difficult, if not impossible, to evaluate with any precision the importance of the moral versus that of the ritual, it seems not very helpful to characterize a religion from this perspective. The distinction between an ethical and a ritual religion is related to the influential distinction that Margaret Mead made between shame and guilt cultures. In the first wrongdoing leads to fear of disclosure and loss of honour, while in the latter the wrongdoer is not so much motivated by the reaction of others as by his own feelings of guilt. The former attitude would be more ritual and the latter more ethical. However, like the moral-ritual dichotomy, the distinction between shame and guilt seems too absolute and too difficult to measure in any detail to be a fruitful tool for historical analysis.[10]

The role of penance and confession has been central in the debate over the nature of medieval religion. The traditional narrative of the history of penance distinguished three major phases. In Late Antiquity a formal ritual of public penance was the norm, which, its ritual and public nature notwithstanding, is often seen as reflecting an ethical stance.[11] In the early Middle Ages private penance was introduced and this new form of penance was associated with a new literary genre: the handbooks for confessors known as penitentials. These books contained long lists of possible kinds of sin together with the appropriate penance to make up for them. As many historians assumed that these lists were to be applied in a mechanical way – i.e. sin x was to be

in the Carolingian world', *Early Medieval Europe* 15 (2007), pp. 402–25; J. Couser, 'Inventing paganism in eighth-century Bavaria', *Early Medieval Europe* 18 (2010), pp. 26–42.

[9] See the monumental study of A. Angenendt, *Geschichte der Religiosität im Mittelalter* (Darmstadt 1997), particularly pp. 1–23, and the work of his pupil H. Lutterbach, 'Intentions- oder Tathaftung? Zum Bußverständnis in den frühmittelalterlichen Bußbüchern', *Frühmittelalterliche Studien* 29 (1995), pp. 120–43, or Lutterbach, 'Die mittelalterlichen Bußbücher – Trägermedien von Einfachreligiosität?', *Zeitschrift für Kirchengeschichte* 114 (2003), pp. 227–44.

[10] See the useful discussion of this topic in R. Künzel, *Beelden en zelfbeelden van middeleeuwse mensen. Historisch-antropologische studies over groepsculturen in de Nederlanden, 7e–13e eeuw* (Nijmegen 1997), pp. 97–110. The concept 'guilt culture' is employed e.g. in the work of Gurevich, *Medieval Popular Culture*, p. 102.

[11] See e.g. Angenendt, *Geschichte der Religiosität im Mittelalter*, p. 628.

remedied by penance y – private penance, or tariffed penance as it is also known, was regarded as ritualistic, unethical and archaic. In the twelfth century, through the innovations of Peter Abelard, things changed for the better. Penance became less formalistic, the stress no longer fell on the proper kind of penance to atone for one's sin, but on the feelings of guilt and remorse of the sinner. From an archaic ritualistic form of penance, a new interiorized ethical form of penance emerged, a development that was seen as intricately linked to the so-called 'discovery of the individual' in the twelfth century.[12] In many studies regarding medieval religion, penance played a crucial role as an indicator of the formal, ritualistic and unethical, or on the other hand the individual, moral and ethical nature of Christianity in a specific period. The following study will argue that many of these assumptions are based on too-easy generalizations of the complex nature and history of penance and confession during the Middle Ages and that it is important first to describe in more detail what we know about medieval penance and confession, before presenting such challenging theses.

Another discussion among historians concerns the importance of penance in medieval culture at large. It has been argued that penance as such was only of minor importance and that penitential tariffs were not used in the everyday contact between a priest and members of his flock, but instead were part of formal proceedings supervised by bishops in their ecclesiastical courts.[13] This has led to the conclusion that penance played a very insignificant role in medieval religion, at least up until the eleventh century.[14] Such a view concurs well with the theory of a thoroughly pagan medieval society touched up with only a veneer of Christianity.

---

[12] C. Morris, *The Discovery of the Individual 1050–1200* (New York 1972); for the importance of intention and penance, see p. 74. For a thoughtful recent assessment of the question of the 'birth of the individual', see W. Pohl, 'Introduction: ego trouble?', in R. Corradini, M. Gillis, R. McKitterick and I. van Renswoude (eds.), *Ego Trouble. Authors and their Identities in the Early Middle Ages*, Forschungen zur Geschichte des Mittelalters 15 (Vienna 2010), pp. 9–21; the threefold scheme forms the outline for H. Lutterbach, *Sexualität im Mittelalter. Eine Kulturstudie anhand von Bußbüchern des 6. bis 12. Jahrhundert*, Beihefte zum Archiv für Kulturgeschichte 43 (Cologne / Weimar / Vienna 1999).

[13] A thesis advanced by Franz Kerff: see his 'Mittelalterliche Quellen und mittelalterliche Wirklichkeit. Zu den Konsequenzen einer jüngst erschienenen Edition für unser Bild kirchlicher Reformbemühungen', *Rheinische Vierteljahrsblätter* 51 (1987), pp. 275–86, and his 'Libri paenitentiales und kirchliche Strafgerichtsbarkeit bis zum Decretum Gratiani. Ein Diskussionsvorschlag', *Zeitschrift der Savigny-Stiftung für Rechtsgeschichte, Kan. Abt.* 75 (1989), pp. 23–57.

[14] A. Murray, 'Confession before 1215', *Transactions of the Royal Historical Society*, 6th series, 3 (1993), pp. 51–81.

In a way such views can be seen as a healthy reaction to earlier views propagating an all too smooth evolution of early medieval penance towards the form of private penance as it developed during the later Middle Ages and the early modern period.[15] Yet the 'minimal view' on penance has been criticized in its turn. The juridical nature of penance has been called into question, while research into military uses of confession as well as into the codicological contexts of penitential texts, i.e. the texts with which they were combined in manuscripts of the period, have demonstrated that penance was more pervasive than the minimalists have been willing to admit.[16] Although there are no easy answers to the question of the ways in which religious confessional ritual played a role in medieval society, simply because we lack any statistical information regarding such questions, this book will try to bring more precision to the question as to who exactly was attracted to penitential procedures or, sometimes, driven to accept them.

In the past the history of penance firmly belonged to the domain of church history. Many books devoted to the topic were therefore written from a confessional background or, as in the case of Henry Charles Lea, from a liberal anticlerical point of view.[17] Particularly Catholic historians have studied the subject, among whom Bernhard Poschmann certainly was the most influential. In his work, published in two important studies of the history of penance in Late Antiquity and the early Middle Ages in the years 1928 and 1930, Poschmann stressed the continuities of penitential practices and concepts as a form of legitimization of the Catholic tradition of auricular confession.[18] For this reason his work concentrated on private penance as the cradle from which modern forms of auricular confession originated. By doing so, Poschmann neglected not only many other ways of doing penance, but

---

[15] As, for example, in the work of Bernhard Poschmann, who stresses continuities with later forms of penance, thereby establishing a legitimizing discourse of continity; for his influence see R. Meens, 'The historiography of early medieval penance', in A. Firey (ed.), *The New History of Penance* (Leiden 2008), pp. 73–95.

[16] D. S. Bachrach, 'Confession in the Regnum Francorum (742–900)', *Journal of Ecclesiastical History* 54 (2003), pp. 3–22; R. Meens, 'The frequency and nature of early medieval penance', in P. Biller and A. J. Minnis (eds.), *Handling Sin. Confession in the Middle Ages*, York Studies in Medieval Theology 2 (Woodbridge 1998), pp. 35–61.

[17] H. C. Lea, *A History of Auricular Confession and Indulgences in the Latin Church*, 2 vols. (Philadelphia 1896).

[18] B. Poschmann, *Die abendländische Kirchenbusse im Ausgang des christlichen Altertums* (Munich 1928) and Poschmann, *Die abendländische Kirchenbusse im frühen Mittelalter*, Breslauer Studien zur historischen Theologie 16 (Breslau 1930); influential also is the English translation of his *Buße und letzte Ölung*, Handbuch der Dogmengeschichte 4.3 (Freiburg im Breisgau 1951), published as *Penance and the Anointing of the Sick* (New York 1964).

most of all he devised the construct 'private penance', which is in many ways inadequate, as this book will contend.[19]

Lately, for a variety of reasons, other historians have developed an interest in the history of penance. They discovered the importance of handbooks for confessors as sources for social and cultural history and with the growing interest in social and cultural issues from the 1970s onwards, penance became of interest, if only because penitential literature provided a lot of information on topics which other kinds of source material hardly ever mentioned. Penitential sources were, for example, mined for the information they contained regarding religious practices that members of the church hierarchy denounced as forms of superstition. They also contain a lot of information on sexual behaviour or dietary habits.[20] Historians, being less interested in a quest for the origins of specific institutions, came to the subject with a greater eye for the diversity that existed on the ground. This tied in with a greater distrust in the possibilities of reconstructing the past on the basis of normative sources, such as law codes or conciliar legislation. Historians became more interested in practice, i.e. the concrete ways in which specific conflicts were handled, and less in the way they should be solved through the application of specific laws. This distrust of normative sources was most obvious in the field of conflict settlement studies, a booming field that drew much of its inspiration from the branch of legal studies known as legal anthropology. In the field of penance this meant that it was no longer of great importance how penance should work according to the normative sources, but rather to try to figure out how it worked in

---

[19] For the neglect of other forms of penance, see R. Price, 'Informal penance in early medieval Christendom,' in K. Cooper and J. Gregory (eds.), *Retribution, Repentance, and Reconciliation*, Studies in Church History 40 (2004), pp. 29–39; for a criticism of the construct of 'private penance', see M. de Jong, 'What was public about public penance? *Paenitentia publica* and justice in the Carolingian world', in *La Giustizia nell'alto medioevo II (secoli IX–XI)*, Settimane di Studio 44 (Spoleto 1997), pp. 863–904, at pp. 864–6 and 893–6; see also S. Hamilton, *The Practice of Penance, 900–1050* (Woodbridge 2001), a work that tries to supersede the private-public distinction.

[20] See, for example, Gurevich, *Medieval Popular Culture*, pp. 78–103; V. Flint, *The Rise of Magic in Early Medieval Europe* (Oxford 1991); M. G. Muzzarelli (ed.), *Una componente della mentalità occidentale: penitenziali nell'alto medio evo*, Il mondo medievale. Studi di storia e storiografia 9 (Bologna 1980); J.-L. Flandrin, *Un temps pour embrasser. Aux origines de la morale sexuelle occidentale (VI–XI siècle)* (Paris 1983); P. Payer, *Sex and the Penitentials. The Development of a Sexual Code, 550–1150* (Toronto 1984); P. Bonnassie, 'Consommation d'aliments immondes et cannibalisme de survie dans l'occident du Haut Moyen Age', *Annales ESC* 44 (1989), pp. 1035–56; R. Meens, 'Pollution in the early Middle Ages: the case of the food regulations in penitentials', *Early Medieval Europe* 4 (1995), pp. 3–19; H. Lutterbach, 'Die Speisegesetzgebung in den mittelalterlichen Bußbüchern (600–1200). Religionsgeschichtliche Perspektiven', *Archiv für Kulturgeschichte* 80 (1998), pp. 1–37.

practice.[21] This interest in practice fostered the historical engagement with diversity on the ground. What mattered were no longer the norms and theories with which bishops and ecclesiastical authors approached penance and confession, but rather the ways in which penance and confession functioned in very specific social circumstances.[22]

The greater interest in diversity also led to a new approach to texts. Whereas in the past editors of medieval texts were at pains to reconstruct the original text as it was composed by the author, lately they have become more interested in the ways a text was read, used, interpreted and altered.[23] Instead of focussing on the original text and eliminating all variant readings that did not reflect the original, they have seen the importance of textual variants, interpolations and omissions as forays into the world of the reader. Important in this context is also the codicological context. Many medieval texts were not read as independent publications, but were part of a manuscript also containing other kinds of texts. For the correct interpretation of a work it is often necessary to look into the other texts that are included in a specific manuscript, because we must assume that texts were not read in isolation, but as part of the codex in which they were being consulted.[24] It matters, for example, if a handbook for penance is included in a liturgical manuscript, or in one containing ecclesiastical and secular legislation. When Archbishop Theodore of Canterbury in the second half of the seventh century proclaimed that menstruating women were not allowed to enter a church building, he clearly moved away from the counsel that Gregory the Great had given to his predecessor Augustine. Gregory had explicitly allowed menstruating women to enter a church and to receive communion, declaring that the Old

---

[21] The title of the book by Sarah Hamilton, *The Practice of Penance*, is paradigmatic in this respect.

[22] See, e.g., M. de Jong, 'Power and humility in Carolingian society: the public penance of Louis the Pious', *Early Medieval Europe* 1 (1992), pp. 29–52 or de Jong, 'Pollution, penance and sanctity: Ekkehard's *Life* of Iso of St Gall', in J. Hill and M. Swann (eds.), *The Community, the Family, and the Saint. Patterns of Power in Early Medieval Europe* (Turnhout 1998), pp. 145–58.

[23] An approach sometimes labelled as 'new philology', see the special issue of *Speculum* 65 (1990) devoted to this approach; fundamental also is B. Cerquiglini, *Éloge de la variante. Histoire critique de la philologie* (Paris 1989). For a recent collection of studies endorsing such an approach, see R. Corradini, M. Diesenberger and M. Niederkorn-Bruck (eds.), *Zwischen Niederschrift und Wiederschrift. Hagiographie und Historiographie im Spannungsfeld von Kompendienüberlieferung und Editionstechnik*, Forschungen zur Geschichte des Mittelalters 18 (Vienna 2010).

[24] For a deliberate attempt to study a specific manuscript as a whole, see Y. Hen and R. Meens (eds.), *The Bobbio Missal. Liturgy and Religious Culture in Merovingian Gaul*, Cambridge Studies in Palaeography and Codicology 11 (Cambridge 2004).

Testament purity regulations concerning menstruation were to be interpreted in a spiritual way. Apparently Theodore felt he could neglect Gregory's spiritual interpretation and proclaim a more literal or cultic one, but to conclude from this that Gregory's more ethical approach remained uninfluential during the early Middle Ages and was superseded by the cultic interpretation of Theodore is too simple.[25] If we look at the manuscripts containing Theodore's statement, we can observe that they often included Gregory's text as well. In some manuscripts Theodore's regulations on this matter were glossed by a reference to Gregory's views to be found elsewhere in the same manuscript, and sometimes they were even replaced by Gregory's text.[26] Only looking at the way these two texts were combined into specific manuscripts allows us to add nuance to the too simplistic view that Gregory still wrote from a late antique, ethical, point of view and that his views were quickly superseded by a cultic interpretation that was typical for the early Middle Ages.

Paying attention to the manuscripts containing penitential works will also help us to avoid too-easy generalizations. Thanks to a better understanding of early medieval palaeography – much of it indebted to the work of the late Bernhard Bischoff – we are in a position to date and locate specific manuscripts more accurately. This, in turn, may provide precious indications for the popularity of a specific text in certain regions or periods and thus contribute to a better understanding of the past. Earlier historians, sometimes, too readily assumed that a rule found in a specific text could be used to illustrate the medieval approach to a particular problem. Now we have the means to assess whether such a rule was disseminated over a wide region and known throughout the Middle Ages, or whether it was confined to a specific region and/or a specific period. To regard the sharing of a cup with a pregnant woman as a sin, for example, is a feature only found in Irish texts and can hardly be regarded as a general feature of medieval religion.[27] In the ninth century within the Carolingian empire a wide spectrum of different opinions existed as to the question of what exactly constituted an incestuous marriage. This was of great social relevance, since it decided whether

---

[25] Flandrin, *Un temps pour embrasser*, p. 81 and A. Angenendt, *Das Frühmittelalter. Die abendländische Christenheit von 400 bis 900* (Stuttgart / Berlin / Cologne, 1990), p. 346.

[26] See R. Meens, 'Ritual purity and the influence of Gregory the Great in the early Middle Ages', in R. Swanson (ed.), *Unity and Diversity in the Church*, Studies in Church History 32 (Oxford 1996), pp. 31–43, at pp. 37–41.

[27] Pace Lutterbach, *Sexualität im Mittelalter*, p. 98, who presents this as a general medieval phenomenon although he refers to only two Irish texts that have a very limited manuscript dissemination.

one was allowed to marry a person within a certain degree of consanguinity and when exactly a marriage had to be dissolved for reasons of
consanguinity. Only a careful investigation of the different texts and their
manuscript transmission will allow for an accurate picture of the diversity
within the Carolingian empire.[28]

Although we are lacking the fullness of source material that would
enable us to answer questions concerning the frequency with which
people confessed their sins, the exact nature of their sins and the ways
in which they atoned for them, when reading the available sources with
an eye for the codicological context and the dissemination of the manuscripts there still remains a lot of documentation containing information
on the practice of penance and confession. In this book many different
kinds of sources will be used, such as treatises on penance, letters, saints'
lives, visions, liturgical texts, monastic rules or conciliar legislation, and
many other kinds of sources could possibly be fruitfully employed as
well. The basis of this study, however, is formed by handbooks for
confessors, those texts meant to inform confessors on how to hear
confession, how to assign a particular form of penance and how to
reconcile the sinner with God and the Christian community. Although
recent historians of penance have been reluctant to use these texts
because of their repetitive and normative character, I think there are
good reasons to use them as the backbone for a study of penance in
the period between 600 and 1200.[29] Although other sources contain a lot
of valuable information, it would be foolish to shy away from those texts
with which confessors were instructed and which they might even have
held in their hands when hearing confession. Many of the manuscripts
containing such texts were of a practical character, so it seems that we
come close to the practice of penance by studying them.[30] In recent
years these texts have been subjected to meticulous textual scrutiny,
particularly in German scholarship.[31] Because of the rather technical
nature of this kind of research, it has not always reached a general
audience, and historians interested in penance or in penitential texts as

[28] As presented in K. Ubl, *Inzestverbot und Gesetzgebung. Die Konstruktion eines Verbrechens (300–1100)* (Berlin / New York 2008), pp. 291–383.

[29] For a reluctance to use these texts, see Hamilton, *The Practice of Penance* and A. Firey, *A Contrite Heart. Prosecution and Redemption in the Carolingian Empire* (Leiden / Boston 2009).

[30] For the practical character of many of these manuscripts, see Meens, 'Frequency and nature' and Meens, 'Penitentials and the practice of penance in the tenth and eleventh centuries', *Early Medieval Europe* (2006), pp. 7–21.

[31] In particular, R. Kottje and his pupils have done a lot of work in this field. In the anglophone world I think of the work of Allen Frantzen. For a short evaluation of this research, see Meens, 'The historiography of early medieval penance', pp. 82–5.

sources for doing cultural history all too often use information that is out of date because a reliable guide to penitential literature is lacking.[32] This book hopes to provide guidance through the thick forest of penitential literature of the period between 600 and 1200.

This book therefore tries to follow the story of penance by charting first of all the history of penitential books in the Middle Ages. The manuscripts diffusion of particular texts is consequently presented as fully as possible. In doing so, this study relies mainly on existing scholarship and although by doing so many a lacuna became manifest, it withstands the temptation to do new research to fill these gaps. This book therefore offers a synthesis of recent research and does not aim to provide new information. Where it does something new, however, is in the interpretation of the material. As indicated above, historians of penance have long tried to fit their material into the mould of a pervasive taxonomy in which the distinction between public and private penance was central. This book argues that this distinction is anachronistic for the period before the late eighth century when it was introduced in Carolingian circles, and even then 'private penance' was not the term Carolingian bishops used. By parting from the concept of 'private penance' for this period, it becomes possible to interpret the existing sources in a new light. This new interpretation emphasizes the social function of penance, particularly in relation to lay people doing penance.

It has already been mentioned that conflict studies is a booming field of research. Historians have observed that rituals of deference and humiliation played an important role in the – often only temporary – settlement of disputes. It has been remarked upon that particularly those rituals in which a party in a conflict would abase himself before the other in order to reach a specific settlement, and which are generally known as a *deditio*, bear a strong resemblance to ecclesiastical rituals of penance.[33] Nevertheless, such rituals of reconciliation are generally regarded as purely secular. This book will attempt to demonstrate that this need not always be the case and that ecclesiastical ritual and the procedures of confession and penance can be part of the reconciliation between

---

[32] To name but one recent example, the discussion of dietary rules in Firey's *A Contrite Heart* is seriously flawed because of the author's ignorance of the so-called *Paenitentiale Oxoniense II*, a text only recently discovered and edited by Kottje (discussed below in Chapter 5). Because she relied solely on the nineteenth-century edition made by Wasserschleben, Firey missed this important work containing a wealth of information on this particular topic.

[33] G. Althoff, *Spielregeln der Politik im Mittelalter. Kommunikation in Frieden und Fehde* (Darmstadt 1997); Althoff, *Die Macht der Rituale. Symbolik und Herrschaft im Mittelalter* (Darmstadt 2003); G. Koziol, *Begging Pardon and Favor. Ritual and Political Order in Early Medieval France* (Ithaca / London 1992).

secular parties.[34] Once we leave the concept of 'private penance' behind, it becomes possible to see the role confessors played as brokers trying to settle disputes between conflicting individuals, families or other social groups. As such this book can therefore be seen as a contribution to the field of dispute settlement studies, stressing the role of ecclesiastical mediation and reconciliation.

This study starts in the sixth century and ends around the year 1200. The reason for choosing these dates is that it allows for an evaluation of two moments that have been regarded as moments of revolutionary changes. As indicated above historians have seen two major breaks in the history of penance, one occurring in the sixth century when late antique penance made way for private penance and one in the twelfth century when private penance evolved from a rather mechanical application of tariffs into an interiorized ethical procedure. In order to assess the exact nature of these changes, it seemed fruitful to look into these periods of change to see what exactly was new and which traditional elements persisted, although it must be stressed that for these 'transition' periods this study relies even more on existing scholarship than for the other periods dealt with here. Geographically this study concentrates on the Latin West. Following the trail of penitential manuals has as a consequence that only those regions where such texts were known will be discussed in this book. Nevertheless this study will treat a major part of Western Europe and over a long period, so that it warrants the title: *Penance in Medieval Europe, 600–1200.*

---

[34] For a later period this has been forcefully argued by P. Hyams, *Rancor and Reconciliation in Medieval England* (Ithaca / London 2003).

2 The late antique legacy

We begin in the year 590 in Rome. At this moment the situation in the former capital of the world can be characterized as simply disastrous. Justinian's attempt to reconquer the western parts of the Roman empire, which started with the destruction of the Vandal kingdom in northern Africa in 533, resulted in Italy in the Gothic Wars. This prolonged confrontation between the troops of the Byzantine generals Belisarius and Narses and the Gothic armies in Italy brought an end to the economic prosperity of the Italian peninsula. Whereas under Gothic rule late Roman structures had continued to function, the Gothic Wars put a definitive end to the prosperity of late antique Italy, leading to famine and plague.[1] In November 589 the waters of the Tiber had risen to such heights that buildings collapsed and ecclesiastical granaries were destroyed. Great amounts of grain had been lost while people were seeing snakes and dragons swimming in the river. In January the plague hit hard, Pope Gelasius II being among its first casualties. The people of Rome looked for guidance to a former prefect of the city, a member of a distinguished Roman family living on the Coelian Hill, the same family from which Pope Felix III (483–92) had come. Gregory the Great, as the scion of this family later came to be known, came to the papal office with serious reservations as he had chosen the contemplative life and was now forced to return to the sorrows of the active life again.[2] His fame, however, seems to have spread fast. Soon after he had become the new bishop of Rome, his namesake, Bishop Gregory of Tours, included an account of Gregory's election in his *Histories*.[3] The bishop of Tours

---

[1] M. Humphries, 'Italy, A.D. 425–605', in A. Cameron, B. Ward-Perkins and M. Whitby (eds.), *The Cambridge Ancient History*, vol. XIV: *Late Antiquity: Empire and Successors, A.D. 425–600* (Cambridge 2000), pp. 525–51.

[2] For Gregory's doubts, see R. A. Markus, *Gregory the Great and His World* (Cambridge 1997), pp. 10–14.

[3] Gregory of Tours, *Historiae*, X, 1, ed. B. Krusch and W. Levison, MGH SS rer. mer. I (Hanover 1956), pp. 477–81.

relates that he was informed about Roman affairs by a deacon who had travelled to Rome in that year, bringing back relics to the town of Tours. Gregory's account informs us of the catastrophes in Rome and the way the newly elected pope tried to remedy them. The new pope saw the plague as a divine punishment for the sins of the people in Rome and organized a penitential procession to atone for these sins.[4] The procession was organized according to the different orders of society: the clerics, the monks, the nuns, the children, the lay people, the widows and the married women all assembled and prayed in a particular church and from there walked in procession to the Santa Maria Maggiore, where the groups should pray together for the remission of sin. Apparently eighty people dropped dead during this procession, yet the pope and his companions persevered in their efforts to appease God. The sermon that Gregory the Great would have preached on that occasion is included in the *Histories*.[5] In this sermon Gregory describes how quickly the plague struck, leaving no time for repentance and atonement. Therefore, everyone should bewail his sins and repent while there still was time, and nobody should despair because of the gravity of his sins, because the inhabitants of Nineveh were able to wash away all their sins in a three-day penance and the murderer on the Cross received the reward of eternal life even at the hour of death. Repentance and sin are central themes in his sermon and it is clear that Gregory put special emphasis on the importance of a good death: that is, being able to confess your sins before death. He certainly regarded dying in a state of sin as an extremely serious matter. 'The blow falls: each victim is snatched away from us before he can bewail his sins and repent. Just think in what state he must appear before the Implacable Judge, having had no chance to lament his deeds', he sermonized.[6] Gregory here reveals that confessing one's sins individually before death was more and more seen as an essential component of a Christian death. This fits a larger pattern which has been observed for the early medieval West in

---

[4] For the development of these penitential processions see G. Nathan, 'Rogation ceremonies in Late Antique Gaul', *Classica et Medievalia* 21 (1998), pp. 276–303.

[5] The authenticity of this sermon has been questioned by O. Chadwick, 'Gregory of Tours and Gregory the Great', *Journal of Theological Studies* 50 (1949), pp. 38–49. See the riposte in M. Heinzelmann, *Gregor von Tours (538–594). 'Zehn Bücher Geschichte.' Historiographie und Gesellschaftskonzept im 6. Jahrhundert* (Darmstadt 1994), p. 70, fn. 76 and p. 72, fn. 83.

[6] Gregory of Tours, *Historiae* X, 1, ed. Krusch and Levison, p. 479; translation from Gregory of Tours, *The History of the Franks*, translated with an introduction by L. Thorpe (Harmondsworth 1974), p. 545.

which the salvation of the soul became increasingly important in the developing Christian deathbed ritual.[7] The penitential procession held in Rome on the other hand shows that there was also a need to atone collectively for the sins of a specific community.

Gregory's sermon as well as the procession organized to appease God's anger therefore exemplify two attitudes towards sin, which are vital for the various ways in which people dealt with the question of sin and redemption in the early Middle Ages: an individual one and a communal one. Sin was an individual matter because it affected the relation between God and the sinner, but it was also a communal one affecting the relation between God and community and sinner and community, thereby creating a triangular relationship between God, sinner and the Christian community. The problem of sin was therefore not only an individual matter but touched upon the whole Christian community. As Gregory's story shows, God could punish a whole town severely for its sins and therefore the community had to find ways to restore the proper relation with the Deity. The Rogations are a particular kind of communal effort to atone for the sins of the community. It was also known in Gaul, instituted there more than a century earlier by Bishop Mamertus of Vienne (c. 461–c. 475).[8] It has been argued that the Roman Rogations differ in kind from the Gallican ones, but both share a preoccupation with sin, God's anger and satisfaction.[9] In this ritual the bishop took pride of place. He controlled the interpretation of what was happening by preaching and organized the penitential procession. The procession, with its stress on the ecclesiastical topography of a town, contributed to the transformation of the late antique city. The distinction between the different orders of society suggests a hierarchical organization of the procession headed by the bishop and in this way created a distinct profile for the head of the local religious community.

---

[7] F. Paxton, *Christianizing Death. The Creation of a Ritual Process in Early Medieval Europe* (Ithaca / London 1990), pp. 47–91.

[8] See Avitus of Vienna, *Homilia in rogationibus*, ed. R. Peiper, MGH AA 6.2 (Berlin 1883), pp. 108–12, translated in D. Shanzer and I. Wood, *Avitus of Vienne. Letters and Selected Prose* (Liverpool 2002), pp. 381–8.

[9] Nathan, 'Rogation ceremonies', stresses the different background to the Roman and Gallican rituals. For the Gallican ones, see I. Wood, 'Liturgy in the Rhône valley and the Bobbio Missal', in Y. Hen and R. Meens (eds.), *The Bobbio Missal. Liturgy and Religious Culture in Merovingian Gaul*, Cambridge Studies in Palaeography and Codicology 11 (Cambridge 2004), pp. 206–18, esp. pp. 206–8; for the further development of the different traditions and the nomenclature, see J. Hill, 'The *Litaniae maiores* and *minores* in Rome, Francia and Anglo-Saxon England', *EME* 9 (2000), pp. 211–46.

The ritual of penance in Late Antiquity

The penitential processions in Rome and Gaul bear witness to the fact that there were more ways to atone for one's sins than the ritual of public penance, the rite that earlier historians of penance privileged to such an extent that it almost seemed as if it was the only way open for sinners to obtain pardon. In the view of historians such as Bernhard Poschmann or Cyrille Vogel there was only one way that guaranteed the remission of sins, only one ecclesiastical ritual that could be seen as a 'sacrament', the authoritative forerunner of the later practice of confessing one's sins.[10] Such a view, however, is still too deeply involved in the polemics between Catholics and Protestants over the legitimacy of the practice of auricular confession. If we stop looking for precedents for later practice, we are able to see a rich variety of ways in which sinners were looking for the remission of their sins as well as ways in which communities and their leaders tried to control and correct the behaviour of individual believers.[11] Origen had listed seven ways to achieve expiation for one's sins, whereas John Cassian, for example, came to a total of twelve. These included, among others, the ritual of baptism, martyrdom, the shedding of tears, the giving of alms, pardoning others or the intercession of saints.[12] It shows that many more or less formal ways of doing penance existed, and it seems hard to believe that in the late antique Christian world, where diversity was the norm and unity mostly a rhetorical construction, only a single approved method for dealing with sin existed.[13] The public ritual of penance was only one of these ways, although a widely known one. There remain, however, many questions as to how regularly such a ritual would be performed. We shall see that in Hippo in Augustine's time there were a specific number of penitents clearly

[10] See e.g. B. Poschmann, *Penance and the Anointing of the Sick* (New York 1964), who does admit that other forms of penance existed, but clearly focusses on the sacramental form of penance and demonstrates a tendency to uniformize the available evidence, or C. Vogel, *Les 'Libri Paenitentiales'*, Typologie des sources du Moyen Âge occidental 27 (Turnhout 1978), p. 34: 'Dans la discipline antique, le processus pénitentiel, non réiterable, s'appliquait avec une rigueur égale à tous les pécheurs, quelle qu'aient été les fautes.'

[11] R. Price, 'Informal penance in early medieval Christendom', in K. Cooper and J. Gregory (eds.), *Retribution, Repentance, and Reconciliation*, Studies in Church History 40 (Woodbridge 2004), pp. 29–38.

[12] John Cassian, *Collationes* XX, 8, ed. M. Petschenig, CSEL 13 (Vienna 2004), pp. 561–565; Origen, *Homélies sur le Lévitique* II, 4, ed. M. Borret, Sources Chrétiennes 286–7 (Paris 1981), pp. 108–10.

[13] See A. Louth, 'Unity and diversity in the Church of the fourth century', in R. Swanson (ed.), *Unity and Diversity in the Church*, Studies in Church History 32 (Oxford 1995), pp. 1–17.

known to the community, but we have to admit that we do not know whether such was also the case in Constantinople, Milan or Arles.

In the late antique Church it was generally possible to do penance for one's sins. Some groups of Christians rejected this possibility and were later labelled as heretical groups whose interpretation of the Christian doctrine was erroneous. The Montanists, or to call them by a less pejorative term the New Prophecy, are such a group.[14] The precise ways in which one could atone for one's sins are not always clear, but we have some texts which inform us about such processes. We should not forget, however, that the Christian world was a diverse one. Ways to do penance probably varied considerably from one region to another and from one period to another. Historians often speak of 'public penance' in this respect to distinguish it from the ritual of private penance as it developed later. Yet sources from the late antique period never speak of public penance, but only of penance as such, although at times they stress its public character, as Ambrose did when commending the penance of Emperor Theodosius.[15] Terms favoured by historians such as 'canonical penance' or 'ecclesiastical penance' are also of a later date.[16]

The ritual of early Christian penance had resulted from discussions of how to deal with people who had broken the rules of the Christian game. As in any community, the basic question was whether people who had transgressed fundamental rules of conduct agreed upon by the group should be excluded from the Christian community, or whether there existed ways to make amends. Before embracing a more severe stance, Tertullian, the early third-century African Church Father, had advocated that a second chance should be given to those who had sinned in a serious way. Penance was a plank of salvation for the shipwrecked Christian. Tertullian offers us the first description of the penitential process, which he calls by the Greek name of *exomologesis*. His description makes it clear that something of an ecclesiastical ritual existed in his time, in which elements such as the prostration of the penitent, a particular penitential dress, sackcloth and ashes and a penitential diet played a part. Furthermore, it is clear that priests, altars and the Christian community played a role in this ritual as well, since Tertullian urges penitents

---

[14] C. Trevett, '"I have heard from some teachers": the second century struggle for forgiveness and reconciliation', in Cooper and Gregory (eds.), *Retribution, Repentance, and Reconciliation*, pp. 5–28, at pp. 23–6.

[15] See below, pp. 21–3.

[16] P. Saint-Roch, *La pénitence dans les conciles et les lettres des papes des origines à la mort de Grégoire le Grand* (Vatican City 1991), p. 15, fn. 1. The council of Toledo of 589 speaks of 'paenitentiam secundum formam canonicam antiquorum', c. 11, ed. J. Vives, *Concilios Visigóticos e Hispano-Romanos* (Barcelona / Madrid 1963), p. 22.

to prostrate themselves in front of the priests, to kneel before the altar
and to ask all their brothers to intervene for them. He further stresses that
the favour of penance was unique.[17] Like baptism it could only be
granted once in a lifetime. Tertullian uses the metaphor of the penitent
knocking on the door of the vestibule to enter the door of forgiveness, a
door that had been closed by baptism but which was ajar for the penitent
Christian and was to be opened only once.[18] This gripping image of the
penitent in a hall knocking on the door to enter an ecclesiastical room
should remind us of the architectural and social setting in which such
a ritual took place. We should not think of churches in the form of a
basilica, but rather of small house churches, as we know them from
Rome and northern Africa.[19] This implies that we are dealing with very
small communities, and the priest mentioned was probably deeply
engaged in local affairs. That the penitent implored all his fellow Christians to intervene for his sins shows that this penitential ritual was to
a high degree a 'public' affair in which the Christian community played a
crucial role, as spectators and as actors. The fact that many sinners
refrained from doing penance for reasons of shame, as Tertullian argues,
underscores the public element in this ritual. The penitent ran the
serious risk of being mocked by people trying to insult him or her, since
some used the ruin of others to exalt themselves, although such an
attitude should, Tertullian stresses, not be found among Christians,
who share the same hope, the same fear, happiness, pain and suffering.[20]
This communal aspect of penance strongly suggests that pressures could
be brought to bear on a sinner to undergo this kind of penance, although
positive proof of such pressure is lacking in Tertullian's text. The reconciliation that this ritual achieved was therefore probably as much a
reconciliation with the local community as the restoration of a proper
relation with God.

Apart from being a means of reconciliation, public penance also had its
disciplinary side. In Tertullian's description such elements are only
hinted at when he discusses, for example, the separation of the sinner

---

[17] The term presbyter is translated as 'prêtre, chef de communauté chrétienne' in Albert
Blaise, *Dictionnaire Latin-Français des auteurs chrétiennes* (Turnhout 1954), p. 661, with
specific reference to Tertullian's *De paenitentia* Bk IX.

[18] For penance as a plank of salvation, Tertullian, *De paenitentia*, IV, 2; for the metaphor of
the door, see VII, 10; for the penitential ritual, ibid. IX, 2–4, ed. C. Munier, *Tertullien,
La pénitence. Introduction, texte critique, traduction et commentaire*, Sources Chrétiennes
316 (Paris 1984), pp. 156, 174 and 180.

[19] See Munier's introduction to *Tertullien*, pp. 59–61; for the persistence of such house
churches in a somewhat later period see K. Bowes, *Private Worship, Public Values, and
Religious Change in Late Antiquity* (Cambridge 2008).

[20] Tertullian, *De paenitentia*, X, 1–4, ed. Munier, p. 182.

from the community of Christians. The disciplinary aspect of penance comes more to the fore in the period after the edict of Milan (312), by which Christianity was tolerated as a religion within the Roman empire. This made it possible for Christian bishops to convene in councils and to issue their decisions. Penance is often found as a prerequisite for returning to the Christian congregation after having committed a serious fault. The council of Ancyra for example, which convened in 314, ruled that men having had sexual relations with animals should live as suppliacants for fifteen years, after which they were allowed to take part in prayer in church; after another five years they were allowed to take part in 'simple communion' and if they persevered they were finally allowed to participate again in communion with offerings.[21] This canon illustrates a process by which sinners were only gradually readmitted as full members of the Christian community. During a period of fifteen years they were apparently not entitled to attend Mass, and only five years later were they readmitted to the Eucharist, but evidently still with reservations since their offerings were not accepted until after a certain lapse of time. These rules, as issued by bodies invested with ecclesiastical authority, implied a certain form of control and discipline to make certain that they were carried out in a proper way. Councils acted as legislative bodies to issue general rulings on disciplinary matters and to determine the period of penance for a specific offence. Somebody however had to oversee the process of assigning such disciplinary measures, to keep an eye on the proper behaviour of the excommunicated person and on the process by which he was to be readmitted into the community. The actual assignment of a period of exclusion, according to the rulings issued by councils from the fifth and sixth centuries, was in principle the task of the local bishop.[22] The church historian Sozomenos, however, informs us that in Constantinople, as well as in other places, the task of hearing confession and of assigning a proportionate penance was delegated to a priest particularly designated for this function.[23] In general, the bishops also seem to have supervised the behaviour of penitents as well as their gradual reintegration into the church, but we should not

---

[21] Council of Ancyra, c. 16, ed. C. H. Turner, Ecclesiae occidentalis monumenta iuris antiquissima canonum et conciliorum graecorum interpretationes Latinae, vol. II, 1 (Oxford 1907), pp. 92–9.

[22] For the central role of the bishop in the penitential process, see Saint-Roch, La pénitence, pp. 30–1; C. Rapp, Holy Bishops in Late Antiquity. The Nature of Christian Leadership in an Age of Transition (Berkeley / Los Angeles / London 2005), pp. 30–2, 38, 46 and 95; K. Uhalde, Expectations of Justice in the Age of Augustine (Philadelphia 2007).

[23] Sozomenos, Historia Ecclesiastica Bks 7, 16, ed. and translated by Günther Christian Hansen, Fontes Christiani 73/3, p. 886.

forget that priests and bishops were not always distinguishable, since our sources use the term 'sacerdos' for both.[24]

Rulings issued by councils are generally known as canons, from the Greek word for rule. As such they form the backbone of early Christian ecclesiastical legislation or canon law. In due time these rulings were gathered in collections of canon law, as for example the *Dionysiana*, a collection compiled by Dionysius Exiguus, a Scythian monk working in Rome in the early sixth century. While we know a lot about how these collections of canon law proliferated, it is far from clear how they were used in actual practice.[25] They were clearly intended as Christian guidelines for a virtuous life and were evidently addressed to the episcopacy, yet whether they functioned, for example, in the *audientia episcopalis*, the episcopal court of law, is questionable.[26] We can assume that bishops in their role of supervisors (the literal meaning of the Greek term *episkopos*) normally decided on the ways to deal with Christians who had broken certain rules, but the setting in which this happened is not always clear. Augustine's biographer, Possidius, paints us a picture of the busy bishop hearing all kinds of cases in the *secretarium* of the cathedral. Apparently the bishop assisted in solving conflicts between Christians, but they also came to express their anger or seek consolation from the bishop. Some came 'after closing hours' to see the bishop in private to confess their sins. The consultation room, pastoral leadership, ecclesiastical discipline and episcopal court in this way all merged together.[27] Many late antique bishops were probably well versed in Roman law and their dealings with delinquent Christians will have been inspired by their knowledge of Roman legal procedures, yet we can also imagine that there was ample room for improvisation and variation. The foremost aspect of their intervention was probably mediation and less the formal application of secular or ecclesiastical law.[28]

---

[24] Rapp, *Holy Bishops*, p. 93: 'For the period of late antiquity, the sources often do not distinguish whether priests or bishops, or both, were involved in the penitential process.'

[25] On late antique canon law collections, see F. Maassen, *Geschichte der Quellen und der Literatur des canonischen Rechts im Abendlande* (Graz 1870; reprint Graz 1956) and L. Kéry, *Canonical Collections of the Early Middle Ages (ca. 400–1140). A Bibliographical Guide to the Manuscripts and Literature* (Washington 1999).

[26] Uhalde, *Expectations of Justice*, pp. 44–76; for the fluid nature of the *audientia episcopalis*, see Rapp, *Holy Bishops*, pp. 242–53; P. Brown, *Power and Persuasion in Late Antiquity. Towards a Christian Empire* (Madison WI / London 1992), p. 100; and C. Humfress, 'Bishops and law courts in Late Antiquity: how (not) to make sense of the legal evidence', *Journal of Early Christian Studies* 19 (2011), pp. 375–400.

[27] Possidius, *Vita Augustini*, ed. W. Geerlings (Paderborn /Munich / etc 2005), pp. 64–6; on the bishop acting as 'judge, arbiter, mediator, or counsellor', see also Uhalde, *Expectations of Justice*, p. 70.

[28] Rapp, *Holy Bishops*, pp. 245–6 and 249–52.

A sermon delivered on a Tuesday after Easter demonstrates that in Hippo around the year 400 penitents were clearly recognizable as such. Augustine mentions a special place for the penitents (*locum paenitentiae*) and apparently at some point in the liturgy they lined up for the imposition of hands by the bishop. Augustine suggests that even in a provincial town such as Hippo, many penitents were to be found (*abundant hic paenitentes*). He distinguishes two groups of penitents: those who chose this state of their own accord and those who were driven to do so after being excommunicated by the bishop. In his sermon the bishop complained that particularly the latter felt honoured by being included among the penitents: they did not want to leave the order of penitents as if they had chosen it themselves. What should be a place of humility had thus turned into a place of vice, i.e. pride. Augustine's sermon nicely illustrates the double nature of penance: it could be chosen by the sinner to atone for their sins, but it could also be a disciplinary tool in the hands of the bishops to correct sinners. Augustine's sermon further illustrates that the shame of being among the penitents could also be turned around into a form of honour.[29] The close affinity between penance and monastic conversion probably contributed to a more elevated view of the state of penance.

The church historian Sozomenos described the ritual of penance as he had seen it in Rome, and from his description it is clear that in Rome as in Hippo penitents were assigned a special place in the church. At the end of Mass the penitents threw themselves on the floor and the bishop joined them with tears in his eyes. He then stood up and the penitents followed suit. It seems that Sozomenos is describing the act of entrance into a penitential state here, for he goes on to explain that the penitents were obliged to fulfil penitential exercises such as fasting for as long as the bishop had decided, and then were acquitted of their sin and allowed to take part fully in the liturgical practices of the community again.[30] From Jerome's letter to Oceanus we learn that the Roman *matrona* Fabiola entered the order of penitents (*ordo paenitentium*) to atone for her bigamous behaviour. Again we can observe that in Rome penitents were assigned a specific place in church. The entry of an honourable lady into the order of penitents seems to have aroused great public interest in the city of Rome. Interestingly, Jerome adds that this episode happened 'ante diem paschae', thereby probably stressing the import of Fabiola's

---

[29] Augustine, *Tractatus habitus tertia feria* (Sermo 232), 8, ed. Suzanne Poque, *Augustin d'Hippone, Sermons pour la Pâque. Introduction, texte critique, traduction et notes*, Sources Chrétiennes 116 (Paris 1966), pp. 274–8.
[30] Sozomenos, *Historia Ecclesiastica* Bk VII, 16, pp. 886–8.

act, choosing to retire from the Christian fold as a penitent right before the most important Christian festival.[31] Jerome presents Fabiola's case as an example of how a Christian even of the highest social standing should not refrain from abasing themself in front of the community. As we have already seen in Hippo, penitents who thus abased themselves could paradoxically gain in prestige.

The best-known case of a person of high social standing doing penance is the act by which the Roman Emperor Theodosius in 390 gained absolution for the massacre among the citizens of Thessalonica, which had taken place on his orders. A great number of citizens of Thessalonica had been killed by Gothic troops as a reprisal for the murder of their general Butherich. Although the penance assigned to the emperor has often been depicted as a show of force on the part of the Christian bishop, it is now conceived as a carefully balanced act between bishop and emperor to redeem Theodosius of the sin and of the political blame he had contracted.[32] In Ambrose's view Theodosius, as a baptized Christian, could not partake of the Eucharist with blood on his hands. Ambrose did his utmost to arrange for a public penance of the emperor, thereby strengthening the political position of his imperial friend.[33] Ambrose's stance was, of course, a courageous one and during these years he did confront the emperor in the case of an imperial demand to hand over Milan churches to the Arians, but it was not totally new.[34]

---

[31] Jerome, letter 77, ed. I. Hilberg, *Sancti Eusebii Hieronymi epistula. Pars II: epistulae LXXI–CXX*, CSEL 55 (Vienna / Leipzig 1912), p. 40.

[32] On the development of the view of this case as a confrontation between bishop and emperor, see R. Schieffer, 'Von Mailand nach Canossa. Ein Beitrag zur Geschichte der christlichen Herrscherbuße von Theodosius d. Gr. bis zu Heinrich IV', *Deutsches Archiv* 28 (1972), pp. 333–70.

[33] The most important source for this episode is Ambrose's letter to Theodosius, written in his own hand so that it was only for the emperor to read, epist. extra coll. 11 [51], ed. M. Zelzer, *Sancti Ambrosi Opera. Pars Decima. Epistularum liber decimus, epistulae extra collectionem, Gesta concili Aquileiensis*, CSEL 82, 3, pp. 212–18; for an English translation, see Ambrose of Milan, *Political Letters and Speeches*, translated by J. H. W. G. Liebeschuetz, Translated Texts for Historians 43 (Liverpool 2005), pp. 262–9. The friendship between emperor and bishop is stressed at the beginning of this letter. See also Paulinus, *Vita Ambrosii*, c. 24, ed. M. Pellegrino (Rome 1961), pp. 84–6. For the interpretation followed here, see E. Dassmann, *Ambrosius von Mailand. Leben und Werk* (Stuttgart 2004), pp. 187–92; see also J. Moorhead, *Ambrose. Church and Society in the Late Roman World* (Harlow 1999), pp. 192–6; N. McLynn, *Ambrose of Milan. Church and Court in a Christian Capital* (Berkeley / Los Angeles / London 1994), pp. 315–30; Brown, *Power and Persuasion*, pp. 109–14; a more political interpretation is advanced by F. Kolb, 'Der Bußakt von Mailand: Zum Verhältnis von Staat und Kirche in der Spätantike', in H. Boockmann, K. Jürgensen and G. Stoltenberg (eds.), *Geschichte und Gegenwart. Festschrift für Karl Dietrich Erdmann* (Neumünster 1980), pp. 41–74.

[34] On the Milan churches controversy, see Dassmann, *Ambrosius*, pp. 92–108; Moorhead, *Ambrose*, pp. 129–56 and McLynn, *Ambrose*.

The church historian Eusebius of Caesarea had already at the beginning of the fourth century written about a Christian emperor, Philip the Arab (244–9), who had been relegated to the place for penitents in church when he wanted to take part in the Eucharist on the feast of Easter. Although there are many grounds to doubt the authenticity of Eusebius's story, it shows that for Eusebius a public penitential act of a Roman emperor was not something that was unthinkable.[35]

As Ambrose had expressed it in a sermon delivered during another contest with an emperor, the emperor was a member of the Church and not someone who was above it (*intra ecclesiam, non supra ecclesiam*).[36] As a member of the Church, a baptized emperor such as Theodosius – which at that time was still something of a novelty – should live according to the strict rules of the Christian faith. The guilt that he had incurred because of the massacre was well known to all Christians and put the bishop in a difficult position. Ambrose could not ignore the emperor's sin, but could he deal with this sinner as he would have done with others? Probably not, although it has been observed that we lack specific knowledge about the ordinary ways of dealing with sinners in Milan in this period.[37] Ambrose could point to biblical precedents of kings doing penance, most of all, of course, the case of David doing penance for his adultery with Bathsheba and his responsibility for the killing of her husband Uriah. Ambrose's arguments might have helped to convince Theodosius that penance could also bring honour, but probably Ambrose also showed him the way out of a precarious political situation, as Neil McLynn has argued.[38] In November the emperor declared that he was willing to undergo public penance. In the address delivered by Ambrose on the death of the penitent emperor five years later, the bishop reminded his audience how the emperor laid down all the imperial insignia, bewailed his sin in public in the basilica and implored absolution with tears and laments. He stressed that the emperor was not ashamed to do what the citizens

[35] Eusebius, *Historia Ecclesiastica*, VI, 34, ed. E. Schwartz, T. Mommsen and F. Winkelmann, *Eusebius Werke: Die Kirchengeschichte* 2.1. Die Griechischen christlichen Schriftsteller der ersten Jahrhunderte, NF 6.2 (Berlin 1999, reprint of the 1st edition), pp. 588–9; cf. Schieffer, 'Von Mailand nach Canossa', pp. 336–8.

[36] Ambrose, *Sermo contra Auxentium*, 36, PL 16, cols. 1007–18, at 1018 B, a statement articulated in the dispute with the Arian bishop Auxentius over the possession of churches in Milan in the years 385–6; for an English translation, see Ambrose, *Political Letters and Speeches*, pp. 142–60 (citation on p. 159); for this conflict, see Moorhead, *Ambrose*, pp. 129–56.

[37] Dassmann, *Ambrosius*, p. 270: 'fehlen exakte dogmatische, kirchenrechtliche und liturgische Auskünfte über Häufigkeit und Modalitäten des kirchlichen Bußverfahrens in Mailand in Ambrosius' Amtszeit' (p. 270).

[38] McLynn, *Ambrose*, pp. 315–30.

were ashamed of: to do penance in public.[39] According to the Church historian Theodoretus, the emperor was allowed to participate in the Mass again as a full member of the Christian community on the following festival of Christmas.[40] His penance, therefore, was a rather short one. It is furthermore unlikely that Theodosius by laying down his imperial insignia had thereby formally renounced imperial power, since there are no signs that the empire did without an emperor during Theodosius's penitence or that imperial authority was in any sense affected by these events. The emperor seems to have been reconciled before Christmas, when he appears to have received communion, although we lack any specific information about this. In Milan in Ambrose's days Maundy Thursday seems to have been the day when penitents were ritually reconciled.[41] The terms of penance and the time of reconciliation seem therefore to have been especially negotiated for imperial use.[42]

There is another episode in Ambrose's life that possibly involves penance by a high-standing official. In the year 396, six years after Theodosius's penance and in the first year of the reign of his successor Honorius, a certain Cresconius sought refuge in a church in Milan, probably Ambrose's basilica, but was arrested and taken away by Arian troops on the order of the *magister militum* Stilicho. According to his biographer Paulinus who had been Ambrose's secretary (*notarius*) in this period, the aged and venerable Ambrose deplored this breach of the right of sanctuary lying in prostration before the altar. When the prisoner was taken to the amphitheatre to be executed, the leopards in the arena refrained from assailing the prisoner but went instead for the soldiers who had been responsible for the breach of sanctuary. This convinced Stilicho of his error, still according to Paulinus, and 'during many days he offered satisfaction to the bishop'. Paulinus carefully crafts this story by opposing an ecclesiastical topograpy (the basilica) with an imperial one (the arena), but unfortunately does not provide any details concerning the way in which Stilicho might have offered satis-faction. It seems, however, that some sort of penitential procedure

---

[39] Ambrose, *De obitu Theodosii*, 34, ed. O. Faller, *Sancti Ambrosii opera. Pars Septima: Explanatio symboli, De sacramentis, De mysteriis, De paenitentia, De excessu fratris, De obitu Valentiniani, De obitu Theodosii*, CSEL 73 (Vienna 1955), pp. 369–401, at p. 388 (translated in Ambrose of Milan, *Political Letters and Speeches*, pp. 174–203, see p. 193).

[40] Theodoretus, *Historia Ecclesiastica*, V, 18, ed. L. Parmentier e.a. SC 530 (Paris 2009), pp. 404–14.

[41] See Ambrose, *Epistola 76*, c. 26, ed. M. Zelzer, *Sancti Ambrosii Opera. Pars Decima. Epistularum liber decimus, epistulae extra collectionem, Gesta concili Aquileiensis*, CSEL 82.3, p. 124; 'erat autem dies quo sese Dominus pro nobis tradidit, quo in ecclesia poenitentia relaxatur' [tr. in Ambrose of Milan, *Political Letters and Speeches*, p. 172].

[42] Dassmann, *Ambrosius*, pp. 190–1.

was envisaged.[43] The fact, however, that Paulinus does not choose to describe this satisfaction in any detail, whereas he laid particular emphasis on the public character of Theodosius's penance, suggests that in this case the atonement offered by Stilicho was even more tailored to the person of the *magister militum* than it had been in the case of Theodosius.

There is a third chapter in which Paulinus discusses Ambrose's attitude towards penance in a more general sense. This is found in a conspicuous position in the part in which he treats the virtues of Ambrose.[44] Paulinus stresses two aspects of the bishop's dealings with sinners. First, the bishop took part of the burden of sin. He compelled the sinner to bewail his sins, but the bishop 'wept with the weeping' and was seen prostrating himself with the prostrated sinner. The second aspect that Paulinus chooses to stress is that Ambrose never talked about the sins confessed to him with anyone, except with the Lord with whom he interceded on behalf of the sinner. Paulinus praises the example of Ambrose who was an intercessor for God and no accuser before men. This statement by Ambrose's biographer underlines one of the central difficulties of the position in which a confessor could find himself. He was not only involved in the vertical relationship between a Christian and his God, but at the same time could not always escape a certain involvement in the more horizontal bonds between a sinner and his fellow men. The fact that Paulinus stresses Ambrose's virtuous conceal-ment of a sinner's crime as an example for later confessors (*bonum relinquens exemplum posteris sacerdotibus*) suggests that it was often difficult to protect a sinner in this way.

The evidence from Ambrose and Augustine suggests that in Milan and Hippo at the end of the fourth century there existed an established ecclesi-astical ritual dealing with sinners in which the bishop played the central role. The bishop, however, acted in cooperation with the local Christian community for whom it was publicly known who the penitents were, if not what they had done. For some there was honour in being a penitent, while even men like the *magister militum* or emperor himself could be subjected to such a ritual. In the cases involving high-profile political figures it seems that bishops adjusted the penitential ritual according to the political

---

[43] Paulinus, *Vita Ambrosii*, c. 34, ed. M. Pellegrino, p. 100; see P. Buc, *The Dangers of Ritual. Between Early Medieval Texts and Social Scientific Theory* (Princeton 2001), pp. 152–3 who speaks simply about Stilicho doing penance and Dassmann, *Ambrosius*, p. 254 who expresses doubts whether this should be regarded as a canonical penance or perhaps some other kind of satisfaction; McLynn, *Ambrose*, p. 364 does not regard this as a form of ecclesiastical penance, but only speaks of Stilicho 'making amends', stressing, however, the strength of Stilicho's position vis à vis Ambrose.

[44] Paulinus, *Vita Ambrosii*, c. 39, ed. M. Pellegrino, pp. 106–8.

circumstances. Whether the rituals enacted in Hippo and in Milan were similar, however, we do not know, although the fact that Augustine had been in Milan and had been taught by Ambrose would suggest that in this case some cross-fertilization had taken place. Still, regional differences in dealing with penitents were probably the rule. At the great meeting of bishops gathering in Nicaea in 325 from many places within the *oikoumene*, for example, disciplinary measures for failing members of the Christian community were established. In the canons promulgated by this famous council, a system of penances becomes visible, in which penitents go through three stages before they are readmitted as full members of the community.[45] Such a system of penitential stages seems to have been quite common in Anatolia. The Greek Church Father Basil advocated a system with four penitential stages and we may assume that Basil's fame helped to establish such a system in the Greek world. In the West, however, we have no signs of the existence of these penitential stages. In Armenia we know that a ritual for public penance existed in the seventh century with two grades of penitents, but in contrast to the system as we know it from the Latin West, in the Armenian church the rites of penance were no episcopal prerogative, but could be ministered by a priest or a teacher (*vardapet*).[46] This suggests that, in general, local solutions were brokered on the basis of some general rules. In specific cases, as we have seen, the resulting forms of dealing with penitent sinners were especially tailored for the occasion.

Gaul in the sixth century: a penitential wasteland?

Late antique and early medieval sermons to the laity often stressed the sinful nature of man and the necessity to make satisfaction for one's sins. Julianus Pomerius the late fifth-century Gallic author in his influential work *De vita contemplativa* (*On the Contemplative Life*) taught that it was not enough for a bishop to teach his congregation by example, i.e. by leading a virtuous life, but that it was also his task to admonish sinners by preaching.[47] The sixth-century collection of sermons known as the Eusebius Gallicanus collection illustrates the importance of penance in preaching in Gaul at this period.[48] Julianus Pomerius's pupil Caesarius,

---

[45] Council of Nicaea, c. 11, ed. Saint-Roch, *La pénitence*, p. 141.

[46] E. Carr, 'Penance among the Armenians: notes on the history of its practice and its theology', *Studia Liturgica* 11 (1976), pp. 65–100, at pp. 65–9.

[47] Julianus Pomerius, *De vita contemplativa* I, 20, PL 59, cols. 415–520, at 430–1; see Rapp, *Holy Bishops*, pp. 51–2.

[48] L. Bailey, '"Our own most severe judges": the power of penance in the Eusebius Gallicanus sermons', in A. Cain and N. Lenski (eds.), *The Power of Religion in Late Antiquity* (Farnham 2009), pp. 201–11.

bishop of Arles in the first half of the sixth century, followed the advice of his teacher and unceasingly preached to his congregation that they should abandon the road of evil, bewail their sins and do penance for them. He presented himself to his flock as the Old Testament prophet Isaiah, who on the Lord's command had to 'cry out unceasingly and lift his voice like a trumpet blast to announce their sins to the people' (Ezekiel 3.18).[49] Caesarius distinguished between daily or lesser sins and deadly sins (*peccata minuta, peccata quotidiana* and *peccata capitalia*).[50] Among the first he reckons eating or drinking to excess, talking too loud when one should be silent or remaining silent when one should speak aloud, harsh treatment of beggars, non-observance of fasting periods, tardiness in rising for church, sexual relations for other reasons than for procreation, failing to visit the sick and the imprisoned, failure to reconcile enemies when there is an opportunity to do so, harshness with one's family and servants, flattery of the powerful, idle talk in church, evil thoughts, a lascivious gaze (*concupiscentia oculorum*) and listening to obscene tales and songs.[51] The capital sins include murder, adultery and honoring pagan cults (*sacrilegium*), as well as false testimony, theft, pride, envy, avarice, anger, frequent abuse of alcohol, fornication and abortion.[52] For such grave sins, serious remedies were in order. Caesarius mentions tears, bewailment, long fasts, generous alms, removal from the Eucharist and the ritual of public penance as means to make up for the sins. Without these the sinner would be condemned to eternal damnation, Caesarius preached.[53] The penitent was also supposed to shave his hair and to wear special clothing, but, Caesarius admonished, it was even more important to change his behaviour and to stop sinning.[54] Interestingly, Caesarius speaks of doing penance in public (*paenitentiam ... publice agentes*), which implies that there were also other ways to atone for one's sins. This applies in particular to the lesser sins, the *peccata minuta*. These could apparently be remedied by

[49] W. Klingshirn, *Caesarius of Arles. The Making of a Christian Community in Late Antique Gaul* (Cambridge 1994), p. 147.

[50] Sermo 179, 2–3, ed. G. Morin, *Sancti Caesarii Arelatensis Sermones nunc primum in unum collecti et ad leges artis criticae ex innumeris Mss. recogniti*, Pars I, 2, CC SL 104 (Turnhout 1953), pp. 724–6; see also sermo 64, ed. G. Morin, *Sancti Caesarii Arelatensis Sermones*, Pars I, 1, CC SL 103 (Turnhout 1953), pp. 275–8; for Caesarius's classification of sins, see C. Vogel, *La discipline pénitentielle en Gaule des origines à la fin du VIIe siècle* (Paris 1952), pp. 86–96 and H. Beck, *The Pastoral Care of Souls in South-East France During the Sixth Century* (Rome 1950), pp. 188–90.

[51] Sermo 64, 2 and 179, 3, ed. Morin, *Sancti Caesarii Arelatensis Sermones* I, 1, pp. 275–6 and I, 2, pp. 725–6.

[52] Sermo 179, 2, ed. Morin, *Sancti Caesarii Arelatensis Sermones* I, 2, pp. 724–5.

[53] Sermo 179, 7, ed. Morin, *Sancti Caesarii Arelatensis Sermones*, I, 2, pp. 727–8.

[54] Sermo 56, 3, ed. Morin, *Sancti Caesarii Arelatensis Sermones*, I, 1, pp. 249–50.

other forms of satisfaction, which Caesarius calls *satisfactio communis, mediocris vel secreta*.[55] Such remedies were to be found in forms of virtuous Christian behaviour. By fasting, distributing alms, caring for the sick and prisoners, acts of hospitality, pardoning others and reconciling enemies a Christian could make amends for his sins and thereby avert punishment in the hereafter.[56]

Gallic councils from the time of Caesarius show that penance was a serious concern for the bishops. The fact that young Christians or married ones chose the life of a penitent appears to have been problematic, probably because of the continence which was demanded of a penitent. The council of Agde (506), convening at the behest of King Alaric II as a kind of national Visigothic council over which Caesarius of Arles presided, gave the advice to be reticent in admitting the young to the procedure of penance because of the weakness of their age.[57] The council of Orléans meeting in 538, at which Caesarius was not present, but which approved of many decisions taken by the council of Agde, confirmed the ruling established at Agde regarding penitents, while it added that for married persons seeking penance one had first to obtain permission of the married partner.[58] Earlier Gallic councils regularly defined severe sanctions for those penitents who had returned to their former way of life.[59]

From Caesarius's sermons it transpires that one solution to such problems was to postpone penance to the end of one's life. This, of course, was a drastic solution to the problems of the penitent who did not live up to his new standard. In earlier days the practical problems involved in leading a Christian way of life were often resolved by postponing baptism to a late stage in life. Penance as a second baptism could also be applied in this way, particularly in a period when child baptism became the rule and postponing baptism was therefore not a real option any more. Penitential rites became a part of the deathbed ritual as it evolved in southern Gaul in the beginning of the sixth century.[60] According to his biographers Caesarius was anxious to

---

[55] Sermo 197, 2, ed. Morin, *Sancti Caesarii Arelatensis Sermones*, I, 2, p. 796.

[56] Sermo 60, 4, ed. Morin, *Sancti Caesarii Arelatensis Sermones*, pp. 265–6.

[57] Council of Agde, c. 15, ed. C. Munier, *Concilia Galliae A. 314 – A. 506*, CC SL 148 (Turnhout 1963), p. 201; for the function of this council and Caesarius's role, see Klingshirn, *Caesarius*, pp. 95–104.

[58] Council of Orléans (538), c. 27, ed. C. de Clercq, *Concilia Galliae A. 511 – A. 695*, CC SL 148A (Turnhout 1963), p. 124.

[59] Councils of Tours (461), c. 8, ed. Munier, *Concilia Galliae*, p. 146; council of Vannes (461–91), c. 3, ed. Munier, *Concilia Galliae*, p. 152; council of Orléans (511), c. 11, ed. de Clercq, *Concilia Galliae*, p. 8.

[60] Paxton, *Christianizing Death*, pp. 48–61.

prevent that 'anyone depart from this world without the remedy of repentance'.[61] In one of his sermons Caesarius discussed the value of this deathbed penance. Apparently many had doubts whether deathbed penance entailed a complete remission of sins. The bishop of Arles distinguished between three cases. If a Christian avoided serious sins and did penance for his venial sins during his life by doing good works, he would be saved, Caesarius taught, even if he did not receive penance at the end of his life. If someone committed not only lesser sins but even serious ones (*capitalia peccata*), he could be saved if he sinned by ignorance and not because he relied on deathbed penance to make up for all his sins. He had, however, to be sincere in his compunction and to be prepared to make up for his sins when he would recover from his illness. In the case that a sinner fully relied on the ritual of deathbed penance to atone for his failings, then it was doubtful, Caesarius taught, whether such a penance would really absolve his sins.[62]

In the fifth and early sixth century the validity of deathbed penance was a point of discussion, particularly among the bishops in southern Gaul. Faustus, bishop of Riez denied the validity of a form of penance in which the sinner did not make satisfaction for his offences. Avitus, bishop of Vienne, argued that any sincere compunction on the part of a sinner could bring forth God's mercy.[63] From the fact that Caesarius and his fellow bishops regularly felt they had to address the problem of sinners postponing their penance to the hour of death, it has been concluded that regular penance was not really an option any more in Caesarius's days. Historians have argued that the practice of penance with its public rituals performed in church had been abandoned because of the severity of this practice and the indifference of sinners. The only penitential remedy that was still being used was the ritual of deathbed penance, the *paenitentia in extremis*.[64]

---

[61] *Vita Caesarii* II,11, ed. G. Morin, *Sancti Caesarii episcopi Arelatensis Opera Omnia nunc primum in unum collecta*, vol. II (Maredsous 1942), pp. 329: 'Et cum nullum sine medicamento paenitentiae de hoc mundi vir dei voluisset recedere, illum praecipue sine hoc remedio non optabat abire', translated in Caesarius of Arles, *Life, Testament, Letters*, translated by W. E. Klingshirn, Translated Texts for Historians 19 (Liverpool 1994), p. 49: 'And although the man of God did not want anyone to depart from this world without the remedy of repentance, he especially did not want Liberius to depart without this remedy.'

[62] Sermo 60, ed. M. J. Delage, *Césaire d'Arles. Sermons au peuple* III, SC 330, pp. 57–69.

[63] Faustus of Riez, *Epistola 5 ad Paulinum*, ed. A. Engelbrecht, *Fausti Reiensis Opera praeter sermones Pseudo-Eusebianos, accedunt Ruricii epistulae*, CSEL 21 (Prague / Vienna / Leipzig 1891), p. 184; Avitus of Vienne, *Epistula ad Gundobadum regem de subita paenitentia*, ed. R. Peiper, MGH AA 6, 2 (Berlin 1882), pp. 29–32 [tr. Shanzer and Wood, *Avitus of Vienne*, pp. 193–201]; see D. Nodes, '*De subitanea paenitentia* in letters of Faustus of Riez and Avitus of Vienne', *Recherches de théologie ancienne et médievale* 55 (1988), pp. 30–40.

[64] Vogel, *La discipline pénitentielle en Gaule*, pp. 118–21 and 195.

For the rest Gaul is characterized as a 'penitential wasteland'. Actually, apart from the discussion about the validity of deathbed penance there is no real indication that penance went out of fashion.[65] We have discussed some famous cases of public penance above, but we do not know how often such a ritual was to be observed in the churches of Late Antiquity and therefore it remains hazardous to speak about a decline of the frequency of penance in the fifth and sixth centuries. The conciliar decisions from Gaul in this period about penitents not fulfilling their obligations or denying the young and the married access to the ritual of penance can also be read as evidence for worries among the bishops of Gaul about people taking on the burdens of penance too easily.[66] Caesarius starts one of his penitential sermons with the words: 'Every time we see some of our brothers and sisters publicly ask for penance', words which, as does the rest of this sermon, suggest a certain familiarity with this ritual among his audience.[67]

That canonical penance did not disappear from Gaul in this period is further revealed by the liturgical manuscripts containing descriptions of this particular ritual.[68] The early sacramentaries containing liturgical *ordines* with their directions for penitential rites are almost exclusively to be found in Merovingian manuscripts. The Old Gelasian Sacramentary, for example, named after Pope Gelasius I and one of the precious early witnesses to genuine Roman liturgical traditions, is preserved in a manuscript written around the year 750 in Merovingian Gaul, probably at the monastery of Jouarre or Chelles. This sacramentary contains an *ordo* describing the way a penitent should be accepted on Ash Wednesday and reconciled on Maundy Thursday. This *ordo* seems to reflect Roman usage, but it is not clear how much this Roman tradition has been adapted to the ways one dealt with sinners in Gaul.[69] The fact that it is found in a manuscript from Gaul and that it was adapted to local taste, however, suggests that there was still a demand for such a ritual in the middle of the eighth century.[70] Because there is no indication for a revival of ancient

---

[65] As argued persuasively in Uhalde, *Expectations of Justice*, pp. 105–34.

[66] Saint-Roch, *La pénitence*, p. 16 refers to the frequency with which Gallic and Spanish councils discussed penitential matters.

[67] Sermo 67, ed. SC 330, pp. 124–35; this passage has been used as support for the argument that penance had become rare and infrequent by Beck, *The Pastoral Care of Souls*, p. 199 and Poschmann, *Die abendländische Kirchenbusse im Ausgang des christlichen Altertums*, p. 116, n. 2.

[68] J. A. Jungmann, *Die lateinischen Bussriten in ihrer geschichtlichen Entwicklung* (Innsbruck 1932), p. 54, fn. 1.

[69] See Jungmann, *Die lateinischen Bussriten*, pp. 13 and 40, 47; Vogel, *La discipline pénitentielle*, pp. 182–97; C. Vogel, *Medieval Liturgy. An Introduction to the Sources* (Washington 1986), p. 67.

[70] It has been argued that the Old Gelasian came to Merovingian France only via Britain; see Y. Hen, 'The liturgy of St Willibrord', *Anglo-Saxon England* 26 (1997), pp. 41–60.

penitential ritual in Gaul around the middle of the eighth century, it seems reasonable to assume that this ritual has somehow remained of interest in Merovingian Gaul up until its 'codification' in the Old Gelasian Sacramentary.[71] The Gelasian Sacramentary influenced a great many eighth-century sacramentaries from Gaul, a family of texts known as the eighth-century Gelasian sacramentaries.[72] These sacramentaries adopted the penitential ritual from the Old Gelasian Sacramentary, with only minor variations.[73] Interestingly, many of these sacramentaries also contain a penitential handbook as these had developed in Ireland and Britain. What this implies for the practice of penance in Gaul in the eighth century will be discussed in another chapter.[74]

Penitential remedies

Rather than supposing that penance was on its decline in Gaul in the sixth century, it seems more convincing to conclude that bishops in Gaul in this period were particularly sensitive to penitential matters. It has recently been argued that the fifth and sixth centuries were a period of heightened liturgical creativity in Gaul and that penance was an important aspect of new liturgical developments.[75] Rogation ceremonies like the one instituted in Rome by Gregory the Great were in Gaul instituted by Bishop Mamertus after an earthquake had struck the city of Vienne. In Vienne these Rogations lasted for no less than three days, filled with prayer, fasting, psalmody and lamentation.[76] The penitential character of

---

[71] For the codification of the liturgy in late Merovingian Gaul, see Y. Hen, *The Royal Patronage of Liturgy in Frankish Gaul. To the Death of Charles the Bald (877)*, Henry Bradshaw Society, Subsidia 3 (London 2001), pp. 28–33.

[72] For which see B. Moreton, *The Eighth-Century Gelasian Sacramentary. A Study in Tradition* (Oxford 1976).

[73] Compare the ritual for public penance in the sacramentaries of Angoulême, ed. P. Saint-Roch, *Liber Sacramentorum Engolismensis. Manuscrit B.N. Lat. 816. Le Sacramentaire Gélasien d'Angoulême*, CC SL 159 C (Turnhout 1987), pp. 37–8 and 81–5); of Autun, ed. O. Heiming, *Liber Sacramentorum Augustodunensis*, CC SL 159 B (Turnhout 1984), pp. 34–5 and 55–6); of Gellone, ed. A. Dumas, *Liber Sacramentorum Gellonensis*, CC SL 159A, pp. 33–4 and 76–9); the Bobbio Missal, nrs. 196–200, ed. E. Lowe, *The Bobbio Missal. A Gallican Mass-Book*, Henry Bradshaw Society 58 (London 1920) and the Gelasian Sacramentary of St Gall, ed. C. Mohlberg, *Das fränkische Sacramentarium Gelasianum in alamannischer Überlieferung (codex Sangall. No. 348)* (3rd edition Münster 1971), pp. 48, 68–73, 92 and 378; see also M. Mansfield, *The Humiliation of Sinners. Public Penance in Thirteenth Century France* (Ithaca / London 1995), p. 169.

[74] See Chapter 4.

[75] Wood, 'Liturgy in the Rhône valley', pp. 207–8; the liturgical creativity of Merovingian Gaul is also stressed in Hen, *The Royal Patronage of Liturgy*, pp. 21–41.

[76] Sidonius Apollinaris, Ep. V.14, ed. W. B. Anderson, *Sidonius Apollinaris. Poems and Letters* (Cambridge MA and London 1965), vol. II, pp. 216–18; see Hen, *Royal Patronage of Liturgy*, p. 24.

this ceremony was stressed by Bishop Avitus, Mamertus's successor in Vienne at the close of the fifth century, who proudly recalled that this ceremony, which had been established at the town of Vienne, soon spread over many other parts of Gaul.[77] It was, for example, also known in Arles as revealed by several sermons preached by Caesarius for this occasion.[78] The council of Orléans of the year 511 declared that all churches should keep to these Rogation days.[79] A pupil of Caesarius, Theodarius, was appointed intercessor for the city of Vienne, if we can believe the ninth-century source informing us about this fact, a position in which he was supposed to mediate for the spiritual well-being of the city.[80] Bishop Gallus of Clermont (525–51) introduced a yearly penitential procession to the grave of St Brioude some 65 kilometres away from Clermont, to be performed in the middle of the penitential season of Lent.[81] In the sixth century, therefore, collective penitential rituals were an important aspect of religious life in southern and central Gaul. They were instigated on the initiative of the local bishop who seems to have played a central role in them, as the sermons delivered on such occasions by for example Avitus or Caesarius reveal. These rituals demonstrated the bishops' leading role in the cities of Gaul and were at the same time a means to establish such a leading position.[82] In such a situation it is difficult to imagine that bishops were unable to impose the ritual of penance on notorious sinners, although it is impossible to establish for this period as for an earlier one the frequency with which this happened.

---

[77] Avitus of Vienne, *Homilia in rogationibus*, ed. Peiper, translation in Shanzer and Wood, *Avitus of Vienne*, pp. 381–8.

[78] Caesarius, *Sermones* 148, 157, 160A, 207, 208, 209, ed. G. Morin, *Sancti Caesarii Arelatensis Sermones nunc primum in unum collecti et ad leges artis criticae ex innumeris Mss. recogniti*, 2 vols. CC SL 104 (Turnhout 1953), vol. II, pp. 605, 641, 658, 828, 832 and 834.

[79] Council of Orléans (511), cc. 27–8, ed. de Clercq, *Concilia Galliae*, pp. 11–12.

[80] *Vita Theudarii* cc. 13–15, ed. B. Krusch, MGH SS rer. mer. III (Hanover 1896), pp. 529–30; discussed in Wood, 'Liturgy of the Rhône valley', p. 208, and Beck, *The Pastoral Care of Souls*, p. 214.

[81] Gregory of Tours, *Historiae* IV, 5, ed. Krusch and Levison, pp. 138–9 and Gregory of Tours, *Liber vitae patrum*, VI, 6, ed. B. Krusch, MGH SS rer. mer. I, 2 (Hanover 1885), pp. 234–5; see Wood, 'Liturgy in the Rhône valley', p. 208.

[82] F. Prinz, 'Die bischöfliche Stadtherrschaft im Frankenreich vom 5. bis zum 7. Jahrhundert', *Historische Zeitschift* 217 (1974), pp. 1–35; M. Heinzelmann, *Bischofsherrschaft in Gallien. Zur Kontinuität römischer Führungsschichten vom 4. bis zum 7. Jahrhundert. Soziale, prosopographische und bildungsgeschichtliche Aspekte* (Munich 1976); R. Kaiser, *Bischofsherrschaft zwischen Königtum und Fürstenmacht. Studien zur bischöflichen Stadtherrschaft im westfranzösischen Reich im frühen und hohen Mittelalter* (Bonn 1981); for a careful reassessment of the concept of *Bischofsherrschaft* see I. Wood, *The Merovingian Kingdoms 450–751* (London / New York 1994), pp. 71–87.

Penance was moreover a regular topic of discussion at Gallic councils in the fifth and sixth centuries. We have already seen Gallic bishops discussing the validity of deathbed penance, but other issues pertaining to penance were regularly addressed.[83] In the collections of canon law of this period, such as the *Statuta Ecclesiae Antiqua*, composed in southern Gaul in the second half of the fifth century – possibly by Gennadius of Marseille – or the *Collectio Vetus Gallica*, composed in Lyon in the decades around the year 600, penance is regularly prescribed as the proper atonement for specific sins.[84] Sins and their remedies were, moreover, at the heart of the reform programme of Caesarius of Arles.[85] Caesarius admonished his audience that a Christian believer had to take care to be in a state of purity when taking communion at the altar, which according to the council of Agde (508) a Christian should do at the Christian festivals of Christmas, Easter and Pentecost.[86] He had to refrain from sexual relations and to atone for his sins by prayers, fasts and alms.[87] If Christians had to atone for their sins every time they took communion, it is clear that Caesarius is not referring to the grand ritual of canonical penance here, but to the other ways to atone for one's sins we mentioned earlier. Caesarius's programme for reform tackled many issues that church leaders had not really addressed before and can be characterized by two major tendencies. First, Caesarius tried

[83] For example at the councils of Orange (441), cc. 3–4 and 12, ed. Munier, *Concilia Galliae*, pp. 78–9 and 81; Vaison (442), cc. 2 and 8, ed. Munier, *Concilia Galliae*, pp. 96 and 100; Arles (442–506), cc. 9–12, 21–5, 28–9 and 52, ed. Munier, *Concilia Galliae*, pp. 115–16, 118–20 and 124; Angers (453), cc. 5 and 12, ed. Munier, *Concilia Galliae*, p. 138; Tours (461), cc. 7–8, ed. Munier, *Concilia Galliae*, p. 146; Vannes (461), cc. 1, 3 and 13, ed. Munier, *Concilia Galliae*, pp. 151–2 and 155; Agde (506), cc. 2, 15, 37, 43–4, 60, ed. Munier, *Concilia Galliae*, pp. 193, 201, 208, 211 and 227; Orleans (511), cc. 7, 11–12, ed. de Clercq, *Concilia Galliae*, pp. 7–8; Epaon (517), cc. 3, 23, 28, 29, 31 and 36, ed. de Clercq, *Concilia Galliae*, pp. 25 and 30–4; Arles (524), c. 3, ed. de Clercq, *Concilia Galliae*, p. 44; Marseille (533), ed. de Clercq, *Concilia Galliae*, p. 85; Orléans (538), cc. 27–8, ed. de Clercq, *Concilia Galliae*, pp. 124; Orléans (541), cc. 8 and 28, ed. de Clercq, *Concilia Galliae*, pp. 134 and 139; Eauze (551), c. 1, ed. de Clercq, *Concilia Galliae*, p. 163; Tours (567), c. 21, ed. de Clercq, *Concilia Galliae*, pp. 184–8; Mâcon (581–3), cc. 12, 19–20, ed. de Clercq, *Concilia Galliae*, pp. 226 and 228; Mâcon (585), c. 8, ed. de Clercq, *Concilia Galliae*, pp. 242–3; Clichy (626/7), c. 9, ed. de Clercq, *Concilia Galliae*, p. 293.

[84] *Statuta Ecclesiae Antiqua*, ed. C. Munier, *Les 'Statuta ecclesiae antiqua': édition, études critiques* (Paris 1960). *Collectio Vetus Gallica*, ed. H. Mordek, *Kirchenrecht und Reform im Frankenreich. Die Collectio Vetus Gallica, die älteste systematische Kanonessammlung des fränkischen Gallien. Studien und Edition*, Beiträge zur Geschichte und Quellenkunde des Mittelalters 1 (Berlin / New York 1975), pp. 341–617.

[85] For Caesarius's programme of reform, see Klingshirn, *Caesarius*, pp. 146–243.

[86] Council of Agde, c. 16, ed. Munier, CS SL 148.

[87] Klingshirn, *Caesarius*, pp. 155–6; for sexual abstinence and attending Mass, see sermons 16,2, 19,3 187,4 and 188,3; for penance as a preparation for Mass, see sermons 202,4 and 227,2.

to persuade the laity to follow forms of religious behaviour more in accordance with the life of religious specialists, such as monks, nuns or clerics. The other important aspect of Caesarius's programme is that it addressed forms of behaviour to be found outside the Roman town of Arles.[88] Although we should be careful not to equate Caesarius's designations for 'rustic' too easily with forms of behaviour by peasants, it seems Caesarius's reform progamme tackled many rural forms of behaviour for their unchristian character. In this way Caesarius branded many cultural habits as 'superstitious' and thus sinful and he was too much of a pastor not to feel the need for advising ways to atone for these sins. Therefore, he recommended practical means to atone for these lesser sins. Many of the forms of superstitious behaviour that Caesarius had castigated were later rejected by church councils in Gaul and thus came to form a part of a catalogue of sins a Christian had to avoid.

Bishops and holy men

Caesarius thus offered his audience several means by which they could make up for their sins. The details of personal virtuous acts were probably left to the discretion of the individual sinner, although he or she might of course have asked religious men or women for advice. The formal ritual of penance and deathbed were supervised and controlled by the bishop and his clergy. Assisted by the community, the bishops acted as intermediaries between the individual sinner and God, and the power to reconcile sinners formed part of what has recently been defined as the pragmatic authority of bishops.[89] Other forms of authority, however, were also sought after for the absolution of sins. Already in the second century people flocked to the prisons in Lyons and Vienne to profit from the intercessory powers of the martyrs locked up for execution. The aura of holiness surrounding the imprisoned martyrs gave them the authority to pray for sinners and even to issue written confirmations of their intercessory powers in the form of *libelli pacis*.[90] Holy men were also credited with intercessory powers by virtue of their ascetic lifestyle and they often took on someone else's burden of sin by the process of vicarious penance.[91] This would have the effect that sinners could feel acquitted from the burden of sin by the powers of a holy man (or woman), without having

[88] Klingshirn, *Caesarius*, pp. 171–243.
[89] For the notion of pragmatic authority, see Rapp, *Holy Bishops*, pp. 23–55; for the administration of penance as part of this pragmatic authority, enhanced, however, with the spiritual authority inherent in the episcopal office, see Rapp, *Holy Bishops*, p. 95.
[90] Rapp, *Holy Bishops*, pp. 85–90.   [91] Rapp, *Holy Bishops*, pp. 81–5.

to go through the episcopally controlled penitential process. On the other hand we should not forget that such distinctions were not always that simple. Someone like Caesarius of Arles would possess pragmatic authority because of his holding episcopal office as well as because of the social standing of his family, but at the same time his monastic background and his ascetic lifestyle would grant him spiritual and ascetic authority enabling him to perform miracles and to forgive sinners.

As can be gleaned from the liturgical rituals surrounding sickness and death, physical afflictions were, particularly in the West, increasingly seen as the consequence of moral failings. Remission of sins, therefore, played an ever-growing role in the liturgy of the dying.[92] In Merovingian Gaul we observe that sickness was often regarded as the consequence of sin. The historiographical and hagiographical works of Gregory of Tours, for example, regularly describe miracles in which people are punished for their sins. Healing miracles, therefore, can be regarded as rituals by which sinners were relieved of the consequences of their sins. Such miracles, taking place mostly on or near the graves of saints in a liturgical setting in the many suburban basilicas of Gaul, often have a public character. The rituals of healing have been examined as processes of reconciliation on at least two levels: the level of the relation of a saint and a sinner and on the other hand that of the relation between a religious community and a sinner. A healing ceremony entailed not so much a physical cure, but 'rather confession, judgment, forgiveness, and reconciliation'.[93] Rituals of exorcism are a subspecies of healing miracles, which have been described as 'drama[s] of authority' and 'dramas of reintegration'. They also occurred in a public setting, and the liturgical process bore a close resemblance to Roman judicial procedures as well as confessional practices, for example when a demon answered demands made in the name of the local saint, a process resembling the interrogation of a criminal or the penitent sinner. Exorcism rituals, therefore, can be regarded as ceremonies aimed at the reintegration of sinners into the Christian community by supernatural means.[94] Many of the healing rituals in Gaul, that we know of, took place in the suburban basilicas, under the supervision of the local bishop. We may assume, however, that in localities priests, monks or other clerics sometimes acted in a similar way, although perhaps not always with the same authority as a bishop.[95]

---

[92] Paxton, *Christianizing Death*.
[93] R. van Dam, *Saints and Their Miracles in Late Antique Gaul* (Princeton 1993), p. 89.
[94] P. Brown, *The Cult of Saints. Its Rise and Function in Latin Christianity* (Chicago 1981), pp. 106–13.
[95] For priests in Merovingian Gaul, see R. Godding, *Prêtres en Gaule mérovingienne*, Subsidia hagiographica 82 (Brussels 2001).

Penance in the afterlife

We have already seen that the Christian community could support the sinner when undertaking penance. Holy men, moreover, could take on a part or even the whole burden of sin by way of vicarious penance. The debate on the validity of deathbed penance revolved around the question whether sins could be absolved without the penitent giving adequate satisfaction. This issue probably related to the controversy that was still raging in southern Gaul initiated by Pelagius and his notions of free will and divine grace.[96] However, in the work of Gregory the Great another aspect comes to the fore: the possibility that sins could be forgiven through expiation in the afterlife. In his *Dialogues* Gregory argues that minor sins can be forgiven in the world to come.[97] Elaborating earlier notions of purgatorial fire by which deceased sinners had to be cleansed of their sins, Gregory not only related visions in which trivial sins were cleansed in purgatorial fire, but he also related how one could assist a deceased person in such a situation. The Roman deacon Paschasius had lived a holy life, yet had backed the wrong candidate for the Roman see. After his death, so Gregory reports, Germanus bishop of Capua saw Paschasius serving as an attendant at the hot baths of Angulus, which, Paschasius confessed, served as a punishment for him backing Lawrence against Pope Symmachus. He implored Germanus to pray for him and when the bishop of Capua did so and returned after a couple of days, Paschasius was no longer to be found in this awful place and this showed that Germanus's prayers had been efficacious.[98] In some cases, therefore, the living could assist the dead to make up for their sins,

---

[96] For the discussion in southern Gaul, see R. Weaver, *Divine Grace and Human Agency. A Study of the Semi-Pelagian Controversy* (Macon GA 1996).

[97] The authenticity of this work has been disputed by F. Clark, *The 'Gregorian' Dialogues and the Origins of Benedictine Monasticism* (Leiden 2003); but see the responses by P. Meyvaert, 'The authentic *Dialogues* of Gregory the Great', *Sacris Erudiri* 43 (2004), pp. 55–129 and A. de Vogüé, 'Is Gregory the Great the author of the "Dialogues"?', *American Benedictine Review* 56 (2005), pp. 309–14; for a brief summary and assessment of the discussion, see S. Pricoco, 'Dialogi: autenticità', in G. Cremascoli and A. Degl'Innocenti (eds.), *Enciclopedia Gregoriana. La vita, l'opera e la fortuna di Gregorio Magno* (Florence 2008), pp. 88–9.

[98] Gregory the Great, *Dialogi* IV, 41–2, ed. A. de Vogüé, *Dialogues*. SC 265 (Paris 1980), pp. 146–54; see J. Le Goff, *La naissance du purgatoire* (Paris 1981), pp. 121–31; C. Carozzi, *Le voyage de l'âme dans l'au-delà d'après la littérature latine (Ve–XIIIe siècle)* (Rome 1994), pp. 43–61. The fact that this episode is set in the context of Roman baths suggests that we are dealing with a text written in a late antique setting, rather than in an insular one as suggested by M. Dunn, 'Gregory the Great, the Vision of Fursey and the origins of purgatory', *Peritia* 14 (2000), pp. 238–54; see also M. Dunn, *The Christianization of the Anglo-Saxons c. 597–c. 700. Discourses of Life, Death and Afterlife* (London 2009), p. 157 endorsing Clark's views on the authenticity of the *Dialogues*.

for which they had not given proper satisfaction during their lifetime. This development, for which we find the earliest evidence in Gregory's *Dialogues*, inaugurated later customs of assisting the dead in the afterlife by means of prayer for which sometimes massive investments to religious institutions were then made.

Gregory's treatment of prayer for the dead has been regarded as an indication that the *Dialogues* could not have been written by this pope. His view of the afterlife as well as his perception of sin would rather resemble the situation in England around the year 670, a period in which Irish conceptions of penance and the cult of Gregory the Great had evolved in Anglo-Saxon England. It has also been suggested that Gregory knew of Irish penitential practice because of his contacts with the Irishman Columbanus, who had moved to the Continent in 590 and who corresponded with Pope Gregory. Instead of assuming, however, that the *Dialogues* are inauthentic or that Gregory knew Irish penitential practice, we should perhaps admit that many elements which we find in Irish penitential practice were not that different from the ways to deal with sins that solicitous pastors as Caesarius of Arles and Gregory the Great had already developed in late antique Gaul and Italy. Historians have tended to stress the differences between late antique forms of penance and those developed in Ireland in the course of the sixth century, but contemporaries of Gregory the Great or Columbanus never seem to have noticed serious differences. Apparently they did not discern important divergences between Irish penitential practice and continental practice. Apart from Columbanus's hagiographer, Jonas of Bobbio, to whom we shall come back later, we have to wait for the Carolingian bishops to comment on such differences. That historians saw more discrepancies between Irish and continental penitential practice than contemporaries did is to be explained by their focus on formal ways of doing penance. If, however, prayers for the dead, intercession of the saints, individual forms of atonement such as the giving of alms, fasting or caring for the sick are included in the discussion, the differences between the ways Irish missionaries dealt with sin and the ways Caesarius of Arles or Gregory the Great did become much less apparent. It is to these Irish ways of dealing with sin that we shall now turn.

3 A new beginning? Penitential practice in the insular world

For over a hundred years historians have taken for granted that private penance originated in Ireland. Since Paul Fournier demonstrated that those penitential handbooks which Hermann Joseph Schmitz still believed to be of Roman origin were actually written in Francia on the basis of earlier texts composed in Ireland and England, it has been generally assumed that penitential handbooks as we know them from the early Middle Ages originated in Ireland and the regions dominated by Celtic-speaking peoples in Britain.[1] There is no doubt that the earliest texts of this new genre do indeed stem from these regions. However, this does not automatically imply that private penance originated with these texts, as so many authors have assumed.[2] As this chapter will demonstrate, there are many uncertainties about the status and the function of penitential handbooks in early medieval Ireland and Wales and their role may at the same time have been more constricted than historians have assumed, but also more far-reaching.

First we have to remember that Christianity had taken root in Ireland at some point in the fifth century. The chronicler Prosper of Aquitaine recorded that in the year 431 a deacon by the name of Palladius had been sent to 'the Irish who believe in Christ' as their first bishop, by Pope Celestine I.[3] As Pope Leo I, with whom Prosper was in close contact, recognized, the introduction of Christianity into Ireland was a unique event, since it meant that Christianity transcended the political

---

[1] P. Fournier, 'Études sur les pénitentiels', *Revue d'histoire et de littérature religieuses* 6 (1901), pp. 289–317, 7 (1902), pp. 59–70 and 121–7, 8 (1903), pp. 528–53 and 9 (1904), pp. 97–103; now published together in P. Fournier, *Mélanges de droit canonique*, ed. T. Kölzer (Aalen 1983).

[2] E.g. B. Poschmann, *Penance and the Anointing of the Sick* (New York 1964) (tr. from *Buße und letzte Ölung*, Handbuch der Dogmengeschichte IV, 3, Freiburg i. Br. 1951), p. 125. C. Vogel, *Le pécheur et la pénitence au Moyen Age. Textes choisis, traduits et présentés par Cyrille Vogel* (Paris 1969), pp. 16–17; K. Hughes, *Early Christian Ireland. Introduction to the Sources* (Ithaca 1972), p. 84; also see the excellent study of B. Yorke, *The Conversion of Britain. Religion, Politics and Society in Britain c. 600–800* (Harlow 2006), pp. 228–9.

[3] Prosper Tiro, *Epitoma Chronicon*, ed. T. Mommsen, MGH AA 9, p. 473.

boundaries of the Roman empire.[4] Whereas in Gaul the position of the
bishop could in many aspects relate to the Roman past, this was much
harder in Ireland where, for example, no towns existed which were
comparable to the late Roman towns as they were found in regions
of the former Roman empire. The earliest phases of the process of
Christianization in Ireland still raise many questions. The relationship
between Palladius and Patrick, for example, is a perennial question in
early Irish history. Palladius was a deacon of the church of Auxerre prior
to his departure for Ireland and was closely connected to the influential
bishop of Auxerre, Germanus, who combatted Pelagianism in Britain.
Palladius probably was acquainted with ways of doing penance as it was
being practised in Gaul in his time, although we have no precise information for Auxerre in the early fifth century. We may perhaps assume
that the bishop played a prominent role in such a penitential procedure.
Patrick, who in later tradition became 'the apostle of the Irish', knew the
concept of penance for serious crimes, as his letter to Coroticus reveals.
In this letter the missionary rebuked a local warlord and his companions
for killing and capturing Christians who had just been baptized. Patrick
forbade Christians to eat and drink with the culprits as well as to accept
alms from them, until they 'perform penance relentlessly enough with
tears poured out to God'.[5] We do not know what forms for doing
penance Patrick would have had in mind, perhaps some formal ritual
under supervision of a bishop, as he seems to imply when alluding to the
power to bind and loose, or other, possibly more monastic, forms of
penance.[6] Even if we do not accept later sources relating that Patrick
spent his formative years in Gaul, it is perfectly possible that Patrick knew
penitential rituals as they were performed in Gaul or Rome from his
native Britain, but such a ritual would look very different in a British
town in the fifth century, where Roman authority had ceased to exist
since the year 410 and post-Roman power structures changed quite
drastically. We know that in Britain Christianity survived the withdrawal
of Roman authority and that ecclesiastical structures somehow survived,
for example because Patrick informs us that his father was a deacon and
that bishops still held authority in his time. Yet we do not have a clear

---

[4] Leo I, *Tractatus* 82.1, ed. A. Chavasse, *Sancti Leonis Magni Pontificis Tractatus septem et nonaginta*, CC SL 138A, pp. 508–9; see T. Charles-Edwards, *Early Christian Ireland* (Cambridge 2000), pp. 206–11.

[5] Patrick, *Letter to Coroticus*, ed. and tr. D. R. Howlett, *The Book of Letters of Saint Patrick the Bishop* (Dublin 1994), pp. 28–9.

[6] For the allusion to the power to bind and loose, see Patrick, *Letter to Coroticus*, pp. 28–9. Patrick's monastic outlook is stressed by Charles-Edwards, *Early Christian Ireland*, pp. 223–5.

picture of the structure of the British Church – or perhaps it would be better to speak of British churches in the plural here – in the fifth century, the time Patrick was raised a Christian and introduced Christianity into Ireland.[7] In the early fifth century British Christianity was in close contact with Gaul, as the career of Pelagius illustrates, who debated the question of predestination and free will with Augustine. Faustus, a British monk, later in his life became bishop of the southern French town of Riez. In the later fifth and sixth centuries, however, such contacts seem to have been less frequent. How Christianity developed in this period in what appears to have been a kind of isolation, we do not know.

The same must, alas, be said for the ecclesiastical organization in Ireland. It has long been assumed that an initially episcopally organized church developed into a church dominated by monastic institutions. Lately this model has been questioned. While some cling to the traditional view – although sometimes disagreeing over the precise period in which this change took place – others nowadays hold a view in which episcopal and monastic forms of authority coexisted in Ireland from a very early stage.[8] Given the dearth of sources for the early period of Irish Christianity as well as the imprecision with which we can date some crucial sources, such as *The First Synod of St. Patrick*, which will be discussed below, it is difficult to gain certainty about the organization of the Irish Church in the fifth and sixth centuries. It seems safe to conclude, however, that monasticism in some of the rich variety of forms developed in Late Antiquity was influential in Ireland from a very early stage onwards.

As we have seen, in monastic circles confessing one's failings to a monk who had travelled further on the road to perfection was an important means to attain the perfect monastic life. We can observe this in the work of John Cassian, the man who played a prominent role in the transmission of Eastern monastic ideals to the West.[9] The Rule of Benedict not only instructed the monks to confess their sins every

---

[7] See C. Stancliffe, 'Christianity amongst the Britons, Dalriadan Irish and Picts', in P. Fouracre (ed.), *The New Cambridge Medieval History*, vol. I (Cambridge 2005), pp. 426–61, at pp. 431–41.

[8] R. Sharpe, 'Some problems concerning the organization of the Church in early medieval Ireland', *Peritia* 3 (1984), pp. 230–70 and C. Etchingham, *Church Organisation in Ireland A.D. 650–1000* (Maynooth 1999) are in favour of a new model in which episcopal and monastic authority are combined, a change still defended by D. Ó Cróinín, *Early Medieval Ireland 400–1200* (London / New York 1995), pp. 149–52 and Charles-Edwards, *Early Christian Ireland*, pp. 241–81.

[9] John Cassian, *Institutiones*, ed. J.-C. Guy, *Jean Cassien, Institutions cénobitiques*, SC 109 (Paris 1965), p. 132; John Cassian, *Collationes* II, 10–12 and XX, ed. M. Petschenig CSEL 13, pp. 48–52 and 553–70.

day in their prayers to God with tears and laments and to correct them henceforward, but also enjoined confession to the abbot of the monastery, all bad thoughts as well as evil deeds committed in secret.[10] Confessing your sins, therefore, was an important aspect of early monasticism by which monks could, through spiritual advice, attain a higher degree of perfection. At the same time knowledge of the failings of their monks offered senior monks and abbots better means to supervise and control the monastic community. Although the Rule of Benedict does not seem to have been known in Ireland in the sixth and seventh centuries, the work of John Cassian probably was. Either through acquaintance with his work or through other monastic traditions, the practice of regular confession would have been known in Ireland at an early stage.[11]

An early cluster of texts

There is a group of four texts which are hard to date or localize, but which are associated with Ireland, Wales or Cornwall and do seem to reflect an early date of composition. These comprise the *Preface of Gildas on Penance*, the *Excerpts of a Book of David* and two synods, one known as the *Synod of North Britain*, the other as the *Synod of the Grove of Victory*. These four texts are transmitted together in two manuscripts written on the Continent in the late ninth and the first half of the tenth century. The manuscript evidence for these texts is therefore rather late and completely continental, but in both manuscripts they are surrounded by a collection of insular texts, which are generally dated to the sixth and seventh centuries.[12] Since the texts are attributed to authorities which were not particularly well known in the ninth century on the Continent, like the Welsh bishop David of Menevia (d. 589/601) or the British author

---

[10] Regula Benedicti 4, 57–8 and 44–8, ed. A. De Vogüé and J. Neufville, *La Règle de Saint Benoît*, SC 181–2 (Paris 1972), vol. 181, pp. 460 and 484.

[11] W. Follet, 'Cassian, contemplation, and medieval Irish hagiography', in G. R. Wieland, C. Ruff and R. G. Arthur (eds.), *Insignis Sophiae Arcator. Essays in Honour of Michael W. Herren on his 65th Birthday* (Turnhout 2006), pp. 87–105; S. Lake, 'Knowledge of the writings of John Cassian in early Anglo-Saxon England', *Anglo-Saxon England* 32 (2003), pp. 27–41. See also Marilyn Dunn, 'Tánaise Ríg: the earliest evidence', *Peritia* 13 (1999), pp. 249–54, who makes a case for the *Regula Magistri*, a text which is generally regarded as an important source of the Rule of Benedict, being written in Ireland; a position she readjusts in M. Dunn, *The Emergence of Monasticism. From the Desert Fathers to the Early Middle Ages* (Oxford 2003), pp. 182–6, where she argues that the *Regula Magistri* may have originated in the Columbanian monastery of Bobbio.

[12] The texts are all edited in L. Bieler (ed. and tr.), *The Irish Penitentials. With an Appendix by D. A. Binchy*, Scriptores Latini Hiberniae 5 (Dublin 1963), pp. 60–73; they are known from mss. Paris, Bibliothèque Nationale, lat. 3182 (s. X^1, written by the Breton scribe Maeloc) and Cambrai, Bibliothèque municipale, 625 (576) (s. IX^2, northern France).

Gildas, it is perfectly possible that we are dealing here with a collection of pristine insular texts, dating perhaps from as early as the sixth century. We know that the *Excerpts of a Book of David* were used in the seventh-century Irish penitential of Cummean and probably also by the sixth-century insular penitential known as the *Paenitentiale Ambrosianum*, so this text can plausibly be dated to the sixth century, while it has definite links with the insular world.[13] The *Paenitentiale Ambrosianum* also refers to the *Synod of the Grove of Victory*, so this text can also be dated to the sixth century.[14] There seems no real reason to doubt that the other texts accompanying this one are from the same historical background.[15]

If we accept these texts as genuine insular texts composed in the sixth or early seventh century, we get a rare glimpse of the uses of penance and ecclesiastical authority in the British Isles in this early period. The *Preface of Gildas on Penance*, for example, can best be regarded as a monastic rule.[16] It deals with matters such as a monk's stealing vestments, offending one another, coming late for the singing of psalms or the proper way to inform the abbot of another monk's misbehaviour.[17] The way to atone for a monk's offences is 'to do penance' for a specific period. The first canon makes clear that 'to do penance' means to fast – the use of Roman measures to specify the amount of food the fasting sinner was allowed to consume in this passage is a further indication of a possible sixth-century date – but the culprit is also excluded from communion for a specific period, although he is allowed to participate in communal life before the end of his period of penance 'lest his soul perish utterly from lacking so long a time the celestial medicine'.[18] The first six canons concern clerics who have indulged in sexual acts, with either men or women. The penance for such an act should last three years, although the rations of food for the offender are adapted to his ecclesiastical status. The priest or deacon who had taken the monastic vow had to accomplish

---

[13] The connection between Cummean, *Paenitentiale Ambrosianum* and the *Excerpta quedam de libro Davidis* is discussed in L. Körntgen, *Studien zu den Quellen der frühmittelalterlichen Bußbücher*, Quellen und Forschungen zum Recht im Mittelalter 7 (Sigmaringen 1993), pp. 22–34.

[14] *P. Ambrosianum* II, 5 and IV, 4, ed. Körntgen, *Studien zu den Quellen*, pp. 260 and 263; see also the discussion at p. 63.

[15] J. F. Kenney, *The Sources for the Early History of Ireland: Ecclesiastical. An Introduction and Guide* (Blackrock 1993, 1st edition New York 1929), pp. 239–40; Bieler, *Irish Penitentials*, p. 3; see M. Lapidge and R. Sharpe, *A Bibliography of Celtic Latin Literature, 400–1200* (Dublin 1985), p. 48.

[16] For this text, see M. W. Herren, 'Gildas and early British monasticism', in A. Bammesberger and A. Wollmann (eds.), *Britain 400–600: Language and History* (Heidelberg 1990), pp. 65–78, at pp. 70–1.

[17] Canons 6, 18, 19 and 27, ed. Bieler, *Irish Penitentials*, pp. 60–4.

[18] Canon 1, ed. Bieler, *Irish Penitentials*, pp. 60–1.

a stricter fast than a monk of a lower grade or a priest or deacon without a monastic vow. A monk who had to do manual labour (*operarius*) was granted a more substantial allowance of food. Reflecting the monk's anxiety to control his thoughts, the intention to sin in this way without putting the thoughts into practice, also required a penance, although it was only half of the three years required for the deed itself. The text gives room, moreover, for the abbot to modify the amount of penance. The author clearly regarded these rules as an indulgence, since he added that the ancient fathers (*antiqui patres*) prescribed twelve years for a priest and six for a deacon sinning in this way.[19] It would be interesting to know who these ancient fathers were. Is the author here referring to conciliar legislation, as for example the council of Ancyra which treats such an offence but prescribes a different penance?[20] If this were so it would mean that in this text ecclesiastical legislation, penitential direction and monastic rules are closely connected.

The *Preface of Gildas* makes clear that it was written for a monastic environment in which some monks had the grade of priests and deacons, but apparently priests and deacons without a monastic vow were also affected by the rules laid down in this text, so these probably were also somehow under the direction of an abbot. Many of the regulations of this text concern disciplinary measures usually laying down a specific penance for a specific offence. It rules, for example, that someone sinning with an animal – probably in a sexual way – should expiate his guilt for a year.[21] It also contains, however, more general rules governing a clerical community. Canon 23, for example, allows sacrifice to be offered for good kings but not for bad ones, while the next canon declares that priests cannot be forbidden to offer sacrifice for their bishop. The last canon suggests that the fact that priests were under the direction of an abbot, but were also subject to episcopal authority, could in some cases cause problems.

Of a different nature are the *Excerpts of a Book of David*. They address mainly secular clergy, particularly priests and bishops, and comprise rulings on inebriety, sexual offences, murder, usury and perjury. Some canons also seem addressed to the laity. The penances described are, however, of a similar nature as those found in the *Preface of Gildas*. The formula 'to do penance' also seems to refer to a period of fasting.[22] Canon 11 dealing with serious crimes, such as clerics of higher grades practicing sexual acts, murder, bestiality and several forms of incest, not

---

[19] Canons 1–5, ed. Bieler, *Irish Penitentials*, pp. 60–1.
[20] Council of Ancyra (314), cc. 36–7, ed. Turner, *Ecclesiae occidentalis monumenta iuris antiquissima*, vol. II, 1, pp. 92–100.
[21] C. 11, ed. Bieler, *Irish Penitentials*, p. 62.   [22] C. 7, ed. Bieler, *Irish Penitentials*, p. 62.

only prescribes a period of fasting but also decrees that the culprit should sleep on the floor for the first year, that during the second year he is allowed to use a stone as a cushion and in the third year of his penance he may sleep on a board. This text looks more like a collection of conciliar decrees and we find no traces of the authority of an abbot in this text. The way it deals with offences, however, is very similar to the one encountered in the *Preface of Gildas* while there also seem to be textual relations between these two texts, although these are still unclear.[23]

The two synods in this collection also address the problem of people who have transgressed rules of Christian behaviour and proclaim in most cases the appropriate penance to atone for their deeds. Both seem to be first and foremost concerned with the behaviour of monks, although the description of certain forms of behaviour suggests that it is not monks who are being addressed here, as these synods deal with matters such as theft, murder, adultery, perjury and the like.[24] The penances decided upon are not characterized in any detail, but are in most cases defined as doing penance for a particular period of time. As in the other documents, this probably denotes a period of fasting.

These four texts probably dating from the sixth century and stemming from the British Church suggest an ecclesiastical organization in which monastic and episcopal forms of authority coexisted. It is impossible to decide whether we are dealing with two rival systems of authority or with one system with two or more poles of authority. What is interesting from our point of view is that all these texts deal with improper behaviour by assigning a proper period of penance to each act. The central element of penance was a period of fasting, which can be alleviated or aggravated by other means. This disciplinary system was first of all intended for the clergy or monks, but many of the canons from these texts were later adopted in the earliest penitential handbooks, thus extending their reach towards lay people. Although three of these texts may have been issued by councils in which bishops probably played an important part, there is no trace of an ecclesiastical ritual centring on the bishop.

The four texts just discussed were probably written in the Celtic-speaking regions of Britain. As we have seen, there existed close contacts between the early Irish Church and the British churches. A probably early Irish text attributed to Ireland's apostle himself, i.e. St Patrick,

---

[23] *Praefatio*, c. 5 and *Excerpta*, c. 10 have close parallels, see Bieler, *Irish Penitentials*, pp. 60 and 70; these have, as far as I can see, never been discussed.

[24] Particularly the *Sinodus Luci Victoriae* deals with such matters, but the last canon makes clear that it aims at persons with a vow of perfection; c. 9, Bieler, *Irish Penitentials*, p. 68; cf. however c. 4, where it is decreed that the sinner should lay down his arms.

can be compared to the British documents just discussed. This text, known as *The First Synod of St. Patrick*, is also known from a Frankish ninth-century manuscript, but again it is probably much older, although it is hard to establish its exact date of origin.[25] It was used in the *Collectio Hibernensis*, the collection of authoritative writings composed in Ireland around the year 700. The text could be seventh century therefore, as has been maintained, but it could also be a fifth-century text, if we believe the attribution to Patrick and two of his fellow bishops, Auxilius and Iserninus.[26] The consensus nowadays seems to be, however, that this is a sixth-century Irish text.[27] The *First Synod of St. Patrick* (*Synodus I S. Patricii*) contains a number of canons regulating the life of the clergy, thereby accentuating episcopal authority. Eleven canons, however, deal with the way of life of the laity and it is in this section (canons 12–22) that we find the imposition of a particular period of penance as the normal procedure to deal with sins. To coerce sinners to accept penance, one could exclude them from taking communion or deny them entrance into a church.[28] To do penance, again, seems to be synonymous with 'to fast', as is implied by the canon specifying the penance by adding 'twenty days on bread only'.[29] So, in this sixth-century Irish text composed in order to enhance episcopal authority, we observe a similar way to deal with sinners that we have also encountered in the monastic *Preface of Gildas*. There are no explicit traces of a specific ecclesiastical ritual dealing with penitents. In this text penance is clearly used as a disciplinary tool. The assignation of a specific penance is used by ecclesiastical authorities to regulate the life of their subjects. It is possible that some sinners did penance on their own initiative, but these canons suggest that temporary excommunication was used to enforce penance upon their subjects. An intriguing canon seems to address the question of the relation between this ecclesiastical disciplinary system and secular courts, as it excommunicates the Christian who goes to a secular court to settle a dispute instead of going to the church to do so.[30] If Bieler's interpretation

---

[25] Ms. Cambridge, Corpus Christi College, 279 (s. IX 2/2, Tours?), Bieler, *Irish Penitentials*, p. 15.

[26] This is the position of the most recent editor of the text, see Bieler, *Irish Penitentials*, p. 2.

[27] Hughes, *Early Christian Ireland*, pp. 68–71; Charles-Edwards, *Early Christian Ireland*, pp. 245–247; A. Breen, 'The date, provenance and authorship of the pseudo-Patrician canonical materials', *ZRG Kan.* 81 (1995), pp. 83–129 at pp 91–6 argues for an early seventh-century date, but possibly on the basis of an earlier text. See also the edition and discussion in M. J. Faris, *The Bishops' Synod ('The First Synod Of St. Patrick')*. *A Symposium with Text, Translation and Commentary* (Liverpool 1976).

[28] See in particular canons 17 and 18, ed. Bieler, *Irish Penitentials*, p. 56.

[29] Canon 15, ed. Bieler, *Irish Penitentials*, p. 56.

[30] Canon 21, ed. Bieler, *Irish Penitentials*, p. 56, but the emendation of *inductum* to *in iudicium* as well as the interpretation of the latter as 'a court' are debatable.

of this canon is correct, this would mean that ecclesiastical penance was used as a means to settle disputes among Christians, at the expense of secular courts.

The early documents discussed so far show that, in the British Church as well as in Ireland, episcopal and monastic forms of authority coexisted and that penance in the form of fasting was generally used as a means to enforce ecclesiastical discipline and possibly also to settle conflicts between Christians. There is no mention of regular confession of sins, nor of the pastoral and educational uses of confession and penance. These aspects, however, are stressed in the penitential handbooks that were composed in this period and to which we shall now turn.

The earliest penitential handbooks

The penitential handbook attributed to Finnian is generally regarded as the oldest text containing detailed guidelines about the penitential tariffs to be imposed for specific sins. Recently, however, it has been convincingly argued that a text of this kind preserved in the *Biblioteca Ambrosiana* in Milan should not be regarded as a work that drew upon the seventh-century Irish penitential of Cummean, but rather as its source. Parallels and references to the four sixth-century British texts support such a view.[31] This penitential handbook, known as the *Paenitentiale Ambrosianum*, was used by the early followers of the Irishman Columbanus in Gaul, and so it can be dated to the sixth or early seventh century.[32] It could therefore be as early as the penitential of Finnian. There are many indications that the *Ambrosianum* was written either in Britain or in Ireland and it thus contributes to our knowledge of the practice of penance in the early insular world. Just like Gildas and Finnian, the author of the *Ambrosianum* wrote a carefully crafted, polished Latin testifying to a continuing tradition of Latin education in the insular world.[33]

The *Ambrosianum* stresses the pastoral significance of penance already by its first words 'through pastoral care' (*pastorali sollicitudine*). The preface further elaborates on the metaphor of the confessor as a physician

---

[31] Körntgen, *Studien zu den Quellen*, pp. 60–4.

[32] Körntgen, *Studien zu den Quellen*, p. 86 dates it to the years 550–650.

[33] The tradition of Latin learning in the insular world has been analysed in great detail in the many studies of David Howlett. I mention only D. Howlett, *The Celtic Latin Tradition of Biblical Style* (Dublin 1995). See the review article A. B. Hood, 'Lighten our darkness – Biblical style in early medieval Britain and Ireland', *Early Medieval Europe* 8 (1999), pp. 283–96 and the response by Howlett in *Early Medieval Europe* 9 (2000), pp. 85–92.

of spiritual wounds. In this text, therefore, the pastoral element of penance aiming at the salvation of the sinner seems much more to the fore than in the documents just discussed. This aspect is also found in the procedure outlined in the text with which a confessor should approach a sinner. If someone sins, he should first be admonished to make satisfaction (*arguatur*). Only if he refuses to do so should he be forced to change his ways by several forms of excommunication. Excommunication here does not entail a grand ecclesiastical ritual, but consists rather of different forms of exclusion from a monastic community. This way to deal with a sinner has a strong monastic flavour.[34] The text is furthermore structured according to the eight vices, as first elaborated by Evagrius of Pontus but promulgated in the West by John Cassian. Evagrius's and Cassian's detailed analysis of a person's desires and thoughts aims at identifying the origin of sinful behaviour, thereby making it possible to prevent sins from happening, and is less interested in the different manifestations of sin.[35] Confession and penance are here clearly intended as a way to correct sins and to lead Christians onwards on the road to perfection – that is, to control their passions. If we look at the canons themselves, it is clear that the text is not intended for monks as such, since it addresses sinful behaviour by bishops, priests, virgins, widows, clerics and lay people. It seems therefore that it tries to extend monastic attitudes towards sins to the secular clergy – although these might, of course, be related to monastic communities. It is remarkable that those canons directed at the laity ignore the refined procedure with which a sinner is generally addressed and seem much more interested in making satisfaction for specific trespasses than in convincing the sinner or in identifying and eradicating the origins of his failings. This is true, for example, for Chapter 2, which deals with fornication.[36] In Chapter 4, which comprises canons dealing with killing, the culprit is simply to be damned, unless he does penance for a fixed period. Someone who deliberately perpetrated murder, employing a ruse in the process, had to fulfil a lifelong form of penance.[37] There is no sign of any interest in the deeper motivation of the killer. We are dealing, therefore, with a text that is concerned with the individual virtues of clerics, which also lays down penances for lay people.

---

[34] Körntgen, *Studien zu den Quellen*, pp. 35–7.
[35] Evagrius, *The Praktikos*, ed. A. Guillaumont and C. Guillaumont, *Évagre le Pontique, Traité pratique ou Le moine* (SC 170–1), vol. II, pp. 506–77. For John Cassian see above, p. 39.
[36] *P. Ambrosianum* II, ed. Körntgen, *Studien zu den Quellen*, p. 260.
[37] *P. Ambrosianum* [IV], 3, ed. Körntgen, *Studien zu den Quellen*, p. 263. See also p. 37.

The penitential handbook of Finnian is of a similar mixed character, since it also aims at the clergy and the laity. It is extant in two manuscripts, one from St Gall and the other from Salzburg, while two manuscripts from Brittany containing early insular material – one of which we have already encountered as containing early texts from the British Isles – preserve some excerpts.[38] Since it was used by Columbanus, it probably dates from the sixth century. Whether this is an Irish text depends partly on our assessment of the author. Two Irish saints have been put forward as the possible author of this text: Finnian of Moville and Finnian of Clonard, while a Breton as well as a British origin have been suggested as well. Almost all scholars agree, however, on the fact that Finnian spent considerable time in Ireland and since the text was used by the Irishman Columbanus we can safely conclude that this penitential was known in Ireland, if not necessarily composed there.[39] Columbanus in one of his letters informs us that Finnian had been in contact with Gildas on matters concerning clerical discipline.[40] These authors therefore seem to have belonged to a close group.

Like the *Ambrosianum* Finnian's penitential demonstrates a sophisticated approach to sins and their penances. It begins, for example, with a number of canons treating sins of the heart and evil thoughts which were not acted upon.[41] In a long canon, drawing upon biblical quotations to demonstrate the seriousness of the sins discussed, Finnian addresses the way clerics should deal with the great sins of wrath, envy, slander, despair and greed. Such sins, 'which kill the soul and plunge it into the depth of hell', should be eradicated from the heart by penance and weeping and by curing these specific sins by their contrary virtues. Patience should thus take the place of anger, restraint of the heart and tongue that

---

[38] Mss. St Gall, Stiftsbibliothek, Cod. 150 and Vienna, Österreichische Nationalbibliothek, lat. 2233; for the latter see R. Meens, 'The Penitential of Finnian and the textual witness of the Paenitentiale Vindobonense B', *Mediaeval Studies* 55 (1993), pp. 243–55; excerpts in Paris, BN, lat 3182 (s. X1) and 12021 (s. X in.)

[39] On the person of Finnian, Vinniau or Ninian, see L. Fleuriot, 'Le "saint" Breton Winniau, et le pénitentiel dit "de Finnian"?', *Études Celtiques* 15 (1978), pp. 607–14; P. Ó Riain, 'Finnian or Winniau?', in P. Ní Chatháin and M. Richter (eds.), *Ireland and Europe. The Early Church / Irland und Europa. Die Kirche im Frühmittelalter* (Stuttgart 1984), pp. 52–7; D. Dumville, 'Gildas and Uinniau', in M. Lapidge and D. Dumville (eds.), *Gildas: New Approaches* (Woodbridge 1984), pp. 207–14; and T. O. Clancy, 'The real St Ninian', *Innes Review* 52 (2001), pp. 1–28; P. Ó Riain, 'Finnio and Winniau: a return to the subject', in J. Carey, J. T. Koch and P.-Y. Lambert (eds.), *Ildánach ildírech. A Festschrift for Proinsias Mac Cana* (Aberystwyth 1999), pp. 187–202, who, while opting for an origin among the Irish colonists in southwestern Britain, reviews the other positions.

[40] Columbanus, *Epistola* I, 7. ed. G. Walker, *Sancti Columbani Opera*, Scriptores Latini Hiberniae, 2 (Dublin 1970), p. 8.

[41] *P. Vinniani*, cc. 1–4, ed. Bieler, *Irish Penitentials*, p. 74.

of slander, liberality that of greed, and so forth.[42] Such a sophisticated approach, however, is again mostly restricted to sinful behaviour by clerics. Finnian makes a clear distinction between clerics and laymen when assigning a form of penance. This distinction is clearly articulated in the sentences concerning violence. If a cleric, for example, plotted to strike or kill his neighbour, but refrained from the act, he should do penance for six months on bread and water and should abstain another half year from wine and meat. A layman sinning in the same way could make satisfaction with only seven days' penance, for 'because he is a man of this world, his guilt in this world is lighter but the reward in the world to come is less'.[43] The last part of Finnian's text addresses lay behaviour and concentrates almost exclusively on the sexual life of the laity. In so doing, it sets a high standard. It censures not only every form of sexual gratification outside of marriage, but also denies any form of remarriage after a matrimonial union has failed. Furthermore, the text requires continence of a couple that remains childless, while it also sets forth a detailed timetable of periods during which a married couple should abstain from sexual intercourse. These clauses display, however, more the character of guidelines than of penitential rulings, in that they lay down a model of marriage, but do not envisage any sanctions for not abiding by these rules.[44]

The *Ambrosianum* and Finnian's penitential, therefore, both clearly envisage lay people receiving penance on the basis of their rules. Does this mean that in the region where these texts were composed, broadly speaking the Celtic-speaking regions of the insular world, lay confession was common practice in the sixth century? This seems hardly plausible. It has been suggested that these penitentials opened up the monastic way of doing penance for the laymen and laywomen who were closely bound to the monastery.[45] Monastic tenants, known as *manaig*, a term which stems from the Latin word for monk, *monachus*, have been described as 'para-monastic' dependants of the church dwelling under a penitential or quasi-penitential regime.[46] Particularly the rules regulating sexual intercourse between a married couple, as formulated in Finnian's penitential, have been seen as an indication of such a quasi-monastic status, since they are hardly compatible with the range of liberties allowed for

---

[42] *P. Vinniani*, c. 29, ed. Bieler, *Irish Penitentials*, p. 84.
[43] *P. Vinniani*, c. 6, ed. Bieler, *Irish Penitentials*, p. 76.
[44] *P. Vinniani*, cc. 36–46, ed. Bieler, *Irish Penitentials*, pp. 86–92; for comments, see Payer, *Sex and the Penitentials*, pp. 20–4.
[45] Etchingham, *Church Organisation*, pp. 290–318.
[46] Etchingham, *Church Organisation*, p. 290 referring to D. Ó Corráin, L. Breatnach and A. Breen, 'The laws of the Irish', *Peritia* 3 (1984), pp. 382–438, at pp. 404–5.

by secular laws in Ireland.[47] Other texts sometimes speak of a *laicus fidelis*, a faithful layman, suggesting that most laymen did not really live up to ecclesiastical standards, while it has even been suggested that in an Irish context *laicus* should be interpreted as 'pagan'.[48] It is hard to get an impression of the religious life of the majority of the Irish in the sixth century or the extent to which pastoral care was provided for them by religious specialists, be they secular or monastic.[49] If we look at the penitential of Finnian and the *Ambrosianum*, we can conclude, however, that the majority of sins of the laity addressed in these texts concern forms of violence and sexuality. Finnian's penitential treats the case of a layman who converts from his evildoing after having committed 'every evil deed', which is glossed as 'committing fornication and shedding blood'. Such a layman should fulfil a three-years' penance during which he must fast, go unarmed and refrain from sexual relations with his wife, in short live the life of a monk.[50] The close connection between the laity, sexuality and bloodshed, as demonstrated in this canon, is further underscored by the *Collectio Hibernensis*, an Irish collection of authoritative sayings which was later seen and employed as a canon-law collection, when it distinguishes between three zones of sanctity. In the two outer zones, which are less holy than the innermost one, layfolk are permitted, but the text distinguishes between the middle zone in which rustic people are allowed to enter who are not much given to iniquity, and the outer zone in which lay people may enter who are adulterous and homicidal.[51]

Whereas traditionally it has been maintained that in Ireland and the neighbouring Celtic-speaking regions the process of private penance had been invented building upon traditions in monastic culture, it is perhaps better to regard the innovations in this field as an opening up of a quasi-monastic state of life for a specific group of the laity to do penance for their sins.[52] The *manaig* were probably among the lay people profiting from this development, but it is hard to establish how many

---

[47] D. Ó Corráin, 'Women in early Irish society', in M. McCurtain and D. Ó Corráin (eds.), *Women in Irish Society. The Historical Dimension* (Dublin 1987), pp. 1–13, at pp. 6–7.

[48] See R. Sharpe, 'Hiberno-Latin *laicus*, Irish *láech* and the devil's men', *Ériu* 30 (1979), pp. 75–92; Etchingham, *Church Organisation*, pp. 298–312.

[49] For the problem in general, see the important collection of articles in J. Blair and R. Sharpe (eds.), *Pastoral Care Before the Parish* (Leicester, London etc. 1992); for the Irish situation, see Etchingham, *Church Organisation* (but see also the critical review by D. Ó Cróinín in *Peritia* 15 (2001), pp. 412–20).

[50] *P. Vinniani* c. 35, ed. Bieler, *Irish Penitentials*, p. 86.

[51] *Collectio Hibernensis* LIV, 5, the long version as cited in H. Wasserschleben (ed.), *Die irische Kanonensammlung* (2nd edn. Leipzig 1885; reprint Aalen 1966), p. 175, fn. e.

[52] Etchingham, *Church Organisation*, p. 317.

other Christians were involved in such a process of penitential cleansing offered by the church. Apart from the *manaig*, however, the texts suggest another group of people profiting from such possibilities to atone for one's sins, since the sins associated with the laity always have important social implications. This is particularly obvious with forms of violence, but acts of fornication discussed in penitential handbooks also often involved a breach of social rules. The texts give clear indications that penance might have been of use in solving disputes resulting from sins of violence and sex. Finnian, for example, decided that a layman who had struck a neighbour and thus shed blood should not only do penance for forty days, but should also give some money to the person he had harmed in compensation. The specific amount of money to be paid should be settled by the priest or a *iustus*, a just man.[53] The term *iustus* might apply to a secular judge here, but might equally be used for a holy man whose position would be perfectly suited to settle local conflicts.[54] The *Ambrosianum* refers to the practice of giving sanctuary for someone who had killed his neighbour by accident (*casu nolens*) as well as to performing a specific penance, while citing Old Testament provisions from the Book of Numbers.[55] The chapter on fornication in the *Ambrosianum* deals first with sexual relations with two classes of 'married' women: nuns (married to Christ) and women married to their husbands. This is an extremely serious offence which together with homosexuality and bestiality warrants the highest penance, i.e. a lifelong penance in a monastery. We do not know whether any compensation to the offended party was offered in the case of adultery, but one can imagine that the fact that the culprit was emasculated, in the sense that he had to refrain from all sexual activity during the rest of his life, could have been regarded as part of a proper satisfaction. Satisfaction to the offended party is mentioned explicitly in the case of adultery with a virgin or a widow. In that case, the *Ambrosianum* demands that the man who dishonoured a woman reconciles himself with her family (*parentibus eius*) by paying the bride-price as it is established in the law. If he is unable to pay he will have to perform a longer penance as the priest will decide, so that 'by the satisfaction of his humility he will heal the sadness of

---

[53] *P. Vinniani* c. 9, ed. Bieler, *Irish Penitentials*, p. 76.

[54] As described by Peter Brown, 'The rise and function of the Holy Man in Late Antiquity', *Journal of Roman Studies* 61 (1971), pp. 80–101, reprinted in P. Brown, *Society and the Holy in Late Antiquity* (Berkeley / Los Angeles / Oxford 1982), pp. 103–52, and see P. Brown, 'The rise and function of the Holy Man in Late Antiquity, 1971–1997', *Journal of Early Christian Studies* 6 (1998), pp. 353–76.

[55] *P. Ambrosianum* IV, 5, ed. Körntgen, *Studien zu den Quellen*, p. 263; parallels in Numbers 35; see the comments by Körntgen, *Studien zu den Quellen*, pp. 73–4.

the friends of the virgin'.[56] The law referred to in this passage is probably the Old Testament law, as found in Exodus 22.16, although early Irish secular law also knows such provisions. It is possible that the *Ambrosianum* here refers to Irish secular law, although it is perhaps more plausible to assume that Irish secular law was influenced by the Old Testament through penitential texts such as the *Ambrosianum*.[57]

Passages such as these seem to indicate that clerics and the whole process of penance and confession also played a part in the settlement of disputes resulting from unlawful sexual relations as well as several forms of violence. Although we have a whole corpus of early Irish law, it is still unclear how such law was actually employed in practice.[58] Study of conflict management in other regions of Europe has suggested that legal prescriptions played only a minor part in the actual settlement of conflicts. Processes of reconciliation and arbitration between offended parties were generally of greater importance than written law and formal legal procedures.[59] It has also been emphasized that religious rituals were frequently employed in the settlement of conflicts, thus conferring greater authority to a specific agreement, providing space and time to negotiate a settlement, while at the same time

---

[56] P. *Ambrosianum* II, 1–2, ed. Körntgen, *Studien zu den Quellen*, p. 260.

[57] L. Bieler, 'The Irish Penitentials: their religious and social background', in *Studia Patristica VIII. Papers presented to the Fourth International Conference on Patristic Studies held at Christ Church, Oxford 1963* (Berlin 1966), pp. 329–39, at pp. 337–8 regards this as a reference to Irish secular law; for the possible Christian influences on Irish secular law, see D. Ó Corráin, 'Irish Vernacular Law and the Old Testament', in P. Ní Chatháin and M. Richter (eds.), *Irland und die Christenheit / Ireland and Christendom* (Stuttgart 1987), pp. 284–307.

[58] For early Irish law, see F. Kelly, *A Guide to Early Irish Law*, Early Irish Law series 3 (Dublin 1991); L. Breatnach, *A Companion to the Corpus Iuris Hibernici*, Early Irish Law Series 5 (Dublin 2005).

[59] This is a large field of study, so I only mention a few important works within it: F. L. Cheyette, 'Suum cuique tribuere', *French Historical Studies* 6 (1970), pp. 287–299; J. Bossy (ed.), *Disputes and Settlements. Law and Human Relations in the West* (Cambridge 1983); W. Davies and P. Fouracre (eds.), *The Settlement of Disputes in Early Medieval Europe* (Cambridge 1986); G. Althoff, *Verwandte, Freunde und Getreue. Zum politischen Stellenwert der Gruppenbindungen im früheren Mittelalter* (Darmstadt 1990); G. Althoff, *Spielregeln der Politik im Mittelalter. Kommunikation in Frieden und Fehde* (Darmstadt 1997); G. Althoff, *Die Macht der Rituale. Symbolik und Herrschaft im Mittelalter* (Darmstadt 2003). Recently it was the theme of two conferences of the Centro del studio del alto medioevo in Spoleto: *La Giustizia nell'Alto Medieovo (secoli V–VIII)*, Settimane di Studio 42 (Spoleto 1995) and *La Giustizia nell'Alto Medioevo (secoli IX–XI)*, Settimane di Studio 44 (Spoleto 1997); Hyams, *Rancor and Reconciliation in Medieval England*. For a bibliographic discussion, see S. D. White, 'From peace to power: the study of disputes in medieval France', in E. Cohen and M. de Jong (eds.), *Medieval Transformations. Texts, Power, and Gifts in Context* (Leiden / Boston / Cologne 2001), pp. 203–218; T. Reuter, 'Peace-breaking, feud, rebellion, resistance: violence and peace in the politics of the Salian era', in T. Reuter, *Medieval Polities and Modern Mentalities*, ed. J. Nelson (Cambridge 2006), pp. 355–87.

offering the opportunity to give in to one's opponent without losing face.[60] Cooperation and arbitration by religious specialists thus becomes indispensable. Whether this is also the case in early medieval Ireland is unclear. There is of course the intriguing corpus of Irish law tracts, most of it composed in the vernacular. Although most of these tracts are preserved in manuscript copies of the fourteenth century and later, they are mainly dated to the seventh and eighth centuries. While it used to be thought that this corpus of secular law preserved a pristine tradition of Irish law, historians nowadays agree more and more on the fact that secular law is greatly indebted to Christian precepts found in the Bible or in canon law.[61] From a chronological point of view the ecclesiastical precepts as found in early conciliar legislation as well as in early penitential handbooks have priority over the vernacular law tracts. This suggests that Christian ideas may have influenced vernacular laws. This does not mean, of course, that all vernacular laws are of biblical inspiration, but should alert us to the possibilities that what seems to be an allusion to vernacular law in an ecclesiastical text may in fact be an allusion to biblical precepts which have found their way into the vernacular Irish law tracts.

Monks and penitent laymen: the penitential of Columbanus

While the *Paenitentiale Ambrosianum* is an anonymous text and the author of the *Paenitentiale Vinniani* remains enigmatic, the author of chronologically the third insular penitential is a well-known historical person. Columbanus was born in Leinster around the middle of the sixth century and educated in the monastery of Bangor. Around the year 590 he followed his inclination to leave his homeland for a *peregrinatio* and took ship for Gaul. There he founded the monasteries of Annegray, Luxeuil and Fontaines. According to his biographer Jonas of Bobbio, who wrote

---

[60] See the seminal article by P. Brown, 'Society and the supernatural: a medieval change', *Daedalus* 104 (1975), pp. 133–51; reprinted in Brown, *Society and the Holy*, pp. 302–32; see also M. de Jong, 'Transformations of penance', in F. Theuws and J. L. Nelson (eds.), *Rituals of Power. From Late Antiquity to the Early Middle Ages* (Leiden / Boston / Cologne 2000), pp. 185–224; M. de Jong, 'Monastic prisoner or opting out? Political coercion and honour in the Frankish kingdoms', in M. de Jong, F. Theuws and C. van Rhijn (eds.), *Topographies of Power in the Early Middle Ages*, Transformation of the Roman World 6 (Leiden 2001), pp. 291–328; R. Meens, 'Sanctuary, penance and dispute settlement under Charlemagne. The conflict between Alcuin and Theodulf of Orléans over a sinful cleric', *Speculum* 82 (2007), pp. 277–300.

[61] Ó Corráin, Breatnach and Breen, 'The laws of the Irish'; M. Gerriets, 'Theft, penitentials, and the compilation of the early Irish laws', *Celtica* 22 (1991), pp. 18–32; Kelly, *A Guide to Early Irish law*, pp. 231–6 holds a somewhat nuanced view on this matter.

shortly after Columbanus had died, Columbanus was very successful at attracting a great many converts. Particularly the 'medicamenta paenitentiae', the remedies of penance, would have drawn many to his new foundations.[62] In Gaul the Irish monk came into conflict with the Frankish episcopacy who summoned him to a council in Chalon-sur-Saône in 603/4 to discuss his idiosyncratic views, particularly those regarding the way of calculating the date of Easter. Columbanus declined the invitation and wrote a letter of excuse in which he asked for tolerance so that he would be allowed 'to enjoy the silence of these woods and to live beside the bones of our seventeen dead brethren, even as up till now we have been allowed to live twelve years among you'.[63] Columbanus seems to have reached some sort of agreement with the Frankish bishops, but when after a couple of years he came into conflict with the royal court of Burgundy he had to leave Gaul. After some wandering he finally ended up in northern Italy where with support of the Lombard king Agilulf he founded the monastery of Bobbio in the year 613. Two years later he died in the same monastery.[64]

Not only do we know quite a lot about Columbanus, but thanks to the continuity of his foundations, where his literary legacy was taken care of, we also know many of the texts that he wrote. We still have six of his letters, thirteen sermons, two monastic rules and his penitential, as well as some poems and hymns, although there is debate about the poems attributed to him.[65] In the letter he wrote to Pope Gregory the Great, probably in the year 600, he indicated that he knew the sins of some Frankish bishops, which suggests that he heard their confessions.[66] The idea of man's sinfulness and the need to atone for these sins is addressed in general terms in Columbanus's sermons and in his *Regula Monachorum*. The latter text is addressed to the individual monk, as the title indicates, for the word *monachus* derives from the Greek word for 'one' (*monos*).[67] It deals mainly with the monk's inner life and is as such

---

[62] *Vita Columbani abbatis discipulorumque eius*, c. I, 10, ed. B. Krusch, MGH SS rer. mer. IV, p. 76.

[63] Columbanus, *Epistola 2*, ed. Walker, *Sancti Columbani Opera*, pp. 16–17 (tr. Walker).

[64] For an overview of his life, see D. Bullough, 'The career of Columbanus', in M. Lapidge (ed.), *Columbanus. Studies on the Latin Writings* (Woodbridge 1997), pp. 1–28.

[65] For an excellent discussion of most of these works, see M. Lapidge (ed.), *Columbanus. Studies on the Latin Writings*. I think the *dubia De homine misero* and *De VIII vitiis principalibus*, ed. Walker, *Sancti Columbani Opera*, pp. 208–12 stand a good chance of being authentic works by Columbanus.

[66] *Epistula I*, 6, ed. Walker, *Sancti Columbani Opera*, p. 8. Walker's translation also interprets this passage as referring to hearing confession.

[67] J. B. Stevenson, 'The monastic rules of Columbanus', in Lapidge (ed.), *Columbanus*, pp. 203–16, at p. 206.

closely related to the *Instructiones* of Columbanus.[68] Columbanus's *Regula Coenobialis* on the other hand is more concerned with the way monks live together, again as its title indicates, for *coenobium* means 'the common life'.[69] This text demonstrates the crucial importance of confessing one's sins and doing penance for them in Columbanian monasticism. There are close connections between this monastic rule and Columbanus's penitential. One manuscript of the rule provides an alternative name for the *Regula Coenobialis*, and calls it 'a book for the daily penances of monks'.[70] In the ninth-century compilation of monastic rules made by Benedict of Aniane, the *Codex Regularum*, the *Regula Coenobialis* is even called a penitential.[71] Some manuscripts of the text contain additions taken from Columbanus's penitential, while the penitential in its turn contains additions that look very much like the rules in the *Regula Coenobialis*.[72]

The importance of penance and confession in the *Regula* is apparent from the very beginning of the text, since the rule starts with the requirement to confess one's sins once every day and stresses the need to confess even the smaller sins, the *parva peccata*.[73] That Columbanus really meant very small sins here is amply illustrated by the contents of this rule, which actually can be called 'a monastic penitential'.[74] It punishes, for example, the monk who forgot to bless his spoon before starting his meal, a monk who cut the table with his knife and the monk who has spilt some bread crumbs when serving dinner.[75] Some of these rules would later be criticized by Columbanus's pupil Agrestius.[76] The normal form of penance set out in the rule is not a period of fasting, as was the case in the other insular documents we have been examining, but corporal punishment in the form of a number of blows. In the later part of this

---

[68] On the authenticity of the last, see C. Stancliffe, 'The thirteen sermons attributed to Columbanus and the question of authorship', in Lapidge (ed.), *Columbanus*, pp. 93–202.

[69] Stevenson, 'The monastic rules of Columbanus', p. 207; A. Diem, *Das monastische Experiment. Die Rolle der Keuschheit bei der Entstehung des westlichen Klosterwesens*, Vita Regularis. Ordnungen und Deutungen religiösen Lebens im Mittelalter 24 (Münster 2005), pp. 240–1.

[70] 'sive liber de quotidianis poenitentiis monachorum', see Walker (ed.), *Sancti Columbani Opera*, p. 142, apparatus, referring to a manuscript from Ochsenhausen, used by Fleming in his edition of the work of Columbanus published in 1667.

[71] 'paenitentialis', see Walker (ed.), *Sancti Columbani Opera*, Introduction, p. xlix.

[72] Walker (ed.), *Sancti Columbani Opera*, Introduction, p. lii; *P. Columbani B*, cc. 26–30, ed. Bieler, *Irish Penitentials*, p. 106.

[73] Columbanus, *Regula Coenobialis*, c. 1, ed. Walker, *Sancti Columbani Opera*, pp. 144–6.

[74] Stevenson, 'The monastic rules of Columbanus', *Columbanus: Studies on the Latin Writings*, p. 207: 'It is thus close to a penitential in some respects.'

[75] Columbanus, *Regula Coenobialis*, c. 1–2, in Walker (ed.), *Sancti Columbani Opera*, p. 146.

[76] Jonas, *Vita Columbani*, c. II, 9, ed. Krusch, p. 124.

rule, a part probably not composed by Columbanus himself but by his successors, fasting becomes a regular form of penance. It has been maintained that Columbanus's claim that not only doing penance but also confessing your sins had a salutary effect on the salvation of one's soul was nothing short of revolutionary.[77] The Rule knows several forms of penance for monks: corporal punishment, solitary confinement, the singing of psalms, fasting, a period of silence, and also penitential ritual labelled 'public penance' (*publica paenitentia*). This entails a ritual in church in which the penitent lies prostrated asking for forgiveness on the floor while his brethren say prayers over him. The abbot seems to grant absolution at the moment in which the penitent is allowed to rise again.[78] Because this part of the rule seems to be a later addition, it does not necessarily bespeak Columbanus's ways of dealing with sin, but might reflect later usage in his monasteries.

We have already seen that Columbanus's *Regula Coenobialis* has close connections with his penitential handbook. This text, which we only know from two late manuscripts written in Bobbio, clearly reflects the monastic outlook of its author.[79] It consists of three parts. The first is devoted to sinning monks, the second to clerics and the third to the laity. What follows is a later addition again concerned with sins of monks. It has been argued that the three parts were originally independent compositions, that they are better understood as a 'file of documents' than as a single text.[80] Even within the parts different layers have been identified, suggesting a composition of the text from loose files, in different stages from 550 to 650.[81] We can discuss which parts were possibly written by Columbanus himself, but what probably mattered to the people using this text was that the text was authorized by the saint. So, if the text was used in Luxueil or any other of the Columbanian foundations, it would acquire the authority of Columbanus. The text was probably composed in Francia, but it undoubtedly draws on an insular tradition, as demonstrated by the fact that it uses the penitential of Finnian.[82]

The penitential is of particular interest because it is the first text which deals with sins of all Christians: monks, clerics and the laity. While in the *Regula Coenobialis* Columbanus had treated mainly minor offences of

---

[77] Diem, *Das monastische Experiment*, p. 244.
[78] *Regula Coenobialis*, c. 15, in Walker (ed.), *Sancti Columbani Opera*, p. 166.
[79] Mss. Turin, Biblioteca Nazionale, G. VII. 16 (s. IX/2, Bobbio) and Turin, Biblioteca Nazionale, G. V. 38 (s. IX–X or X in., Bobbio), see Bieler (ed.), *Irish Penitentials*, p. 15.
[80] T. Charles-Edwards, 'The penitential of Columbanus', in Lapidge (ed.), *Columbanus*, pp. 217–39, at p. 225.
[81] Charles-Edwards, 'The penitential of Columbanus', pp. 235–6.
[82] Charles-Edwards, 'The penitential of Columbanus', pp. 220–5.

monks, the first part of his penitential deals with serious ones: murder, homosexual acts, breaking a monastic vow, theft, perjury, bloodshed and false testimony committed by monks. The parts addressing sinning clerics and laymen treat the same kind of offences and add sexual relations with women, forms of sorcery, masturbation and sex with animals. Like Finnian, Columbanus also considers sinful thoughts that have not been acted upon; interestingly enough he discusses this topic not only with regard to monks, but also in the clerical and lay part.[83] As the range of offences already indicates, the penitential deals mainly with sinful behaviour that had important social consequences. In the monastic part there is no mention of reconciliation with the offended party, not even in the case of murder. Only the regulation discussing false testimony demands the return of the object under discussion.[84] This is different in the other two sections. The cleric or layman who killed his neighbour had to go into exile and on his return he had to make atonement to the parents of the person he had murdered, taking the place of their child and fulfilling their wishes.[85] In the case of theft, they had to make restitution before doing penance.[86] A layman who had committed adultery, moreover, had to pay the price of chastity (*praetium pudicitiae*) to the offended husband. In the case of sexual relations with an unwedded woman, he had to pay her relatives or could choose to marry the woman if her relatives agreed. In the case of bloodshed, a layman had to pay for the damage he had caused and if he was unable to pay, he had to do the victim's work and to call in a doctor.[87] For people living in the world, therefore, reconciliation with the offended party seems to have been of greater importance in the penitential process than it was for monks. The most important development, however, was that Columbanus in his part for the laity treated the same topics as in the other two. This indicates that in principle he laid down the same demands for the laity as for the clergy and monks. He was the first who censured masturbation by a wedded husband, drunkenness, participation in pagan feasts and, as we have seen, the desire to fornicate.[88] Whereas the earlier insular penitentials had penalized only those offences of lay people which had social repercussions and for which penance formed one of the means to restore social relations, Columbanus went further and demanded that lay people lived a life that was modelled on that of a monk and had to perform

---

[83] *P. Columbani* B 11 and 23, ed. Bieler, *Irish Penitentials*, pp. 100 and 104.
[84] *P. Columbani* A 8, ed. Bieler, *Irish Penitentials*, p. 96.
[85] *P. Columbani* B 1 and 13, ed. Bieler, *Irish Penitentials*, pp. 98 and 102.
[86] *P. Columbani* B 7 and 19, ed. Bieler, *Irish Penitentials*, pp. 100 and 102.
[87] *P. Columbani* B 14, 16 and 21, ed. Bieler, *Irish Penitentials*, pp. 102–4.
[88] *P. Columbani* B 17, 22–24, ed. Bieler, *Irish Penitentials*, pp. 102–4.

penance – although a lesser one than was demanded of monks and clerics – if they did not comply to the monastic ideal.[89] Columbanus's goals seem contradictory, for while he thus diminishes the distance between monks and the laity, his view of the monastic life seems to enhance the distinction between the monastery and the world. The solution of this seeming contradiction perhaps lies once again in the group of lay people addressed in his penitential. The purity and holiness of Columbanian monasteries seem to have attracted many laymen and laywomen, who wanted to be 'the neighbour of St Columbanus', to borrow the felicitous title of Barbara Rosenwein's study of the relations between the monastery of Cluny and its donors.[90] The close ties entertained by the royal family and leading aristocratic families with Columbanian monasticism entailed in the eyes of Columbanus that they conformed their moral life to the ideals propagated by Columbanus and his fellow monks. When the Burgundian court did not live up to Columbanus's expectations, the close relationship between the two parties came to an end.[91]

Cummean's penitential

Columbanus's penitential has taken us outside of the insular world into Francia and northern Italy, a region to which we shall return in the next chapter. The inspiration for his penitential was, however, mainly insular, as its dependence on Finnian's work clearly demonstrates. That the abolition of a clear distinction between laity, clergy and monks was not confined to Columbanus's foundations in Francia and Lombard Italy is demonstrated by a somewhat younger penitential handbook written by the Irishman Cummean. Two manuscripts containing this text refer to its author as 'cumianus longus', which has enabled historians to identify this author with Cummaine Fota, possibly bishop of Clonfert, who according to the Annals of Ulster died in 662.[92] Possibly this is the same Cummean who wrote a famous letter to abbot Ségéne of Iona regarding the controversy over the date of Easter.[93] Unfortunately we

---

[89] See Diem, *Das monastische Experiment*, pp. 247–8.
[90] B. Rosenwein, *To be the Neighbor of St. Peter. The Social Meaning of Cluny's Property, 909–1049* (Ithaca 1989).
[91] Bullough, 'The career of Columbanus', pp. 14–16.
[92] Bieler (ed.), *Irish Penitentials*, p. 6 and Körntgen, *Studien*, p. 7. S. MacAirt and G. Mac Niocaill (eds.), *Annals of Ulster (to AD 1131). Part I: Text and Translation* (Dublin 1983), pp. 132–3.
[93] Charles-Edwards, *Early Christian Ireland*, p. 265; see D. Ó Cróinín and M. Walsh, *Cummian's Letter 'De Controversia Paschali' and the 'De Ratione Computandi'* (Toronto 1988), pp. 13 and 217 and D. Ó Cróinín, s.v. Cummian in *Lexikon des Mittelalters* 3, cols. 370–1.

know next to nothing about this 'exasperatingly enigmatic figure' and it is troubling that one manuscript of the penitential describes him as an abbot, while in the Irish annals he is clearly a bishop.[94] If the identification of the author is correct, then we are dealing with a seventh-century Irish text. The fact that Cummean is nowhere cited in the *Collectio Hibernensis*, the compilation made in Ireland around the year 700 which cites Gildas, Finnian's penitential and the seventh-century Anglo-Saxon penitential rulings by Theodore of Canterbury, suggests that it was not regarded as an authoritative text in the years around 700.[95] The same might be concluded from the fact that although Cummean was a source of inspiration for the penitential decisions of Theodore of Canterbury as collected by the *Discipulus Umbrensium*, his name was nowhere mentioned, but his work was referred to as *libellus Scottorum*, a booklet of the Irish.[96] The fact that Cummeanus seems not to have been regarded as an authority in either the *Collectio Hibernensis* or in the U-version of Theodore's penitential indicates that his work was of recent origin when these texts were composed, probably both somewhere around the year 700. So we may date Cummean's penitential to the second half of the seventh century.

Cummean's penitential is inspired by the Ambrosian one as far as its canons are concerned and also for its structure, which like the *P. Ambrosianum* follows the classification of vices by John Cassian. Cummean's prologue, however, which provides biblical justification for twelve ways to obtain remission for sins, also draws independently on Cassian. Cassian's work was meant for a monastic audience, as it gave advice for monks on how to advance on the road to perfection. As such it was more interested in a monk's urges and motives than in his actual behaviour, which was no more than a window granting insight into the monk's inner life. Cassian's outlook has been preserved to a considerable degree in the *Paenitentiale Ambrosianum*, but Cummean was apparently more interested in forms of behaviour and their remedies. In many cases he shortens and simplifies the regulations as set forth in the *Ambrosianum* in such a way as to provide only the details of the offence and the

---

[94] Citation from Ó Cróinín and Walsh, *Cummian's Letter*, p. 12, providing, however, 661 as the year of his death; ms. Sang. 150, a. p. 285 notes 'Prefatio Cummeani abbatis in Scothia ortus', see Bieler, *Irish Penitentials*, p. 108, critical apparatus.

[95] Wasserschleben, Foreword to the 1885 edition, p. xx; for the use of Theodore in the *Collectio Hibernensis*, see R. Flechner, 'The making of the Canons of Theodore', *Peritia* 17–18 (2003–4), pp. 121–43, at pp. 131–4.

[96] For the Discipulus's use of Cummean, see T. Charles-Edwards, 'The penitential of Theodore and the *Iudicia Theodori*', in M. Lapidge (ed.), *Archbishop Theodore. Commemorative Studies on his Life and Influence* (Cambridge 1995), pp. 141–74, at pp. 151–5.

penance the sinner had to fulfil. He also used Finnian's penitential in this way, simplifying Finnian's elaborate formulations to a bare minimum.[97] Cummean's penitential is the first text of this kind that is no longer addressed to specific groups within Christian society. It contains rules for all Christians, although the severity of the penances is adapted to the position of the sinner in Christian society.[98]

Thanks to its dependence on the Ambrosian penitential and Cassian's work, the *Paenitentiale Cummeani* has a strongly monastic outlook, not only because of its structure but also because of the character of specific canons. It censures, for example, eating before the canonical hour, wet dreams or coming late for singing psalms.[99] The section dedicated to boy's games (*de ludis puerilibus*), dealing mainly with sexual acts, also has a strong monastic flavour, as the references to the rules of our fathers (*statuta patrum nostrorum*) confirm.[100] The penitential further contains detailed rules about how to handle the Eucharist. One should take care, for example, to keep it in a safe place so that it cannot be consumed by mice or worms; and if a worm is found in the Eucharist, it shall be burned and the ashes shall be buried beneath the altar.[101] This section seems to aim mainly at clerics who had to handle the Eucharist on a frequent basis, clerics who in seventh-century Ireland could very well be living in a monastic community. It is striking, though, that the sections dealing with strong monastically flavoured vices such as sadness (*tristitia*), languor (*acedia*) and vainglory (*iactantia*) receive only scant attention, and that they focus on those manifestations of these vices which might obstruct social life within a community.[102]

Most of the canons of Cummean's penitential would fit a monastic community. The canons which explicitly address lay people are mainly concerned with sexual mores. Chapter 2 on fornication, for example, deals with a layman having sexual intercourse with a married woman, a virgin or a woman slave. There are, however, no indications that other forms of satisfaction are required apart from doing penance, so in this respect Cummean differs from Columbanus. In the case of sex with a female slave, Cummean required that the slave be sold, or in the case

[97] Compare Finnian 39–40 and 42–5, ed. Bieler, *Irish Penitentials*, pp. 88 and 90 with *P. Cummeani* II, 26–7 and 29; the shorter version of Finnian printed synoptically by Bieler is in fact a reception of the text of Cummean in the *Paenitentiale Vindobonense B*, see Meens, 'The penitential of Finnian'.

[98] Charles-Edwards, 'The penitential of Columbanus', p. 218.

[99] *P. Cummeani* I, 5; II, 15; (IX), 6–7, ed. Bieler, *Irish Penitentials*, pp. 112, 114 and 126.

[100] *P. Cummeani* (X): 'Ponamus nunc de ludis puerilibus priorum statuta patrum nostrorum', ed. Bieler, *Irish Penitentials*, pp. 126–8.

[101] *P. Cummeani* (XI), 1 and 19–20, ed. Bieler, *Irish Penitentials*, pp. 130–2.

[102] *P. Cummeani* (V)–(VII), ed. Bieler, *Irish Penitentials*, pp. 120–2.

of her begetting a child that she be set free. This does look more like an extra penance or a way to prevent further offences, rather than a form of reconciliation. Like Finnian, Cummean provides guidelines for married couples without any suggestions for penances for breaking them.[103] Forms of satisfaction to the offended party are mentioned in the chapter dealing with violence, which is partly devoted to misdeeds committed by laymen, but some canons look as if they are more geared towards a monastic community. The canon determining that someone who crippled a person by a blow should fast for half a year but first of all should pay the medical expenses and the 'price of the wound' could very well relate to a lay offender. The canons dealing with cursing, verbal abuse and feelings of anger, and which require a reconciliation with the person who aroused such feelings, might apply more to a monastic community.[104] The fact that it is hard to define exactly which offenders Cummean's penitential is targeting in its individual canons might suggest its usefulness in settings where distinctions between monks, clerics and laymen were somewhat fluid, as seems to have been the case in Ireland in the seventh century, where clerics were often living in a monastery and where lay people were closely attached to monastic settlements.

As we have noted above, Cummean's penitential was not regarded as an authoritative text by the compilers of the *Collectio Hibernensis*, nor by Eoda or the Discipulus Umbrensium when editing the *iudicia* of Theodore of Canterbury. His work was however well received on the European mainland, where as we shall see many of Cummean's sentences were adopted in later works. Cummean's work survives as a complete text only in a single manuscript, written in Lorsch in the second half of the ninth century. A fragment written in Mainz or Fulda in second quarter of the ninth century has recently been found in Marburg, while a twelfth-century manuscript from southern Germany contains some excerpts. Fortunately Cummean's work in its entirety was included in a collection of penitentials made in the tenth century, so that we have three early medieval manuscript witnesses to the text.[105] Cummean was an authority not only for many continental penitentials, but also

---

[103] *P. Cummeani* II, 22–31, ed. Bieler, *Irish Penitentials*, p. 116.
[104] *P. Cummeani* (IV), ed. Bieler, *Irish Penitentials*, pp. 118–20.
[105] Mss. Vatican, Biblioteca Vaticana, Vat. pal. lat. 485 (written between 860 and 875 in Lorsch); fragment Marburg, Hessisches Staatsarchiv, Hr 4, 7 (s. IX 2/4, Mainz-Fulda); excerpts in Munich, Bayerische Staatsbibliothek, Clm 12888; tenth-century collection Oxford, Bodleian Library, Bodl. 311 (s. X, Northern France); see Bieler (ed.), *Irish Penitentials*, pp. 13–15 and 17–19; fuller description in Körntgen, *Studien zu den Quellen*, pp. 91–8; for the Marburg fragment, see R. Kottje, 'Das älteste Zeugnis für das Paenitentiale Cummeani', *Deutsches Archiv* 61 (2005), pp. 585–9, which gives an up-to-date overview of the manuscript tradition.

in Ireland itself since he was quoted in the – probably Irish – *Paenitentiale Bigotianum* and the *Old Irish Penitential*.

Penance and the Céli Dé

While most Irish penitentials have influenced later continental traditions, this is not true for the texts just mentioned: the *Paenitentiale Bigotianum* and the *Old Irish Penitential*. The *Paenitentiale Bigotianum* was known on the European mainland, since its only two surviving manuscript copies were written there.[106] It has even been argued that this is probably a text composed on the Continent, since it shows knowledge of the Rule of St Benedict, a text thought by Bieler to be unknown in Ireland.[107] Yet the *Collectio Hibernensis* and the Irish text known as *De duodecim abusivis saeculi* both know Benedict's Rule, so there is no reason to assume that this is not an Irish text.[108] The *Bigotianum* contains an elaborate prologue dealing with sin and forgiveness, in which it cites authors such as Gregory the Great, Origen, Cassian, Isidore of Seville and Cummean. It further consists mainly of rules taken from Cummean's penitential and from the penitential rulings of Theodore of Canterbury, a text that was known in Ireland around the year 700.[109] In some places excerpts from Book 5 of the *Vitae Patrum (Verba Seniorum)* are added.[110] The *Bigotianum* is generally dated between the late seventh and ninth

---

[106] Paris, BNF, lat. 3182 (codex Bigotianus) (s. X1, Brittany) and Cambrai, Bibliothèque municipale 625 (567) (s. IX ex.), Bieler, *Irish Penitentials*, pp. 12–13.

[107] Bieler, *Irish Penitentials*, p. 10.

[108] For the use of Chapter 7 of the *Regula Benedicti* as a model for *De duodecim abusivis*, see S. Hellmann (ed.), 'Pseudo-Cyprianus: *De XII abusivis saeculi*', Texte und Untersuchungen zur Geschichte der altchristlichen Literatur 34 (1909), pp. 1–61, at p. 5; Aidan Breen points at the possibility that the *Regula Magistri*, on which Benedict drew, may have been used here: A. Breen, '*De XII Abusivis*: text and transmission', in P. Ní Chatháin and M. Richter (eds.), *Ireland and Europe in the Early Middle Ages: Texts and Transmission / Irland und Europa im früheren Mittelalter: Texte und Überlieferung* (Dublin 2002), pp. 78–94, at p. 80. For the use of the *Regula Benedicti* in the *Collectio Hibernensis*, see H. Wasserschleben (ed.), *Die irische Kanonensammlung* (2nd edn. Leipzig 1885), p. 149; Kenney, *The Sources for the Early History of Ireland*, p. 241 and T. Charles-Edwards, 'The pastoral role of the church in the early Irish laws', in J. Blair and R. Sharpe (eds.), *Pastoral Care Before the Parish* (Leicester / London etc. 1992), pp. 63–80, p. 74, fn. 64, also argue for an Irish provenance of the *Bigotianum*.

[109] According to Bieler, *Irish Penitentials*, p. 285, Finnian's penitential would also have been used, but in all cases a similar canon can be found in Cummean's work. See *P. Bigotianum* II, 4 (Finn. 35 and Cumm. II, 22), *P. Bigotianum* II, 5, 5–6 (Finn. 37–8 and Cumm. II, 24–5) and Bigot II, 11, 2 (Finn. 48 and Cumm. II, 33). There seems therefore no reason to assume that Finnian was used; for the use of Theodore in the version of the *Discipulus Umbrensium* (U), see Charles-Edwards, 'The penitential of Theodore', p. 142.

[110] Bieler, *Irish Penitentials*, p. 10.

centuries.[111] It must be prior to the late eighth century, though, since it was used for the production of the *Old Irish Penitential*, the only extant Irish penitential in the vernacular. Although the *Old Irish Penitential* has been preserved in a fifteenth-century manuscript, it is linguistically dated to the end of the eighth century, so this would set a *terminus ante quem* for the *Paenitentiale Bigotianum*.[112] The *Old Irish Penitential* has been related to the Céli Dé movement, a monastic movement in Ireland with at its centre Mael Ruain, founding abbot of the monastery of Tallaght near Dublin.[113] The interest of this monastic group in penitential matters is clear from the monastic rule of the Céli Dé and the account of the teachings of Mael Ruain.[114] The fact that the *Bigotianum* and Cummean's penitential were used for the *Old Irish Penitential* shows that these texts were known and carried weight among the Céli Dé. One might consider the possibility that the *Bigotianum* was also related to the Céli Dé.

The Céli Dé was a monastic movement very much concerned with the distinctions between the inner and the outer. This anxiety over boundaries of the monastic world was expressed in a number of ways, among them being a remarkable concern for ritual purity.[115] Both in the Bigotian penitential and in the Old Irish one, this is expressed in rules which forbade drinking something which had been touched by a layman or laywoman. This entailed a one-day's penance, but if the woman was pregnant or had had sex the penance increased to forty days. The same penance was required for the monk who slept in the same house as a layperson.[116] A similar attitude regarding the purity of

---

[111] Vogel, *Les 'Libri Paenitentiales'*, p. 72: 'VIIIe s./IXe s.'; Kenney, *The Sources for the Early History of Ireland*, p. 241: 'the end of the seventh or in the eighth century'; Bieler peculiarly does not discuss the date of composition; Lapidge and Sharpe, *Bibliography of Celtic Latin Literature*, p. 157, date it to the first half of the eighth century.

[112] D. A. Binchy, 'The Old Irish Penitential', in Bieler (ed.), *Irish Penitentials*, pp. 258–74, at p. 258.

[113] Binchy, 'The Old Irish Penitential', in Bieler (ed.), *Irish Penitentials*, pp. 47–9 and recently W. Follet, *Céli Dé in Ireland. Monastic Writing and Identity in the Early Middle Ages*, Studies in Celtic History 23 (Woodbridge 2006), pp. 124–8.

[114] *The Rule of the Céli Dé*, ed. Reeves, 'On the Céli Dé', *Transactions of the Royal Irish Academy* 24 (1873), pp. 205–15; 'The monastery of Tallaght', ed. E. Gwynn and W. J. Purton, *Proceedings of the Royal Irish Academy* 29 C (1911), pp. 115–80; see Follet, *Céli Dé*, pp. 195–9. I also profited a lot from the PhD thesis by the late Stefanie Morgyn Wagner, 'Ritual purity and the Céli Dé. Sin, theology and practice in the eighth and ninth centuries' (University of Edinburgh 2005), who tragically passed away at an early age before being able to see her work published.

[115] Analysed by Morgyn Wagner, 'Ritual purity and the Céli Dé'; cf. Charles-Edwards, *Early Christian Ireland*, p. 7.

[116] *P. Bigotianum* I, 5, 6–7, ed. Bieler, *Irish Penitentials*, pp. 216–18; I interpret *P. Bigotianum* I, 5, 6, 2 differently from Bieler's translation; *Old Irish Penitential*, I, 3, ed. Bieler, *Irish Penitentials*, p. 260, is of the same import.

clerics is found in the first canons of a late ninth-century penitential, which possibly were taken from an Irish penitential related to the Céli Dé movement.[117] Such rules are also found in a text known as the *Canones Hibernenses I*, a collection of canons usually dated to the seventh century, but preserved only in a tenth-century manuscript from Brittany.[118] The stress on the purity of the monk or cleric that is implied in these canons suggests that this text was also related to the Céli Dé movement. It consists of a set of rules determining the penance for several forms of killing and of dietary taboos. The text that follows in the manuscript, a tract called *De arreis*, which contains a set of commutations, i.e. rules for the transformation of one form of penance into another, has connections to an Old Irish text of this kind, which has been related to the Céli Dé movement.[119] So we might be dealing with two additional texts related to this movement, in which penance plays a cardinal role.[120]

The earliest disciplinary documents from the early British Church, which we have been discussing at the beginning of this chapter, are concerned with ecclesiastical discipline among monks, the clergy and the laity. The normal way to make up for specific trespasses is to do penance for a limited period of time. Rules for the imposition of penance are, however, often interspersed with other directions governing the ecclesiastical organization. *The First Synod of St. Patrick*, for example, also rules that there should be no vagrant cleric in a community, while the *Preface of Gildas on Penance* states that one is allowed to offer sacrifice for good kings, but not for bad kings, a rule later adopted in Cummean's penitential.[121] In the penitential handbooks we have been discussing so far, we can sometimes observe the same mixture of penitential rules and more general rules governing the ecclesiastical community. Finnian, for example, ruled that Christians should give money for the redemption of captives as well as for the poor and the needy, while his elaborate

---

[117] R. Meens, "'Aliud benitenciale": the ninth-century *Paenitentiale Vindobonense C*', *Mediaeval Studies* 66 (2004), pp. 1–26, at pp. 7–8.

[118] *Canones Hibernenses* I, 21–4, ed. Bieler, *Irish Penitentials*, p. 162. Ms. Paris, BNF, lat. 12021 (s. X in., Brittany), Bieler, *Irish Penitentials*, p. 14. The text is dated to the seventh century by Bieler, *Irish Penitentials*, p. 9; Vogel, *Les 'Libri Paenitentiales'*, p. 63; Kenney, *The Sources for the Early History of Ireland*, p. 244; Lapidge and Sharpe, *Bibliography of Celtic Latin Literature*, p. 154.

[119] Follet, *Céli Dé*, pp. 126–8.

[120] Not mentioned by Follet, *Céli Dé*.

[121] *First Synod of St. Patrick*, c. 3, ed. Bieler, *Irish Penitentials*, p. 54; see the comments in M. J. Faris, *The Bishops' Synod: ('The First Synod of St. Patrick'); [Collectio canonum Hibernensis]: A Symposium with Text Translation and Commentary* (Liverpool 1976), pp. 33–4; *Preface of Gildas*, c. 23, ed. Bieler, *Irish Penitentials*, p. 62; *P. Cummeani* (IX), 11, ed. Bieler, *Irish Penitentials*, p. 126.

directions for the sexual life of married people do not mention any sanctions.[122] This suggests that penitential rules were closely related to rules governing the church at large. Penance therefore seems not to have been a purely pastoral tool, but apparently also was a major factor contributing to the organization of the life of the Christian community in general. Penitential rules found their way into the *Collectio Hibernensis* among ecclesiastical laws and authoritative sayings. From a very early period, therefore, penitential rulings and texts of a more legal nature seem to be closely related. We have already seen that penance probably also played a role in the settlement of disputes, particularly in cases involving bloodshed and illicit sexual relations.

Penitents on Iona

So far, we have only been looking at the contents of penitential handbooks and normative texts, such as *The First Synod of St. Patrick*. The main reason for this is that we have a decent number of texts of this nature and that they contain useful information concerning the attitudes towards penance. However, although I do think that such texts had practical implications, one could argue that their normative character makes them less useful as sources for historical enquiry. Therefore, we are fortunate that other sources can be used to enrich our normative sources. The *Life of Columba*, for example, written by Adomnán, abbot of Iona from 679 to 704, contains precious information regarding penitents living at the monastery of Iona and therefore will provide some idea of how sinners were dealt with in one of the most important Irish monasteries.[123] Adomnán emphasized that Columba had been taught by Finnian, whom we have met as the author of a penitential, so the attention Adomnán pays to the topic of penance need not surprise us.[124] Adomnán describes several ways in which a penitent came into contact with the holy man. We see a young student in the monastery being chastised by Columba for his disobedience. The saint foretells that he will be able to do penance for his sins before his death, so apparently this young sinner postponed his penance until later in his life.[125] In another case the holy man sent out a fellow monk to interrogate his mother who had sinned in secret and was unwilling to admit her sin. When her son interrogated her she finally confessed her sin and, after doing

---

[122] *P. of Finnian*, cc. 32 and 41–6, ed. Bieler, *Irish Penitentials*, pp. 86 and 88–92.

[123] Briefly and lucidly discussed in Charles-Edwards, *Early Christian Ireland*, p. 248.

[124] *Vita Columbae* II, 1, ed. A. O. and M. A. Anderson, *Adomnán's Life of Columba* (Oxford 1991) p. 94; the saint Findbarr is usually identified as Finnian.

[125] *Vita Columbae* III, 21, ed. Anderson and Anderson, *Life of Columba*, pp. 212–14.

penance according to the judgment of Columba, she was healed.[126] At one time Columba during his travels embarrassed a priest in the monastery of Trevett by challenging him for saying Mass in a sinful state, and the priest was forced to confess his sins in public.[127] When travelling on the island of Rathlin, Columba was approached by a layman who complained about the fact that his wife would not sleep with him. The saint called for the man's wife who declared that she would do anything, 'take on all the whole management of the house or cross the sea to live in a monastery of nuns', if only she would not have to sleep with her husband. The saint proposed to fast and pray together, and on the next day the wife declared that the one she detested yesterday, she now loved. This little episode illuminates the rules in penitential handbooks concerning the sexual life of the married. Like Finnian's penitential it stresses the indissolubility of a marriage, but it also shows that in such circumstances confessors acted more like marriage counsellors than judges. Although the couple agrees to fast for a while, there is no mention of confessing sins or assigning a specific penance, which agrees with what we have observed in penitential books.

In the last two instances the saint was travelling and intervened in a local situation or was approached to solve a matrimonial conflict. Often, however, sinners travelled to the island of Iona to seek intervention. Such was the case for a certain Librán who had killed a man and broken an oath. He travelled to Iona 'to expiate his sins in pilgrimage', where he confessed his sins to the saint and promised to do anything required by the laws of penance, an expression which probably refers to the decrees of a penitential handbook. In the *Old Irish Penitential* there is a reference to a penitential ruling by Colum Cille, so Adomnán is possibly alluding here to a penitential written by or attributed to Columba.[128] Columba assigned the penitent Librán a penance of seven years in a monastery on the nearby island of Tiree, an extremely heavy penance for a layman. Columbanus, for example, had assigned a three years' penance for a layman killing someone. The breaking of an oath, however, was regarded as an extremely serious crime in Irish penitentials requiring a penance of seven years or even until death.[129] Doing penance in another monastery is a punishment we find in penitential handbooks as well. It was only after the fulfilment of his seven years of penance that the culprit was allowed

[126] *Vita Columbae* I, 17, ed. Anderson and Anderson, *Life of Columba*, pp. 40–2.
[127] *Vita Columbae* I, 40, ed. Anderson and Anderson, *Life of Columba*, pp. 72–4.
[128] *Old Irish Penitential* III, 12, ed. Bieler, *Irish Penitentials*, p. 267; for the probability that Columba had written a penitential, see Charles-Edwards, 'The penitential of Columbanus', p. 229.
[129] *P. Columbani* B 13 and 20, ed. Bieler, *Irish Penitentials*, pp. 102–4; *P. Vinniani* c. 22, ed. Bieler, *Irish Penitentials*, p. 80.

to take part in the Eucharist. Columba furthermore decreed that the sinner after completion of these seven years should return to the man whom he had deceived by breaking his oath. He was to make up for his debt, but was aided by the saint who gave him a splendid sword decorated with carved ivory. After having completed this duty, he was to return to his parents to fulfil his filial duty in taking care of his aged parents, a requirement similar to the one we encountered in Columbanus's penitential, where, however, a murderer had to fulfil such a duty for the parents of his victim.[130] After completing this task, he returned to Iona, where he became a monk and a member of the monastic *familia* of Columba.[131] This story nicely illustrates several aspects of penitential practice among laypeople as we have encountered them in penitential handbooks: confession of sins to a religious authority, assignment of a specific period of penance according to certain rules, penance to be fulfilled in a monastery, offering compensation to the injured party with help of the confessor and the filial duties required of someone by social practice. The close affinity between life as a penitent and that of a monk is exemplified by the final entry of the sinner into Columba's monastic family, but at the same time this shows that in Columba's monasteries a clear distinction was maintained between real monks and penitents.

The monastery of Columba on the isle of Tiree to which Librán was sent to perform his seven years of penance seems to have been specifically devoted to accommodating penitents.[132] There is even an indication that there was at least one other monastery on that island where penitent laymen could atone for their sins. Adomnán relates how Findchán, the founder of the monastery Artchain on Tiree, received as a pilgrim the king Áid the Black, who had a lot of blood on his hands. The purport of the story seems to be that Findchán was too easy on Áid, even consecrating him a priest for reasons of worldly love (*carnaliter amans*). The hand with which he consecrated him, however, would rot away, while Áid would return to his former violent and murderous life, like a dog returning to his vomit, and come to a violent end.[133] Adomnán's story

---

[130] *P. Columbani* B 13, ed. Bieler, *Irish Penitentials*, p. 102; discussed above, p. 56.

[131] *Vita Columbae* II, 39, ed. Anderson and Anderson, *Life of Columba*, pp. 154–162.

[132] *Vita Columbae* I, 30, ed. Anderson and Anderson, *Life of Columba*, p. 58, see the comments by Richard Sharpe in Adomnán of Iona, *Life of St. Columba*, translated by Richard Sharpe (Harmondsworth 1995), p. 303; A. MacDonald, "Adomnán's Vita Columbae and the early churches of Tiree," in J. Wooding (ed.), *Adomnán of Iona. Theologian, Lawmaker, Peacemaker* (Dublin 2010), pp. 219–236, at p. 222.

[133] *Vita Columbae* I, 36, ed. Anderson and Anderson, *Life of Columba*, pp. 64–66; a rivalry with other monastic foundations on Tiree is also suggested by *Vita Columbae* III, 8, ed. Anderson and Anderson, *Life of Columba*, pp. 192–194, where Columba's foundation is saved from a pestilence, 'while many in the other monasteries of the island' perished.

should perhaps be read as a critique of the lenient way sinners were welcomed at the rival monastery of Artchain. It also hints at the idea that sinners should not live on Iona itself. This is also suggested by another episode, in which Columba took great care that a layman who had committed fratricide and had slept with his mother would not set foot on the island of Iona. Adomnán informs us that this sinner swore not to eat with anyone until he had spoken to Columba. This has been interpreted as referring to the Irish custom of fasting to coerce someone, but might also reflect an anxiety that monks would be polluted by contact with such a sinner.[134] For this case, involving such serious sins as fratricide and sexual relations with one's mother, Columba judged that he do penance for twelve years in exile.[135]

Fear of pollution of the monastery of Iona might also explain the fact that we find no reference to women visiting the island. Irish penitentials only address men and their sins and nowhere explicitly refer to women. This might be accounted for by the fact that, as we have seen, they restrict themselves mainly to a discussion of sins concerning violence and sexuality as far as the laity is concerned, and we may question whether women had the power to sin in these ways. Possibly their wrongdoings in such respects were regarded as actually falling under the responsibility of their father or husband. The presence of penitent women among a community of monks and penitents would, certainly, have caused specific problems and it is easy to imagine that monks were reluctant to admit them. Moreover, Irish and British Christianity developed views in which women were regarded as physically impure when they were menstruating and such impurity could pollute the sacred spaces within a monastery, as well as monks being in contact with such women.[136] These factors might explain why women were not welcome in a male monastic community such as that of Iona.

Another interpretation of this episode is offered by L. Bitel, *Isle of the Saints. Monastic Settlement and Christian Community in Early Ireland* (Ithaca and London 1990), p. 171.

[134] On fasting as a means of coercion, see comments by Sharpe, *Life of St. Columba*, p. 283; on a sinner polluting the island of Iona, see A. Angenendt, 'Die irische Peregrinatio und ihre Auswirkungen auf dem Kontinent vor dem Jahre 800', in H. Löwe (ed.), *Die Iren und Europa im früheren Mittelalter* (Stuttgart 1982), 2 vols., vol. I, pp. 52–79, at p. 57 and T. Charles-Edwards, 'The social background to Irish *peregrinatio*', *Celtica* 11 (1976), pp. 43–59, at pp. 50–1.

[135] *Vita Columbae* I, 22, ed. Anderson and Anderson, *Life of Columba*, pp. 48–50.

[136] As argued in R. Meens, 'A background to Augustine's mission to Anglo-Saxon England', *Anglo-Saxon England* 22 (1994), pp. 5–17; see also R. Meens, 'Questioning ritual purity. The influence of Gregory the Great's answers to Augustine's queries about childbirth, menstruation and sexuality', in R. Gameson (ed.), *St. Augustine and the Conversion of England* (Stroud 1999), pp. 174–86.

Whether penitent women were welcome in female monasteries is a question that needs further investigation. The *Life of Brigit* relates an intriguing case which indicates that female ascetics judged female sins. A woman accused one of the followers of St Patrick of having had sexual relations with her as a result of which a son was born. When the woman declared this, Brigit confronted her for telling a lie, and then the head and tongue of the woman swelled up. Miraculously the infant then declared that the cleric was not the father and identified the real father. When the angry crowd wanted to burn the liar, Brigit interfered once again and demanded that the woman was to do penance. Once the woman accepted penance, her head and tongue lost their swelling. This text therefore suggests that Brigit, as a female ascetic, played a crucial role in the penitential process of women, an impression that is further enhanced by an intriguing aspect of the story. The text explicitly draws attention to the fact that although the cleric in question is a follower of Patrick, the case was only resolved in Patrick's absence.[137] In another chapter we find Brigit acting as a 'marriage counsellor', when a man turned to her for help because his wife did not love him. Water blessed by the saint changed this situation.[138] So it seems that saintly women could play similar roles to those of men.[139] Although in hagiographic texts we do find sinning women, mostly nuns, it is obvious that we have no penitential handbooks written with a specific stress on women and their sins. Perhaps this was because female ascetics did not travel as *peregrinae* to the Continent, where the chances that a text survived were apparently greater?[140]

The *Life of Columba* reveals ways in which the norms we encountered in penitential texts could be put into practice. Although the exact nature of the sins is not always revealed, we meet the familiar offences that we encountered in penitential handbooks when dealing with the laity: violence, killing, forms of fornication and the sexual life of the married. In accordance with the rules found in penitential texts, the sexual life of the married is not subject to sanctions or penances, while the other offences are. In the latter case sinners are sentenced to years of penance, involving doing penance in a monastery or in exile and compensating the offended

---

[137] *Vita Brigitae*, c. 40, ed. and tr. Donncha Ó hAodha (Dublin 1978), p. 31; see for a somewhat different interpretation of Patrick's absence R. Chapman Stacey, *Dark Speech. The Performance of Law in Early Ireland* (Philadelphia 2007), pp. 144–5.

[138] *Vita Brigitae*, c. 45, ed. Ó hAodha, p. 32.

[139] For other instances taken from hagiography, see L. Bitel, 'Women's monastic enclosures in early Ireland: a study of female spirituality and male monastic mentalities', *Journal of Medieval History* 12 (1986), pp. 15–36, at pp. 24–5.

[140] For sinning nuns, see Bitel, 'Women's monastic enclosures', pp. 32–3.

parties. We should of course be cautious of considering Adomnán's work as a simple description of reality. However, given that it concurs so well with the contents of the Irish penitentials, it seems difficult to deny that these latter texts were used in assigning penances to sinners, although for the laity they probably applied only to those men and women closely related to a monastic community or those guilty of very serious crimes. Furthermore, it is uncertain whether such a view is true for all of Ireland and for every monastic community. We have already seen that on one small island such as Tiree different attitudes towards sinners could exist. It is furthermore revealing that Columba was a pupil of Finnian, that Columbanus knew Finnian's work thoroughly, that Cummean was probably in touch with Ségéne the abbot of Iona, the monastery founded by Columba, and that Cummean's work formed the basis for the *Bigotianum* and the *Old Irish Penitential*. This gives the impression that we are actually dealing with a closely knit group of monasteries and authors, whose work has come down to us. While it is probable that some works have been lost, such as the penitential attributed to Columba to which we find an allusion in the *Old Irish Penitential*, we do not know whether the remaining texts are the tip of an iceberg, or whether they represent a reliable sample of Irish penitential literature. As we have noticed, the manuscript evidence of the Irish penitentials is entirely continental. It seems, therefore, that those texts which were associated with Columbanus and his foundations in Gaul and northern Italy and those associated with the mission from Iona to northern parts of Britain stood a much better chance of survival than other Irish penitentials. It is to the influence of Irish penitential practices in these regions that we shall now turn, taking the texts influenced by Irish texts as our guide.

4   Insular texts on the move: penance in Francia and England

In the last chapter we saw that some Irish monasteries opened up ways for the laity to atone for their sins. This applied mostly to serious sins such as killing someone or having sex with someone you were not allowed to have such relations with. For people with close links to a monastery, such as the lay tenants or supporters of monastic institutions, more guidelines helping them to lead a Christian life would be offered. Such guidelines were codified in texts we call penitentials that were written in Ireland and adjacent territories in Britain. We have seen that Columbanus probably took a file of such texts with him when he travelled to Francia, where these were collected and with some other material fitting the local situation turned into a text later known as Columbanus's penitential. In England Cummean's penitential was known as a 'libellus scottorum'. This shows that Irish monks following the urge to leave their home country took penitential texts with them. In Ireland the desire to leave your country for a *peregrinatio*, that is the ascetic practice of leaving your family and relatives to follow the way of Christ, was particularly strong.[1] From the late seventh century onwards, English monks would follow in their wake. In travelling abroad Irish and Anglo-Saxon clerics seem to have taken penitential texts and attitudes with them, but had to adapt these to the new surrounding in which they found themselves. It is to the dissemination of insular penitential ideas and their adaptation to new circumstances that we shall now turn.

Columbanus and his pupils

When Jonas of Bobbio wrote the *Life of Columbanus* in the three years between 639 and 642, he stressed the impact the Irish *peregrinus* had on

---

[1] For the concept of *peregrinatio*, see Charles-Edwards, 'The social background to Irish *peregrinatio*'; Angenendt, 'Die irische *peregrinatio*'.

penitential discipline in Gaul.[2] When Columbanus arrived in Gaul, Jonas wrote, 'the strength of religion had almost vanished there because of the frequent invasions by enemies from abroad and because of the neglect from the side of the local episcopacy'. This was particularly discernible in the fact that 'the remedies of penance and the love of the ascetic life were barely to be found'.[3] When Columbanus had founded the monastery of Luxeuil, people flocked to his foundation for the remedy of sin in such numbers that Columbanus felt obliged to establish another monastery at a place called Fontaines.[4] This image of an Irish saint bringing penitential remedies to a region where ancient forms of penance had declined proved attractive to many historians.[5] It is, however, hardly in line with what we know about ecclesiastical life in Gaul in the sixth century, as we have seen in Chapter 2. Penance was a major theme in ecclesiastical life in the fifth and sixth centuries, while the bishops at the close of the sixth century could hardly be accused of negligence. In this period King Guntram and the bishop of Lyon had called together the bishops of the kingdom of Burgundy in two major councils in Mâcon in the years 581/3 and 585. Shortly thereafter the bishop of Lyon cooperated in the composition of a major collection of canon law, known as the *Collectio Vetus Gallica*.[6] Something of the implementation of this reform can be seen in the council of Auxerre (585–92), whereby the local bishop Aunacharius disseminated the decisions of the council of Mâcon (585) among the local clergy.[7] Columbanus, therefore, did not enter an ecclesiastical void, but instead a vibrant Merovingian church.

[2] On the date of the *Vita Columbani*, see Jonas de Bobbio, *Vie de Saint Colomban et de ses disciples*, introduced, translated and with notes by A. de Vogüé (Bégrolles-en-Mauges 1988), pp. 20–1; I. Wood, *The Missionary Life. Saints and the Evangelization of Europe, 400–1050* (Harlow 2001), p. 31, dates the first book of the *Vita* to *c.* 641/2 on the basis of C. Rohr, 'Hagiographie als historische Quelle: Ereignisgeschichte und Wunderberichte', *MIÖG* 103 (1995), pp. 229–64, at p. 233.

[3] *Vita Columbani*, c. 5, ed. Krusch, p. 51: 'A brittanicis ergo sinibus progressi, ad gallias tendunt, ubi tunc vel ob frequentia hostium externorum vel neglegentia praesulum religionis virtus pene abolita habebatur. Fides tantum manebat christiana, nam penitentiae medicamenta et mortificationis amor vix vel paucis in ea repperiebatur locis.'

[4] *Vita Columbani*, c. 10, ed. Krusch, p. 76: 'Quod beatus Columbanus cernens, undique ad paenitentiae medicamenta plebes concurrere et unius caenubii septa tantum conversantum cohortem absque difficultate non teneri.'

[5] B. Poschmann, *Die abendländische Kirchenbuße im frühen Mittelalter*, pp. 63–4.

[6] For the collection, see the monumental study by H. Mordek, *Kirchenrecht und Reform im Frankenreich. Die Collectio Vetus Gallica, die älteste systematische Kanonessammlung des fränkischen Gallien. Studien und Edition*, Beiträge zur Geschichte und Quellenkunde des Mittelalters 1 (Berlin / New York 1975).

[7] R. Meens, 'Reforming the clergy: a context for the use of the Bobbio penitential', in Hen and Meens (eds.), *The Bobbio Missal*, pp. 154–67.

Why then did Jonas emphasize Columbanus's contribution to the field of penance? It is now generally accepted that Jonas did not provide an impartial history of Columbanus's career. He chose, for example, to leave out an account of the difficulties Columbanus encountered with the bishops in Gaul over the date on which he celebrated the feast of Easter, difficulties about which we are well informed because Columbanus discussed them in his letters. Shortly after Columbanus had died, his monasteries must have adopted the Gallic calculation method and it probably was not appropriate to present the saint as a staunch defender of the Irish calculation of Easter to an audience that had just decided to switch to a new one. Moreover, Jonas's account of the relations between Columbanus and the Burgundian kings was written with hindsight, skipping over some delicate questions.[8] We should therefore ask whether Jonas's stress on penance perhaps reflects a later preoccupation with this topic.[9] As we have seen in the last chapter, Columbanus's texts demonstrate the importance of the concept of penance in his monasteries. He wrote a monastic rule which can be regarded as a monastic penitential, while he also had a hand in the penitential which goes under his name. It can also be shown that this topic was of continuing interest in the Columbanian foundations. The *Regula Coenobialis* as well as his penitential show signs of a later redaction, most probably executed in Columbanus's monasteries after the death of their founder.

We can therefore conclude that Jonas's stress on the importance of penance in Columbanian monasticism is supported by other evidence and that it consequently not only reflects the views of Columbanus himself, but also those of his successors. Particularly his penitential shows that lay people could benefit from forms of penance provided for by a monastery. The monastic life as envisaged by Columbanus seems moreover of a different nature to forms of monasticism to be found in Gaul at that time. Columbanian monasticism was characterized by a stress on the (sexual) purity of the monks and the power of their intercessory prayer.[10] For this reason the monastery was much less open to the laity, if compared to the suburban monasteries of Merovingian Gaul. Supported by royal and aristocratic benefactions, Columbanian monasteries were furthermore to be found in the countryside, away from episcopal centres.

---

[8] Wood, *The Missionary Life*, p. 32: 'Jonas' picture of Columbanian monasticism may also reflect the norms of his own day rather more exactly than the original ideas of the founder'; Charles-Edwards, *Early Christian Ireland*, pp. 344–90, adds nuance to this view.

[9] As suggested by Charles-Edwards, 'The penitential of Columbanus', p. 219.

[10] Diem, *Das monastische Experiment*; and Charles-Edwards, *Early Christian Ireland*, p. 382.

The fact that Jonas felt free to discuss the penitential achievements of Columbanus suggests that the monastic penitential regime introduced by Columbanus was not regarded as something radically new. As far as we know, it was not part of the complaints raised against Columbanus by the Frankish bishops at the council of Chalon, nor by the attacks of the Columbanian monk Agrestius on the monastic *familia* of the Irish *peregrinus* in the 620s.[11] Traditionally this apparent easy reception of Columbanian penance has been explained by the gradual disappearance of public penance in the fifth and sixth centuries.[12] We have seen, however, that there is no real reason to assume a decline in ecclesiastical attention for the theme of penance in Merovingian Gaul. It is rather the existence of a wide variety of forms in which one could atone for one's sins that should be regarded as the background against which the introduction of new ways to deal with sin was not seen as problematic. The fact moreover that Columbanian monasteries were often found away from episcopal cities surely helped in preventing tensions from arising over this topic. What it was exactly that attracted people to Columbanian forms of penance remains unclear. We may assume that the personality of the saint, whom we can regard as one of the last living 'holy men' who had been so important for the late antique Church, played a part, as did the purity of the monks and the power of their intercessory prayer.[13] Perhaps the 'measurability' of sins, penances and their commutations was another factor contributing to the success of the Columbanian movement. The fact that sins could be measured and accounted for by specific forms of penances, which could be changed into another 'currency', for example a certain number of prayers or amount of alms, by the process of commutations, could perhaps induce powerful lay people to establish a bond with these monasteries for the benefit of their soul (*pro remedia animae*) by handing over land and sometimes their children, possibly as part of the atonement for sins.[14] The prayers of the pure monks said in return would then assure their salvation.

---

[11] See Charles-Edwards, *Early Christian Ireland*, pp. 364–5 and 368–9.

[12] Poschmann, *Die abendländische Kirchenbuße im frühen Mittelalter*, p. 64. Vogel, *La discipline pénitentielle en Gaule*.

[13] For Columbanus as 'the last holy man', see A. Diem, 'Monks, kings, and the transformation of sanctity: Jonas of Bobbio and the end of the holy man', *Speculum* 82 (2007), pp. 521–59.

[14] For the importance of gift-giving for the establishment of social relations, see Rosenwein, *To be the Neighbor of St. Peter*, for giving away your children, see M. de Jong, *In Samuel's Image. Child Oblation in the Early Medieval West* (Leiden / New York / Cologne 1996); a useful reassessment of the literature on gift-giving is A. Bijsterveld, 'The medieval gift as agent of social bonding and power', in A. Bijsterveld, *Do ut des. Gift Giving, 'Memoria', and Conflict Management in the Medieval Low Countries* (Hilversum 2007), pp. 17–50.

There might be another factor contributing to the success of the Columbanian movement. Suburban basilicas comprising the venerated graves of renowned Gallic saints such as St Medard at Soissons or St Martin at Tours had been places of refuge for people seeking sanctuary. Conciliar and royal legislation, as well as the power of the saint buried in the church, protected the fugitive against his enemies, but such protection was not always adequate. The council of Mâcon of the year 585, for example, criticized powerful men, censured here as 'pseudo-Christians', for having violently captured people who had sought refuge in a church.[15] This might relate to the famous case of the royal treasurer Eberulf seeking refuge in the basilica of St Martin in Tours after being accused by King Guntram of the murder of his brother Chilperic in 584. The king sent a certain Claudius with 300 men to capture the treasurer, who hid in the church of St Martin accompanied by his own followers. In the end it came to bloodshed in the atrium of the church in which Eberulf had his brains smashed out and Claudius in turn was killed by Eberulf's men. Gregory of Tours relates this story in great detail, trying to explain why St Martin had not protected the refugee at his grave and thereby justifying his own role in the conflict.[16] This episode shows that the repeated injunctions to guarantee the safety of people seeking refuge in a church were no mere formulas but necessary in order to safeguard the sanctity of church buildings. In the course of the seventh century, monasteries seem in part to have taken over the role of suburban basilicas as places of refuge. They offered places of internal exile for the aristocracy to retreat from the political arena without losing face.[17] In Columbanian monasteries entry into the inner precincts was taboo and this might have assisted in turning them into places of retreat, and therefore of penance.

The fact that the inner precincts of the monastery were inaccessible to anybody except the monks themselves is stressed in two places by Jonas. In the first instance King Theuderic accused the Irish *peregrinus* for digressing from the normal custom in his country by forbidding entry into the *septa secretiora* to every Christian.[18] In his reply Columbanus

---

[15] Council of Mâcon (585), c. 8, ed. C. De Clercq, *Concilia Galliae A.511–A.695*, CC SL 148A (Turnhout 1963), pp. 242–3.

[16] See Gregory of Tours, *Historiae* VII, 22 and 23, ed. Krusch and Levison, pp. 303–311; see for an analysis of this episode R. Meens, 'The sanctity of the basilica of St. Martin. Gregory of Tours and the practice of sanctuary in the Merovingian period', in R. Corradini, R. Meens, C. Pössel and P. Shaw (eds.), *Texts and Identities in the Early Middle Ages* (Vienna 2006), pp. 277–87.

[17] De Jong, 'Monastic prisoners or opting out?'

[18] *Vita Columbani*, I, 19: 'intra septa secretiora omnibus christianis aditus non pateret', ed. Krusch, p. 88.

declared that it was his custom to deny entry into the inner parts of the monastery to lay people or to people who were not leading a religious life, even as the king insisted that he had the right to enter every part of the monastic settlement that he had himself endowed.[19] The sacral character of the inner parts of the monastery is further emphasized by the episode in the *Vita Columbani* where a group of warriors is sent by the king to Luxeuil to capture the Irish saint. After entering the inner parts of the monastery (*septa monasterii*), the soldiers were unable to see Columbanus, who was sitting in the churchyard (*in atrio ecclesiae*) reading a book. Though they passed him by several times and some of them even touched his feet in doing so, they just could not discover the saint: a wonderful sight (*expectaculum pulcherrimum*) Jonas calls it.[20] When Columbanus finally left his monastery, Jonas stresses the fact that he did this of his own free will, out of compassion for the soldiers who were sent to capture him, and that no one from outside the monastery was able to accomplish anything on his own strength within the *septa secretiora*.[21] The last episode shows that even in Columbanian monasteries warriors could enter to capture an enemy, but Jonas at least wants his readers to believe that such an action was of no avail. In the *Vita Columbani*, Jonas, therefore, stresses the inaccessibility of the inner parts of Columbanian monasteries for outsiders, thus enhancing their appeal to political refugees.

We have seen that in an Irish context perpetrators of crimes threatening the social order could do penance in a monastery and after fulfilling their penance and with help of a monastic authority could return to the world. Can such a scenario be envisaged in Columbanus's foundations in Gaul and Italy? Columbanus's penitential, as we have seen in the last chapter, clearly envisaged lay sinners confessing their sins, doing penance and offering compensation to the injured party in cases of crimes which shocked the social order. This would fit a picture of a monastically mediated penance being part of a process of reconciliation in the world. The structure of Columbanus's penitential makes it clear that this text continued to be used in his foundations after Columbanus's death in 615. The fact that Columbanus's penitential survives from two manuscripts written in Bobbio indicates that his text remained authoritative in this monastery in northern Italy. That his work was also of continued interest in his foundations in Burgundy is suggested by a group of texts that built on the groundwork laid out by Columbanus, the group of the so-called 'simple Frankish penitentials'.

---

[19] *Vita Columbani*, I, 19, ed. Krusch, p. 88.   [20] *Vita Columbani*, I, 20, ed. Krusch, p. 90.
[21] *Vita Columbani*, I, 20, ed. Krusch, p. 91.

The 'simple Frankish penitentials' (*libri paenitentiales simplices*) form a group of eight closely related texts, which are all extant in one or two manuscript copies.[22] The earliest manuscripts containing these works date from the late seventh or early eighth century, while the latest were copied in the tenth century.[23] Since they all contain a corpus of shared material, they must go back to a common source, which probably was composed in a place with close connections to the foundations of Columbanus. Since this common material comprises as its most recent source several canons from the council of Auxerre, a Burgundian origin of the common source of this group seems perfectly plausible, while a date in the early first half of the seventh century might be possible.[24] Interestingly, the best witness to this group, the *Paenitentiale Burgundense*, is transmitted in a manuscript which also contains the council of Auxerre.[25]

It has long been recognized that this group of texts uses Columbanus's penitential as its main source, enriched by conciliar legislation. The most recent council used is that held shortly after 585 in Auxerre under the direction of Bishop Aunacharius, but late antique councils are also used, such as the council of Ancyra (314) or Nicaea (325). The fact that Columbanus's penitential was combined with ecclesiastical legislation raises some interesting points. First, it shows that the Columbanian practice of penance did not remain an isolated phenomenon, but was

---

[22] See the synoptical edition of these texts in R. Kottje (ed.), *Paenitentialia minora Franciae et Italiae saeculi VIII–IX*, CC SL 156 (Turnhout 1994), pp. 1–60, bearing out the similarities between these texts. It concerns the following texts:

Paenitentiale Bobbiense, ed. Kottje, *Paenitentialia minora*, pp. 66–71;
Paenitentiale Burgundense, ed. Kottje, *Paenitentialia minora*, pp. 61–5;
Paenitentiale Floriacense, ed. Kottje, *Paenitentialia minora*, pp. 95–103;
Paenitentiale Hubertense, ed. Kottje, *Paenitentialia minora*, pp. 105–15;
Paenitentiale Oxoniense I, ed. Kottje, *Paenitentialia minora*, pp. 87–93;
Paenitentiale Parisiense simplex, ed. Kottje, *Paenitentialia minora*, pp. 73–9;
Paenitentiale Sangallense simplex, ed. Kottje, *Paenitentialia minora*, pp. 117–21;
Paenitentiale Sletstatense, ed. Kottje, *Paenitentialia minora*, pp. 81–5.

[23] Earliest mss. Paris, BN, lat. 13246 (s. VII ex. or VIII; containing the *P. Bobbiense*) and 7193 (s. VIII med.; containing the *P. Parisiense simplex*); latest ms. Oxford, Bodleian, Bodl. 311 (s. X; containing the *P. Oxoniense I*); the early date for the ms. Paris lat. 13246 has been advanced by R. McKitterick, 'The scripts of the Bobbio Missal', in Hen and Meens (eds.), *The Bobbio Missal*, pp. 19–52.

[24] According to Kottje, *Paenitentialia Minora*, p. XXIV the *Discipulus Umbrensium* version of Theodore's penitential was also used, pushing the date of origin into the eighth century; see however Meens, 'Reforming the clergy', p. 160, where I argue that there is no need to regard Theodore's penitential as the source for *P. Burgundense* c. 6.

[25] Ms. Brussels, KB, 10127–44 (s. VIII–IX, northern France); for this manuscript, see Y. Hen, 'Knowledge of canon law among rural priests: the evidence of two Carolingian manuscripts from around 800', *Journal of Theological Studies* NS 50 (1999), pp. 117–34.

fruitfully combined with existing ecclesiastical rules. As his followers did
not hesitate to use other monastic rules, besides the two composed by
Columbanus, they also seem not to have doubted that his penitential
rulings could be combined with existing conciliar legislation. The Irish
impetus of Columbanus was therefore quickly taken on by Frankish
monks and aristocrats, forging a movement known by historians as
'Hiberno-Frankish monasticism' (*irofränkisches Mönchtum*).[26] The
'simple Frankish penitentials' in this way combined the Burgundian
movement for Church reform with Columbanian monasticism.[27] In this
context it is significant that the council of Auxerre was not a meeting
between bishops, as is generally the case for Merovingian councils whose
decrees have survived, but is actually the first synod held by a bishop to
educate and discipline his clergy. As such it is the earliest text known to
us of a meeting of a bishop with his suffragan clerics. In this meeting
Aunacharius disseminated the decisions of the council of Mâcon (585)
among his clergy.[28] Its concern for clerical discipline is shared by the
'simple Frankish penitentials', which cite mainly canons from the part
of Columbanus's penitential devoted to sinning clerics. Another impli-
cation of the combination of Columbanian penitential sentences and
conciliar legislation is that, by some at least, no major opposition was
felt between ecclesiastical legislation as it was found in collections of
conciliar decrees and penitential rulings.[29] This can only be explained
by the fact that the canonical rules, which had gained new emphasis in
the sixth century when the *Collectio Vetus Gallica* had systematized
existing canonical legislation, were applied in a way that was not felt to
be totally different from the ways in which Columbanus's penitential
rulings were employed. Historians who maintain that already in the
seventh century a clear-cut distinction existed between public and private
penance have to stress the continuities of Columbanus's approach with
the ancient practice of public penance or to assume the existence of

---

[26] For this movement, see F. Prinz, *Frühes Mönchtum im Frankenreich. Kultur und Gesellschaft
in Gallien, den Rheinlanden und Bayern am Beispiel der monastischen Entwicklung (4. bis 8.
Jahrhundert)* (Darmstadt 1988, 2nd edition); the notion of Iro-Frankish monasticism was
criticized by A. Dierkens, 'Prolégomènes à une histoire des relations culturelles entre les
îles britanniques et le continent pendant le Haut Moyen Age. La diffusion du
monachisme dit colombanien ou iro-franc dans quelques monastères de la région
parisienne au VIIe siècle et la politique religieuse de la reine Bathilde', in H. Atsma
(ed.), *La Neustrie. Les pays au nord de la Loire de 650 à 850*, 2 vols., Beihefte der Francia 16
(Sigmaringen 1989), vol. II, pp. 371–94; the notion of Iro-Frankish monasticism is
applied usefully in Charles-Edwards, *Early Christian Ireland*, p. 389.

[27] Meens, 'Reforming the clergy'.

[28] O. Pontal, *Histoire des conciles mérovingiens* (Paris 1989), p. 192.

[29] Already observed by Poschmann, *Die abendländische Kirchenbuße im frühen Mittelalter*,
p. 81.

private penance in Gaul already before the arrival of Columbanus in order to explain this phenomenon.[30] If we admit, however, that in Gaul a wide variety of ways to atone for your sins existed, and that there is no reason to speak of private penance in the case of the Irish way of dealing with sin, the smooth combination of ecclesiastical legislation and penitential rulings becomes easier to understand.

There is another interesting aspect to some of these 'simple Frankish penitentials', which throws light on their use. The *P. Burgundense*, for example, is preserved in a late eighth-century manuscript containing a rich collection of canon law and liturgical texts, which has been described as a 'small handbook for the use of rural priests'.[31] As such it illustrates the relations of penance with the fields of canon law and liturgy. The Bobbio penitential, which was not composed in Bobbio but more probably in Burgundy, is included in a highly interesting manuscript, known as the Bobbio Missal. Again, this manuscript can be regarded as a handbook for a priest as it contains liturgical *formulae* enabling one to say Mass, to baptize, to visit the sick and the dying, to bless a matrimonial bed and to hear confession.[32] This manuscript differs from the one containing the *P. Burgundense* in that it contains mostly material of a liturgical or catechetical nature. It is also the earliest manuscript in which we find evidence for a liturgical elaboration of the process of hearing confession, since it contains two prayers to be said over a penitent, probably after he had confessed his sins.[33] Interestingly, one of these prayers is derived from the liturgy of public penance as it is found in the Old Gelasian Sacramentary.[34] Possibly, therefore, the compiler of this

---

[30] On continuities with public penance, see Poschmann, *Die abendländische Kirchenbuße im frühen Mittelalter*, pp. 24–37, e.g. p. 24: 'Bei aller Gegensätzlichkeit aber in Bezug auf die äußere Gestaltung bleibt bestehen, daß das eigentliche Wesen der kirchlichen Buße durch das Abgehen von den alten kirchenrechtlichen Bestimmungen nich alteriert worden ist'; on the existence of private penance, see E. Göller, 'Studien über das gallische Bußwesen zur Zeit des Cäsarius von Arles und Gregors des Grossen', *Archiv für katholisches Kirchenrecht* 109 (1929), pp. 3–126.

[31] Hen, 'Knowledge of canon law among rural priests', p. 128; see also D. Bullough, 'The Carolingian liturgical experience', in R. Swanson (ed.), *Continuity and Change in Christian Worship*, Studies in Church History 35 (Woodbridge 1999), pp. 29–64, at p. 48.

[32] See A. Wilmart, 'Notice du Missel de Bobbio', in A. Wilmart, E. A. Lowe and H. A. Wilson (eds.), *The Bobbio Missal. Notes and Studies*, Henry Bradshaw Society 61 (London 1924), pp. 38–9 (reprinted in 1991 in one volume with E. A. Lowe (ed.), *The Bobbio Missal. A Gallican Mass-book (Ms. Paris. Lat. 13246)*, Henry Bradshaw Society 58); see also the collections of essays in Hen and Meens (eds.), *The Bobbio Missal*.

[33] Lowe (ed.), *The Bobbio Missal*, nrs. 578 and 579.

[34] Nr. 578; see *Sacramentarium Gelasianum* no 1702, ed. L. C. Mohlberg (in collaboration with L. Eizenhöfer und P. Siffrin), *Liber Sacramentorum Romanae Aecclesiae Ordines Anni Circuli (Cod. Vat. reg. 316/Paris Bibl. Nat. 7193, 41/56)*

manuscript had access to the penitential ritual as it is given in the Old Gelasian Sacramentary and thought it appropriate to use a prayer from this ritual when hearing confession.

Whereas this combination of liturgical elements taken from the Old Gelasian penitential ritual and a 'simple Frankish penitential' does not really need to surprise us, another penitential of this group is found in the manuscript which is central to the liturgy of 'canonical penance' in the early Middle Ages: the Old Gelasian Sacramentary itself. This sacramentary, as we have already seen, contains an *ordo* for the admission of a penitent on Ash Wednesday and his reconciliation on Maundy Thursday, but the manuscript, now split and preserved in Paris and the Vatican, originally also contained the *P. Parisiense simplex*.[35] This fact not only shows that in the middle of the eighth century when this manuscript was written in the nunnery of Chelles or Jouarre, the liturgy of canonical penance was still known, but it also raises questions about how the penitential in this manuscript might have been used. The Gelasian Sacramentary is a *de luxe* manuscript which one would associate with a bishop or important monastery. Perhaps it was written for the dioceses of Paris or Meaux.[36] It has been argued that the *Gelasianum* came to France from England, conveyed by contact with England established by the Merovingian queen Balthild, of Anglo-Saxon descent.[37] The presence of the penitential in this manuscript is to be explained through contacts with Columbanian monasticism. Bertila, the abbess of Chelles, who formerly had been a nun in the monastery of Jouarre, had close relations with the Columbanian monastic movement.[38] Her *Vita* relates how Bertila 'persuaded the *familia* of the monastery as well as the people in the neighbourhood (*vicinos propinquos*) through holy communion to do penance for their sins after having done confession'.[39] Such an attitude would fit a Columbanian monastery, where women could hold formidable positions, including hearing confessions of the nuns in the monastery,

---

(Sacramentarium Gelasianum), Rerum Ecclesiasticarum Documenta, Series Maior: Fontes IV (Rome 1968), p. 248.

[35] Ed. Kottje, *Paenitentialia minora*, pp. 73–9; it is preserved in Ms. Paris, BNF, lat. 7193 (s. VIII med.), which originally formed one ms. with Vat. Reg. lat. 316: see introduction, Kottje, *Paenitentialia minora*, p. 26.

[36] Hen, *Culture and Religion in Merovingian Gaul*, p. 45.

[37] Y. Hen, 'Rome, Anglo-Saxon England and the formation of the Frankish liturgy', *Revue Bénédictine* 112 (2002), pp. 301–22.

[38] Prinz, *Frühes Mönchtum im Frankenreich*, p. 175.

[39] *Vita Bertilae abbatissae Calensis*, c. 6, ed. W. Levison, MGH SS rer. mer. VI (Hanover / Leipzig 1913), p. 106: 'Familiam quoque monasterii sive vicinos propinquos per sanctam communionem attrahebat ut, datis confessionibus, paenitentiam pro peccatis suis agerent' (translation in J. A. McNamara and J. E. Halborg, *Sainted Women of the Dark Ages* (Durham / London 1992), pp. 279–88, part. p. 285).

as demonstrated by abbess Burgundofara.[40] The fact that we find a liturgical text regulating the admission and reconciliation of a penitent and a text containing specifications for the assignment of penance in one and the same manuscript written in a nun's scriptorium raises an interesting set of questions. Were both texts used in hearing confession and apportioning penances? Does this imply that a liturgical ritual was used to hear confession regulated by a penitential? Was it necessarily a bishop who administered such rites, or possibly an abbess? The occurrence of the rite of canonical penance that some have regarded as the classical expression of late antique public penance in a manuscript which also contains a copy of a penitential of Columbanian stock again demonstrates that the two forms of penance were not seen as being in opposition to each other, but rather as smoothly complementing one another. This is another indication that there was no single ritual for the imposition of penance, but that it could take many forms, using late antique and insular patterns.

At a council in Chalon-sur-Saône held in the years 647–53 the bishops decreed that penance for sins was a useful remedy for the soul for everyone. When someone had confessed his sins, priests or bishops – the Latin is ambiguous here in using the word *sacerdos*, which can mean both – should impose penance.[41] It has been suggested that a council making such an obvious statement must somehow have been reacting to a new development. The fact that among the bishops attending this council there were former monks from Columbanian Luxeuil, such as Donatus of Besançon and Chagnoald of Laon, while others present, such as Eligius of Noyon, were closely connected to the Columbanian monastic movement, implies that this new development must have concerned the introduction of insular forms of penance.[42] Whether the council of Chalon was indeed reacting in defence of Columbanian ways of dealing with penitents seems questionable, since this would mean that an opposition was felt between insular and traditional Gallic ways of dealing with penitents, for which there is no firm evidence. The interest in penance at Chalon was probably stirred by the dispute about Bishop

---

[40] *Vita Columbani*, II, 19 and 22, ed. Krusch, pp. 139–42; see the translation in McNamara and Halborg, *Sainted Women of the Dark Ages*, pp. 171–5, although they unnecessarily seem to deny the nature of such confessions by questioning their 'sacramental dimension', cf. G. Muschiol, *Famula Dei: Zur Liturgie in merowingischen Frauenklöstern* (Münster 1994), pp. 222–63; G. Muschiol, 'Men, women and liturgical practice in the early medieval West', in L. Brubaker and J. Smith (eds.), *Gender in the Early Medieval World. East and West, 300–900* (Cambridge 2004), pp. 198–216, at pp. 210–11.

[41] Council of Chalon, c. 8, ed. C. De Clercq, *Concilia Galliae A.511–A.695*, CC SL 148A (Turnhout 1963), p. 304.

[42] Poschmann, *Die abendländische Kirchenbuße im frühen Mittelalter*, pp. 75–6; Vogel, *Les 'Libri Paenitentiales'*, pp. 35–6.

Theudorius of Arles, who had not turned up at the council, although he had travelled to the town of Chalon. Apparently the bishop knew that some painful topics were going to be raised concerning his own lifestyle and for that reason chose to stay away. The council then sent him a letter which has survived as an appendix to its decrees, in which it censures the bishop for his indecent way of life which was contrary to canonical regulations. The council had also seen a written document signed by the bishop and corroborated by his 'comprovincials' (*cumprovinciales*) in which he professed himself to be a penitent. Therefore, the council decided, he could no longer hold or rule the bishopric entrusted to him, because someone who had publicly confessed to be a penitent could not at the same time hold the position of a bishop.[43] The canon issued at Chalon about penance being a useful remedy for all, if it addressed an actual problem at all, probably tackled the question of a bishop doing penance, rather than the ways of dealing with penitents as they had been practised in Columbanian monasteries.

Irish *peregrini* and penitential visions

That Columbanus had an impact on monasticism in Francia and in northern Italy is well established. Historians of penance have highlighted his impact on ways of dealing with sin. What then did Columbanus bring that was really new? First of all he seems to have conveyed a renewed emphasis on sin and penance in monastic life, an emphasis which he extended to the laity attached to his monastic houses. Furthermore he introduced the fixed correlation of specific sins to specific forms of penance, as exemplified in his penitential. This made it possible to calculate precise forms of atonement. The possibilities to transform one form of penance into another provided opportunities to replace periods of fasting, the normal currency of penance, to making gifts of alms and land to make up for one's sins. The purity of Columbanian monks made them into a perfect vehicle to pray for the well-being of others, thus attracting the support of the laity for their foundations. The laity maintaining close relations with a monastery were, moreover, expected to order their life increasingly according to monastic principles.

We have seen in the last chapter that his monastic rule and penitential are closely interconnected. We can therefore imagine that Columbanus's influence on monasticism and penitential practice went hand in hand. This would mean that his penitential practice spread mostly in northern

---

[43] See the letter attached to the council of Chalon, ed. de Clercq, *Concilia Galliae A.511– A.695*, pp. 309–10; the matter is briefly discussed in Pontal, *Die Synoden in Merowingerreich*, pp. 193–7.

France and around Bobbio.[44] Columbanus's influence also reached the Neustrian royal court, where many of his followers held important positions. In the correspondence of this group of courtiers associated with the Merovingian king Chlothar II the author often identified himself as *peccator*, a sinner.[45] The manuscript tradition of the simple Frankish penitentials suggests that his penitential teachings were influential mainly in the north of France and Burgundy where the earliest manuscripts containing these texts were written.[46] Early in the eighth century such a text was also known at the monastery of Corbie, where with its help the *Excarpsus Cummeani* was being put together.[47]

Columbanus, however, was not the only Irish monk who travelled to the Continent, although he is definitively the one about whom we are best informed. Fursa, another Irishman, left his native country for East Anglia where he built a monastery at a place called Cnobheresburg.[48] After a while he departed from there to Gaul where he was received with due honour by the Neustrian king Clovis II and the mayor of the palace Erchinoald. The latter supported him to found a monastery at Lagny, where he died only a few years later, close to the middle of the seventh century. Fursa's body was interred by Erchinoald at a place which later became known as a typically Irish monastery: *Peronna Scottorum*: Péronne of the Irish.[49]

---

[44] For Columbanian monasticism, see Prinz, *Frühes Mönchtum*; H. B. Clarke and M. Brennan (eds.), *Columbanus and Merovingian Monasticism* (Oxford 1981); Wood, *The Merovingian Kingdoms*, pp. 184–9; Diem, *Das monastische Experiment*; Charles-Edwards, *Early Christian Ireland*, pp. 344–90 and B. Rosenwein, *Emotional Communities in the Early Middle Ages* (Ithaca / London 2006), pp. 130–5.

[45] Rosenwein, *Emotional Communities*, p. 139.

[46] Mss. Brussels, KB, 10127–44 (s. VIII–IX, northern France) containing the *Paenitentiale Burgundense*; Paris, BN, lat. 13246 (s. VII ex. or VIII, Burgundy, possibly Vienne) containing the *Paenitentiale Bobbiense*; Paris, BN, lat. 7193 (s. VIII med., Jouarre or Chelles) containing the *P. Parisiense simplex*.

[47] *Paenitentiale Excarpsus Cummeani*, ed. Schmitz II, pp. 597–644; see F. B. Asbach, 'Das Poenitentiale Remense und der sogen. Excarpsus Cummeani: Überlieferung, Quellen und Entwicklung zweier kontinentaler Bußbücher aus dem 1. Hälfte des 8. Jahrhunderts' (dissertation, Regensburg, 1975), pp. 95–8; for the origin of the *Excarpsus Cummeani* in Corbie, see L. Körntgen, 'Der *Excarpsus Cummeani*, ein Bußbuch aus Corbie', in O. Münsch and T. Zotz (eds.), *Scientia veritatis. Festschrift für Hubert Mordek zum 65. Geburtstag* (Ostfildern 2004), pp. 59–75.

[48] Bede, *Historia Ecclesiastica Gentis Anglorum* III, 19, ed. Colgrave and Mynors, p. 270; on the identification of this place, see J. M. Wallace-Hadrill, *Bede's Ecclesiastical History of the English People. A Historical Commentary* (Oxford 1988), p. 113.

[49] On Fursa and his monastic *familia*, see Ian Wood, *The Merovingian Kingdoms*, pp. 189–90; A. Dierkens, *Abbayes et chapitres entre Sambre et Meuse (VIIe–IXe Siècles)* (Sigmaringen 1985), pp. 303–9, with important reservations; M. Richter, *Ireland and Her Neighbours in the Seventh Century* (Dublin 1999), pp. 126–33. For the *Vita Fursei*, ed. B. Krusch in MGH SS rer. mer. 4 (Hanover / Leipzig 1902), pp. 434–40, but unfortunately the visions are left out here; the visions are edited in C. Carozzi, *Le voyage de l'âme dans l'au-delà d'après la littérature latine (Ve–XIIIe siècle)* (Rome 1994),

We do not learn about Fursa hearing confessions and imposing penance the way Columbanus had done, but interestingly enough his *Vita* contains a long episode relating visions of the afterlife Fursa had had in his early years in Ireland. According to one of the best-informed historians in this field, the *Vita Fursei* was the *point de départ* of a new literary genre, the 'voyages of the soul'.[50] In Fursa's visions penance is a major theme, while the idea of combatting vices with their contrary virtues, which we find expressed here, is also found in Columbanus's work as well as in the Irish penitentials of Finnian and Cummean.[51] The *Vita* relates, moreover, how demons came after Fursa to claim his soul with charges which show that the demons clearly 'knew their *Penitentials*', as Peter Brown observed.[52] One of the claims made against Fursa was that he had accepted gifts from the unjust, a claim that his guardian angel could only counter with the assertion that Fursa had thought that every one of them had done penance. The devil replied that he should have probed the sincerity of their penance before accepting gifts, because 'gifts blind the wise and pervert the words of the just' (Deuteronomy 16.19). This episode not only shows that the author of the *Vita Fursei*, probably a monk of Lagny or Péronne writing shortly after Fursa's death, was acquainted with insular ways of imposing penances, but it also demonstrates that gift-giving to holy men and monasteries was closely connected to the concept of penance.[53]

The *Vita Fursei* contains another intriguing episode shedding light on a penitential debate. In the afterlife Fursa met two bishops, Beonanus and Meldanus, who instructed him on the negligence of the doctors of the Church. These doctors often were lecherous, avaricious, grudging and even violent men, so the bishops said. Often they held small crimes for serious ones, while they thought lightly about pride, avarice, envy, false testimony and blasphemy. One of the small crimes the importance of which was being exaggerated was that of 'nocturnal illusions' – by which we will have to understand nocturnal emissions, a feature that was problematic in monastic circles from very early on.[54] Many, moreover, the two bishops continued, refrained from kinds of food that God had

pp. 677–92, who discusses them extensively on pp. 99–138; another edition was prepared by M. P. Ciccarese, 'Le visioni di S. Fursa', *Romanobarbarica: Contributi allo studio dei rapporti culturali tra mondo latino e mondo barbarico* 8 (1984/1985), pp. 231–303.

[50] Carozzi, *Le voyage de l'âme*, p. 99.   [51] Carozzi, *Le voyage de l'âme*, p. 113.

[52] P. Brown, *The Rise of Western Christendom. Triumph and Diversity, A.D. 200–1000* (2nd edition, Oxford 2003), p. 259.

[53] For the date of the text, see Dierkens, *Abbayes et chapitres*, p. 304, n. 147 dating the *Vita* to the years 656/657.

[54] D. Brakke, 'The problematization of nocturnal emissions in early Christian Syria, Egypt, and Gaul', *Journal of Early Christian Studies* 3 (1995), pp. 419–60; C. Leyser, 'Masculinity in flux: nocturnal emission and the limits of celibacy in the early Middle

allowed man to eat.[55] This criticism of the evaluation of specific sins reminds one of the penitential regulations concerning diet and sexual purity that we find, for example, in Cummean's penitential.[56] It concerns two topics that Gregory the Great also had problems with, as his replies to questions from Augustine of Canterbury demonstrate. Apparently Irish and British forms of Christianity had developed a greater sensitivity with regard to matters relating to ritual purity and the author of the *Vita Fursei* here seems to react to some of these.[57] The similarities with the work of Columbanus and Irish penitentials might tempt one to conclude that the author of the *Visio* was acquainted with Columbanus's, Finnian's and Cummean's work.[58] A relation between Fursa and Columbanus is suggested by the fact that Eligius of Noyon, who was closely related to the Columbanian movement, participated in the translation of the saint's body to Péronne.[59] Yet there is no real proof demonstrating that Fursa or the author of the *Visio* knew specific Irish penitential texts. We can, however, safely conclude that for this Irish *peregrinus* and his foundation in Gaul, penance was a major theme and that it is highly likely that he was acquainted with Irish penitential texts with their detailed descriptions of sins and their atonement.

The vision of Fursa can be read as a penitential vision in another sense as well. On his way back Fursa is scorched by purgatorial fire because of the fact that he had accepted a cloak from a sinner on his deathbed. The angel accompanying him explained that he should not have accepted this cloak nor allowed a burial in a holy place, but instead should have preached penance to this sinner. When Fursa finally returned to his terrestrial body, the mark of this wound was still to be seen, making the experience of the soul manifest in the flesh.[60] This contact with

Ages', in D. Hadley (ed.), *Masculinity in Medieval Europe* (London / New York 1999), pp. 103–20.

[55] *Visio Fursei*, c. 13, ed. Carozzi, *Le voyage de l'âme*, p. 688.

[56] P. *Cummeani* II, 15 (nocturnal pollutions) and (XI), 12–18 (dietary rules), ed. Bieler, *Irish Penitentials*, pp. 114 and 130; an allusion to a discussion about dietary rules is also to be found in the *Vita Columbani* (eating fish).

[57] For the sensitivity to matters relating to ritual purity in insular texts, see Meens, 'A background to Augustine's mission' and Meens, 'The uses of the Old Testament in early medieval canon law', in Y. Hen and M. Innes (eds.), *The Uses of the Past in Early Medieval Europe* (Cambridge 2000), pp. 67–77.

[58] As e.g. Carozzi, *Le voyage de l'âme*, p. 114.

[59] For Eligius's relationship to Columbanian monasticism, see Prinz, *Frühes Mönchtum*, pp. 132–4 and Rosenwein, *Emotional Communities*, p. 133; it is not mentioned in G. Scheibelreiter, 'Ein Gallorömer in Flandern: Eligius von Noyon', in W. Pohl (ed.), *Die Suche nach den Ursprüngen. Von der Bedeutung des frühen Mittelalters* (Vienna 2004), pp. 117–28.

[60] *Visio Fursei*, ed. Carozzi, *Le voyage de l'âme*, pp. 691–2; and see the comments on pp. 104–5.

purgatorial fire cleansed Fursa of sin and turned him into a person fit to preach the faith to others.[61]

A text written some two decades later can also be read as a penitential vision, but in a different way. It concerns a layman who had confessed his sins and had entered a monastery to do penance for them. This man, called Barontus, had entered the monastery of Longoretus, near Bourges, and fell ill. During his illness he toured the afterlife accompanied by the archangel Raphael. As with Fursey, demons wanted to capture his soul, but Raphael protected him and and in the end called in the help of St Peter, who happened to be the patron of the monastery of Longoretus. Before Peter, demons accused Barontus of serious sins (*principalia vitia*): he had had three wives and had nonetheless committed adultery. Moreover, the demons were proud to announce that they had succeeded in persuading him to commit many more sins and they listed Barontus's sins from his infancy, some of which he had himself forgotten about. When St Peter asked Barontus whether that was true, he had to confess that the demons were right. But at that point Peter himself took over the defence and argued that Barontus had made up for his faults by giving alms, confessing his sins to priests, doing penance and even leaving his hair in Peter's monastery, leaving everything behind and commending himself to the service of Christ.[62] The demons were not impressed and only left Barontus in peace after Peter got angry and threatened them with the three keys he held in his hands, a scene vividly depicted in a ninth-century manuscript containing this text (see Figure 1).[63] Apparently it was at this moment only that Barontus's sins were really forgiven and the three keys acted as a symbol for the power of the apostle to loose and bind on earth, in heaven and in hell.[64]

The text of the *Visio Baronti* is clearly influenced by Gregory the Great's vision of the afterlife, while there are also some resemblances to the *Vita Fursei*.[65] The resemblances with the *Vita Fursei* suggest that

---

[61] Carozzi, *Le voyage de l'âme*, pp. 136–7.

[62] *Visio Baronti*, c. 12, ed. W. Levison, MGH SS rer. mer. V, p. 386: 'Etsi aliquid contrarium aegit, elymosinam fecit – elemosyna enim de morte liberat – et sua peccata sacerdotibus est confessus et paenitentiam ex ipsa peccata aegit et insuper sua coma in meo monasterio deposuit et omnia propter Deum dereliquid et semet ipsum in servitio Christia tradidit.'

[63] For this manuscript, see L. Nees, 'The illustrated manuscript of the *Visio Baronti* [*Revelatio Baronti*] in St Petersburg (Russian National Library, cod. lat. Oct. v.I.5)', in C. Cubitt, *Court Culture in the Early Middle Ages. The Proceedings of the First Alcuin Conference* (Turnhout 2003), pp. 91–126.

[64] Carozzi, *Le voyage de l'âme*, p. 158.

[65] Carozzi, *Le voyage de l'âme*, pp. 150–5.

1. Ms. St Petersburg, National Library, Cod. lat. Oct. v.1.5, f. 10v: St Peter drives away the demons (*Visio Baronti*).

the author of the *Visio Baronti* was somehow connected to Fursa or his foundations in Gaul. The mere fact that two texts both describing in great detail a journey to the afterlife were composed within such a brief time-span within the same region suggests at least some form of affinity between the two. The *Visio Baronti* has been interpreted as a text closely connected with the insular practice of tariffed penance.[66] There are, therefore, indications that the *Visio Baronti* is influenced by insular conceptions of penance, even if the account of the founder of the monastery of Longoretus, St Cyran being in close contact with an Irish bishop named Falvius is of a later date and therefore suspect.[67] We see a noble layman confessing his sins and entering a monastery as atonement for his sins. However, there is a striking difference with the situation of penitents as we have encountered them on Iona. On Iona penitents seem to have spent their time in penance in a specific monastery before being admitted as full members of Columba's community, but the *Visio Baronti* stresses the fact that Barontus is a full member of the community of Longoretus,

---

[66] Y. Hen, 'The structure and aims of the *Visio Baronti*', *Journal of Theological Studies*, NS 47 (1996), pp. 477–97, see in particular pp. 488–92.

[67] *Vita Sigiramni*, c. 9, ed. B. Krusch, MGH SS rer. mer. IV, p. 611.

and the idea of a holy community of monks is very much emphasized in the text. Yet the *Visio* also suggests that Barontus did not sleep among his fellow monks but apart, together with his son, which may indicate that recently converted laymen were full members of the monastic group, yet somehow standing apart from the rest of the community.[68]

Columbanus and Fursa are Irish ecclesiastics travelling on the European mainland about whom we are fairly well informed. About others we know next to nothing. Kilian, an Irish bishop, worked with two associates, the priest Colonatus and the deacon Totnanus in the region of Würzburg among the Thuringians in the 680s. The *Passio* of Kilian, written at least seventy years later, related how Kilian and his companions came into conflict with the ruling house of the region over the fact that duke Gozbert, whom Kilian had converted to the Christian faith, had married his brother's widow. The duke complied with Kilian's wish to separate from his wife. The thus despised woman, however, took revenge on the religious counsellors of her husband and had them killed in secret. While there may have been a local cult of these martyrs, it was only after the establishment of a bishopric in Würzburg by Boniface in 742 that the cult of Kilian gained in importance. What Kilian actually preached in Würzburg we shall probably never know, but the fact that he criticized the marital behaviour of rulers concurs with Columbanus's attitude in such matters. Since Kilian did not succeed in establishing an enduring ecclesiastical institution in Würzburg, most of what he might have achieved did not last in an institutional form.[69] It was not until later when Anglo-Saxon missionaries like Willibrord and Boniface were active in this region that we are better informed about Christianity in the Main region. After Willibrord's activities in the region Anglo-Saxon influence is paramount, and we may infer that at least at this point tariffed penance with the penitential handbooks was introduced.

Only in the eighth century do we find Irish ecclesiastics further east, about whom we are better informed. The most important is without doubt the Irish *peregrinus* Virgil of Salzburg who was one of the most effective opponents of Boniface. He outlived the Anglo-Saxon missionary and was a figure of major ecclesiastical and intellectual importance. For a long period he held the position of abbot of St Peter in Salzburg (from 747/9) and bishop of Salzburg (from 749) until his

---

[68] *Visio* c. 1, ed. MGH, pp. 377–8; see Carozzi, *Le voyage de l'âme*, p. 169.

[69] For Kilian, see K. Schäferdiek, 'Kilian von Würzburg: Gestalt und Gestaltung eines Heiligen', in H. Keller and N. Staubach (eds.), *Iconologia Sacra: Mythos, Bildkunst und Dichtung in der Religions- und Sozialgeschichte Alteuropas. Festschrift für Karl Hauck zum 75. Geburtstag*, Arbeiten zur Frühmittelalterforschung 23 (Berlin 1994), pp. 313–40.

death in 784.[70] His close connections with Columba's foundation on Iona are demonstrated by the fact that he included names of the monks of Iona in the *liber confraternitatum* of Salzburg, while these connections may also explain the existence of two copies of Adomnán's *De locis sanctis* at Salzburg early in the ninth century.[71] At the end of the eighth century the penitentials of Finnian and Cummean were known in Salzburg and it is tempting to assume that these must have come from Ireland through Virgil or his companions. Under his successor Arn these texts were still respected and used to enrich the *Excarpsus Cummeani* and Theodore's penitential.[72]

Penance in Anglo-Saxon England

Following the traces of some Irish *peregrini* on the Continent, we have with Virgil in Salzburg reached the end of the eighth century. The Anglo-Saxon missionaries Willibrord and Boniface have already crossed our path, yet it is important to see what they knew of the new penitential books produced in the insular world. Therefore we have to turn our attention to England in the seventh and early eighth centuries. We have already observed that Cummean's penitential was probably known in England in the seventh century, where it was referred to as a *libellus scottorum*. That Irish texts relating to ecclesiastical norms and discipline were known in England need not surprise us in view of the impact of Irish monks on early Christianity in England. Particularly in the north the monastic *familia* of Iona, through its foundations in Lindisfarne and other places, took part in the Christianization of the Anglo-Saxons.[73] Bede provides a glowing account of Bishop Aidan, the monk from Iona who founded the monastery of Lindisfarne, and his pastoral work among the English. According to Bede Aidan attracted many monks from

---

[70] Wood, *The Missionary Life*, pp. 145–6; see H. Wolfram, 'Virgil als Abt und Bischof von Salzburg', in H. Dopsch and R. Juffinger (eds.), *Virgil von Salzburg. Missionar und Gelehrter* (Salzburg 1985), pp. 342–56.

[71] Ms. Vienna, Österreichische Nationalbibliothek, lat. 458; see H. Löwe, 'Salzburg als Zentrum literarischen Schaffens im 8. Jahrhundert', in Löwe, *Religiosität und Bildung im frühen Mittelalter. Ausgewählte Aufsätze*, ed. T. Struve (Weimar 1994), pp. 1–45 (originally published in *Mitteilungen der Gesellschaft für Salzburger Landeskunde* 115 (1975).

[72] See R. Meens, 'Kanonisches Recht in Salzburg am Ende des 8. Jahrhunderts. Das Zeugnis des *Paenitentiale Vindobonense B*', *Zeitschrift der Savigny-Stiftung für Rechtsgeschichte Kanonistische Abteilung* 82 (1996), pp. 13–34.

[73] B. Yorke, *The Conversion of Britain. Religion, Politics and Society in Britain c. 600–800* (Harlow 2006), pp. 123–4; J. Blair, *The Church in Anglo-Saxon Society* (Oxford 2005), pp. 43–9; R. Fletcher, *The Conversion of Europe. From Paganism to Christianity, 371–1386 AD* (London 1997), pp. 162–9.

Ireland to 'preach the word of faith with great devotion' to the English.[74] One may presume that they also sermonized on such themes as repentance and penance, as Bede depicted St Cuthbert visiting remote villages and through his preaching inciting the local population to confess their sins and to wash these away with the fruits of penance.[75] Cuthbert even managed to exhort ravens to contrition and atonement.[76] It seems obvious that the monks from Ireland active in England would use the penitential handbooks they were familiar with, although in fact there is little evidence for the availability of such texts in early Anglo-Saxon England, apart from the reference to Cummean's penitential by Theodore of Canterbury. The most informative source for attitudes towards penitential discipline is the collection of penitential sentences which went back to the teaching of Theodore of Canterbury. Before looking in closer detail at this collection, or rather the various collections related to this archbishop of Canterbury, something should be said about Theodore himself.

Of the authors of penitential handbooks, Theodore is without doubt the most interesting figure.[77] Born in 602 in the Greek-speaking town of Tarsus in Cilicia, he probably received his education in Antioch, Edessa and Constantinople. At some point he travelled to Rome where he probably stayed in the Greek monastery *Ad aquas Salvias*. These were turbulent times in Rome as the monothelete controversy, originating from an attempt by Emperor Heraclius and the patriarch Sergius to solve the problem of Christ's nature by shifting the attention to His will, was troubling ecclesiastical unity. In 649 Pope Martin I called together a council in the Lateran to discuss these matters, a council in which Theodore took part, if he is indeed identical with the *Theodorus monachus* included in the list of signatories connected to the *acta* of the council. In the aftermath of the council Martin was arrested on the behest of

---

[74] Bede, *Historia Ecclesiastica Gentis Anglorum* III, 3, ed. Colgrave and Mynors, p. 220.

[75] Bede, *Historia Ecclesiastica Gentis Anglorum* IV, 27, ed. Colgrave and Mynors, p. 432; see also Bede, *Vita Cuthberti*, chapters 9, 16 and 22, ed. B. Colgrave, *Two Lives of St. Cuthbert* (Cambridge 1940), pp. 184–6, 206–12 and 228–30.

[76] Bede, *Vita Cuthberti*, chapter 20, ed. Colgrave, pp. 222–4.

[77] For a fascinating account of Theodore's career, see M. Lapidge, 'The career of Archbishop Theodore', in M. Lapidge, *Archbishop Theodore. Commemorative Studies on his Life and Influence* (Cambridge 1995), pp. 1–29; this is a brief survey based on the much more detailed account in B. Bischoff and M. Lapidge, *Biblical Commentaries from the Canterbury School of Theodore and Hadrian* (Cambridge 1994), pp. 5–81 and 133–89; much of Theodore's career prior to his arrival in England derives from Michael Lapidge's ingenious analysis of the biblical glosses edited by him and Bernhard Bischoff. For a critique of this reconstruction, see M. Gorman, 'Theodore of Canterbury, Hadrian of Nisida and Michael Lapidge', *Scriptorium* 50 (1996), pp. 184–92.

Emperor Constans II, taken to Constantinople and tried on grounds of treason, one of the more gruesome episodes in the history of the papacy. His death sentence was commuted to lifelong exile. In the year 664 the archbishop of Canterbury Deusdedit died and his chosen successor Wigheard was sent to Rome for consecration by the pope. Unfortunately Wigheard died of the plague, and Pope Vitalian chose to send the Greek monk Theodore to Canterbury as the next archbishop. He was to be accompanied by the North-African monk Hadrian who had to take care that Theodore would not introduce anything 'contrary to the faith and in the manner of the Greeks' in the English Church.[78] Theodore was consecrated in 668 and left for England at the age of sixty-six.

Although Theodore was already in old age when he arrived in Canterbury, he acted swiftly and energetically. He made a tour of England, installed new bishops and convoked councils. His attempt to reorganize the vast diocese of York into smaller units brought him into a long-lasting conflict with its bishop, Wilfrid. Together with his companion Hadrian he established a school at Canterbury which Bede praised highly: 'because both of them were extremely learned in sacred and secular literature, they attracted a crowd of students into whose minds they daily poured the streams of wholesome learning. They gave their hearers instruction not only in the books of holy Scripture but also in the art of metre, astronomy, and ecclesiastical computation. As evidence of this, some of their students still survive who know Latin and Greek just as well as their native tongue.'[79] There may be some exaggeration in this praise, but we have evidence in glossaries that can be related to the school of Canterbury demonstrating that Theodore's and Hadrian's teachings included knowledge of texts and subjects which were not known in England, or other parts of Western Europe, in this period.[80]

Theodore's concerns for ecclesiastical organization and teaching are paramount in the cluster of texts generally known as Theodore's penitential, which occasionally are unhelpfully referred to as Pseudo-Theodorian.[81] In fact, we are dealing with five different traditions which all contain *Iudicia Theodori*, but in different formulations and combinations.[82]

---

[78] Bede, *Historia Ecclesiastica Gentis Anglorum* IV, 1, ed. Colgrave and Mynors, p. 330; probably the pope alludes to Theodore's involvement in the monothelete controversy, see Lapidge, 'The career of Theodore', p. 25.

[79] Bede, *Historia Ecclesiastica Gentis Anglorum* IV, 2, ed. Colgrave and Mynors, pp. 332–4.

[80] Bischoff and Lapidge, *Biblical Commentaries*.

[81] This is particularly unhelpful because it can cause confusion with the ninth-century Pseudo-Theodorian penitential discussed below at p. 136.

[82] For these five traditions see R. Kottje, 'Paenitentiale Theodori', in *Handwörterbuch zur deutschen Rechtsgeschichte* 3 (Berlin 1984), cols. 1413–16; Flechner, 'The making of the canons of Theodore', distinguishes seven recensions, seeing the Theodorian material in

The relationship between these strands and their relative chronology still remains unclear. It had been argued that the tradition known as *Capitula Dacheriana* (D), named after its first editor Jean-Luc d'Achéry, is the earliest surviving version. Although this tradition only survives in a manuscript from the tenth century, it was probably used in Ireland by the compilers of the *Collectio Hibernensis* already at the end of the seventh or very early in the eighth century.[83] It has recently been put forward that the *Capitula Dacheriana* as well as the tradition known as the *Canones Cottoniani* (Co) and the *Canones Gregorii* (G) must have been composed prior to the council of Hertford (673), because they do not conform to the rules for remarriage after divorce on grounds of adultery formulated at this council over which Theodore himself presided.[84] From this group, the *Canones Gregorii* are the most influential as regards the number of surviving manuscripts as well as its influence on other texts.[85] This may be the result of its attribution to Pope Gregory the Great, which possibly came about by a deliberate attempt to confer Gregory's authority on Theodore's sentences, or by an accidental event in the transmission of the text.[86]

From the Theodorian traditions, the one edited by a *Discipulus Umbrensium* and known by this name (U) had by far the greatest influence (see Figure 2). This U-version is distinct from all other versions

the mss. Cologne, Dombibliothek 210 and Paris, BN lat. 12444 as a separate version; according to P. W. Finsterwalder, *Die Canones Theodori Cantuariensis und ihre Überlieferungsformen*, Untersuchungen zu den Bußbüchern des 7., 8. und 9. Jahrhunderts 1 (Weimar 1929), pp. 74–6, both are excerpted from the so-called *Discipulus Umbrensium* version. K. Zechiel-Eckes has demonstrated that in the Cologne manuscript Theodore's penitential was drawn upon extensively to create the *Collection in Two Books*, see K. Zechiel-Eckes, 'Zur kirchlichen Rechtspraxis im späteren 8. Jahrhundert. Die Zwei-Bücher Sammlung der Kölner Dom-Handschrift 210 (fols. 122–151)', in H. Finger (ed.), *Mittelalterliche Handschriften der Kölner Dombibliothek. Zweites Symposium der Diözesan- und Dombibliothek Köln zu den Dom-Manuskripten (1. bis 2. Dezember 2006)* (Cologne 2008), pp. 187–229.

83 T. Charles-Edwards, 'The penitential of Theodore and the *Iudicia Theodori*', in Lapidge (ed.), *Archbishop Theodore*, pp. 141–74, at p. 142, but see the comments by Flechner, 'The making of the canons of Theodore', p. 134; for the date of the *Collectio Hibernensis*, see Richter, *Ireland and Her Neighbours*, p. 216.

84 Flechner, 'The making of the canons of Theodore', p. 124.

85 For the fourteen mss. of this text, see Appendix 1; it was used in the *P. Sangallense tripartitum*, the *P. Capitula Iudiciorum*, the *P. Merseburgense A* and the *P. Vallicellianum I*, see R. Meens, *Het tripartite boeteboek. Overlevering en betekenis van vroegmiddeleeuwse biechtvoorschriften (met editie en vertaling van vier tripartita)*, Middeleeuwse Studies en Bronnen 41 (Hilversum 1994), pp. 87–94 and 152–6 and G. Hägele, *Das Paenitentiale Vallicellianum I. Ein oberitalienischer Zweig der frühmittelalterlichen kontinentalen Bußbücher. Überlieferung, Verbreitung und Quellen*, Quellen und Forschungen zum Recht im Mittelalter 3 (Sigmaringen 1984), pp. 71–4.

86 The latter possibility is mentioned by Flechner, 'The making of the canons of Theodore', p. 124, fn. 12; the first by Meens, 'Ritual purity and the influence of Gregory the Great', p. 37.

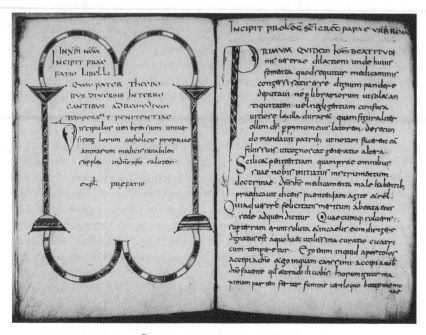

2. Ms. Vienna, Österreichische Nationalbibliothek, Ms. lat. 2195:
the beginning of Theodore's penitential.

in that it is arranged in two books, the first of which mainly contains
penitential rulings, while Book 2 consists mostly of rules of church
discipline. The first part can be considered a penitential and the second
has more the character of a canon law book or a collection of episcopal
statutes. The prologue of the *Discipulus Umbrensium* refers to three
persons involved in the production of this text. Theodore as the authority behind the sentences, a priest called Eoda, who as a pupil of Theodore played a role in the transmission of these rules, and lastly a
Discipulus Umbrensium who took care of the final redaction, ordering
the confused state in which he had found Theodore's rules. This
suggests that the *Discipulus* was working with one or more of the other
traditions in which the material was not systematically arranged. The
U-version was clearly in existence in the first half of the eighth century
when it was used at the monastery of Corbie to supplement the canon
law collection known as the *Collectio Vetus Gallica*.[87] The multitude

---

[87] See Mordek, *Kirchenrecht und Reform*, p. 86.

of manuscripts containing the U-version of Theodore's penitential, as well as the use of its sentences in later works, demonstrate that this version was very widely known.[88]

Theodore's penitential rulings are unique for the number of traditions in which they are to be found. The existence of these different traditions is probably the result of the way in which Theodore's *iudicia* have come into being. They were not composed by a single author, as Finnian's penitential had been, nor compiled on the basis of existing files as in the case of the penitential of Columbanus, but reflect Theodore's teaching. The texts as we know them are most probably reflections of reports of pupils relating Theodore's teachings. This explains the diverging traditions, which must already have existed at quite an early stage as well as the fact that a core of teachings is to be found in all traditions. Theodore's background is evident in the texts from the fact that they regularly refer to the customs of the Greeks and the Romans as well as to the specific authority of Greek authors such as Basil the Great or Gregory of Nazianze.[89] This brings us to an interesting point. Apparently, Theodore did not see fundamental differences between the way sins were treated in the East and in England. He probably knew Cummean's penitential, a text he possibly came to know through Irish students who sat at his feet. If, as historians have supposed, a fundamental difference had indeed existed between the ancient forms of public penance and private penance as it had developed in Ireland, it would be difficult to understand Theodore's apparently easy acceptance of Irish penitentials without assuming that 'Theodore went Celtic'.[90] Theodore was certainly aware of major differences between existing ways to deal with penitents. He refers, for example, to differences between the Romans and the Greeks when it comes to the place of reconciliation. The Romans reconciled penitents in the apse, while the Greeks did not. Furthermore, he mentioned that the reconciliation of penitents had to take place on Maundy Thursday under the supervision of a bishop and only in cases of necessity was a priest allowed to step in, but apparently this was not a ritual that was to be found everywhere. Theodore went on to say that

---

[88] For the twenty-five medieval mss. of this text, see Appendix 1; it was used in the *Excarpsus Cummeani*, the *P. Remense*, the *P. Vindobonense B* and *Vindobonense C*, the *P. Capitula Iudiciorum*, for which see Asbach, 'Das Poenitentiale Remense', pp. 117–24 and 175–6; Meens, *Tripartite boeteboek*, pp. 122–3 and 152–6; and R. Meens, '"Aliud benitenciale"', pp. 9–10.

[89] See Bischoff and Lapidge, *Biblical Commentaries*, pp. 150–5.

[90] Cf. Charles-Edwards, 'The penitential of Theodore', p. 170: 'Theodore's penitential is not, therefore, to be summed up in terms of Theodore going Celtic.'

reconciliation was not required 'in this province' (*in hac provincia*), because no public penance (*publica penitentia*) existed there.[91] Theodore thus reveals that he was familiar with a ritual of public penance and that he had observed that it was not in use in England in his time. This demonstrates that Theodore was well aware of major differences between ways to deal with penitents as he had encountered them among the Greeks, in Rome and in England, yet he did not feel that the ways developed in Ireland to deal with penitents and introduced into England by Irish missionaries were fundamentally different and could not be reconciled with Mediterranean practices. This accords well with our analysis of insular penance, where we found no real secrecy or privacy, which according to some earlier historians distinguished it from late antique forms of penance.

The penitential decisions of Theodore are, again, also a nice example of the smoothness with which penance and ecclesiastical legislation went together. Theodorian penitentials, for example, contain not only rules about the reconciliation of sinners, but also rules about ordination, the position of an abbot in relation to his community and the bishop, the proper age at which a boy or a girl could choose the monastic life without parental consent, and the grades of consanguinity within which one could marry.[92] The *Discipulus Umbrensium* tried to separate the penitential decisions from the canonical ones, but still included disciplinary rules among the penitential ones.[93] Theodore's penitential rulings also seem to have played a role in settling conflicts with the party offended by a sinner. Theodore apparently regarded laymen as capable of manifold sins. He mentions people doing many bad things: murder, theft and adultery with women and animals. Such sinners were to enter a monastery and to do penance until their death.[94] There is no mention of satisfaction for the offended party here, but Theodore ruled elsewhere that in the case of bloodshed to avenge a close relative penances could be reduced, while in another place he states that paying a financial compensation to the relatives of the person killed would halve the

---

[91] *P. Theodori U* I, 13, ed. Finsterwalder, *Die Canones Theodori Cantuariensis*, p. 306; only the U-version contains this material, but see also *P. Theodori Co* 190–1 on the reconciliation on Maundy Thursday, ed. Finsterwalder, *Die Canones Theodori Cantuariensis*, p. 283.

[92] See *P. Theodori G* 1–4, 13–16, 20–2, 43 and 78, ed. Finsterwalder, *Die Canones Theodori Cantuariensis*, pp. 253, 254, 256 and 261.

[93] See e.g. *P. Theodori U* I, 5, 11 excusing a monk for disobedience when his superior demanded him to pray for deceased heretics, among which Christians adhering to the Irish calculation of the date of Easter are included: see *U* I, 5, 3, ed. Finsterwalder, *Die Canones Theodori Cantuariensis*, pp. 295–6.

[94] *P. Theodori G* 98, ed. Finsterwalder, *Die Canones Theodori Cantuariensis*, p. 263.

penance.[95] In the case of religious people being killed, the murderers were delivered to the king or bishop for judgment.[96] Reconciliation with an offended party is also required in the case of theft. If a thief returns the stolen property and reconciles himself with the offended party, his penance will be shortened considerably (*multum breviabit*); if not, he has to fulfil the full period of penance, which may extend to seven years of fasting.[97] These clauses clearly demonstrate that the process of doing penance was closely related to means of reconciliation with the offended party, and we may safely infer that such a reconciliation must have taken a public form.

Although Theodore addressed matters that would require some form of public ritual to reconcile an offended party, the fact that he provides room for the possibility that a culprit would not seek reconciliation and therefore had to fulfil a harsher penance suggests some secrecy in confessing one's sins. This would mean that sinners came to confess their sins not only when forced by social pressure, but possibly also on their own volition. Such an eagerness to confess one's sins without pressure from another party explains the occurrence of minor sins in Theodore's penitential, where he dealt, for example, with someone vomiting because of overeating (U I, 1, 8) or with the question whether absorbing one's own blood with saliva (because of bleeding gums) was to be considered as a sin (U I, 7, 11). Theodore is also the first one to assign penance for forms of sexual behaviour by married couples, which would presuppose knowledge of intimate acts between man and wife by a confessor.[98] Such sins were not addressed in earlier penitential books, at least not in those parts affecting lay people. So this text contains several indications that people came to confession on their own initiative. However, Theodore was apparently also concerned with matters pertaining to ecclesiastical discipline. He addressed matters such as the keeping of the Sunday's observance or honouring the Lenten period, superstitious practices which are found under the rubric of 'Of the worship of idols', dietary restrictions or the proper rules for marriage and divorce. Another important aspect of his teachings was the ways in which one should deal

---

[95] *P. Theodori U* I, 4, 1–2, ed. Finsterwalder, *Die Canones Theodori Cantuariensis*, p. 294; *P. Theodori Co* 130–1, ed. Finsterwalder, *Die Canones Theodori Cantuariensis*, pp. 279–80; *P. Theodori G* 111–12, ed. Finsterwalder, *Die Canones Theodori Cantuariensis*, p. 263.

[96] *P. Theodori G* 108, ed. Finsterwalder, *Die Canones Theodori Cantuariensis*, p. 263 (should be numbered 108–9, but the number 109 has disappeared because of a misprint).

[97] *P. Theodori G* 39, ed. Finsterwalder, *Die Canones Theodori Cantuariensis*, p. 256; *P. Theodori U* I, 3, 3, ed. Finsterwalder, *Die Canones Theodori Cantuariensis*, p. 293.

[98] *P. Theodori U* I, 14, 19–23, ed. Finsterwalder, *Die Canones Theodori Cantuariensis*, p. 309; for Theodore's innovations in this respect, see Payer, *Sex and the Penitentials*, pp. 25 and 29.

with heretics, a term he used for those who did not follow the Roman way of calculating the date of Easter.

We do not know whether Theodore distinguished in his teachings between canon law, ecclesiastical regulations and penitential discipline, but in the texts in which his sentences have been handed down such distinctions are not to be found. This suggests, therefore, that in practice these three fields were not carefully distinguished. It is hard to assess the influence of Theodore's work. There are no early English manuscripts of his penitential decisions, but the fact that we still have no less than five textual traditions relating his teachings, all of a relatively early date, suggests that interest in his work was fairly widespread already at an early date. Shortly after his death he was cited as an authority in the *Collectio Hibernensis* and one version of his *iudicia* was added to an important collection of canon law in northern Gaul: the *Collectio Vetus Gallica*. His sentences were adopted in a great number of handbooks of penance from the eighth to the eleventh centuries. While Bede had not mentioned Theodore's contribution to the field of penance, Paul the Deacon writing his *History of the Lombards* in the final years of the eighth century praised the archbishop chiefly for the fact that he had carefully drafted a list of penances for sinners.[99] Theodore's fame in the early Middle Ages therefore rested not only on the glowing description in Bede's *History of the English Church and People*, but also on his judgments in the field of penance.

There is another penitential handbook that might have originated in Anglo-Saxon England. The attribution of a penitential to Bede is probably spurious, but the penitential attributed to Egbert of York stands a good chance of being English.[100] As in the case of Theodore's

---

[99] Paul the Deacon, *Historia Langobardorum* V, 30, ed. L. Bethman and G. Waitz, MGH SS rer. Lang. (Hanover 1878), p. 154; a somewhat earlier date for the composition of Paul's history is suggested by R. McKitterick, *History and Memory in the Carolingian World* (Cambridge 2004), p. 77.

[100] For an edition of the text, see H. Wasserschleben, *Die Bussordnungen der abendländischen Kirche* (Halle 1851), pp. 231–47; the attribution of a penitential to Bede and Egbert has sparked off a whole discussion, see M. L. W. Laistner, 'Was Bede the author of a penitential?', in Laistner, *The Intellectual Heritage of the Early Middle Ages. Selected Essays*, ed. C. G. Starr, (1957; New York 1983), pp. 165–77 (originally in *Harvard Theological Review* 31 (1938), pp. 263–74); A. Frantzen, 'The penitentials attributed to Bede', *Speculum* 58 (1983), pp. 573–97; J.-P. Bouhot, 'Les pénitentiels attribués à Bède le Vénérable et à Egbert d'York', *Revue d'histoire des textes* 16 (1986), pp. 141–69; R. Haggenmüller, *Die Überlieferung der Beda und Egbert zugeschriebenen Bußbücher* (Frankfurt a.M. / Bern / etc. 1991); R. Haggenmüller, 'Frühmittelalterliche Bußbücher – Paenitentialien – und das Kloster Lorsch', *Geschichtsblätter Kreis Bergstraße* 25 (1992), pp. 125–54; and D. Bullough, *Alcuin. Achievement and Reputation. Being Part of the Ford Lectures Delivered in Oxford in Hilary Term 1980* (Leiden / Boston 2004), p. 236.

penitential, the extant manuscripts are almost exclusively written on the Continent, with an early concentration in the monastery of Lorsch.[101] This has led Reinhold Haggenmüller, to whom we are indebted for the most detailed investigation of the manuscript tradition of this text, to the conclusion that this penitential was composed near this monastery in the Middle Rhine area, probably in Anglo-Saxon circles.[102] Yet a 'manuscript of singular importance', now preserved in the Vatican Library, which was already in Lorsch in the first half of the ninth century, was written in an English hand around the year 800, possibly in England.[103] Since this early manuscript which also contains an ancient text version was possibly taken from England to Lorsch, an English provenance of the text itself is plausible, although a close investigation of the sources of this penitential would be necessary to confirm or reject this view. The fact that its prologue cites Gregory the Great and Theodore of Canterbury as established authorities might support an English origin.

The Vatican manuscript containing the penitential attributed to Egbert (see Figure 3) consists of two small codicological units of which the one with the penitential consists of a single quire containing only this text. Some additions were later made in Lorsch on the final folio. The codicological details show that the penitential attributed to Egbert is transmitted here in a booklet, measuring 25 by 18.5 cm and consisting of one quire of nine folios.[104] Such a format suggests why early copies

---

[101] It is known from ten extant manuscripts, see Haggenmüller, *Die Überlieferung der Beda und Egbert zugeschriebenen Bußbücher*, p. 149:

Vatican, BAV, Pal. lat. 554 (s. VIII–IX, England / insular circles on the Continent?)
Vienna, Österreichische Nationalbibliothek, lat. 2223 (s. VIII–IX, Main-region)
Vatican, BAV, Pal. lat. 485 (860–75, Lorsch)
Sélestat, Bibliothèque Humaniste, 132 (s. IX 2/3, Mainz?)
St Gall, Stiftsbibliothek, 677 (s. X med., St Gall)
Vatican, BAV, Pal. lat. 294 (s. X / XI, probably Lorsch)
Oxford, Bodleian Library, Bodl. 718 (s. X–XI, England, possibly Exeter)
Cambridge, Corpus Christi College, 265 (s. XI/1, England?); s. XI/2 according to
H. Mordek, *Bibliotheca capitularium regum Francorum manuscripta. Überlieferung und Traditionszusammenhang der fränkischen Herrschererlasse*, MGH Hilfsmittel 15 (Munich 1995), pp. 95–7.
Munich, Bayerische Staatsbibliothek, Clm 22288 (s. XII 1, Bamberg?)
Oxford, Bodleian Library, Barlow 37 (s. XIII in., England).

[102] Haggenmüller, *Die Überlieferung der Beda und Egbert zugeschriebenen Bußbücher*, p. 298.

[103] Quotation from Frantzen, 'The penitentials attributed to Bede', p. 576; for the ms. Vat. pal. lat. 554, see B. Bischoff, *Lorsch im Spiegel seiner Handschriften*, Münchener Beiträge zur Mediävistik und Renaissance-Forschung (Munich 1974), pp. 112–13.

[104] See the description in Haggenmüller, *Die Überlieferung der Beda und Egbert zugeschriebenen Bußbücher*, pp. 108–9.

3. *P. Egberti*, Vat. Pal. lat. 554, f. 5r: the beginning of the Egbert penitential.

made in a similar way probably have perished. If penitential texts were copied on single quires and remained unbound, they would run a high risk of getting damaged or lost, particularly when being used intensively. In this case we are fortunate that this precious copy has survived, demonstrating the way in which these texts might have served in the early phases of Anglo-Saxon missions on the Continent.

This eighth-century penitential contains a remarkable prologue stressing the need for confessors to be careful in assigning a specific penance and admonishing them to always keep the subtle differences between particular offences in mind as well as those between different perpetrators of such deeds. Everyone should not be weighed on the same balance: the confessor should always distinguish according to a person's wealth (rich or poor), status (free or unfree, married or unmarried, cleric or lay etc.), age and health when deciding on an appropriate penance.[105] The prologue further stresses the need for mercy and the importance of sincerity on the part of the penitent. As such it seems particularly concerned with the motives of people coming to confession. The penitential proper contains many provisions for clerics and carefully distinguishes its penances according to ecclesiastical rank (bishop, priest, deacon, subdeacon and cleric). When discussing specifically lay behaviour, it deals with sexual rules within marriage, following Theodore's guidelines that provide penances for married couples involved in sexual acts not approved of by the authors of our manuals. Although it apparently used Theodore's penitential judgments, this work seems more particularly concerned with penance and confession, for it leaves out the canonical rules supplied by Theodore. In its canons concerning violent and fraudulent behaviour by lay people, moreover, the lack of any demand for secular compensation is striking.[106] This text, therefore, seems to be focussed more exclusively on people coming to confession, their motives for sinning and the sincerity of their penance than earlier texts at which we have been looking. Such a stress on the more pastoral aspects of penance is supported by the list of books that a priest should have at his disposition that is mentioned in the prologue. It refers to a psalter, a lectionary, an antiphonary, a sacramentary, a baptismal tract, a martyrology, a sermon collection and a computus, a work enabling a priest to organize the liturgical year. These are all books necessary to fulfil a priest's liturgical functions and it is among these that a penitential is also mentioned.[107] It has been argued that this booklist is of continental origin, since we know such lists only from texts originating from Francia, but one should note that all continental parallels are of a

---

[105] *P. Ps.-Egberti*, prologue, ed. Wasserschleben, *Bussordnungen*, p. 232.
[106] Noted by A. Frantzen, *The Literature of Penance in Anglo-Saxon England* (New Brunswick 1983), p. 76.
[107] *P. Ps.-Egberti*, prologue, ed. Wasserschleben, *Bussordnungen*, p. 232.

somewhat later date.[108] The penitential attributed to Egbert, therefore, clearly draws penance into a pastoral context and this feature would seem to fit an Anglo-Saxon provenance better than an origin in Anglo-Saxon circles on the Contintent in a missionary context.

Handbooks for confession as they had developed in the Celtic-speaking world of Ireland, Wales and Cornwall were thus found in specific circles on the Continent and in Anglo-Saxon England by the end of the seventh century. Visionary literature painting a 'penitential' view of the afterlife demonstrates knowledge of descriptions of sins as we find them in such penitential literature. An ecclesiastical foundation with ties to Ireland, as Salzburg was at the end of the eighth century, clearly was well acquainted with Irish penitential books. Irish works must have been known in Anglo-Saxon England as well, although they have left few specific traces. Theodore of Canterbury, however, connected to such texts when he taught about penance in Canterbury. His teachings were promulgated in different versions that attest to an early and lively interest in Theodore's opinions on such matters in England, Ireland and the Continent. A penitential handbook attributed to Egbert of York probably orginated in England. This work and Theodore's penitential rulings suggest that some people confessed individual shortcomings on a voluntary basis. This is a sign indicating a more pastoral setting for hearing confession than any we have encountered before.

---

[108] For the list as 'continental' in character, see Frantzen, *Literature of Penance*, pp. 74–5; Frantzen, 'The penitentials attributed to Bede', pp. 584–5. The earliest parallel is the *Capitula de examinandis ecclesiasticis*, from 802, ed. A. Boretius, MGH Cap. reg. Franc. I (Hanover 1883), pp. 109–11; for a discussion of this text, see the introduction to the *Capitula Frisingensia secunda*, a text deriving from the *Capitula de examinandis ecclesiasticis*, ed. R. Pokorny, MGH Cap. Ep. 3 (Hanover 1995), pp. 206–11, at p. 206.

5   Penance and the Carolingian Reforms

We have seen in the last chapter that penitential handbooks from Ireland were known in England and on the European mainland from the late sixth century onward. Probably they had been introduced there by Irish monks during their *peregrinatio*. Apart from particular historical figures such as Columbanus and Fursa, the influence of whom we have sketched above, there might have been more about whom we do not know a lot. However, the evidence for the existence of penitential handbooks and the practice of hearing confession that these texts presuppose, dating from the seventh and early eighth centuries, is scarce.[1] Although, for example, Cummean's penitential was used in a couple of eighth- and ninth-century texts, only one manuscript – and a rather late one – containing this text has survived.[2] There are good reasons for this lack of manuscript evidence. As is clear from the case of the penitential attributed to Egbert, the manuscripts may have remained unbound, existing only as loose quires. This would endanger their preservation for future generations, while the fact that they probably were written in an insular script, which at some point was no longer easy to read, may also have contributed to the bad state of survival of these texts.[3] At the Carolingian councils of the first half of the ninth century, penitential handbooks came under fire and, as we shall see in this chapter, the council of Paris (829) actually called for the destruction of such books. It is not very probable that such an inquisition had much success, but it goes to show that we must reckon with the fact that many penitential handbooks did not survive the ravages of time.

Nevertheless, even if there are grounds for assuming that for various reasons a lot of manuscripts containing these texts have disappeared,

---

[1] R. Kottje, 'Überlieferung und Rezeption der irischen Bußbücher auf dem Kontinent', in H. Löwe (ed.), *Die Iren und Europa im früheren Mittelalter*, vol. I (Stuttgart 1982), pp. 511–24.

[2] Ms. Vat. Pal. Lat 485 (Lorsch 860–75), in the ms. Oxford Bodleian 311 (s. X) used by Bieler for his edition, it is included as part of a bigger compilation.

[3] Kottje, 'Überlieferung und Rezeption', vol. I, p. 521.

compared to the surviving manuscripts from the late eighth and ninth centuries containing penitential handbooks, the contrast is striking. In the Carolingian period we can perceive an upsurge in surviving penitential manuscripts, which is surely related to the general increase in book production that we can observe in this era.[4] It is also related, however, to the special attention the Carolingians devoted to matters pertaining to religious life, a movement that is often referred to as the Carolingian Renaissance or the Carolingian Reforms.[5] The Carolingians were not the first to do so, as the Merovingian king Guntram had, for example, fostered religious reform in the years prior to Columbanus's arrival in Gaul, as we saw in the previous chapter. Yet the Carolingian family from an early period onward seems to have grasped the possibilities of a close cooperation with missionaries from abroad and through them with the papacy, a cooperation which not only facilitated their seizure of royal power in 751, but also gave them more control over ecclesiastical affairs. The emphasis on the Christian religion was also an important factor that helped to shape the identity of the Franks as a people.[6]

Willibrord and penance

Already before they became kings, members of the Carolingian family demonstrated a particular interest in religious affairs, as was well understood by Willibrord who upon his arrival in Frisia in 690 turned not to the Frisian king nor to the Merovingian ruler, but to the powerful mayor of the palace, Pippin II.[7] Pippin welcomed him warmly and seems to have grasped the opportunity of combining political lordship with

---

[4] D. Ganz, 'Book production in the Carolingian empire and the spread of Caroline minuscule', in R. McKitterick (ed.), *The New Cambridge Medieval History*, vol. II, *c. 700–c. 900* (Cambridge 1995), pp. 786–808.

[5] This cultural movement has raised a lot of historical interest, for which in general see J. Contreni, 'The Carolingian Renaissance: education and literary culture', in McKitterick (ed.), *The New Cambridge Medieval History*, vol. II, pp. 709–57 and M. de Jong, 'Charlemagne's Church', in J. Story (ed.), *Charlemagne. Empire and Society* (Manchester 2005), pp. 103–35.

[6] For the importance of religion as an element of Frankish identity, see M. de Jong, 'Sacrum palatium et ecclesia. L'autorité religieuse royale sous les Carolingiens (790–840)', *Annales HSS* 58 (2003), pp. 1243–69.

[7] A. Angenendt, '"Er war der Erste...". Willibrords historische Stellung', in P. Bange and A. Weiler (eds.), *Willibrord, zijn wereld en zijn werk. Voordrachten gehouden tijdens het Willibrordcongres Nijmegen, 28–30 september 1989*, Middeleeuwse Studies 6 (Nijmegen 1990), pp. 13–34, at pp. 17–18; P. Fouracre, *The Age of Charles Martel* (Harlow 2000), pp. 126–7.

Christianization.[8] Interestingly, the sources characterize one of Pippin's major opponents, the Frisian king Radbod, always as a pagan although in many respects he can be regarded as simply another aristocrat in the frontier regions of the Frankish kingdom, whose behaviour did not differ significantly from that of other aristocrats in frontier regions.[9] Willibrord, who had grown up in Northumbria at a time when this region was still dominated by Irish forms of Christianity and who had spent ten years of his life in Ireland at the monastery at Rath Melsigi before undertaking his mission to Frisia, must have been acquainted with penitential handbooks as these had been composed in Ireland in the sixth and seventh centuries. Whether he had a chance to get to know Theodorian texts on penance is unclear.[10] An eighth-century penitential that has only recently been discovered in an Oxford manuscript and is therefore named the *Paenitentiale Oxoniense II* is clearly related to Frisian practices.[11] In its complete form it is known only from a relatively late manuscript, but some fragments and its use in eighth- and ninth-century penitentials firmly establish its eighth-century date.[12] Parallels with Frisian practices demonstrate that it was composed for use in Frisia. It discusses, for example, the practice of a mother travelling with an army that does not accept her newborn child. Whether we should think here about women following an army of their own free will or as captives remains unclear. If the mother does not accept the child by lifting it from the ground and feeding it, she can determine for herself whether to do penance or not.[13] This unique clause, which has no parallels in other penitential texts, seems to allude to

---

[8] Alcuin, *Vita Willibrordi*, c. 5, ed. W. Levison, MGH SS rer. Mer. VII (Hanover / Leipzig 1920), pp. 120–1; Beda, *Historia Ecclesiastica Gentis Anglorum* V, 10, ed. Colgrave and Mynors, p. 480.

[9] W. S. van Egmond, 'Radbod van de Friezen, een aristocraat in de periferie', *Millennium* 19 (2005), pp. 24–44.

[10] For Willibrord's possible knowledge of penitential texts, see R. Meens, 'Het heilige bezoedeld. Opvattingen over het heilige en het onreine in de vroegmiddeleeuwse religieuze mentaliteit', in P. Bange and A. Weiler (eds.), *Willibrord, zijn wereld en zijn werk. Voordrachten gehouden tijdens het Willibrordcongres Nijmegen, 28–30 september 1989*, Middeleeuwse Studies 6 (Nijmegen 1990), pp. 237–55, at pp. 241–2.

[11] It was discovered by Asbach, 'Das Poenitentiale Remense'; it is edited in Kottje, *Paenitentialia minora*, pp. 179–205; for a discussion of its importance, see Körntgen, *Studien zu den Quellen*, pp. 90–205.

[12] Ms. Oxford, Bodleian Library, Bodl. 311 (s. X, N-W France); fragments Darmstadt, Hessische Landes- und Hochschulbibliothek, Hs. 895 Fragm. and Stuttgart, Württembergische Landesbibliothek, Cod. fragm. 100 A (both from the same manuscript written s. VIII/IX in Northern Italy and once kept in Konstanz); see Kottje, *Paenitentialia minora*, p. xlvi; for a detailed analysis, Körntgen, *Studien zu den Quellen*, pp. 90–108, and see pp. 113–21 for its use in other penitential books.

[13] P. *Oxoniense II*, c. 31, ed. Kottje, *Paenitentialia minora*, p. 196. One should probably read: 'et non eum sustulerit a terra'.

a practice of infanticide before the child had been fed for the first time. Such a practice is also known from the *Lex Frisionum* and the ninth-century *Life of Liudger*.[14] The *P. Oxoniense II* clearly is a text which was meant to be used in a society where Christians and non-Christians lived together, as is demonstrated by the clause prescribing a four weeks' penance for Christians who helped their neighbours in preparing a funeral pyre.[15] Since this text may very well stem from the first half of the eighth century, there seems to be no reason to exclude the possibility that the *Paenitentiale Oxoniense II* was used or even composed by Willibrord himself.[16] The use that was made of this text in the *Iudicium Clementis* – a clearly later text that has sometimes been attributed to Willibrord, who in 695 received the name Clemens from Pope Sergius – might explain why this text was attributed to Clemens. This would in turn mean that the *Oxoniense* penitential might have been attributed to Clemens and therefore to Willibrord.[17]

Willibrord's penitential, if we may call it thus, is remarkable for a number of reasons. First, it is the earliest penitential handbook we know of which deals almost exclusively with offences of the laity. Only canons 66–73 at the end of the text are concerned with clerical failings, particularly in their dealings with the Eucharist, but these are probably a later addition.[18] The fact that this text was composed for penitent layfolk who had only recently been converted to the Christian faith may account for its lenient attitude. In the prologue the author censures prevailing methods of assigning penances to sinners for their harshness. Sinners willing to do penance should not be burdened with heavy fasts, but should instead be accepted with clemency and mildness.[19] The penances assigned for specific offences here are indeed much lighter than in other texts, expressed in weeks where elsewhere months and years are the

---

[14] *Lex Frisionum* V, ed. H. Siems, *Studien zur Lex Frisionum* (Ebelsbach 1980), supplement; *Vita Liudgeri* I, 6–7, ed. W. Diekamp, *Die Geschichtsquellen des Bistums Münster*, vol. IV (Münster 1881), pp. 10–11. See also R. Meens, 'Children and confession in the early Middle Ages', in D. Wood (ed.), *The Church and Childhood*, Studies in Church History 31 (Oxford 1994), pp. 53–65.

[15] *P. Oxoniense II*, c. 41, ed. Kottje, *Paenitentialia minora*, pp. 197–8.

[16] See R. Meens, 'Willibrords boeteboek?', *Tijdschrift voor Geschiedenis* 106 (1993), pp. 163–78; R. Meens, 'Christentum und Heidentum aus der Sicht Willibrords? Überlegungen zum *Paenitentiale Oxoniense II*', in M. Polfer (ed.), *L'évangélisation des régions entre Meuse et Moselle et la fondation de l'abbaye d'Echternach (Ve–IXe siècle). Actes des 10es Journées Lotharingiennes*, Publications de la Section Historique de l'Institut G.-D. de Luxembourg 117 (Luxembourg 2000), pp. 415–28; and R. Meens, 'Het christendom van Willibrord en Bonifatius', *Trajecta* 15 (2006), pp. 342–58, at p. 345.

[17] Meens, 'Willibrord's boeteboek?', pp. 176–7.

[18] Körntgen, *Studien zu den Quellen*, p. 109.

[19] *P. Oxoniense II*, prol., ed. Kottje, *Paenitentialia minora*, p. 182.

norm. The text also speaks about the unfree (*servi et ancillae*) confessing their sins and being willing to do penance for them. The confessor should assign them half the penance he would assign free men and women (*liberi et ingenui*). The reference to the unfree 'seeking' penance suggests that they did so on their own accord. Because the free could rest whenever they wanted while the unfree could not, and because the unfree did not have the possibility to pay for their sins, they should fast less.[20] Apparently, the author foresaw that free men and women could pay, i.e. give alms, for their sins. He also refers to people who offer to fast for the sake of others for payment, a practice that he criticizes severely. Neither the sinner nor the one who offers to fulfil someone else's penance are to be counted among the Christians.[21] The same kind of criticism was aired at the council of Cloveshoe (747).[22] The fact that some thought it was possible to perform someone else's penance demonstrates that penance was not a strictly private affair. The *Oxoniense* penitential relates in this context how people saw others accepting penance and then approached these with the offer to fulfil the kind of penance inflicted upon them by the priest for them. This presupposes that the act of accepting penance could easily be observed by others. That the laity attached particular value to confessing their sins is indicated by the sentence dealing with warriors who sought penance before going to battle. They should be treated in the same manner as those who were dying, but in case they returned safe and sound, they should confess all their sins and do penance for them.[23]

The *Oxoniense* penitential occasionally considers sins in which there was no offended party, such as predicting the future or eating food that was regarded as impure.[24] Most of its provisions, however, deal with 'social sins', such as adultery, unlawful marriages, theft and murder. The penitential orders illicit marriages to be dissolved and in cases of theft and murder compensation and returning the stolen goods are part and parcel of the penitential process. This indicates that also in this context reconciliation with the offended party was an important aspect of

---

[20] P. *Oxoniense II*, c. 63, ed. Kottje, *Paenitentialia minora*, p. 203.

[21] Cc. 61–2, ed. Kottje, *Paenitentialia minora*, pp. 202–3.

[22] Council of Cloveshoe, c. 27, ed. A. Haddan and W. Stubbs, *Councils and Ecclesiastical Documents Relating to Great Britain and Ireland*, vol. III (Oxford 1871; repr. 1964), p. 373; see the comments in C. Cubitt, *Anglo-Saxon Church Councils c. 650–c. 850* (London / New York 1995), p. 101.

[23] P. *Oxoniense II*, c. 45, ed. Kottje, *Paenitentialia minora*, p. 198; for the importance of penance to warriors, see Bachrach, 'Confession in the Regnum Francorum' and Bachrach, *Religion and the Conduct of War c. 300 – c. 1215* (Woodbridge 2003), pp. 43–62.

[24] P. *Oxoniense II*, cc. 24–5 and 52–8, ed. Kottje, *Paenitentialia minora*, pp. 195 and 200–1.

ecclesiastical penance.[25] Canon 10 of the text closely allies excommunication with confessing one's sins and accepting penance, suggesting that excommunication was used as a tool with which one could force a sinner into accepting penance.[26] Churches should also refuse to accept gifts from sinners as alms or to redeem captives when the donors refused to confess their sins and to do penance for them.[27] This clause again reveals that a relation with ecclesiastical institutions through gift-giving mattered and that leading a Christian life and therefore confessing one's sins were an important aspect of such a relation.

The *Oxoniense* penitential deals with some very specific types of behaviour which seem to be related to the region of the Frisians, but it is also revealing to look at the topics it does not deal with. While it discusses fortune-telling and eating sacrificial food related to pagan feasts, it does not contain the kind of detailed list of 'superstitious practices' that we find in Theodore's handbook or in the earliest generation of Frankish penitentials. Conspicuously lacking also is the theme of sexual relations within marriage. The work discusses adultery and illicit marriages, but is nowhere concerned with forms of sexual conduct within marriage which should be confessed. The fact that this text does not want to regulate the sexual life of the married might be related to the lenient approach to the laity's sins that is so clearly evident in this work.

Boniface and the Carolingian Reforms

In some respects Willibrord's relationship with the Carolingian family seems to have been comparable to Columbanus's affiliation with the Merovingians. Perhaps the relationship between a royal family and a 'holy man' was even one of the main attractions for Charlemagne's forefathers in supporting Willibrord. In this way they acquired a status that could be compared to the Merovingian kings. Unlike Columbanus, however, Willibrord seems to have accommodated well to local circumstances. There are no indications that he ran into serious trouble with the Pippinids, not even when Charles Martel the son of a concubine insisted upon his rights of succession.[28] The many gifts from local landowners to Willibrord testify to his good relations with the local elites.[29]

---

[25] E.g. cc. 6, 18–20, ed. Kottje, *Paenitentialia minora*, pp. 192 and 195.

[26] *P. Oxoniense II*, c. 10, ed. Kottje, *Paenitentialia minora*, pp. 193–4.

[27] *P. Oxoniense II*, c. 64, ed. Kottje, *Paenitentialia minora*, pp. 203–4.

[28] Fouracre, *Charles Martel*, pp. 62–4; A. Fischer, *Karl Martell. Der Beginn der karolingischen Herrschaft* (Stuttgart 2012), pp. 53–4.

[29] M. Costambeys, 'An aristocratic community on the northern Frankish frontier 690–726', *Early Medieval Europe* 3 (1994), pp. 39–62.

There is one person, however, with whom Willibrord came into serious conflict, and that is his kinsman Boniface. According to Boniface's biographer, who clearly portrayed the conflict in euphemistic terms, 'after a long period of discussion, a dispute between them (Boniface and Willibrord) was born and a harmonious difference of opinion of a beautiful sort'.[30] The dispute allegedly centred on Willibrord's request made to Boniface to act as his *chorepiscopus*. Boniface declined the offer and left for Thuringia and Hessen. The affair seems to indicate a more serious conflict than that over the right age for episcopal anointment, the reason advanced by the *Vita Bonifatii*. What exactly the arguments between the two men may have been we shall probably never know. While Willibald hints at the existence of a controversy without informing us about its details, Alcuin, the biographer of Willibrord, does not even mention Boniface and his cooperation with the protagonist of the *Vita*.[31] It is, however, perfectly possible that differences of opinion as to the ways in which one should deal with the moral failings of recently converted Christians played a role in the differences of views between the two missionaries.[32]

From Boniface's letters as well as from the councils over which he presided and some documents related to these, it is clear that Boniface's attitude towards sinning Christians was much harsher than the one we encountered in 'Willibrord's penitential'. In the councils convening under his authority penance was something that could be forced upon unwilling sinners, while for clerics penance could consist of incarceration and flagellation.[33] In the Synod of Soissons secular authorities were called

---

[30] Willibald, *Vita Bonifatii*, V, ed. R. Rau, *Briefe des Bonifatius. Willibalds Leben des Bonifatius. Nebst einigen zeitgenössischen Dokumenten*, Ausgewählte Quellen zur deutschen Geschichte des Mittelalters. Freiherr vom Stein-Gedächtnisausgabe, vol. ivb (Darmstadt 1968), p. 486: 'inter eos orta est contentio et consona pulchrae discretionis facta dissensio'.

[31] See Wood, *The Missionary Life*, pp. 86–8.

[32] On the conflict between Boniface and Willibrord, see T. Schieffer, *Winfrid-Bonifatius und die christliche Grundlegung Europas* (Darmstadt 1980), pp. 118–19; A. Weiler, *Willibrords Missie. Christendom en cultuur in de zevende en achtste eeuw* (Hilversum 1989), pp. 158–9; M. Mostert, *754, Bonifatius bij Dokkum vermoord* (Hilversum 1999), pp. 44–5; L. von Padberg, *Bonifatius. Missionar und Reformer* (Munich 2003), pp. 35–6; for a related possible divergence of opinion, see R. Meens, 'With one foot in the font. The failed baptism of the Frisian king Radbod and the eighth century discussion about the fate of unbaptized forefathers', in P. Moran and I. Warntjes (eds.), *Culture and Tradition in Medieval Ireland. A Festschrift for Dáibhí Ó Cróinín* (Turnhout 2014) (in press).

[33] See e.g. *Concilium Germanicum* (742/3), cc. 1d and 6, ed. Rau, *Briefe des Bonifatius*, pp. 378 and 380. For the councils convened under Boniface's authority, see U. Nonn, 'Castitas et vitae et fidei et doctrinae – Bonifatius und die Reformkonzilien', in F. J. Felten, J. Jarnut and L. von Padberg (eds.), *Bonifatius. Leben und Nachwirken (754–2004)* (Wiesbaden 2007), pp. 271–80.

upon to punish infractors of these ecclesiastical decisions.[34] During his conflict with the Irishman Clemens and the Frankish wandering Bishop Aldebert, Boniface also called in secular power in order to secure their downfall.[35] Boniface, clearly, was a missionary with high standards, who relied partly on secular power to enforce his interpretation of ecclesiastical rules upon clerics and lay people alike, and penance seems to have been an important aspect of his reform efforts.[36] This may have been a way to ingratiate himself with the Carolingian mayors of the palace.[37]

There is a penitential handbook dating from this period which can possibly be associated with Boniface and his circle. In the second quarter of the eighth century an ambitious new handbook was conceived at the northern French monastery of Corbie, a handbook which, because historians in the past thought it had been composed by the Irish abbot Cummean, is known as the *Excarpsus Cummeani*.[38] Boniface had close connections with this monastery, particularly with its abbot Grimo, from whom he received canon law texts.[39] At this time monks in Corbie were updating an ancient collection of canon law, which we now know as the *Collectio Vetus Gallica*, with excerpts taken from works such as the *Collectio Hibernensis*, the *Regula Coenobialis* of Columbanus, the penitential of Theodore of Canterbury and the council of Rome from the year 721, paying particular attention to the theme of penance.[40] It is hard to fathom

---

[34] Council of Soissons (744), c. 10, ed. Rau, *Briefe des Bonifatius*, pp. 386–8.

[35] For Boniface's conflict with these 'heretics', see M. Innes, '"Immune from heresy": defining the boundaries of Carolingian Christianity', in P. Fouracre and D. Ganz (eds.), *Frankland. The Franks and the World of the Early Middle Ages. Essays in Honour of Dame Jinty Nelson* (Manchester 2008), pp. 101–25 and S. Meeder, 'Boniface and the Irish heresy of Clemens', *Church History* 80 (2011), pp. 251–80.

[36] On the use of the concept of reform in this context see the caveat formulated by T. Reuter, '"Kirchenreform" und "Kirchenpolitik" im Zeitalter Karl Martells: Begriffe und Wirklichkeit', in J. Jarnut, U. Nonn and M. Richter (eds.), *Karl Martell in seiner Zeit* (Sigmaringen 1994), pp. 35–59.

[37] M. de Jong, 'Bonifatius: een Angelsaksische priester-monnik en het Frankische hof', *Millennium* 19 (2005), pp. 5–23.

[38] *Excarpsus Cummeani*, ed. H. Schmitz, *Die Bussbücher und das kanonische Bussverfahren* (Düsseldorf 1898), pp. 597–644; for its Corbie origin, see Körntgen, 'Der *Excarpsus Cummeani*, ein Bußbuch aus Corbie', and Körntgen, 'Kanonisches recht und Busspraxis. Zu Kontext und Funktion des Paenitentiale Excarpsus Cummeani', in W. P. Müller and M. E. Sommar (eds.), *Medieval Church Law and the Origins of the Western Legal Tradition. A Tribute to Kenneth Pennington* (Washington 2006), pp. 17–32.

[39] M. Glatthaar, *Bonifatius und das Sakrileg. Zur politischen Dimension eines Rechtsbegriffs*, Freiburger Beiträge zur mittelalterlichen Geschichte 17 (Frankfurt a.M. etc. 2004), pp. 386–9, argues that Boniface may have received the so-called *Libellus Responsionum* of Gregory the Great from Grimo; for the connections between Boniface and Corbie, see D. Ganz, *Corbie in the Carolingian Renaissance* (Sigmaringen 1990), p. 20.

[40] On this important collection, see Mordek, *Kirchenrecht und Reform im Frankenreich*; for the Corbie revision, see pp. 86–94.

that Boniface, who had a keen interest in canon law and who corresponded with the abbot of Corbie about canonical matters, would not have known about this ambitious enterprise.[41] It was apparently in the same context that the *Excarpsus Cummeani* was composed and therefore Boniface would probably also have known about this penitential handbook, particularly in view of Boniface's efforts to reform the moral life of the clergy and the laity. An analysis of the way this text was composed reveals that it was carefully crafted from three different traditions of texts, always judiciously selecting one particular interpretation among the three.[42] A comparison of this penitential with the reform themes evident in Boniface's letters demonstrates many parallels between the two.[43] There are therefore good reasons to associate this penitential handbook with Boniface and his reform activities.[44]

Using the penitentials of Theodore, Cummean and one of the 'simple Frankish penitentials', the *Excarpsus Cummeani* deals with a whole range of topics. It is an extremely comprehensive handbook, adopting almost all of the sentences from these three traditions, and therefore treating a great many topics. Remarkable is its insistence on the moral failings of the clergy.[45] It starts, for example, with guidance on how to deal with inebriety and carefully distinguishes between the penances for bishops, monks, priests, deacons and the laity giving in to such a vice. In contrast to the penitential associated with Willibrord, the *Excarpsus* draws clear distinctions between the penance imposed for every ecclesiastical grade for each major sin. It is also concerned, however, with sins of the laity and, again in contrast to Willibrord's penitential, carefully examines the sexual life of the married and religious practices which were regarded as pagan or superstitious. In these respects the *Excarpsus* follows the lead of Columbanus and Theodore of Canterbury in demanding of the laity a compliance with ecclesiastical regulations, in a way that until then was reserved mainly for the clergy. From Theodore's penitential the *Excarpsus* adopted many sentences that were of a more general nature and had no direct connection to the hearing of confession. It adopted, for example, Theodore's rule that one was allowed to wash one's hair on a

---

[41] Glatthaar, *Bonifatius und das Sakrileg*, p. 392.

[42] Meens, *Tripartite boeteboek*, pp. 269–97 and 314.

[43] R. Meens, 'Aspekte der Christianisierung des Volkes', in F. J. Felten, J. Jarnut and L. von Padberg (eds.), *Bonifatius. Leben und Nachwirken (754–2004)* (Wiesbaden 2007), pp. 211–29, at pp. 219–27.

[44] Meens, 'Het christendom van Willibrord en Bonifatius'; a connection with Boniface and his activities is also, albeit more cautiously, suggested by Körntgen, 'Kanonisches Recht und Busspraxis', pp. 29–31.

[45] Körntgen, 'Kanonisches Recht und Busspraxis', pp. 22–7.

Sunday.[46] It also ruled that one was not to accept the Eucharist from the hands of a priest who was unable to say prayers or to read from Scripture, and included Theodore's regulations for moving a church building to another location.[47] So, there seems to be no strict demarcation between penitential rules and a broader conception of ecclesiastical regulations. The fluid boundary between what we now tend to see as penitential texts and canon law proper is exemplified by the fact that the *Excarpsus* adopted canons taken from canon law collections and that the Corbie redaction of the *Collectio Vetus Gallica* adopted sentences from Theodore's penitential, possibly even some excerpts from the *Excarpsus Cummeani*.[48] Does this mean that the *Excarpsus* should be regarded as a kind of canon law collection? It seems more plausible to regard it as a text assisting priests in dealing with their communities by informing them about important ecclesiastical decrees as well as by establishing guidelines to deal with penance and confession. Thus, it combined the function of a penitential handbook with that of the later episcopal statutes, which were developed from the late eighth century onwards.[49]

The *Excarpsus Cummeani* was a huge success. This is not only attested by the more than twenty surviving manuscripts written in the eighth and ninth centuries, but also by the fact that many penitential handbooks from this period drew upon the *Excarpsus Cummeani* as a source.[50] The oldest manuscripts containing this work attest that by the ninth century it was fairly well known in southern Germany and in northern France, regions which were closely related to the activities of Boniface and his circle, with two ninth-century manuscripts copied in Mainz, the episcopal town where Boniface resided.[51] In a number of manuscripts, the *Excarpsus* was combined with the *Collectio Vetus Gallica*, and such a combination with a collection of canon law may have contributed to the popularity of the *Excarpsus Cummeani*. The popularity of this work

---

[46] *Excarpsus Cummeani* XII, 6, ed. Schmitz, *Die Bussbücher und das kanonische Bussverfahren*, pp. 636, quoting *P. Theodori U* II, 8, 8, ed. Finsterwalder, *Die Canones Theodori Cantuariensis*, p. 323.

[47] *Excarpsus Cummeani* XIV, 3 and 18, ed. Schmitz, *Die Bussbücher und das kanonische Bussverfahren*, pp. 640 and 642, quoting *P. Theodori U* II, 2, 10 and U II, 1, 1, ed. Finsterwalder, *Die Canones Theodori Cantuariensis*, pp. 314 and 311.

[48] See Mordek, *Kirchenrecht und Reform*, p. 235.

[49] On these see P. Brommer, '*Capitula Episcoporum*'. *Die bischöflichen Kapitularien des 9. und 10. Jahrhunderts*, Typologie des sources 43 (Turnhout 1985) and recently C. van Rhijn, *Shepherds of the Lord. Priests and Episcopal Statutes in the Carolingian Period* (Turnhout 2007).

[50] For the list of mss., see Appendix 2; Meens, *Tripartite boeteboek*, pp. 44–6; Körntgen, 'Kanonisches Recht und Busspraxis', pp. 19–20.

[51] Mss. Oxford, Bodleian Library, Bodl. 572 (Mainz, s. IX in.) and Sélestat, Bibliothèque Humaniste, Ms. 132 (Mainz?, s. IX 3/4), see Meens, *Tripartite boeteboek*, p. 45.

may also be a result of the Carolingian efforts to discipline Frankish Christians, cleric and lay, initiated by Boniface.

Unity and diversity

The composition and the dissemination of the *Excarpsus Cummeani* seem to have been closely related to the efforts initiated by Boniface and his circle to reform the Frankish Church. Penance in the view of Boniface and his companions was an important means to educate and to discipline the clergy and through them the populace at large. The *Excarpsus* drew on a variety of sources, but strove to choose the most authoritative sentences from its sources to present to its readers. During the second half of the eighth century the issues of authority and uniformity would occupy the minds of many authors of penitential texts. By the beginning of the ninth century Carolingian rulers and leading churchmen were struggling with these issues in a more general sense. This would prove to be crucial also for further developments in the field of penance.[52]

While churchmen were using the *Excarpsus Cummeani* other texts were being composed and copied for the benefit of being used in a similar context. They were building mainly on the same set of sources as had been used for the *Excarpsus Cummeani*: the penitential of Cummean, one of the Theodorian strands of sentences and an exemplar from the group of Frankish penitentials building on that of Columbanus. In the second half of the eighth century, probably in a northern French region, the so-called *Paenitentiale Sangallense tripartitum* was written. The author of this text clearly worried about the differences of opinion he encountered in his sources and therefore presented his material in three distinct parts. The basis for each series was provided by one of the basic sources of the work. It distinguishes between the first series following a Frankish penitential from the Columbanian tradition, a second one presenting Theodorian *iudicia* and finally a series drawing on Cummean's penitential. By distinguishing the same topics within these parts, the author put particular emphasis on the differences between the series.[53] Another author

---

[52] On the theme of unity and diversity in the Carolingian Church, see R. Kottje, 'Einheit und Vielfalt des kirchlichen Lebens in der Karolingerzeit', *Zeitschrift für Kirchengeschichte* 76 (1965), pp. 323–42 and R. McKitterick, 'Unity and diversity in the Carolingian Church', in R. Swanson (ed.), *Unity and Diversity in the Church*, Studies in Church History 32 (Oxford 1996), pp. 59–82; for an interesting recent approach, see the chapter on the Carolingian attitudes towards incest in Ubl, *Inzestverbot und Gesetzgebung. Die Konstruktion eines Verbrechens*, pp. 291–383.

[53] For this penitential, see Meens, *Tripartite boeteboek*, pp. 73–104; it is called Sangallense because its only manuscript witness in now preserved in St Gall in the Stiftsbibliothek,

writing a little bit later in the same geographical area went even further than this. He used the tripartite St Gall penitential and the *Excarpsus Cummeani* to fabricate a text in which for every sinful act three traditions were juxtaposed in a systematic way. This text is now known as the *Paenitentiale Capitula Iudiciorum* and must have been fairly popular as its eight surviving manuscript witnesses testify.[54] It was well known in Italy where it was not only copied a few times but also used for the composition of new penitential books and canon law collections.

In northern France as well as in Salzburg at the end of the eighth century, penitential handbooks were composed which used the *Excarpsus* as their base, but enriched this already rather full text with a lot of extra material taken from essentially the same sources. These texts thereby reintroduced the differences that the author of the *Excarpsus* had tried to iron out.[55] Another text known as the *Paenitentiale Merseburgense A*, possibly written somewhere in France or in northern Italy, its main area of dissemination, made use of the same three sources as the *Excarpsus*, but did not distinguish them explicitly.[56] A penitential handbook in two books and therefore known as the *Paenitentiale in duobus libris*, composed in the second half of the eighth or early ninth century, used essentially the same material but enriched it with sentences from Willibrord's penitential.[57] None of these texts, however, was as successful as the *Excarpsus Cummeani*. Most of them we only know from a single manuscript witness.[58] They show, however, that in many areas in the second half

Cod. 150 (s. IX 2/4, St Gall). This is a ms. containing several codicological units, which were all written in St Gall but in different periods.

[54] *P. Capitula Iudiciorum*, for which see L. Mahadevan, 'Überlieferung und Verbreitung des Bussbuchs "Capitula Iudiciorum"', *ZRG Kan. Abt.* 72 (1986), pp. 17–75 and Meens, *Tripartite boeteboek*, pp. 138–76. It survives in the following manuscripts: Kynžvart, Zámecká Knihovna, 20 K 20 (s. XII 1/2, St Blasien); London, British Library, Add. 16413 (s. XI in., southern Italy); Munich, Bayerische Staatsbibliothek, Clm 6333 (s. VIII ex., northeastern France); Paris, Bibliothèque Nationale de France, nouv. acq. lat. 281 (s. X/XI, northern Italy, south of France?); St Gall, Stiftsbibliothek, Ms. 150 (s. VIII/IX or IX in., St Gall); Vatican, Biblioteca Apostolica Vaticana, Vat. lat. 5751 (s. IX ex. or IX/X, Verona/Bobbio?); Vercelli, Biblioteca Capitolare, CCIII (32) (s. IX 4/4, possibly copied in northern Italy in a hand that is regarded as northern French, see Mahadevan, 'Überlieferung', p. 72); Vienna, Österreichische Nationalbibliothek, ms. 2223 (s. IX in., Main region).

[55] *P. Remense* and *P. Vindobonense B*, for which see Asbach, 'Das Poenitentiale Remense' and Meens, *Tripartite boeteboek*; pp. 105–37 and Meens, 'Kanonisches Recht in Salzburg', pp. 13–34.

[56] *P. Merseburgense A*, see Hägele; for a possible Italian origin of this text, see Meens, '"Aliud benitenciale"', p. 19.

[57] *P. in duobus libris*, see Körntgen, *Studien zu den Quellen*, pp. 206–16 and Meens, *Tripartite boeteboek*, pp. 43–4.

[58] Except for the *P. Capitula Iudiciorum* and the *P. Merseburgense A*, which are known from eight and three manuscripts respectively.

of the eighth century, compilers of penitential handbooks were using the same set of sources and tried to get to grips with the different traditions that they represented. In coping with these traditions most of these authors arranged the canons according to their origin, but some presented their material in a systematic way, weaving together the sentences on murder, fornication, theft and so on from their respective sources and thereby demonstrating the variety in penances that their sources assigned. Some attributed the sentences explicitly to their sources, others did not so distinguish between the series they presented to their readers.

Another tradition of penitential texts was known mainly in the Rhine-Main area, from where it spread to eastern France and later to Italy, western France and England. These texts were attributed to two outstanding authorities from the Anglo-Saxon Church: Bede the Venerable and Egbert Archbishop of York. While the latter may have been a genuinely English text, the former was probably produced in the Rhineland, possibly in the monastery of Lorsch.[59] Since the earliest manuscripts of these works stem from around 800, we can conclude that they were composed in the second half of the eighth century. In this case the authority of Bede and Egbert, the alleged authors, seems to have been authoritative and even while these two texts were subsequently forged into one single work, a process neatly analysed by Reinhold Haggenmüller, there does not seem to have been a specific need to attribute singular sentences to one of these (alleged) authors.[60]

The penitential handbooks compiled in the second half of the eighth century reveal a dynamic activity in the composition of these works. This should obviously be seen in the context of the royal and courtly interest in the religious life of the Franks. From an early period onwards religious authority was an integral part of the practice of ruling of the Carolingian family, as is evident in the close cooperation of Willibrord and Boniface with members of the Carolingian dynasty. The cooperation between the Carolingian family and the papacy is well known, although it may not always have been as close as later Carolingian sources want us to believe.[61] The influential capitulary that Charlemagne issued in 789, the *Admonitio Generalis*, clearly demonstrates the importance that

---

[59] There has been ample discussion about the authorship of these texts: see Chapter 4, n. 100 and pp. 96–100.

[60] Although it is hard to be sure on the basis of the existent editions, in which the different strands of transmission have been confused, see Haggenmüller, *Die Überlieferung der Beda und Egbert zugeschriebenen Bußbücher*, pp. 119–28.

[61] See the careful analysis in R. McKitterick, 'Kingship and the writing of history', in McKitterick, *History and Memory in the Carolingian World* (Cambridge 2004), pp. 133–55.

Charlemagne and his advisors attached to the proper Christian way of life of his subjects.[62] This stress on the proper Christian behaviour of the Frankish people stood behind the effort to raise religious and educational standards in the eighth and ninth centuries which is known as the Carolingian Renaissance or the Carolingian Reforms, both of them not really adequate terms.[63] A desire to raise the level of religious instruction was one of the main forces behind the increase in book production in this period.[64] The power and material resources at the command of the Carolingians made such an endeavour possible on a hitherto unprecedented scale.

In the second half of the eighth century we can therefore see the beginnings of an increase in the production of manuscripts meant to be used in pastoral care, often including penitential handbooks.[65] We have evidence that penitential books were regularly part of the collection of liturgical books available at a country church.[66] The growing production of manuscripts went hand in hand with an increase in new compilations of penitential texts and a greater awareness of the different traditions on which these were based. Carolingian Reforming circles put great emphasis on authority and uniformity. For these reasons they prescribed the Rule of Benedict as the sole rule monks should live by. In the field of liturgy they tried to impose the Roman sacramentary which Pope Hadrian had sent to Charlemagne, while the canon law collection known as the *Collectio Dionysio-Hadriana* was meant to displace all other collections as the authoritative text in this field.[67] It therefore does not come as a surprise that the rich variety of penitential rulings provoked discussion among the ecclesiastical elite. The first signs that diversity was felt as a problem comes from a text now only found in the collection of

---

[62] *Admonitio Generalis*, ed. H. Mordek, K. Zechiel-Eckes and M. Glatthaar, *Die Admonitio generalis Karls des Großen*, MGH Fontes Iuris Germanici Antiqui in usum scholarum separatim editi 16 (Hanover 2012). Its religious aspects are discussed in T. M. Buck, *Admonitio und Praedicatio. Zur religions-pastoralen Dimension von Kapitularien und kapitulariennahen Texten (507–814)* (Frankfurt 1997).

[63] For an entry into the vast literature on this theme, see n. 5.

[64] D. Ganz, 'Book production in the Carolingian Empire', pp. 801–6.

[65] Meens, 'The frequency and nature'; Hen, 'Knowledge of canon law among rural priests'; Bullough, 'The Carolingian liturgical experience'.

[66] C. Hammer, 'Country churches. Clerical inventories and the Carolingian renaissance in Bavaria', *Church History* 49 (1980), pp. 5–19; J.-P. Devroey, *Le polyptyque et les listes de cens de l'abbaye de Saint-Remi de Reims (IXe–XIe siècles)*, Travaux de l'Académie Nationale de Reims 163 (Reims 1984), pp. 14, 46, 53; A. Hase, *Mittelalterliche Bücherverzeichnisse aus Kloster Lorsch. Einleitung, Edition und Kommentar* (Wiesbaden 2002), p. 353.

[67] R. Schieffer, '"Redeamus ad fontem". Rom als Hort authentischer Überlieferung im frühen Mittelalter', in A. Angenendt and R. Schieffer, *Roma: Caput et Fons* (Opladen 1989), pp. 45–70.

capitularies assembled by Ansegisus, the abbot of the monastery Fontanelle, finished early in the year 827.[68] Where Ansegisus took this text from is uncertain, but most historians agree that it must be from a text prior to 813.[69] It states that it is yet to be decided by which penitential or how penitents are to be judged.[70] Although it is not clear who is addressing whom in this text, it is evident that the variety of penitentials and their authority were seen as a problem. In 813 precisely this issue was discussed at the council of Tours. The bishops assembled there at the behest of the aging Emperor Charlemagne addressed the question of how penitents should be judged, because priests were applying varying penances and did not always make the right distinctions when doing so. The bishops decided therefore to postpone their decision in making a choice for an authoritative penitential handbook to a meeting in the 'sacred palace'.[71] In Chalon-sur-Saône the bishops criticized penitential handbooks explicitly: 'we should repudiate and eliminate totally those booklets which they call penitentials, of which the errors are as certain as the authors are uncertain'.[72] In Reims it was decided that bishops and priests should examine how they judged penitents and decide on the length of their penance, a decree which also implies that there were problems with the proper authorities by which penitents should be corrected.[73] The council of Arles merely decreed that whoever committed a public crime should be judged in public and had to perform public penance.[74]

The four councils meeting in 813, in which there was discussion of the right ways to judge penitents and the proper texts by which they should be judged, form part of five reform councils convening at the behest of Charlemagne to discuss problems in the Carolingian Church. It is striking that the fifth council convening in Mainz did not discuss the ways in which penance should be imposed, although this clearly seemed to be a part of the agenda that Charlemagne had devised for these councils.[75] How can these differences be explained? Worries about the

---

[68] *Collectio Capitularium Ansegisi*, ed. G. Schmitz, *Die Kapitulariensammlung des Ansegis*, MGH Cap. N.S. I (Hanover 1996).

[69] See Boretius who edited the text in MGH Cap. I, p. 178; Schmitz, *Die Kapitulariensammlung*, pp. 29–30.

[70] *Collectio Capitularium Ansegisis*, Appendix I, 30, ed. Schmitz, p. 668: 'De iudicio poenitentiae ad interrogandum reliquimus, per quem paenitentialem vel qualiter iudicent paenitentes.'

[71] Council of Tours (813), c. 22, ed. A. Werminghoff, MGH Concilia II, 1, p. 289.

[72] Council of Chalon (813), c. 38, ed. A. Werminghoff, MGH Conc. II, 1, p. 281.

[73] Council of Reims (813), c. 16, ed. A. Werminghoff, MGH Conc. II, 1, p. 255.

[74] Council of Arles (813), c. 26, ed. A. Werminghoff, MGH Conc. II, 1, p. 253.

[75] On these councils see W. Hartmann, *Die Synoden der Karolingerzeit im Frankenreich und in Italien*, Konziliengeschichte, Reihe A: Darstellungen (Paderborn / Munich / Vienna / Zürich 1989), pp. 128–40; G. Schmitz, 'Die Reformkonzilien von 813 und die

proper penitential rules to follow seem to have been most acute at Tours, Chalon and Reims. This seems to reflect the regional peculiarities of these councils. The compilation and use of penitential texts in the eighth and early ninth centuries were mainly confined to the northern and eastern parts of the Carolingian realm. It was in these regions that Irish and English monks had left their marks in the religious landscape and in these regions we find most of the manuscripts containing penitential texts.[76] South of the Loire such texts were virtually unknown. In this region a legal tradition which had its roots in conciliar legislation and late Roman law is thought to have persisted well into the ninth century.[77] In this legal culture written documents and late Roman law texts such as the *Lex Romana Visigothorum*, a compendium of the *Codex Theodosianus*, played a central role. In Arles therefore, there was no tension between dealing with penitents on the basis of episcopal authority as found in canon law collections and dealing with them with the help of penitential handbooks and the bishops assembled in Arles seem to have been content with stating the obvious: a public crime should be judged in public. In Mainz on the other hand, where mainly bishops from the Rhineland and Bavaria met, the use of penitential handbooks was apparently so obvious that one felt no need to discuss their lack of authority. It was therefore exactly in the regions where the canonical tradition met the penitential tradition that bishops seem to have encountered problems in dealing with penitents. In Tours there had been a conflict in the early ninth century between Theodulf, archbishop of Orléans and Alcuin, then abbot of St Martin in Tours. This dispute had been partly about the applicability of the public legal system or the less public penitential tradition, Theodulf defending the legal tradition and Alcuin the penitential one.[78] That bishops in Tours were discussing the proper texts to be used in penitential matters, therefore, does not come as a surprise. In the huge metropolitan province of Reims, there were probably similar

---

Sammlung des Benedictus Levita', *Deutsches Archiv* 56 (2000), pp. 1–31; and D. Hägermann, *Karl der Große. Herrscher des Abendlandes: Biographie* (third edn, Berlin 2006), pp. 609–13.

[76] Kottje, 'Überlieferung und Rezeption'.

[77] J. Busch, *Vom Amtswalten zum Königsdienst. Beobachtungen zur 'Staatssprache' des Frühmittelalters am Beispiel des Wortes 'administratio'*, MGH Studien und Texte 42 (Hanover 2007), pp. 42–57; A. Rio, *Legal Practice and the Written Word in the Early Middle Ages. Frankish Formulae, c. 500–1000* (Cambridge 2009), esp. pp. 193–7 commenting on the absence of formulary collections from southern Gaul; I. Wood, 'Administration, law and culture in Merovingian Gaul', in R. McKitterick (ed.), *The Uses of Literacy in Early Medieval Europe* (Cambridge 1990), pp. 63–81 is more sceptical concerning cultural continuity in the south.

[78] For this dispute, see Meens, 'Sanctuary, penance, and dispute settlement', esp. pp. 298–9.

clashes between dealing with delinquents on the basis of canon law or penitential handbooks. Bishops were most outspoken in Chalon. There are indications that the canons decreed by the council of Chalon were composed by Theodulf of Orléans, which might explain the fact that this council did not meet in a metropolitan see. Although the argument for Theodulf's redactorship is not watertight, it would explain the extremely critical attitude concerning penitential handbooks as it was formulated by the council, given Theodulf's southern background and the conflict over jurisdiction he had fought with Alcuin.[79]

In Tours the bishops had decided to delay their decision regarding the choice of an authoritative penitential handbook to a meeting in 'the sacred palace'. Later that year such a meeting took place in the palace in the presence of Charlemagne, where the results of the five reform councils were being discussed. Unfortunately, the capitulary issued by Charlemagne on this occasion has not been preserved.[80] We have, however, a text composed by the attending bishops which was meant to serve as a basis for issuing a royal capitulary, a text known as the *Concordia Episcoporum*. This document contains only one clause regarding the proper way of judging penitents, and it indicates that the bishops in Aachen had not come to an agreement, because they decreed that they were pleased by all the decisions in the reform councils touching upon the subject of dealing with penitents and that they all seemed worthy of compliance.[81] Apparently, no decision had been taken concerning the proper texts to be used in assigning penitential sentences. Two other texts, the exact nature of which is enigmatic, although it seems sure that they are not the capitulary issued by Charlemagne in 813, contain excerpts of the five reform councils. Reading these excerpts there is no

---

[79] On Theodulf as possible author of these canons, see E. Dahlhaus-Berg, *Nova antiquitas et antiqua novitas. Typologische Exegese und isidorianisches Geschichtsbild bei Theodulf von Orléans*, Kölner Historische Abhandlungen 23 (Cologne / Vienna 1975), pp. 221–35. The argument is not totally incontrovertible, particularly in the light of the recent doubt regarding the attribution of the so-called second episcopal statute of Theodulf, for which see R. Pokorny, 'Exkurs II: Ist Theodulf II tatsächlich ein Kapitular Theodulfs von Orléans?', in R. Pokorny (ed.), *Capitula Episcoporum* IV, MGH Cap. Ep. IV (Hanover 2005), pp. 96–100.

[80] The chronicle of Moissac reports on the issuing of a capitulary containing forty-six clauses dealing with the Church and the Christian people, *Chronicon Moissiacense*, ed. G. H. Pertz, MGH SS 1 (Hanover 1826), p. 310; see also K. Ubl, *Inzestverbot und Gesetzgebung*, p. 286.

[81] *Concordia Episcoporum* (813), c. 27: 'De modo et observatione dandae penitentiae, sicut omnibus istis conventibus, qui anno praesente celebrati sunt, visum est, ita nobis placet et observatione dignum ducimus', ed. A. Werminghoff, MGH Conc. II, 1, p. 300. A meeting in Aachen discussing the outcome of the reform councils in the presence of the emperor is mentioned in the *Annales regni Francorum* anno 813, ed. G. H. Pertz and F. Kurze, MGH SS rer. Germ. 6 (Hanover 1895), p. 138.

indication that choosing an authoritative penitential handbook was an important issue, since only the decree of the council of Arles is cited here.[82] The council of Chalon with its fierce censure of penitential handbooks seems therefore to be an exception. In the area where the tradition of penitential handbooks was confronted with an existing legal culture in which Roman and canon law were dominant, it seems that the lack of uniformity posed a problem to bishops. In southern Gaul, where penitentials were virtually unknown, there was no need to discuss the proper penitential handbook, while in the Rhineland and bishoprics east of the Rhine the diversity of penitential decisions was not felt to be such a central problem. This diversity of attitudes towards penitential texts, as apparent in these councils, seemingly was an impediment for the bishops and the emperor to reach a uniform solution in this matter.

Public and secret penance

Another issue that was discussed at the reform councils in 813 is often seen in relation to the question of the authority of penitential texts. The council of Chalon lamented the fact that 'in many places people no longer do penance according to the old decrees of the canons and in excommunicating and reconciling the old ritual is no longer applied'. It went on to state that someone who sinned in public should do penance in public, and that he should be excluded from taking Holy Communion and be reconciled according to the canons.[83] In some other texts prior to the reform councils of 813, it had already been stated that public sins required public penance. The earliest reference to this principle is to be found in a late eighth-century penitential, the *Paenitentiale Remense*. It decrees that who sinned in public should also do penance in public, and who sinned in secret should do penance in secret.[84] It is unclear how exactly we have to understand this clause. It appears in the context of clerical fornication and seems to refer specifically to priests whose sexual sins have become generally known. It does not seem likely that the penitential is referring particularly to the application of a specific liturgical penitential rite here as we know it from, for example, the Old Gelasian Sacramentary. Probably it refers simply to the deposition of a priest or to him remaining in office but

---

[82] For these texts, see G. Schmitz (ed.), *Die Kapitulariensammlung des Ansegis*, MGH (Hanover 1996), pp. 27–8.

[83] Council of Chalon, c. 25, ed. MGH Conciliae II, 1, p. 278.

[84] *P. Remense* IV, 50–1: 'Si publice peccaverint, publice peniteant. Si occulte peccaverint, occulte peniteant', ed. Asbach, 'Das Poenitentiale Remense', supplement, p. 30.

doing penance in secret. It is interesting, however, that the notion that a public sin requires a public form of penance is expressed in this text which has been explicitly connected to the Carolingian court, as one of its early manuscripts, now kept in Paris, was written by a scribe with courtly connections.[85]

That penance was an important topic around the year 800 is amply demonstrated by the *Collectio Dacheriana*, a collection of ecclesiastical regulations made in Lyon, possibly under the supervision of Agobard of Lyon and, as has been suggested, his disciple Florus.[86] This important collection of canon law – of which a scholarly edition is still awaited – is divided into three books, the first one of which is completely devoted to penance.[87] The author nowhere refers to clauses taken from penitential handbooks, but presents solely conciliar decisions as well as papal letters with regard to penance. He clearly had a narrow view of what constituted canon law and tried to assemble every useful canon from what he regarded as proper canon law, thereby expressing some concern about using canons from local councils.[88] This collection of penitential rulings differs fundamentally from the penitential handbooks that we have been discussing, and many of the canons reflect a penitential process in which bishops play a pivotal role. Because they are taken from the late antique ecumenical councils, from African, Spanish and Merovingian local councils as well as from papal letters, they reflect the variety of late antique penance, but it seems difficult to imagine how this rich collection functioned in the process of dealing with sin and correction in the early ninth-century Frankish Church. In at least some manuscripts the *Collectio Dacheriana* has been enriched by adding a penitential. Such a combination provided the user with a legal framework which perhaps was used more as a theoretical exercise, while the practical canons of the penitential then provided rules for dealing with people confessing

---

[85] Paris, BN, lat. 1603, see Asbach, 'Das Poenitentiale Remense', supplement, pp. 30–1; Mordek, *Kirchenrecht und Reform*, pp. 281–3.

[86] Mordek, *Kirchenrecht und Reform im Frankenreich*, pp. 259–63; for Florus, see K. Zechiel-Eckes, *Florus von Lyon als Kirchenpolitiker und Publizist. Studien zur Persönlichkeit eines karolingischen 'Intellektuellen' am Beispiel der Auseinandersetzung mit Amalarius (835–838) und des Prädestinationsstreits* (Stuttgart 1999), whose chronology of Florus's biography makes his participation in the composition of the *Dacheriana* highly unlikely, see particularly pp. 13–14.

[87] *Collectio Dacheriana*, ed. L d'Achery and L.-F.-J. de la Barre, *Spicilegium sive collectio veterum aliquot scriptorum qui in Galliae bibliothecis delituerant* (Paris 1723), pp. 509–64; for general information on this collection, see Kéry, *Canonical collections of the Early Middle Ages*, pp. 87–92; and A. Firey, 'Ghostly recensions in early medieval canon law: the problem of the *Collectio Dacheriana* and its shades', *Tijdschrift voor Rechtsgeschiedenis* 68 (2000), pp. 63–82.

[88] *Praefatio*, ed. d'Achery and de la Barre, *Spicilegium*, p. 512.

their sins.[89] This engagement with late antique ecclesiastical legislation in the field of penance was probably one of the main sources of inspiration for the critique of existing forms of penance that we encounter in 813. It is noteworthy that during the ninth century knowledge of the *Dacheriana* was mainly confined to southern parts of France, regions where penitential books were very rare. In the more northern parts Reims was an important centre of dissemination, if we can judge by the surviving manuscripts.[90]

The notion that public sins required public penance was then alluded to in three of the five reform councils. As we have seen the bishops in Arles decreed that those who had been convicted of a public crime should be judged in public and should do public penance.[91] This suggests that there were possibilities to do penance in a non-public, or perhaps a less public, way. The council of Chalon lamented the fact that 'doing penance in the old way' in many places had fallen out of use and added that one should seek help from the emperor on the question of how someone who had sinned in public should do penance in public.[92] The council of Reims also issued a decree on this matter which stated that a distinction had to be upheld among penitents who should do penance in public and those who could do so in secret.[93] The main problem was therefore not, as some historians have concluded, that secret penance as exemplified by the penitential handbooks had to be replaced by a return to the ancient ritual of public penance. The problem was rather that people who had sinned in public should be seen to do penance.[94] And, interestingly, it was again particularly at the councils of Reims and Chalon that these problems seem to have been felt to be most urgent.

---

[89] Mss. containing the *Collectio Dacheriana* and a penitential proper, Paris, BNF, lat. 2341 (s. IX 2/4, Orléans?), with the sixth book of Halitgar's penitential and the *P. additivum Pseudo-Bedae-Egberti*, Vienna, ÖNB, lat. 2231 (Italy/southern France, s.IX/X) and Monte Cassino. Arch. dell'Abbazia, 554 (Italy, s. X) with the *Paenitentiale in duobus libris*, see R. Kottje, *Die Bussbücher Halitgars von Cambrai und des Hrabanus Maurus. Ihre Überlieferung und ihre Quellen*, Beiträge zur Geschichte und Quellenkunde des Mittelalters 8 (Berlin / New York 1980), pp. 50–1 and Körntgen, *Studien zu den Quellen*, pp. 207–8.

[90] See Kéry, *Canonical collections*, pp. 87–91, mentioning twenty-nine mss. from the ninth century of which ten are located in southern France or the Rhone region; another centre for dissemination of this text seems to be Reims where nine mss. appear to have been written in this period. See also R. Kottje, 'Einheit und Vielfalt', p. 339.

[91] Arles, c. 26, MGH Conc. II, 1, p. 253. See above p. 115.

[92] Chalon, c. 25, ed. MGH Conc. II, 1, p. 278.

[93] Reims, c. 31, ed. MGH Conc. II, 1, p. 256.

[94] For the view that the critique of penitential handbooks was closely connected to the demand for public penance, see e.g. C. Vogel, *Les Libri Paenitentiales*, pp. 39–41.

These councils do not seem to indicate that ecclesiastical penance was in a crisis, but rather that penance had spread to so many fields in which it could be applied that the bishops worried about this proliferation of penance in its manifold manifestations. The fact that the council of Chalon criticized the decline of the old way of doing penance is perhaps to be explained by the influence of the *Collectio Dacheriana*, with its stress on canonically approved authorities, a collection which had been composed in nearby Lyon, the actual metropolitan see of this council. The diversity of forms in which penance could be done is indicated by the reform councils themselves. The council of Chalon ruled that bishops and abbots who had tonsured men for the sake of confiscating their property were to do penance 'canonice sive regulari', according to the canons or the monastic Rule.[95] Canon 34 ruled that a priest should not be led by personal sympathies or enmities when laying down a specific penance, but should do so on the basis of the sacred canons, Holy Scripture or ecclesiastical custom, thereby providing a wide array of texts that could be used in assigning a penance. The bishops added, however, that not only the length of the penance should be considered, but also the enthusiasm and the corporal afflictions with which penance was undertaken.[96] Such an evaluation of the sinner's intentions increased, of course, the room for individual judgment on the part of the confessor. The bishops in Chalon clearly struggled with people who thought that by abstaining from meat and wine or by providing alms they could sin without further complications. The council therefore insisted that an inner conversion was indispensable. Such a critique may have been directed at a mechanical application of the tariffs to be found in penitential handbooks, the more so since these books were heavily criticized in this council. But there were other forms of penance that the bishops in Chalon did not approve of. The bishops also criticized clerics and lay people for going on a pilgrimage to 'Rome, Tours and other places' to obtain forgiveness of their sins.[97] Again it is the lack of inner conversion that is criticized here, but the canon also stresses the need to confess one's sins to the priest to whose *parochia* the sinner belongs. Because of the ambivalence of the terms *sacerdos* and *parochia* it is possible that the bishops are here referring exclusively to episcopal authority, but it could just as well mean, or have been interpreted as, referring to priests and their parish church. In Chalon there was also a discussion about the

---

[95] Chalon, c. 7, ed. MGH Conc. II, 1, p. 275.
[96] Chalon, cc. 34–6, ed. MGH Conc. II, 1, p. 280, echoing the preface of the *Collectio Dacheriana*, ed. d'Achery and de la Barre, *Spicilegium*, p. 510.
[97] Chalon, c. 45, ed. MGH Conc. II, 1, p. 282.

justification of a confession to God without any mediation by a cleric. Some, so the council concluded, are of the opinion that sins should only be confessed to God (Deo solummodo), others that sins should be confessed to priests. While stressing the educational character of priestly confession, the bishops decided that confession to God alone also had the power to forgive sins.[98]

Confession and penance were therefore important topics discussed in Chalon and in this respect this council stands apart from the other reform councils of the same year. This might have been a result of the influence of Theodulf of Orléans, at that time one of the leading personalities in the Carolingian Church. When discussing penance the council hints at the existence of several competing ways in which forgiveness of sins could be achieved – confession to a priest, monastic penitence, pilgrimage or confession to God alone – and while examining these, no firm conclusions seem to have been reached. The ancient way of doing penance is stressed by the bishops but is not promoted as the sole response to sin. A general trend in Chalon is that penitential acts should be joined by a contrite heart (cor contritum) and that an adherence to penitential acts that is only outward behaviour was unacceptable to the bishops assembled at Chalon.

As the bishops in Chalon seem to have been unable to come to a clear-cut response addressing the existing variety of views on penance, the same can be said about the other councils. It is difficult to conclude from the canons of these councils that the Carolingian Church tried to reintroduce the ancient Roman liturgy of penance. Three councils addressed the question as to when someone should perform penance in public. The council of Reims was mostly interested in the proper way priests were to hear confession and assign penances.[99] In Mainz the bishops appear not to have discussed penance at all. The documents closely related to these reform councils do not come to any firm conclusions either. The reform councils therefore seem first of all to bear witness to the variety of penitential practices in the Carolingian world. Particularly the council of Chalon hints at the existence of several forms in which sinners were seeking absolution for their sins. The different ways in which Carolingian bishops dealt with penitential matters in 813 shows not only that a variety of penitential practices existed, but that ecclesiastical views could also differ significantly.

Given the enormous geographical range covered by the Carolingian empire in the ninth century, it should not come as a surprise that all kinds

---

[98] Chalon, c. 33, ed. MGH Conc. II, 1, p. 280; see A. Teetaert, *La confession aux laïcs dans l'Église latine depuis le VIIIe jusqu'au XIVe siècle* (Paris / Louvain 1926).

[99] Reims, cc. 12, 13 and 16, ed. MGH Conc. II, 1, p. 255.

of different attitudes towards sins and their correction existed within the empire. Leading personalities in the Carolingian Church sometimes worried about the diversity that existed within the Church and tried to ensure greater uniformity in several other fields as well: monastic observance, law, chant, liturgy and the like, where a Roman provenance was generally regarded as a guarantee for authenticity.[100] These efforts to create a greater uniformity were only partially successful, a fact that should not come as a surprise given the immense efforts needed, for example, to provide all bishoprics, monasteries and country churches with the proper books to be used.[101] In a society where all texts had to be copied by hand, the production of texts alone required an effort that superseded even the rich resources the Carolingians put at the disposal of the Church. Nonetheless, even if the Carolingians did not succeed in creating a uniform Church, the enormous number of books that were copied in the late eighth and ninth centuries to provide churches and monasteries with the necessary tools to address the needs of the mass of believers in the empire was an astonishing accomplishment in itself.[102]

Royal penance

At the end of the reign of Charlemagne penance was a topic about which opinions seem to have conflicted. The ensuing discussion about the proper way of doing penance and the proper texts to be used in the process must have boosted interest in the subject of penance in royal circles. Another incentive for the Carolingian kings' interest in sinfulness came from the ideology in which the prosperity of the realm was closely related to the moral state of the king and his people. In a letter of advice written around 775 to the young king Charlemagne by a certain Cathwulf, the author, probably an Anglo-Saxon cleric, underlines the importance of a just ruler in describing the positive effects that such a ruler brought about: the air will be quiet and peaceful, the earth and the sea will bring forth ample fruits, the king will reign over many peoples and his enemies will fall before his person. Rule by an unjust king, however, will cause conflicts in the royal family, famine, plague, infertility of the land and military defeat.[103] Such ideas possibly had an Irish

---

[100] Schieffer, '"Redeamus ad fontem"'.
[101] Kottje, 'Einheit und Vielfalt'; McKitterick, 'Unity and diversity'.
[102] For Carolingian manuscripts production, see D. Ganz, 'Book production in the Carolingian empire'; in general the work of Bernhard Bischoff is indispensable for our knowledge of Carolingian manuscripts.
[103] Cathwulf, *Epistola Ad Karolum*, ed. E. Dümmler, MGH Epistolae IV (Berlin 1895), pp. 501–5. For this letter, see J. Story, 'Cathwulf, kingship, and the royal abbey of Saint-

background, since they can also be found in the *Collectio Hibernensis* and in the text known as *De XII abusivis saeculi*, on the twelve abuses of the world, a text attributed to Cyprian of Carthage but composed in Ireland.[104] These Irish texts were well known in Francia, and Alcuin in 799 addressed Charlemagne in similar terms, linking his religious duties to the well-being of the realm.[105] During the ninth century this ideology stressing the connection between royal behaviour and the well-being of the realm was a regular feature of *Mirrors of Princes*, texts meant to be used in the education of princes and kings in order to prepare and guide them for kingship.[106] The king was also, however, to take care of the behaviour of his subjects. If they were straying from the Christian path, he should correct them in order that God's wrath would not fall upon his kingdom. Charlemagne demonstrated the importance of religious factors in governing the kingdom by including big chunks from the canon law collection that he had acquired in Rome, the *Collectio Dionysio-Hadriana*, in the *Admonitio Generalis*, the influential royal capitulary laying out the principal rules by which his subjects should abide.

That Charlemagne attached great importance to the correct moral behaviour of his subjects is further shown by his reactions to serious adversities that befell his kingdom. For example, when, in 778/9, shortly after he had received Cathwulf's letter, a great famine afflicted many parts of his kingdom, Charlemagne issued a capitulary in which he ordered that bishops, priests, monks and nuns, canons, counts and paupers fulfil all kinds of penitential actions, mostly fasting and giving alms, appropriate to their social function in order to please God. They were to act in this way 'for our lord the king, for the army of the Franks and for the present tribulation'.[107] When he observed in 805 that all

Denis', *Speculum* 74 (1999), pp. 1–21 and M. Garrison, 'Letters to a king and biblical exempla: the examples of Cathuulf and Clemens Peregrinus', *Early Medieval Europe* 7 (1998), pp. 305–28.

[104] See R. Meens, 'Politics, mirrors of princes and the Bible: sins, kings and the well-being of the realm', *Early Medieval Europe* 7 (1998), pp. 345–57; H. H. Anton, 'Königsvorstellungen bei Iren und Franken im Vergleich', in F.-R. Erkens, *Das frühmittelalterliche Königtum. Ideelle und religiöse Grundlagen*, Ergänzungsbände zum Reallexikon der Germanischen Altertumskunde 49 (Berlin / New York 2005), pp. 270–330.

[105] Alcuin, *Epistola* 177, ed. E. Dümmler, MGH Epistolae IV, pp. 292–3.

[106] For these texts, see H. H. Anton, *Fürstenspiegel und Herrscherethos in der Karolingerzeit*, Bonner historische Forschungen 32 (Bonn 1968) and J. Smith, *Europe after Rome. A New Cultural History* (Oxford 2005), pp. 239–52.

[107] *Capitulare Haristallense secundum speciale (Second capitulary of Herstal)*, ed. H. Mordek, 'Karls des Großen zweites Kapitular von Herstal und die Hungersnot der Jahre 778/ 770', *Deutsches Archiv* 61 (2005), pp. 1–52, at p. 50; see also Hägermann, *Karl der Große*, pp. 167–8.

kinds of disasters befell his empire – bad harvests resulting from bad weather, plagues and enemy invasions – Charlemagne ordered three empire-wide three-day fasts by which the people were to make up for their sins and regain God's grace.[108] Apparently he did the same five years later, as we can learn from a letter that Archbishop Riculf of Mainz addressed to his suffragan Bishop Egino of Konstanz, which unfortunately has only partially survived.[109] That such royal letters were not unfamiliar and were held to be important may be concluded from the fact that a very similar letter has been included in a ninth-century collection of formularies providing its users with exemplary letters.[110] These texts document that ruling justly was important and that the emperor had to be aware of his own behaviour, as well as that of his subjects, in order to retain divine grace.

Such an emphasis on the responsibility of the king for the religious state of his kingdom was further strengthened by a late Roman military tradition formed around triumphal rulership.[111] Fighting a battle was not merely a military operation. In such a situation much depended on divine favour and therefore religious rituals were needed to secure this favour. The Roman emperor played an important role in securing the favour of the Gods; Christian emperors and kings later adopted this role seeking the support of the Christian God. We can see that Charlemagne also went to war anticipating divine assistance. In a letter to his queen Fastrada he described how he and his men supported the army in their invasion of Avar territory in 805 with fasts and litanies, and he invited his wife to add her share to these endeavours.[112] Such religious rituals have strong penitential overtones and this strongly suggests that in the eyes of Charlemagne the themes of sin, grace and success in war were closely connected.

This stress on the close connection between sins and the well-being of the realm did not disappear under Charlemagne's successor, Louis the Pious. In recent historiography, Louis has been salvaged from the conventional slighting interpretation of him as merely being the little son of a

---

[108] *Karoli ad Ghaerbaldum episcopum epistola*, ed. A. Boretius, MGH Capitularia I, pp. 245–6; see Meens, 'Politics, mirrors of princes and the Bible', p. 345.

[109] Riculf of Mainz, *Epistola ad Eginonem*, ed. A. Boretius, MGH Cap. I, p. 249.

[110] *Formulae Salicae Merkelianae*, nr. 63, ed. K. Zeumer, MGH Formulae, p. 262; for the ninth-century date of this collection, see Rio, *Legal Practice and the Written Word*, pp. 128–32.

[111] M. McCormick, *Eternal Victory. Triumphal Rulership in Late Antiquity and the Early Medieval West* (Cambridge 1986); McCormick, 'The liturgy of war in the early Middle Ages: crisis, litanies, and the Carolingian monarchy', *Viator* 15 (1984), pp. 1–24; D. S. Bachrach, *Religion and the Conduct of War*, pp. 32–43.

[112] Letter of Charlemagne to Fastrada, ed. Dümmler, MGH Epistolae IV, pp. 528–9.

great father.[113] Whereas traditionally historians, often thinking in terms
of 'state versus church', tended to criticize Louis's domination by ecclesiastical leaders, lately historians with a better understanding of the close
connection between 'church' and 'state' in the Carolingian era have
emphasized how Louis cooperated with ecclesiastical leaders to enhance
the position of the emperor.[114] In 822 Louis took a remarkable step when
reconciling himself with 'those brothers whom he had ordered, against
their will, to be tonsured' and trying to make up for his behaviour in the
case of the revolt of Bernhard of Italy, abbot Adalhard of Corbie and the
latter's brother Wala. At an assembly in Attigny held in August after
deliberations with the attending bishops and members of the secular
elite, he confessed his sins in public and performed penance.[115] This is
the first penance by a ruler that we hear of since Ambrose forced
Emperor Theodosius to do penance, if we leave apart the deathbed
penances of Visigothic kings and the penance forced upon King Wamba
in 680 in order to remove him from the throne.[116] Louis's royal gesture
has been viewed as a sign of his weakness, of his being under the influence of the bishops, but also as a sign of royal strength.[117] What is clear,
however, is that penance here, as we have seen in other cases as well, is
used as part of a process of reconciliation after a conflict, this time
between the emperor on the one hand and on the other some of his
family members and their supporting magnates. All the sources stress in
some way or another public aspects of this royal penance.[118] The *Royal
Frankish Annals*, one of the major court-centred historical works of the
period, and the Astronomer, the author of a *Life of Louis*, both stress the
fact that the emperor confessed his sins in public, while the Annals of
Fulda and St Bertin emphasize the fact that the king did public penance

---

[113] Most influential in this respect was P. Godman and R. Collins (eds.), *Charlemagne's Heir. New Perspectives on the Reign of Louis the Pious (814–840)* (Oxford 1990).

[114] The first step towards this rehabilitation was T. F. X. Noble, 'Louis the Pious and his piety reconsidered', *Revue Belge de philologie et d'histoire* 58 (1980), pp. 297–316; for recent work on Louis, see M. de Jong, *The Penitential State. Authority and Atonement in the Age of Louis the Pious, 814–840* (Cambridge 2009) and C. Booker, *Past Convictions. The Penance of Louis the Pious and the Decline of the Carolingians* (Philadelphia 2009).

[115] *Annales Regni Francorum*, a. 822, ed. Pertz and Kurze, MGH SS rer. Germ. 6 (Hanover 1895), p. 158; translation in P. E. Dutton (ed.), *Carolingian Civilization. A Reader* (Peterborough, Ontario 1993), p. 181.

[116] See De Jong, *The Penitential State*, p. 244.

[117] The idea of Louis's penance as an act of strength was first proposed in M. de Jong, 'Power and humility in Carolingian society', pp. 31–2; it is now argued more comprehensively in her *The Penitential State*, pp. 35–6.

[118] *Annales Regni Francorum*; *Annales Fuldenses*, ed. Pertz and Kurze, MGH SS rer. Germ. 7 (Hanover 1891), p. 22; *Annales Sithienses*, ed. G. Waitz, MGH SS 13 (Hanover 1881), p. 38; Astronomer, *Vita Hludowici imperatoris*, c. 35, ed. F. Tremp, MGH SS rer. Germ. 64 (Hanover 1995), p. 406.

for crimes he had also committed in public. This royal penance has therefore always been regarded as a public penance, and rightfully so. But we have to ask what exactly was meant by public penance here. Apparently the confession of sins was professed in public, but did the penitential ritual follow the rite as we know it from the *Gelasianum Vetus*? Unfortunately, there is no way of telling, but the fact that this penance was not imposed during Lent and that there are no indications that a period of penance elapsed before Louis was reconciled – the *Royal Frankish Annals* inform us that Louis went hunting right after the assembly at Attigny – suggests that it was not. Only the Astronomer, writing however considerably later, informs us of the penitential acts of the emperor: giving alms, (paying for) prayers by servants of God and providing satisfaction himself. There is no indication that this penance somehow impeded the emperor in his duties.

Things would be more difficult for the emperor when in 833 he was again doing penance in public. This moment of deep crisis shook the Carolingian empire. It happened in the aftermath of the defeat of the emperor in the battle of the so-called Field of Lies against his revolting sons, Lothar and Louis. In the political discourse in the buildup to this event, the close relationship between the king and the well-being of the realm that we have just observed had risen to extremely high levels. In this context much stress was put upon the royal palace as a place that had to remain free from any form of pollution.[119] The palace was by some described as a brothel, where not only all kinds of fornication were being committed, but also people were involved in sorcery and other crimes.[120] Agobard of Lyon explicitly connected the state of the royal bed with that of the palace, of the kingdom and of the name of the Franks.[121] This stress on the purity of the royal palace was related to efforts to improve the religious life of the Franks. In 828 the Emperor Louis together with his eldest son and co-emperor Lothar summoned four great synods in Mainz, Paris, Lyon and Toulouse. They did so to discuss the recent string of disastrous events that had befallen the Carolingian empire comprising military defeat in the Spanish March and problems with the Danes in the north. The councils should not only find out in what ways God had been offended, but they should also help to placate Him by

[119] See e.g. the *Capitulare de disciplina palatii Aquisgranensis*, dated to around 820, ed. A. Boretius, MGH Capit. I, pp. 297–8.

[120] Paschasius Radbertus, *Epitaphium Arsenii*, c. 8, ed. E. Dümmler, *Abhandlungen der kaiserlichen Akademie der Wissenschaften zu Berlin, phil.-hist. Klasse* (Berlin 1900), p. 69.

[121] Agobard of Lyon, *Liber apologeticus* I, 1, ed. L. van Acker, *Agobardi Lugdunensi Opera Omnia*, CC CM 52 (Turnhout 1981), p. 311: 'videntes maculatum stratum paternum, sordidatum palatium, confusum regnum et obscuratum nomen Francorum'.

proper ways of atonement. In the turbulent years between 828 and 833, when the Frankish empire was riven apart by internal political strife and attacked by external enemies, ideas of sin, penance, reconciliation and regaining God's grace were at the centre of political debate leading one of the main experts in this field to speak of the Frankish kingdom in this period as a 'penitential state'.[122]

Since penitential themes dominated political discourse at the Frankish court around the year 830, it seems appropriate that a publicly staged penitential ritual was at the heart of the conflict. In 833 Louis the Pious, pressed by his sons Lothar and Louis, was forced to do public penance in the church of St Médard in Soissons. Louis confessed his sins, had them written down on a piece of parchment, prostrated himself on a hair shirt in front of the main altar and asked for the imposition of a public and ecclesiastical penance.[123] The bishops assembled there, among whom Agobard of Lyon and Ebo of Reims were the leading figures, imposed penance on the emperor and thereby divested him of his imperial office. As a sign of this, the emperor laid down his military belt (*cingulum militiae*), the token of his ability to command an army, and his secular attire and placed these on the altar.[124] The bishops assembled at Soissons did their utmost to follow canonical precepts. They stressed that they were following ancient forms of penance, they took official records of every action, they made sure that Louis's confession was put to parchment and laid on the altar, and emphasized that the ritual was irreversible. Nevertheless, although everything that happened in Soissons was laid out in detail in advance, the magnates involved in the process were not sure about its outcome. Recent research has shown how much such rituals were stage-set and were meant to communicate political decisions as well as ensure consent.[125] However, even if this was so, it was extremely important that everyone agreed on what had actually happened and to ensure that one's interpretation of the events became the dominant one.[126] For the latter, written accounts formed an important arena in which to impose one's reading of a particular ritual.[127] In spite of all the

---

[122] De Jong, *The Penitential State*.

[123] *Episcoporum de poenitentia, quam Hludowicus imperator professus est, Relatio Compendiensis*, ed. A. Boretius and V. Krause, MGH Capit. II, pp. 51–5.

[124] *Episcoporum de poenitentia, quam Hludowicus imperator professus est, Relatio Compendiensis*, p. 55.

[125] Althoff, *Spielregeln der Politik* is still fundamental; see also Althoff, *Die Macht der Rituale* and C. Garnier and H. Kamp (eds.), *Spielregeln der Mächtigen. Mittelalterliche Politik zwischen Gewohnheit und Konvention* (Darmstadt 2010).

[126] As argued by Buc, *The Dangers of Ritual*.

[127] The arena of Louis's penance is thoroughly explored by De Jong, *The Penitential State* and Booker, *Past Convictions*.

rhetoric stressing the conformity of Louis's penance to ancient models and ecclesiastical legislation, the penance of Louis was something spectacularly new. Theodosius had done penance for his sins, but he had not been deposed because of them, whereas Louis was. In 822 there had been no discussion at all about deposing Louis because of the fact that he had done public penance, yet now the bishop emphasized that 'after such a serious penance, nobody is allowed to return to secular service'.[128] That the bishops were not completely sure about their position is revealed by the fact that they unsuccessfully tried to force Louis to monastic conversion, a step that would make a return to a secular position of power as good as impossible.

The bishops in Soissons were right in their assessment of the situation. Louis's penance proved to be reversible and within a year the humiliated emperor was back on the throne again. In March 834 in the church of St Denis bishops reconciled the emperor with the Church and reinvested him with his arms. One source even explicitly connects this reconciliation with heavenly signs: according to the Astronomer, at this moment the flooding rains and the raging storms subsided.[129] Again we can observe how flexible penitential traditions were. This episode involving the emperor of the West shows how penitential rituals could be used in specific conflicts not only to reconcile opposing parties, but also to humiliate and to rule out an opponent. Lothar and his party had tried to use the ritual of public penance to remove Louis from office, but when the tides had changed it was no problem to reconcile the emperor to the Church and to reinvest him with his imperial office. Of course, this is a special case involving the highest echelons in Frankish society. We can imagine that this was a spectacular case that instigated the use of penance or penitential elements in the settling of secular disputes.[130] In regard to what we have seen in earlier chapters it makes more sense, however, to regard Louis's penance as a spectacular specimen of an existing tradition of using penitence in such conflicts. It reveals the diversity of penitential rituals that one could apply as well as the malleability of tradition that

---

[128] *Episcoporum de poenitentia, quam Hludowicus imperator professus est, Relatio Compendiensis*, p. 55: 'post tantam talemque poenitentiam nemo ultra ad militiam saecularem redeat'.

[129] Astronomer, *Vita Hludowici imperatoris*, c. 51, ed. Tremp, *Thegan, Die Taten Kaiser Ludwigs / Astronomus, Das Leben Kaiser Ludwigs*, pp. 488–90.

[130] As argued by G. Althoff, *Macht der Rituale*, pp. 61–2 and 69: 'Rituelle Handlungen der Kirchenbuße dienten also als Bausteine der Kreation eines Rituals, das es erlaubte Konflikte gütlich beizulegen'. Koziol, *Begging Pardon and Favor*, p. 19: 'Laymen and laywomen knew what it meant to prostrate themselves and beg God's grace and forgiveness in penance. They therefore understood that when they knelt to beg favor or forgiveness from a lord who claimed to hold his authority "by the grace of God", they were countenancing that claim by approaching him as they approached God.'

went with it: instead of using a fixed legal tradition of public penance, the bishops in 833 felt the need to invent such a tradition in order to secure their position.

Reform penitentials

In discussing the reform councils of 813 we observed a tension between a broadly southern tradition in which ancient canonical sources were being used in penitential matters – a tradition culminating in the *Collectio Dacheriana* – and a more northern tradition building on penitential handbooks deriving from insular sources. This tension was probably even more acute at a period of heightened political strife such as occurred in the years around 830, a period culminating in the public penance of Louis the Pious in Soissons in 833. At the council of Paris in 829 penance was again an important topic on the agenda. This feature should be regarded in conjunction with the importance of public penance in dealing with Louis the Pious in those critical years.[131] The introduction to the council, penned by Jonas of Orléans, stressed the theme of sins, kings and the well-being of the realm, a theme that was developed more fully in the second book of this council devoted to kingship.[132] This explicit reference to the responsibility of the ruler for the well-being of the kingdom was clearly related to the ensuing political development in which Louis was held accountable for the disasters befalling the Frankish empire. Many of the bishops attending the Paris council were to play a crucial role in Louis's penance.

At this council the bishops sharply criticized penitential handbooks, which they wanted to abolish altogether. These books were written 'contra canonicam auctoritatem', contrary to the authority of the canons, and did not heal the wound of the sinner but rather caressed them, so the bishops wrote.[133] Archbishop Ebo of Reims, one of the main opponents of Louis the Pious in the years to come and the scapegoat who was made to bear all the consequences after the revolt of Louis's sons broke down, was one of the bishops attending this council. Ebo was also the one who asked one of the other attendants of this council, Halitgar Bishop of Cambrai, to compose a penitential handbook that was in full accordance with the canons. Ebo was appalled by the diversity of existing penitentials, by their inconsistency and lack of

---

[131] De Jong, *The Penitential State*, pp. 176–84.
[132] Meens, 'Politics, mirrors of princes and the Bible', p. 355.
[133] Council of Paris (829), c. I, 32, ed. A. Werminghoff, MGH Conc. II, 2 (Hanover / Leipzig 1908), p. 633.

authority, and he therefore requested Halitgar to excerpt the canons and
the writing of the Fathers to compose a penitential to assist the priests
hearing confession.[134] Halitgar complied with this wish and produced a
penitential in six books of which the first five consisted mainly of
excerpts taken from Julianus Pomerius, Gregory the Great and the
important Carolingian canonical collections, the *Collectio Dacheriana*
and the *Dionysio-Hadriana*.[135] Apparently, however, Halitgar felt that
such a collection could not fulfil all the demands from the clergy hearing
confession and therefore he added a sixth book, particularly for 'the
simpler minds among them who were unable to understand the bigger
issues'.[136] This sixth book was an existing penitential in the traditional
sense, although belonging to the group in which the various traditions
were neatly distinguished in different series of canons. Halitgar claimed
that he took this penitential from the Roman archive and in this way
provided the text with Roman authority.[137] There is no hard evidence
establishing the date when Halitgar composed this work. If we take Ebo's
role at the council of Paris into account as well as his role in the
circumstances leading up to the penance of Louis the Pious in 833, it
seems more probable that he encouraged Halitgar to compose this
penitential in the late 820s than earlier in his career. In a text emanating
from a diocesan synod that met shortly after the council of Paris (829),
the presiding bishop mentioned a penitential which he had spread
among his clergy.[138] Probably the penitential referred to here is Halitgar's penitential, which is also included in the sole manuscript containing this text. Wilfried Hartmann concluded that we are probably dealing
with a diocesan synod presided over by Halitgar himself. If he is right,
then it stands to reason that Halitgar shortly after 829 referred to his
work which was still fairly recent at this point, thus suggesting a date for
the penitential in the late 820s.[139] Hartmann's views about the role of
Halitgar in this diocesan synod have not won general approval, but even

---

[134] Letter of Ebo to Halitgar, ed. Dümmler, MGH Epp. V (Berlin 1899), p. 617.
[135] For a thorough study of Halitgar's work, see R. Kottje, *Die Bussbücher Halitgars von Cambrai und des Hrabanus Maurus*.
[136] Halitgar's preface, ed. Schmitz, *Die Bussbücher und das kanonische Bussverfahren*, p. 266: 'simplicioribus qui majora non valent capere'.
[137] For the tradition of a Roman penitential, see Meens, 'The historiography of early medieval penance', pp. 74–82.
[138] *Capitula Neustrica tertia*, c. 2, ed. R. Pokorny, MGH Cap. Ep. III (Hanover 1995), p. 65.
[139] W. Hartmann, 'Neue Texte zur bischöflichen Reformgesetzgebung aus den Jahren 829–31. Vier Diözesansynoden Halitgars von Cambrai', *Deutsches Archiv* 35 (1979), pp. 368–94; R. Kottje, 'Ein Fragment des "Paenitentiale" Halitgars von Cambrai aus einem Frühdruck der "Institutionen" Justinians', *Sacris Erudiri* 44 (2005), pp. 241–6, at p. 243, thinks it is possible that the work was composed immediately after 829.

if we suppose that this text was issued by another northern French bishop in those years, this would still support a date for Halitgar's penitential in the late 820s rather than an earlier date.[140]

This reform penitential composed by the bishop of Cambrai was extremely successful. It survives in sixty-nine manuscripts, most of which were written in the ninth and tenth centuries.[141] Although such a wide dissemination attests to the influence of the Carolingian Reform movement, the geographical distribution of the manuscripts demonstrates that some regions remained unaffected by it. That part of the reason for the success of Halitgar's work may lie in its adoption of an existing penitential as Book 6 is suggested by the fact that in quite a lot of manuscripts Halitgar's work is combined with still other penitential handbooks of a more traditional kind. Halitgar's handbook cannot be said to have replaced the existing tradition of pre-reform penitentials, but his influence was nevertheless remarkable.[142]

After the restoration of Louis the Pious, Ebo of Reims was held accountable for the public humiliation the emperor had had to undergo. Consequently Ebo was deposed from office and exiled to the monastery of Fulda. The manuscripts of Halitgar's penitential demonstrate that it had an early centre of dissemination in Fulda, so we must conclude that Ebo promoted this handbook when in exile.[143] While in exile Ebo must have met the then abbot of Fulda, Hrabanus Maurus. Whether this meeting was an incentive for Hrabanus to engage with penitential literature is unknown. Although there is evidence that Hrabanus knew Halitgar's penitential by the year 850, there is no sign that he used it when composing two penitential handbooks himself.[144] Hrabanus composed these two texts as responses to requests from fellow bishops concerning penitential matters. Although they originated as long letters, their manuscript transmission demonstrates that they were in fact regarded as guidelines for confessors, since they were included in manuscripts containing other penitential handbooks. The earliest of Hrabanus's works on penance is the so-called *Paenitentiale ad Otgarium*, which he composed at

---

[140] Pokorny has aired doubts about the attribution to Halitgar, see MGH Cap. Ep. III, pp. 63–4; I suggested that the text might equally well have been issued by Ebo of Reims, who seems to have been more involved in the promotion of Halitgar's work than Halitgar himself, as the number of early manuscripts containing Halitgar's penitential from the Reims region testifies: see Meens, *Tripartite boeteboek*, p. 62, n. 179; for Ebo's role in the dissemination of the mss., see Kottje, *Die Bussbücher Halitgars*, p. 251.

[141] The manuscript tradition has been charted thoroughly in Kottje, *Die Bussbücher Halitgars*, pp. 13–110; for a list of Halitgar mss., see Appendix 4.

[142] Kottje, *Die Bussbücher Halitgars*.

[143] Kottje, *Die Bussbücher Halitgars*, p. 251.

[144] See Kottje, *Die Bussbücher Halitgars*, pp. 200–1.

the request of Archbishop Otgar of Mainz in or shortly after 841.[145] This work was written solely on the basis of texts with impeccable authority: the Bible, Church Fathers and conciliary decrees which he took mainly from two authoritative canon law collections: the *Collectio Dionysio-Hadriana* and the *Hispana*.[146] It had only limited impact. It was never drawn upon in later works and only three manuscripts with this work survive, all of them written in the Middle Rhine region, not far from Mainz, the original destination of the work.[147]

The first question Hrabanus dealt with in his penitential concerns sinning priests and whether it was permitted to reinstate them to office after they had confessed and fulfilled their penance. The urgency of the question, which Hrabanus tried to answer in full using a whole dossier of canonical and patristical texts, seems to be related to the discussion about the reinstallation of Ebo as archbishop of Reims in the year 840.[148] The discussion about the reinstitution of Ebo was still urgent when Hrabanus composed the penitential for Heribald, bishop of Auxerre, in or shortly after 853.[149] In this work, he not only adopted the part about sinning priests from his earlier penitential, but also devoted a chapter to an explicit discussion of the reinstitution of Ebo of Reims on the see of Reims. Heribald had taken part in the council of Soissons in 853, where it was decided that all the priests consecrated by Ebo during his short period in office after his rehabilitation (840–1) were to be deposed. It was this question which apparently troubled Heribald and about which he sought Hrabanus's advice. In this second penitential, Hrabanus recirculated parts of his earlier handbook and canons from the council of Mainz (847), over which he had presided. His attitude towards the acceptability of canonical resources seems to have become less restricted, however. In his penitential to Otgar Hrabanus had restricted his sources to the Bible, Church Fathers and well-established canonical sources. The council of Mainz in 847, deliberating under the direction of Hrabanus, referred to the reform councils of 813, as it stressed that penance should be established according to the Bible, the ancient conciliar decisions or ecclesiastical custom, but it left out the

[145] Kottje, *Die Bussbücher Halitgars*, p. 6, ed. PL 112, 1397–424.
[146] Kottje, *Die Bussbücher Halitgars*, pp. 190–250 and 253.
[147] Mss. Wolfenbüttel, Herzog August Bibliothek, 656 Helmsted (s. IX med. Mainz); Vatican, Biblioteca Apostolica Vaticana, Ottob. lat. 3295 (S. IX 3/4, Rhine/Main region); Düsseldorf, Universitätsbibliothek, B. 113 (s. IX 3/4, Middle Rhine region, possibly Lower Rhine); see Kottje, *Die Bussbücher Halitgars*, pp. 139–41.
[148] Kottje, *Die Bussbücher Halitgars*, pp. 228–30; for Ebo's reinstallation, see Booker, *Past Convictions*, pp. 191–5.
[149] Hrabanus Maurus, *Paenitentiale ad Heribaldum*, ed. PL 110, cols. 467–94.

part of the text explicitly condemning penitential books. This may indicate a shift in Hrabanus's thinking, as his use of the penitential sentences of Theodore and Egbert in the later penitential to Heribald suggests, although he employed these sources with some reservations.[150] The manuscript tradition suggests that this work had more success than Hrabanus's first manual of this kind. The penitential written for Heribald still survives in twelve manuscripts dating from the ninth to the twelfth centuries, and it was also regularly cited in later texts.[151] The manuscript context suggests that Hrabanus's work was more useful for bishops and clerics with an interest in ecclesiastical law than for parish priests.[152]

The penitentials of Halitgar and Hrabanus Maurus clearly tried to live up to one of the main criticisms directed at the existing penitentials, i.e. their dubious authority. Both authors based their texts on the well-established sources of ecclesiastical authorities, particularly conciliary and papal decisions. Yet even these texts, with the exception of Hrabanus's penitential to Otgar, at some points used penitential decisions attributed to authors such as Theodore of Canterbury or the Venerable Bede. The same can be said about a work in four books, known as the *Quadripartitus*, which has been attributed in the past to both Halitgar and Hrabanus. Its author can no longer be identified, but it was composed in the second or third quarter of the ninth century in northern Gaul, possibly in the neighbourhood of Reims, and should be regarded as another book reflecting the ambitions of Carolingian Reform circles. Like Halitgar's penitential, which was one of its main sources of

---

[150] Kottje, *Die Bussbücher Halitgars*, pp. 204–12 and 253; R. Haggenmüller, 'Zur Rezeption der Beda und Egbert zugeschriebenen Bußbücher', in H. Mordek (ed.), *Aus Archiven und Bibliotheken. Festschrift für Raymund Kottje zum 65. Geburtstag* (Frankfurt a.M. / Bern / etc. 1992), pp. 149–59.

[151] It is preserved in the following mss.: Heiligenkreuz, Stiftsbibliothek, Ms. 217 (s. X ex., Germany, western parts); Cologne, Dombibliothek, 118 (s. IX ex., near Reims); Cologne, Dombibliothek, 120 (s. X in., eastern France); Kynžvart, Zámecká Knihovna, 20 K 20 (s. XII 1/2, St Blasien); Munich, Bayerische Staatsbibliothek, Clm 3851 (s. IX ex., eastern France); Munich, Bayerische Staatsbibliothek, Clm 3853 (s. X 2/2, southern Germany, Augsburg?); Munich, Bayerische Staatsbibliothek, Clm 3909 (1138–43, Augsburg); Paris, BNF, lat. 3878 (s. X ex., northeastern France, region of Liège?); Salzburg, Stiftsbibliothek St Peter, Ms. a IX 32 (s. XI 1/2, Cologne?); St Gall, Stiftsbibliothek, Ms. 676 (XI ex., St Blasien/Schaffhausen); Stuttgart, Württembergische Landesbibliothek, Cod. HB VI 107 (s. XI ex., southwestern part of Germany, region of the Lake Constance); Zürich, Zentralbibliothek, Ms. Car. C 123 (s. IX med.–3/4, Alemannia, Reichenau?); see Kottje, *Die Bussbücher Halitgars*, pp. 13–83 and Meens, *Tripartite boeteboek*, pp. 65–6. For the reception of the penitential in later works, Kottje, *Die Bussbücher Halitgars*, p. 254.

[152] Most of the manuscripts containing the *P. Heribaldum* are to be found among books with a strong episcopal or canonical stamp: see Meens, 'Frequency and nature'.

inspiration, it included a great many sentences from canon law collections such as the *Collectio Dacheriana*.[153] Its stress on the proper authorities is strengthened by the inclusion of a list of twenty-four approved authorities used in this work.[154] The fact that this work lacks a clear indication of its compiler demonstrates that it was the authority of the canons which mattered to Carolingian Reformers, not the identity of the author of a penitential. The *Quadripartitus* was not particularly influential. It survives in nine manuscripts all dating from before the thirteenth century.[155] It was however one of the sources used by Regino of Prüm when he wrote his handbook for the visitation of priests as well as by six canon law collections.[156]

The reform penitentials discussed so far, in their effort to use only approved authorities, show many similarities with canon law collections, and sometimes it is even hard to establish the character of a particular text.[157] Two other texts emanating from the Carolingian Reform movement are more clearly recognizable as penitential handbooks. The penitential attributed to Pope Gregory, which is commonly known as the penitential of Pseudo-Gregory III – although the attribution does not refer to a specific Gregory – includes parts of Ebo's letter to Halitgar lamenting the lack of uniformity among penitential books and decisions as well as their lack of authority. It is, therefore, counted among the books inspired by the Carolingian Reforms. This book, however, composed probably around the middle of the ninth century or a little later in the northern Frankish regions, contains almost no decisions from well-established canon law collections, but draws mostly upon existing penitential traditions. It refers to the authority of Theodore of Canterbury, Bede and Egbert.[158] It had a fairly limited distribution

---

[153] F. Kerff, *Der Quadripartitus. Ein Handbuch der karolingischen Kirchenreform. Überlieferung, Quellen und Rezeption*, Quellen und Forschungen zum Recht im Mittelalter 1 (Sigmaringen 1982), pp. 61–4.

[154] Kerff, *Quadripartitus*, p. 54.

[155] Mss. Antwerpen, Museum Plantin-Moretus/Prentenkabinet, M 82 (66) (s. XII 1/2, northeastern France); Monte Cassino, Archivio dell'Abbazia, cod. 541 (ext. 541) (s. XI in., southern Italy, Monte Cassino?); Oxford, Bodleian Library, Bodl. 718 (s. X–XI, England, perhaps Exeter); Stuttgart, Württembergische Landesbibliothek, Cod. HB VII 62 (s. IX ex., region of Lake Constance, perhaps Reichenau); Trier, Stadtbibliothek, Ms. 1084/115 (s. XI, was preserved in Trier in the twelfth century); Vatican, Biblioteca Apostolica Vaticana, Vat. lat. 1347 (s. IX med.-3/4, Reims); Vatican, Biblioteca Apostolica Vaticana, Vat. lat. 1352 (s. XI 2/2, Italy); Vendôme, Bibliothèque Municipale, Ms. 55 (s. XI, Vendôme?); Vienna, Österreichische Nationalbibliothek, lat. 12886 (theol. 387) (s. XII 1/2, Austria).

[156] Kerff, *Quadripartitus*, pp. 69–76.

[157] Kerff, *Quadripartitus*, pp. 83–4.

[158] See F. Kerff, 'Das Paenitentiale Pseudo-Gregorii III. Ein Zeugnis karolingischer Reformbestrebungen', *ZRG Kan Abt.* 69 (1983), pp. 46–63; the text is edited by

and is known from only two complete manuscripts and surviving fragments from another.[159]

Another text composed in ninth-century Francia is often associated with the Carolingian Reform programme. It concerns the penitential known as Pseudo-Theodore, although this name is a bit misleading, since the attribution of the text is only to be found as an eleventh- or early twelfth-century remark added on to the text in a single manuscript.[160] On the basis of the sources it draws upon, it can be dated to the second quarter of the ninth century and its origin probably must be sought in the northeastern parts of the Frankish realms, somewhere near Reims and Mainz.[161] In contrast to the other penitentials related to the Carolingian Reform movement, this text seems to be of a different nature. It does not appear to attach great value to the authority of the canons, since it almost never identifies these. Moreover, as well as making use of Halitgar's work, it draws heavily on traditional penitentials, such as the *Excarpsus Cummeani* and Theodore's penitential.[162]

Also drawing on penitential sentences was another ninth-century penitential, the so-called *Paenitentiale Vallicellianum I*.[163] This text was a reworking of an earlier text, known as the *Paenitentiale Merseburgense A*, using essentially the same penitential decrees, but no longer presenting these in a historical order, i.e. organized by its sources, but in a systematic order so that decrees concerning the same kind of offences were grouped together.[164] The compiler of the *Vallicellianum* penitential, however, showed that he worried about the authority of his decrees by

F. Kerff, 'Das Paenitentiale Pseudo-Gregorii. Eine kritische Edition', in Mordek (ed.), *Aus Archiven und Bibliotheken*, pp. 161–88.

[159] Mss. Montpellier, Bibliothèque Interuniversitaire, Médecine H 137 (s. XI, France) and Ghent, Universiteitsbibliotheek, Hs. 506, ff. 67r–73v (s. IX/2); for some reason or other Kerff did not include the complete text found in the latter manuscript in his edition, although he used the fragment to be found on ff. 110–11 of the same manuscript, as already observed in R. Kottje, '"Buße oder Strafe?". Zur "Iustitia" in den "Libri Paenitentiales"', in *La Giustizia nell'alto medioevo (secoli V–VIII)*, Settimane di Studio 42 (Spoleto 1995), pp. 443–74, at p. 449, n. 17. For a careful description of the Ghent ms., see Mordek, *Bibliotheca capitularium*, pp. 127–30.

[160] Ms. Cambridge, Corpus Christi College, 190; see the discussion in C. van Rhijn (ed.), *Paenitentiale Pseudo-Theodori*, CC SL 156 B (Turnhout 2009), pp. xiv–xvii.

[161] Van Rhijn, *Paenitentiale Pseudo-Theodori*, pp. ix–xiv; see also the discussion in C. van Rhijn and M. Saan, 'Correcting sinners, correcting texts: a context for the *Paenitentiale pseudo-Theodori*', *Early Medieval Europe* 14 (2006), pp. 23–40, at p. 37.

[162] Van Rhijn, *Paenitentiale Pseudo-Theodori*, pp. xvii–xx; Van Rhijn and Saan, 'Correcting sinners', p. 25.

[163] Hägele, *Paenitentiale Vallicellianum I*, p. 93, dates it in the late ninth or early tenth century, which seems a bit late. I think there is no reason to exclude any date in the second half of the ninth century.

[164] Hägele, *Paenitentiale Vallicellianum I*, pp. 59–63.

adding inscriptions in which he identified the decrees that he took from the Merseburg penitential, with canons from authoritative early Christian councils, such as those of Nicaea, Ancyra or Neocaesarea. This painstaking work which the compiler completed with the help of at least two canon law collections – probably the *Collectio Herovalliana* and the collection of Cresconius – demonstrates that the authority of its canons mattered greatly to the compiler. As such this text can be counted among the texts reflecting the worries of Carolingian bishops concerning the dubious authority of penitential texts.[165] It was mainly known in Italy, as its eight surviving manuscripts, dating from the tenth to the end of the twelfth century, testify.[166]

So we can conclude that although Halitgar's penitential clearly was the most influential text composed in reaction to the criticism aired against penitential texts at Carolingian councils, in the ninth century traditional penitential manuals were still being used for the composition of new ones. There are indications that a priest had difficulties in hearing confession using the central reform penitentials of Halitgar, Hrabanus or the *Quadripartitus*, which limit themselves to genuinely authoritative texts that they found in approved collections of canon law. Halitgar already added especially for the 'simple priests' a traditional penitential to his work, which might explain at least in part its wide dissemination. We have seen how other texts were created during the ninth century which were of a more traditional kind in the sense that they included many sentences from earlier penitential texts. Moreover we can observe that earlier penitential texts continued to be copied and to be reworked, indicating that they continued to meet a certain demand for such texts.[167] Minor texts were also being composed as additions to

---

[165] Hägele, *Paenitentiale Vallicellianum I*, p. 81: 'Man könnte geneigt sein, hierin einen verspäteten Ausfluß karolingischer Reformbestrebungen zu sehen.'

[166] Mss. Barcelona, Biblioteca de la Universidad, Ms. 228 (s. X 2/2, northern Italy); Florence, Biblioteca Medicea Laurenziana, Ms. Ashburnham 1814 (s. XI, possibly copied from a northern Italian exemplar); Milan, Biblioteca Ambrosiana, Ms. I 145 inf. (s. XII, Milan?); Paris, Bibliothèque Nationale de France, lat. 14993 (s. XII/XIII, France); Rome, Biblioteca Vallicelliana, E 15 (s. XI 1/2, Rome?); Rome, Biblioteca Vallicelliana, F 54 (s. XII 1/2, middle Italy); Vercelli, Biblioteca Capitolare, CXLIII (159) (s. X 2/2, northern Italy); Vercelli, Biblioteca Capitolare, CLXXIX (152) (s. XII/XIII, Vercelli); see Hägele, *Paenitentiale Vallicellianum I*, pp. 21–31; for the localization of Paris 14993, see R. Pokorny and M. Stratmann, MGH Cap. Ep. II, p. 173.

[167] For the continuing process of copying earlier texts, see R. Kottje, 'Busspraxis und Bussritus', in *Segni e riti nella chiesa altomedievale occidentale*, Settimane di studio 33 (Spoleto 1987), pp. 369–95; for the reworking of earlier texts in the ninth century, see L. Körntgen, 'Bußbuch und Bußpraxis in der zweiten Hälfte des 9. Jahrhunderts', in W. Hartmann (ed.), *Recht und Gericht in Kirche und Welt um 900*, Schriften des Historischen Kollegs, Kolloquien 69 (Munich 2007), pp. 197–215.

existing compilations, surviving in small and simple manuscripts again showing the precariousness of their chances for survival.[168] Another indicator that what the reformers thought of as proper canon law did not always suffice in the eyes of those using these texts is revealed when we look at the manuscripts containing them. Many reform penitentials – as we have seen in the case of the influential canon law collection, the *Collectio Dacheriana* – were in fact combined with traditional ones. In the third quarter of the ninth century, for example, in a manuscript that may have been written in Alsace and is now preserved in Zürich, Halitgar's penitential was combined with the penitential attributed to Bede.[169] At the end of the ninth century in northern France a manuscript was produced which combined Halitgar with the penitential in which the penitentials attributed to Bede and Egbert had been blended into a well-ordered text, the so-called *Paenitentiale mixtum pseudo-Bedae-Egberti*.[170] In some texts moreover the canon of authoritative texts had started to include works by Theodore of Canterbury, Bede and Egbert, a tendency that we can also observe in the centuries to come.

Under the Carolingians, penance had become an important, and in some circumstances even crucial, factor in religion, society and politics. God's grace had to be preserved by leading a life pleasing to God and by atoning for every serious misdeed. This was no longer true only for religious men and women, but also for lay people, kings as well as persons of a lesser status. The ways in which one did penance were the subject of ample discussions at ecclesiastical councils and many penitential handbooks bear witness to the efforts of their authors to provide sure and authoritative guidelines for priests hearing confession. These texts also show, however, that the Carolingians did not reach a single solution. In practice as in theory, a great variety of approaches continued to exist. Our sources do suggest, however, that bishops during the ninth century gained more control over the process of confession and penance. Furthermore, they suggest that penance became a regular feature of ecclesiastical life. Every Christian was supposed to confess his or her sins in times of tribulation and at least three times a year as a preparation for the important liturgical feasts of

[168] Meens, "'Aliud benitenciale'".
[169] Ms. Zürich, Zentralbibliothek, Ms. Car. C 176 (D 64), part I (ff. 1–136), see Kottje, *Die Bussbücher Halitgars*, pp. 82–3; Haggenmüller, *Überlieferung der Beda und Egbert zugeschrieben Bußbücher*, pp. 115–16.
[170] Ms. Munich, Bayerische Staatsbibliothek, Clm 14532, see Kottje, *Die Bussbücher Halitgars*, pp. 41–2; Haggenmüller, *Die Überlieferung der Beda und Egbert zugeschrieben Bußbücher*, pp. 80–1.

Christmas, Easter and Pentecost.[171] Whether such demands were met in practice remains questionable, but the fact that they were expressed is surely significant. Penitential handbooks still discussed major sins disrupting the social fabric, but minor sins were now also of importance, not only for the clergy but also for the laity. This suggests that penance had become a regular feature of Christian life in the sense that all Christians were supposed to confess their sins regularly, i.e. between one and three times a year. The explosion in penitential texts and manuscripts that we have discussed in this chapter reflects the growing importance of penance in everyday life. This growth also led to a need to provide a script for hearing confession, a need that was met by the development of liturgical *ordines*, which strengthened ecclesiastical control over the whole process. That this increasing importance led to differences of opinion on how to deal with sinning Christians is understandable, given the variety of options that were available at the time. The ardent efforts of ecclesiastical leaders, first and foremost the powerful Carolingian bishops, to provide unity could not, however, eliminate the rich diversity that continued to exist on the ground.

---

[171] See e.g. the council of Tours (813), c. 50, ed. MGH Conc. 2.1, p. 293; many penitentials require married couples to abstain from sexual intercourse before these three major feasts to prepare for receiving communion on these festivals, see Payer, *Sex and the Penitentials*, pp. 127–8 and J. Brundage, *Law, Sex, and Christian Society in Medieval Europe* (Chicago / London 1987), pp. 158–9; episcopal capitularies seem to regard receiving communion three times a year as a kind of minimum. In his widely distributed First Capitulary, Theodulf of Orléans urged all Christians to communicate every Sunday in Lent plus Maundy Thursday, Good Friday, Holy Saturday and Easter Sunday, thereby indicating that receiving communion on Easter was considered normal, see c. 41 of the *First Capitulary of Theodulf*, ed. P. Brommer, MGH Cap. Ep. I, p. 138; see also the tenth-century *Capitula Helmstadensia*, c. 9, ed. R. Pokorny, MGH Ep. Cap. 3, p. 186 and the capitulary by Ruotger of Trier, c. 25, MGH Cap. Ep. I, p. 69; the close connection between communion and confession is addressed in all these sources, see Meens, 'Frequency and nature', pp. 37–8.

6 New penitential territories: the tenth and eleventh centuries

In the Carolingian Church penance had become a regular feature of the life of the clergy and the laity. As a consequence many penitential books were composed to assist priests in their task of hearing confession. Such penitential manuals had been copied in large quantities and were available in the small collections of books of country churches. After this blossoming of penitential literature, which was characterized by a production of new texts, distributing these texts by copying them and discussing their models and functions, the tenth and eleventh centuries form a contrast. In the northern Frankish regions, the centre of production and discussions of penitential texts during the Carolingian era, we no longer see a thriving production of new penitential texts. This decrease fits in with a more general decline in the production of texts and manuscripts that has been observed for this period.[1] This decline can partly be explained by the extensive production of texts and manuscripts in the preceding era, which seems to have met many demands. Given the fact that parchment manuscripts are durable products, the Carolingian copies probably remained in use in the following centuries. A well-stocked parish bookshelf did not need instant renewal. The conservative nature of the tenth- and eleventh-century liturgical developments did not create a need for new texts, as is shown, for instance, by the fact that earlier penitential handbooks continued to be reproduced. The penitentials attributed to Bede and Egbert, for example, were copied at least eighteen times in this period.[2]

Already in their early history, penitential handbooks had close relations to collections of canon law. Because there was no established criterion to determine whether or not a text had canonical status in the field of Church law, the boundaries between penitential handbooks and collections of canon law proper were most of the time fluid. Penitentials instructed confessors about what the Church regarded as unlawful

---

[1] C. Leonardi, 'Intellectual life', in T. Reuter (ed.), *The New Cambridge Medieval History*, vol. III: *c. 900–c. 1024* (Cambridge 1999), pp. 186–211, at p. 186.
[2] Meens, 'Penitentials and the practice of penance', pp. 14–15.

behaviour. In the ninth century episcopal capitularies had been developed that partly took over these functions of a penitential book. These episcopal books stressed episcopal authority over the priesthood and the laity. Such texts also marked a growing awareness of the boundary between canon law collections and penitential handbooks. Yet the Carolingian Reform penitentials, particularly those of Hrabanus Maurus and Halitgar of Cambrai, had brought the two traditions closer together again by including authoritative legal material in their penitential handbooks. After the disappearance of the Carolingian rulers, within the region formerly under their control, two crucial new texts again connected ecclesiastical legislation closely with penitential concerns.

Regino of Prüm and synodal inquisitions

Shortly after the year 900, Regino of Prüm, after his resignation as abbot of the important Eifel monastery of Prüm, finished a work positioning itself on the borderline of canon law and penitential discipline. In his famous *Two Books on Synodal Investigations and Ecclesiastical Instruction*, dedicated to Archbishop Hatto of Mainz (891–913), he collected sentences from various councils and decrees of the holy fathers, in order to inform bishops in a convenient way about the proper rules for Christian life.[3] This work was meant to epitomize ecclesiastical legislation for bishops touring their diocese so that they did not need to carry around bulky volumes containing such legislation. As such Regino placed himself in the Carolingian tradition of providing authoritative ecclesiastical rules for a Christian life. However, Regino had fewer qualms about the authorities he cited than his predecessors Halitgar and Hrabanus had had. While most of his sources did derive from authoritative texts, such as councils and books from the Church Fathers, he had some misgivings about using Frankish capitularies and decisions of ninth-century church councils.[4] Apart from

---

[3] Regino of Prüm, *Libri duo de synodalibus causis et disciplinis ecclesiasticis, Praefatio*, ed. H. Wasserschleben, *Reginonis libri duo de synodalibus causis et disciplinis ecclesiasticis* (Leipzig 1840), p. 1; there is a recent German translation by Wilfried Hartmann with accompanying Latin text based on Wasserschleben's edition, *Das Sendhandbuch des Regino von Prüm*, AQ 42 (Darmstadt 2004), pp. 20–1. The preface has been translated into English in R. Somerville and B. Brasington, *Prefaces to Canon Law Books in Latin Christianity. Selected Translations, 500–1245* (New Haven / London 1998), pp. 92–4. For a good introduction to the text, see W. Hartmann, *Kirche und Kirchenrecht um 900. Die Bedeutung de spätkarolingischen Zeit für Tradition und Innovation im kirchlichen Recht*, Schriften der MGH 58 (Hanover 2008), pp. 149–62.

[4] Regino, *Praefatio*, ed. Wasserschleben, *Reginonis libri*, p. 2; H. Siems, 'In ordine posuimus: Begrifflichkeit und Rechtsanwendung in Reginos Sendhandbuch', in W. Hartmann (ed.), *Recht und Gericht in Kirche und Welt um 900*, Schriften des Historischen Kollegs. Kolloquien 69 (Munich 2007), pp. 67–90, at p. 73.

these sources Regino also cited some texts attributed to councils allegedly held at Rouen and Nantes, for which we have no other evidence. It is still unclear whether Regino knew conciliar texts that have left no other traces in the historical record, or whether he did not refrain from forging new texts where he felt that new regulation was needed.[5] That Regino did not share the negative Carolingian views on traditional penitential handbooks is shown by one of the questions he includes in order to investigate the knowledge and behaviour of priests: they should be asked whether they possessed the penitentials of Theodore, Bede or 'the Roman penitential' and also whether they heard confession and decided on a particular penance according to the book.[6] He thus endorsed the use of penitential handbooks promoting those possessing a particular authority. When speaking of the penitential of Bede Regino apparently had the so-called *Bede-Egbert mixtum* penitential in mind, which he used as one of the sources of his work, while the 'Roman penitential' to which he refers might have been Book 6 of Halitgar of Cambrai.[7]

Regino's work was composed to be used in episcopal visitations and thus to function in the context of episcopal authority. In the second half of the ninth century we find the earliest sources informing us about bishops travelling through their dioceses and inquiring into the religious life of the priesthood as well as the laity. Probably this institution of the episcopal synodal inquiry was somehow related to the use in Carolingian politics of bishops as *missi dominici*, those members of the ecclesiastical and secular elite sent out by the court to keep an eye on local affairs.[8] Particularly when a bishop was asked to act as a *missus* in his own diocese, his subjects would have become acquainted with the bishop intervening at the local level.[9] Such actions would have required a more active role

---

[5] The best discussion is in W. Hartmann, 'Die Capita incerta im Sendhandbuch Reginos von Prüm', in O. Münsch and T. Zotz (eds.), *Scientia veritatis. Festschrift für Hubert Mordek zum 65. Geburtstag* (Ostfildern 2004), pp. 207–26.

[6] Regino, *Libri duo de synodalibus causis et disciplinis ecclesiasticis*, Inquisitio, 96: 'Si habeat poenitentialem Romanum vel a Theodoro episcopo aut a venerabili Beda editum, ut secundum quod ibi scriptum est, aut interroget confitentem, aut confesso modum poenitentiae imponat?', ed. Wasserschleben, *Reginonis libri*, p. 26; Hartmann, *Das Sendhandbuch des Regino von Prüm*, pp. 38–9; for the identity of these three texts, see Körntgen, 'Bußbuch und Bußpraxis', pp. 201–2 and Meens, 'The historiography of early medieval penance', p. 77.

[7] Haggenmüller, 'Zur Rezeption der Beda und Egbert zugeschriebenen Bußbücher', pp. 155–6.

[8] On the *missi dominici*, see now R. McKitterick, *Charlemagne. The Formation of a European Identity* (Cambridge 2008), pp. 256–66.

[9] R. Schieffer, 'Zur Entstehung des Sendgerichts im 9. Jahrhundert', in W. P. Müller and M. E. Sommar (eds.), *Medieval Church Law and the Origins of the Western Legal Tradition. A Tribute to Kenneth Pennington* (Washington DC 2006), pp. 50–6; W. Hartmann, 'Probleme des geistlichen Gerichts im 10. und 11. Jahrhunderts: Bischöfe und

for bishops in the localities, a role already envisaged as such in the episcopal capitularies from the first half of the ninth century. The synodal inquisition was, of course, also closely related to the bishop's task of visiting his diocese in order to confer the ministry of confirmation, and to the canonical rule that bishops should hold diocesan synods once or twice a year.[10]

At the beginning of the second book, dealing with the laity, Regino describes how such a visitation was to take place. The bishop's visit should be prepared by an archdeacon or archpriest one or two days prior to the bishop's arrival. This person had to announce the visitation and call together the community, threatening anyone who remained absent with excommunication. Together with the priests in the service of the bishop, he should settle minor cases so as not to burden the visitation proper. The bishop came to the community, so Regino stresses, as the vicar of Christ and should therefore be welcomed with joy, fear and the greatest honour. Seven trustworthy members of the community should swear on holy relics that they would inform the bishop of all things contrary to God's will that had occurred at the local level. Then Regino presents an extensive list of eighty-nine questions which should be put to these witnesses. The topics dealt with in this list and the order in which they are advanced closely resemble those of a penitential book and seem to be based on such a text. The rest of the second book then comprises authoritative texts providing guidelines on how to deal with these offences. These guidelines partly stem from penitential handbooks, which Regino clearly regarded as authoritative texts.

The description of the procedures of an episcopal visitation by Regino can be enriched by some details revealed in the biography of Ulrich, the bishop of Augsburg in the years 923–73. This *Life* was written at the end of the tenth century by Gerhard, a priest from the circle of Ulrich. Gerhard depicts how a bishop should visit his diocese every four years in order to judge (*regere*), to preach and to administer the sacrament of baptismal confirmation. According to Gerhard this

---

Synoden als Richter im ostfränkisch-deutschen Reich', in *La Giustizia nell'alto medioevo (secoli IX–XI)*, Settimana di Studio 44 (Spoleto 1997), pp. 631–72.

[10] For the episcopal task of travelling around in his diocese for the sake of granting confirmation, see e.g. *Concilium Germanicum* (742), c. 3 and the council of Soissons (744), c. 4, ed. R. Rau, *Briefe des Bonifatius. Willibalds Leben des Bonifatius. Nebst einigen zeitgenössischen Dokumenten*, Ausgewählte Quellen zur deutschen Geschichte des Mittelalters. Freiherr vom Stein-Gedächtnisausgabe 4b (Darmstadt 1968), pp. 378–80 and 386. The council of Cloveshoe, c. 3, ed. Haddan and Stubbs, *Councils and Ecclesiastical Documents Relating to Great Britain and Ireland*, vol. III, pp. 363–4. For the close connection between these canons, see Cubitt, *Anglo-Saxon Church Councils*, pp. 103–4.

was a joyful yet necessary occasion. When the bishop arrived he was
welcomed with all honour, accompanied by the ringing of the church
bells. After Mass was sung, the bishop invited the trustworthy and
prudent men from the village for an interrogation under oath about
the religious life in their community. If the bishop found out that
someone had offended ecclesiastical rules, he hastened to bring him
back to the road of justice according to the judgment of the clerics,
probably in a kind of ecclesiastical tribunal. However, Gerhard conceded that the bishop's authority was not always uncontested. When a
case proved to be so difficult that it could not be dealt with by his
subordinates, the bishop himself took great care that the case was
settled with the help of all his companions. Sometimes such strife was
set loose by someone who would not accept the bishop's justice that the
case could not be settled before nightfall. In such a case, Gerhard
relates, the procedure was continued by candlelight and the person
contesting his judgment was silenced by the reading of ecclesiastical
regulations (*regulas canonicas*).[11] What kind of text Gerhard envisaged
to have been read by the bishop by candlelight, we do not know for
certain. It might have been Regino's handbook, although no manuscript
of this text is known from Augsburg.[12] Possibly Gerhard was thinking of
a manuscript like Munich, Clm 3853, one of the most comprehensive
collections of ecclesiastical and secular law of this period and possibly
coming from Augsburg.[13] This manuscript not only contains part of
Halitgar's penitential, the so-called mixtum version of the Bede-Egbert
penitential and Hraban's penitential for Heribald, but also conciliar
legislation, a canon law collection in seventy-seven chapters, the
Bavarian and the Alemannic law codes, and the collection of capitularies made by Ansegisus.[14] A close connection between this particular
manuscript and the episcopal visitation is demonstrated by its inclusion
of an elaborate instruction on how to conduct such a visitation.[15]

[11] *Vita sancti Oudalrici episcopi Augustani auctore Gerhardo*, c. 6, ed. G. Waitz, in
Lebensbeschreibungen einiger Bischöfe des 10.–12. Jahrhunderts, tr. Hatto Kallfelz,
Ausgewählte Quellen 22 (second edition, Darmstadt 1986), pp. 78–80; see also
Hartmann, *Kirche und Kirchenrecht*, pp. 311–14.
[12] For the mss. see Kéry, *Canonical Collections of the Early Middle Ages*, pp. 129–31.
[13] Mordek, *Bibliotheca*, p. 288: 'ein imposantes Opus ..., das ... zu den umfangreichsten
Kompendien des frühmittelalterlichen kirchlichen und weltlichen Rechts gehört.' For a
detailed description of the ms., Mordek, *Bibliotheca*, pp. 287–305.
[14] See the comments in Meens, 'Penitentials and the practice of penance', p. 19.
[15] Published in A. Koeniger, *Die Sendgerichte in Deutschland* (Munich 1907), pp. 191–4 as
the 'Augsburger Sendordnung'. For comments, see W. Hartmann, 'Zu Effektivität und
Aktualität von Reginos Sendhandbuch', in Müller and Sommar (eds.), *Medieval Church
Law*, pp. 33–49, at p. 37.

The *Life of Ulrich of Augsburg* and Regino's handbook make clear that an episcopal visitation was a grand affair with the bishop visiting a local community as a powerful lord. The liturgical setting of this procedure, with the Mass, the bishop preaching and administering confirmation, the ritual role of a book of canons and the orchestration of the church bells clearly enhanced the bishop's authority. The fact that Gerhard acknowledges that some did fervently oppose the bishop's judgment demonstrates, however, that an episcopal visitation was sometimes regarded as an infraction of local traditions and rights. An episcopal visitation should, therefore, be regarded as a powerful tool in the hands of bishops for exerting influence in their diocese at a local level. Regino's handbook shows that penitential canons could play a role in such a show of force and we can assume that manuscripts containing a combination of canon law and penitential handbooks, sometimes even combined with secular law, as in the case of the manuscript from Munich just discussed, were employed in such a setting.

How regular a feature of ecclesiastical life such a visitation actually was is hard to establish. The *Life of Ulrich* speaks of a four-year cycle.[16] Regino, unfortunately, does not specify how often a bishop should make the round of his diocese. In the thirteenth century an active archbishop like Eudes Rigaud, archbishop of Rouen, visited the deaneries in his diocese only between one and three times during his twenty-one years in office, although we should keep in mind that in his time archdeacons were also active in overseeing the local clergy through visitations.[17] So we may surmise that in Regino's time the frequency was less. Another question is how widespread the practice was. Regino's work is, apart from some surviving fragments, extant in eleven manuscripts, all but one of them from the tenth and eleventh centuries. Most of these come from the Rhineland area or from the archbishopric of Trier, although its use in other texts indicates a somewhat wider diffusion.[18] Regino's work was apparently mainly used in the region of Trier and the Rhineland. Of course, this does not mean that bishops only visited their diocese in regions where Regino's handbook was known, as the *Life of Ulrich of*

---

[16] *Vita sancti Oudalrici*, c. 6, ed. Waitz, p. 78: 'cum quarto anno secundum constitutionem canonum ministerium suum adimplendum', a formulation which, just like the accompanying German translation, suggests a four-year cycle. Koeniger, *Die Sendgerichte in Deutschland*, pp. 117–18, fn. 3, however, translates this as 'in the fourth year of his episcopate'.

[17] A. Davis, *The Holy Bureaucrat. Eudes Rigaud and Religious Reform in Thirteenth-Century Normandy* (Ithaca / London 2006), pp. 111–12.

[18] Kéry, *Canonical Collections*, pp. 129–31 and Hartmann, *Kirche und Kirchenrecht*, pp. 158–62; Hamilton, *The Practice of Penance*, p. 30, mentions only seven manuscripts.

Augsburg demonstrates, but it is also risky to assume that an episcopal visitation as we know it from Regino's work was a general feature of the Latin Church in the tenth century. Regino's work does show, however, that bishops sometimes intervened in local communities and that they used the instruments of penance, penitential decisions and excommunication in the process.[19] The reference in the *Life of Ulrich of Augsburg* to an obstinate litigant opposing the bishop suggests that the settling of a dispute at a synodal inquisition need not have been a harmonious procedure. A bishop arrived in a locality as a powerful person, who had access to religious authority as well as secular power.

Regino's handbook demonstrates that topics touched upon in traditional Carolingian penitential handbooks, were also of concern to a bishop. The newly established institution of the synodal inquisition, which we know to have been employed in some regions in the Frankish world, dealt with such issues on the basis of a broad corpus of canon law which often included penitential sentences. Regino's handbook also informs us about other instances in which penitential sentences were of primary importance. In the first book, Regino deals extensively with the topic of confession and penance.[20] From this discussion it is clear that Regino took a practice of yearly confession before the beginning of Lent for granted, because he urges priests to admonish their flocks to confess their sins, great and small, before the beginning of Lent and to accept the penances assigned by the priest. Regino stresses the fact that everyone should confess to their own priest (*ad proprium sacerdotem*), demonstrating that for him the practice of confession was closely linked to a parochial system.[21] He also includes liturgical instructions for the hearing of confession, incorporating a long list of questions about people's sins with their appropriate penances: in this way, his text resembles a traditional penitential handbook.[22]

Regino further stresses the role of priests in local communities. He instructs them to check whether Christians from other parishes were coming to Mass in their church out of disrespect for their own priest. If this was the case they should send them away and force them to return to

---

[19] For excommunication, see S. Hamilton, '*Absoluimus uos uice beati petri apostolorum principis*: episcopal authority and the reconciliation of excommunicants in England and Francia c. 900–1150', in P. Fouracre and D. Ganz (eds.), *Frankland. The Franks and the World of the Early Middle Ages. Essays in Honour of Dame Jinty Nelson* (Manchester 2008), pp. 209–41.

[20] Regino, *Libri duo*, I, 292–319; *Das Sendhandbuch des Regino von Prüm*, ed. Hartmann, pp. 152–76.

[21] Regino, *Libri duo*, I, 292, ed. Hartmann, p. 152.

[22] Regino, *Libri duo*, I, 303–4, ed. Hartmann, pp. 156–70; see the short discussion in Hamilton, *The Practice of Penance*, pp. 38–44.

their own parishes. Priests should also check whether there were any conflicts among members of the community. In a case of conflict, they should try to reconcile the opposing parties, and if this proved to be impossible they should send them away from the church. It is probably no accident that Regino included a canon from a clearly monastic context right after this sentence stressing the conciliatory role of the priest in the local community. This canon decrees that someone who did not try to correct a mortal sinner or refrained from denouncing the latter's sins should do penance himself for as long as he did not contradict the sinner.[23] Clearly Regino is cherishing an ideal of parishes as close-knit harmonious communities under the tight control of priests and, in the final instance, bishops. Yet his work also reveals that priests often held a more ambiguous role in the local community. In his questionnaire, he includes two questions regarding local ties preventing a priest from reporting a sinner to the bishop or inciting him to absolve a sinner without him fulfilling the appropriate penance. Apparently a priest was sometimes willing to act in such ways for reasons of temporal gain, friendship or consanguinity.[24] However, it is clear from Regino's work that for priests in local communities, penance was an important tool to encourage church discipline and for the settling of conflicts within the community.[25]

Regino also knew the practice of public penance. He cites a canon from a fifth-century African council requiring an imposition of hands for those whose sins had become known. He goes on to describe a ritual for the laying on of hands to penitents, which should take place *caput quadragesimae*, at the beginning of Lent, a text for which no precedent had been identified, so it was perhaps composed by Regino himself on the basis of current practice. In this ritual penitents were to present themselves to the bishop through an act of prostration, going barefoot and wearing sackcloth. In assigning a specific penance to the penitents the bishop was assisted by deans, that is the archpriests of the parishes, so Regino explains. After the penance had been established, the bishop led the penitents into the church where they received his laying on of hands,

---

[23] Regino, *Libri duo*, II, 421 and 422, ed. Hartmann, p. 448.

[24] Regino, *Libri duo*, I questionnaire, nrs. 38–9, ed. Hartmann, p. 30; for ways in which priests were tied to local communities, see C. van Rhijn, 'Priests and the Carolingian reforms: the bottlenecks of local *correctio*', in R. Corradini, R. Meens, C. Pössel and P. Shaw (eds.), *Texts and Identities in the Early Middle Ages*, Forschungen zur Geschichte des Mittelalters 12 (Vienna 2006), pp. 219–37.

[25] See also R. Meens, 'Die Bußbücher und das Recht im 9. und 10. Jahrhundert. Kontinuität und Wandel', in W. Hartmann (ed.), *Recht und Gericht in Kirche und Welt um 900* (Munich 2007), pp. 217–33, at p. 228.

a sprinkling of holy water, ashes and sackcloth, before they were driven out of the church again. On Maundy Thursday they were then presented at the entrance of the church in order to be readmitted into the Christian community. The elaborate liturgy, in which penitent Christians were banished from the church and later readmitted, emphasized the authority of the bishop, who clearly played the leading part in this ritual.[26]

Burchard of Worms

Regino's collection was one of the main sources for Burchard, bishop of Worms, when he composed his huge and influential compendium of canon law in twenty books, known as Burchard's *Decretum*.[27] This collection, which was probably composed in the second decade of the eleventh century, was extremely influential.[28] We know of seventy-seven manuscripts containing this work, while twenty-four fragments have been identified.[29] Fifty-five of these manuscripts were copied in the eleventh century, a number which, particularly given the size of the collection, is an astonishing figure. The other manuscripts are mainly from the twelfth century. Geographically Burchard's work seems to have been chiefly known in Germany and particularly Italy. No less than thirty-seven manuscripts have been identified as having been copied in Italy, while fourteen were written in Germany.[30] These figures should,

[26] Regino, *Libri duo*, I, 293–5, ed. Hartmann, pp. 152–4; see for an analysis Hamilton, *The Practice of Penance*, pp. 34–8, who stresses the importance of penance for episcopal authority.

[27] For a bibliography on Burchard's *Decretum*, see Kéry, *Canonical Collections of the Early Middle Ages*, pp. 149–55 and L. Fowler-Magerl, *Clavis canonum. Selected Canon Law Collections Before 1140. Access with Data Processing*, MGH Hilfsmittel 21 (Hanover 2005), p. 90.

[28] For the date of the collection, see Kéry, *Canonical Collections of the Early Middle Ages*, p. 133; G. Austin, *Shaping Church Law Around the Year 1000. The Decretum of Burchard of Worms* (Farnham 2009), p. 20, and H. Hoffmann and R. Pokorny, *Das Dekret des Bisschofs Burchard von Worms. Textstufen – Frühe Verbreitung – Vorlagen*, MGH Hilfsmittel 12 (Munich 1991), pp. 12–13. The demonstration that the two Vatican mss. (Vat. pal. lat. 585 and 586) were written in Worms under Burchard's supervision undermined the traditional earlier date (1008–12).

[29] Listed in Kéry, *Canonical Collections of the Early Middle Ages*, pp. 134–44; two mss. mentioned there – Paris, BN lat. 4283 and Troyes, Bibliothèque municipale, 1386 – originally formed one manuscript and are therefore counted as one; to the list of seventy-seven mss. found there, the ms. Nijmegen, Universiteitsbibliotheek Ms. 185 should be added; see G. Huisman, *Catalogus van de middeleeuwse handschriften in de Universiteitsbibliotheek Nijmegen* (Leuven 1997), pp. 77–82.

[30] I base my argument here upon the descriptions in Kéry, *Canonical Collections of the Early Middle Ages*. I only counted the manuscripts with a 'Schriftheimat', not those with a provenance from these regions. Since almost half of the mss. have no established palaeographical origin, there are surely even more mss. with an Italian origin.

of course, be handled with care, because of the number of manuscripts that are of unknown origin and because quite a few manuscripts have not survived, but it seems significant nevertheless that only one manuscript has been identified as being copied in France.[31] That Burchard's *Decretum* was not unknown in France, however, is clear from the fact that it is mentioned in a number of book lists and library catalogues from France.[32] It was also used by Ivo of Chartres (1040–115) when he composed his *Decretum* at the end of the eleventh century.[33] Other avid readers of Burchard include Anselm of Lucca, Bonizo of Sutri and Gratian.[34] Although Burchard's text was clearly known in France, overall the manuscript diffusion and its use by later authors strongly suggest that the main area of dissemination was Italy and Germany.

Burchard's collection of canon law, we may therefore conclude, was hugely successful, although more in the regions dominated by the Ottonian and Salian kings and emperors than in those where the Capetian kings tried to impose their rule. This success was surely partly because of the fact that Burchard and his team managed to assemble such a wealth of canonical material and to present this in a useful way. Burchard's *Decretum* is generally regarded as a canon law collection, and its use by famous compilers of canon law collections such as Ivo of Chartres and Gratian demonstrates that it was definitely used as such. This assessment contributed to a depreciation of the function of the *Decretum* in pastoral care.[35] It is difficult to imagine that this huge collection was available in parish churches for the use of local priests, and it has therefore been suggested that it was intended and used as a kind of reference work by the bishop and his entourage.[36] This would fit a more general pattern of change, suggesting that penitential manuscripts were written more for an episcopal and juridical audience than for a priestly and pastoral one.[37] Nevertheless, when reading this huge

---

R. Reynolds, 'Penitentials in south and central Italian canon law manuscripts of the tenth and eleventh centuries', *Early Medieval Europe* 14 (2006), pp. 65–84, at pp. 82–3 lists thirty-six Italian manuscripts containing Burchard.

[31] Ms. Orléans, Bibliothèque municipale, 229, see Kéry, *Canonical Collections of the Early Middle Ages*, p. 136. C. Rolker, *Canon Law and the Letters of Ivo of Chartres* (Cambridge 2010), pp. 68–9, reaches a somewhat more optimistic view of the number of Burchard's manuscripts in (northern) France by including manuscripts with a French provenance, although it is not always certain that these mss. were already in France by the eleventh or twelfth centuries. Nonetheless, he still agrees on the rather meagre distribution of Burchard mss. in France.

[32] Listed in Kéry, *Canonical Collections of the Early Middle Ages*, pp. 145–7.

[33] Rolker, *Canon Law and the Letters of Ivo of Chartres*, pp. 108–12.

[34] Hamilton, *The Practice of Penance*, pp. 27–8.

[35] Hamilton, *The Practice of Penance*, p. 44.   [36] Hamilton, *The Practice of Penance*, p. 44.

[37] Hamilton, *The Practice of Penance*, p. 48.

collection it becomes clear that penance formed its major theme. Book 19 of the collection, also known as the *Corrector sive Medicus*, is completely devoted to the theme of penance and includes one of the most detailed penitential handbooks that still survive. Burchard expressly stated that this book should teach any priest, even a less educated one (*simplicem*), how to correct and heal the spiritual wounds of his parishioners.[38] To enhance the practical value of his work, Burchard added tables of contents for each book and numbered rubrics to make it easier to consult.[39] The work therefore was intended for local priests as a 'guide for penances in the parish', although Burchard also hints at the use of his work in schools.[40] Moreover, we should not take it for granted that Burchard devoted a whole book to the subject of penance, as this does in fact require some explanation.[41] The nineteenth book is organized in the form of one long questionnaire. Burchard adopted this scheme from Regino but attached far greater importance to it. With the help of the canons that he had assembled in the other books, he enriched his list of questions to the penitent. In doing so, he adapted his canonistic material to a penitential setting and made his grand collection subservient to a penitential use.[42] The nineteenth book, therefore, should not be seen as a kind of appendix, as the sixth book of Halitgar's penitential had been, but rather as the culmination of the whole work.[43]

Burchard's *Corrector sive Medicus* was the result of an attempt to put the available knowledge of canon law at the disposal of a confessor, culminating in the lengthy list of questions that the confessor put to a penitent. To the material culled from existing ecclesiastical legislation Burchard added a lot of interesting new material, providing us with a rare view of

[38] The 1584 Cologne edition of the *Decretum*, based on the two Vatican mss. that have now been identified as being produced in Worms in Burchard's lifetime, provide the best text of this work. It was reproduced by Migne in PL 140, cols. 537–1065, and has now been reprinted: G. Fransen and T. Kölzer (eds.), *Burchard von Worms: Decretorum libri XX* (Aalen 1992). For the sake of convenience, I shall cite here the edition of Book 19 in Schmitz, *Die Bussbücher und das kanonische Bussverfahren*, pp. 393–467, here p. 407.

[39] Austin, *Shaping Church Law*, pp. 91–101; for the use of such devices to provide easier access to written texts, see M. Mostert, 'What happened to literacy in the Middle Ages? Scriptural evidence for the history of the western literate mentality', *Tijdschrift voor Geschiedenis* 108 (1995), pp. 323–5.

[40] G. Austin, 'Jurisprudence in the service of pastoral care. The *Decretum* of Burchard of Worms', *Speculum* 79 (2004), pp. 929–59, at p. 932; and Austin, *Shaping Church Law*, pp. 237–8.

[41] L. Körntgen, 'Canon law and the practice of penance: Burchard of Worms's penitential', *Early Medieval Europe* 14 (2006), pp. 103–17, at p. 106.

[42] Körntgen, 'Canon law and the practice of penance', pp. 110–12.

[43] For Halitgar's sixth book, see above p. 131.

medieval popular culture of his time.[44] In one of his questions, for example, Burchard asked: 'Have you done what some women are accustomed to do? When there is no rain when it is needed, they assemble a group of girls and they choose a little girl as their leader. They take off her clothes and take the naked girl to a place outside of the village where the herb henbane is to be found, which in the German language is called *belisa*. They make the naked girl dig up the herb with the little finger of her right hand and when it is dug up with root and all, they tie it to the little toe of her right foot. Holding twigs in their hands they then guide the little girl, dragging the herb behind her, to the nearest river and with the twigs sprinkle her with water. And so with these incantations they hope to bring forth rain. Thereafter they escort the naked maiden from the river back to the village, while she walks backward in the manner of a crab. If you have done this or consented to this, you should do penance for twenty days on bread and water.'[45] Here Burchard describes with almost ethnographic precision a ritual for which there is no other historical evidence. The details he mentions, such as the use of the little finger of the right hand or the backward-walking procession together with the allusion to the vernacular term for the herb in question, strongly suggest that Burchard is here describing an authentic ritual, of which he had some personal knowledge.[46] It is perfectly possible that the fact that Burchard as a bishop took great interest in the well-being of his *familia* in Worms, for which he issued special legislation, led to closer contact with the daily life of the laity than monastic authors of an earlier age had had.[47] Another factor leading to a more detailed knowledge of popular behaviour and beliefs is probably to be found in the practice of episcopal visitations. If Burchard travelled around his diocese and investigated erroneous beliefs and practices, he may have become well informed about these. Burchard's particular interest in episcopal visitations is clearly demonstrated by his detailed knowledge of Regino's work.

---

[44] Gurevich used Burchard's work as a major source in his *Medieval Popular Culture*, pp. 78–103.

[45] *P. Burchardi*, bk. 19, c. 194, ed. Schmitz, *Die Bussbücher und das kanonische Bussverfahren*, p. 452; for a slightly different translation, see J. T. McNeill and H. Gamer, *Medieval Handbooks of Penance. A Translation of the Principal 'Libri Poenitentiales' and Selections from Related Documents* (New York 1938, repr. 1990), p. 341.

[46] For criteria enabling historians to evaluate the authenticity of descriptions of specific religious rituals that were condemned by ecclesiastical authorities, see R. Künzel, 'Paganisme, syncrétisme et culture religieuse populaire au Haut Moyen Age', *Annales ESC* 47 (1992), pp. 1055–69; for background, see Blöcker, 'Wetterzauber: Zu einem Glaubenskomplex des frühen Mittelalters'.

[47] As argued by Körntgen, 'Canon law and the practice of penance', p. 110.

Like Regino, Burchard knew the practice of public penance. He adopts
Regino's script for the expulsion of penitents on Ash Wednesday, with
only a few minor alterations.[48] He distinguishes public penance from
doing penance in secret (*absconse*).[49] Exactly how priests had to distinguish between these forms is hard to fathom. Burchard adopts the
Carolingian paradigm that public sins had to be reconciled by public
penance.[50] Yet he cites a canon issued at the council of Mainz (852) that
those who had secretly committed the sin of incest, that is marrying
someone who was related to someone in such a degree that ecclesiastical
legislation had forbidden it, and secretly confessed this to a priest, should
be treated as if the sin had been public.[51] This canon nicely exemplifies
some of the problems involved in distinguishing between public and
secret sins. We see here a secret confession touching, however, on a very
public occasion, a wedding, while the fact that the wedded couple was
related probably was also to some degree public knowledge. Apparently
Burchard regarded this as a public sin, although it was confessed in
secret. If we look at the descriptions offered by Burchard, and by Regino,
of the ritual of public penance and its less public counterpart, then it is
obvious that we are not dealing with two totally different processes, but
rather with corresponding procedures set in different contexts. Both
procedures centre upon the beginning of Lent. It is at this moment that
people are expected to confess their sins before their priest or to submit
to the ritual of public penance before the bishop. It seems that for
penance in the parish there was also need for a ritual in which the
penitents were received, albeit a less elaborate one than before the
bishop. Parochial penitents seem to be less visible as sinners, yet they
seem to have been identifiable.

It is probable, therefore, that what was happening in the villages was
more or less an imitation of the grander ritual of the bishop at a local
level. This is exemplified by the story about Iso's parents included in the
monastic chronicle written by Ekkehard IV of St Gall around the middle
of the eleventh century. In this story Ekkehard relates how a lay couple
after forty days of abstinence from food and sex had intercourse on Holy

---

[48] *P. Burchardi*, bk. 19, c. 26, ed. Schmitz, *Die Bussbücher und das kanonische Bussverfahren*,
pp. 462–3; for a careful comparison with Regino's text, see Hamilton, *The Practice of
Penance*, pp. 34–8.

[49] *P. Burchardi*, bk. 19, c. 37, ed. Fransen and Kölzer, 206v; this part is omitted from
Schmitz's edition of book 19.

[50] *P. Burchardi*, bk. 19, c. 40, ed. Fransen and Kölzer, 206v.

[51] *P. Burchardi*, bk. 19, c. 36, ed. Fransen and Kölzer, 206v; Burchard drew this canon
from the council of Mainz (852), c. 10, ed. W. Hartmann, MGH Conc. 3 (Hanover
1984), pp. 247–8; footnote 61, stating that this canon was not adopted by Burchard,
should be corrected. Cf. Ubl, *Inzestverbot*, pp. 318–19.

Saturday, tempted by the devil. The Christian calendar forbade sex on such a holy day and the couple was well aware of this.[52] They immediately began to lament their sin with a loud voice and prostrated themselves in sackcloth and ashes – which they had just stopped wearing – barefoot and weeping before the local priest in front of the community. The priest accepted their repentance, forgave them and imposed as a penance, referred to here as *punitio* (punishment), that they remain in front of the church for a day and a night as 'excommunicated'. Eager to receive communion on Easter Day, the couple went to the priest of the neighbouring village, where they again made their sin known to the priest and the community, asking him that they would be admitted to communion the next day. He reproached them in harsh terms for such temerity. Nevertheless, he blessed them before sending them home. The next morning the couple stood in front of the church and followed at the rear end of the procession leading up to the church before Mass began. The priest led them into the church and brought them to a place at the far end of the church. During Mass the couple refrained from asking for communion, but when everyone had received communion the priest from the neighbouring village entered the church, led them to the altar and offered them the Eucharist. He ordered them to lay down their penitential garb and to dress in their best clothes and then blessed and kissed them before leaving in a hurry. When later that day the couple sent a servant with gifts to thank the priest, it turned out that he had not left the village.[53]

This story was meant to illustrate the holiness of Iso, a famous teacher of the St Gall monastery, but in doing so paints a small vignette of penitential liturgy in a village setting as a monastic chronicler imagined it around the middle of the eleventh century. It has been argued that this story is so far removed from the legal prescriptions regarding penance that it cannot be taken seriously as a historical source. The fact that the neat distinction between public and private penance is nowhere visible in this story would lead to the conclusion that the author had no real

---

[52] For the relation between the Christian calendar and sexual abstinence see Flandrin, *Un temps pour embrasser*; Payer, *Sex and the Penitentials* and Brundage, *Law, Sex, and Christian Society*.

[53] Ekkehard IV of St Gallen, *Casus Sancti Galli*, c. 30, ed. H. Haefele, AQ 10 (Darmstadt 1980), pp. 70–2; for a discussion of this case see M. de Jong, 'Pollution, penance and sanctity: Ekkehard's *Life* of Iso of St. Gall', in J. Hill and Mary Swan (eds.), *The Community, the Family and the Saint. Patterns of Power in Early Medieval Europe* (Turnhout 1998), pp. 145–58 and S. Hamilton, 'The unique favour of penance: the Church and the people c. 800 – c. 1100', in P. Linehan and J. Nelson (eds.), *The Medieval World* (London and New York 2001), pp. 229–45.

knowledge about penitential practice.[54] This is surely taking the normative evidence too seriously, or perhaps not seriously enough. As we have
seen, the distinction between public penance and less public forms is not
as neat as some would like to believe. Burchard and Regino seem to
envisage a kind of penitential liturgy taking place at the beginning of Lent
at a parochial level. Ekkehard's description would then more or less
accurately reflect such a penitential liturgy in which elements of public
penance were employed. Liturgical sources, in particular, suggest that in
practice a simple distinction between public and private penance was not
feasible, as the next paragraph will show.

Liturgies of penance

In the last chapter we saw that liturgical instructions as to how to deal
with penitents survive from the eighth century onwards. Sometimes these
were included in liturgical books, which could contain a penitential
handbook, as for example, in the *Old Gelasian Sacramentary*. In the
eighth and ninth centuries such *ordines* are often to be found as prefaces
to penitential books. Burchard also begins his nineteenth book with such
a liturgical *ordo*. His *ordo* is closely related to an important liturgical text:
the so-called *Pontificale Romano-Germanicum*, written in the neighbouring diocese of Mainz around the middle of the tenth century. This text
can be characterized as the earliest well-organized pontifical, a liturgical
book designed specifically to be employed by a bishop in order to fulfil
his liturgical duties.[55] It contains three penitential rites: the rite for a
formal entry into penance on Ash Wednesday, the rite for the reconciliation of penitents on Maundy Thursday and a rite for penance 'in the
normal way' (*more solito*).[56] These describe rather long and complex
rituals, containing prayers and psalms, acts of humiliation and scripts
for interrogating and educating penitents. There is quite a lot of overlap
between them. The first two clearly aim at some form of public penance,
while the third one, describing 'penance in the normal way', suggests a
more pastoral and personal setting. It is not always easy to reconstruct,

---

[54] F. Kerff, 'Libri paenitentiales und kirchliche Strafgerichtsbarkeit bis zum *Decretum Gratiani*. Ein Diskussionsvorschlag', *ZRG Kan. Abt.* 75 (1989), pp. 23–57, at p. 36.

[55] E. Palazzo, *Le Moyen Age. Des origines au XIIIe siècle*, Histoire des livres liturgiques (Paris 1993), pp. 210–15. N. K. Rasmussen, *Les pontificaux du haut Moyen Age. Genèse du livre de l'évêque. Texte mise au point par Marcel Haverals*, Spicilegium Sacrum Lovaniense, Études et documents 49 (Leuven 1998).

[56] *Roman Germanic Pontifical* cxix, 44–80, xcix, 224–51 and cxxxvi, ed. C. Vogel and R. Elze, *Le Pontifical Romano-Germanique du dixième siècle*, 3 vols., Studi e Testi 226, 227 and 269 (Vatican City 1963–72), vol. II, pp. 14–23, 59–67 and 234–45. The best discussion of these rites is in Hamilton, *The Practice of Penance*, pp. 107–28.

however, exactly how they were to be performed. It remains uncertain, for instance, where the rites should take place – in or outside of the church? – or how many penitents might have been involved. Moreover, although they occur in an episcopal book, the rites were not necessarily administered by the bishop, but could also be performed by a priest and in case of necessity even by a deacon. The rites for Ash Wednesday and Maundy Thursday are clearly more public in the sense that they devote more attention to gestures like prostration and genuflection, whereas the 'normal penance' seems to be more geared towards an individual confession. The latter also includes a questionnaire which is similar to the one found in Burchard's penitential, although much shorter. This little penitential book, incorporated in a liturgical text, deals with the sins that are familiar in the penitential tradition. They include acts which by their nature are public, such as killing someone in public or hitting someone in such a way as to lead to bloodshed or fractured bones.[57] Again, this suggests that the secret-public dichotomy was not that easy to maintain in practice.

The penitential rituals of the *Roman-Germanic Pontifical* seem to have been somewhat indefinite for medieval readers just as they are for modern ones, as we can tell from the variants found in the manuscript tradition of this text. The surviving manuscripts show a quite remarkable diversity in the formulation and organization of the penitential rites. Only a minority of the manuscripts, for example, contain all three penitential rites.[58] In some copies, apparently made for monastic communities, it is no longer the bishop who is presiding over the whole process, but the abbot.[59] In the past, liturgical specialists tended to pay no heed to such discrepancies because they were mainly interested in the original version of the work. Nowadays such diversity is more and more read as an indication of a rich and diverse liturgical practice. The penitential rites of the *Roman-Germanic Pontifical* have been regarded as the standard text for this period.[60] This assessment was partly based on the number of surviving manuscripts of this text, reaching the impressive total of some fifty manuscripts.[61] The attention paid to this text, however, was also

---

[57] *Roman Germanic Pontifical* cxxxvi, 13, ed. Vogel and Elze, pp. 237–8.
[58] Hamilton, *The Practice of Penance*, p. 135.
[59] Hamilton, *The Practice of Penance*, pp. 129–30, referring to mss. Bamberg, Staatsbibliothek, Cod. Lit. 55 and Wolfenbüttel, Herzog August Bibliothek, Cod. Guelf. 141 Helmstadt.
[60] C. Vogel, 'Les rites de la pénitence publique aux Xe et XIe siècle', in P. Gallais and Y.-J. Riou (eds.), *Mélanges René Crozet* (Poitiers 1966), vol. I, pp. 137–44.
[61] Vogel and Elze, *Le Pontifical Romano-Germanique*, vol III, p. 7. Hamilton, *The Practice of Penance*, p. 106, speaks of thirty-eight mss.

motivated by the fact that this pontifical lay at the basis of the later Roman Pontifical, turning it into a focus for liturgical studies with its strong emphasis on things Roman. The rapid diffusion of this text within the Ottonian realm has been explained by imperial patronage. The Ottonian emperors would have promoted this specific liturgical compos-ition as the Carolingians had promoted the *Gregorian Sacramentary*.[62] Yet the diffusion of the manuscripts suggests that even within the Otto-nian empire, the *Roman-Germanic Pontifical* was not accepted every-where. Its main areas of distribution (or production?) were the archbishoprics of Mainz and Salzburg, besides Italy in general. In the archdioceses of Cologne and Trier, however, very close to the Mainz region where the work originated, its influence can hardly be traced.[63]

In fact the penitential liturgy of the tenth and eleventh centuries is even richer than the textual tradition of the *Roman-Germanic Pontifical* sug-gests. In the monastery of Fulda, which had close links with the archiepiscopal see in Mainz, an *ordo* for private (secret?) or annual penance (*ordo privatae seu annualis poenitentiae*) was included in a sacramentary, which resembled in many ways the ritual for Ash Wednesday as it is encountered in the *Roman-Germanic Pontifical*. This rather public ceremony is here called private or annual penance possibly because of the absence of the bishop from the ritual. There are clearly elements pointing to the fact that we are dealing with lay people confess-ing their sins to the abbot or monk-priests from the monastery, as for example the well-known miniature illustrating the penitential ritual clearly shows. We see here a bishop (or abbot wearing pontificalia) in front of a group of laymen and laywomen, bowing their heads in front of the religious man. The lay people here are clearly distinguished from the monks assisting the bishop/abbot. This miniature, probably the earliest depiction of a penitential rite, is accompanying a confession formula in the vernacular, which also suggests that these texts were being used for lay confession.[64] There are many common elements in the Fulda peni-tential rites and the *Roman-Germanic Pontifical*, yet there does not seem to be a direct link between the two texts. The similarities should rather be explained by the elaboration of similar rituals on the basis of a common stock of available prayers and ritual gestures. The same can be concluded about another important family of penitential liturgy: the so-called

---

[62] Palazzo, *Le Moyen Age*, p. 213.   [63] Hamilton, *The Practice of Penance*, pp. 131–2.

[64] For a brief discussion of this miniature, see Hamilton, *The Practice of Penance*, pp. 148–9 and E. Palazzo, *Les sacramentaires de Fulda. Étude sur l'iconographie et la liturgie à l'époque ottonienne*, Liturgiewissenschaftliche Quellen und Forschungen 77 (Aschendorff, Münster 1994), p. 98.

Northern-French rite. It has recently been suggested that this penitential rite is not only of an earlier date than has generally been assumed, but that it was also developed independently from the *Roman-Germanic Pontifical* using the same set of sources.[65] It differs from the Mainz composition in its stress on episcopal authority. Whereas in the *Roman-Germanic Pontifical* the bishop prostrates himself and concedes his own sinfulness, in the Northern-French rite the bishop does not in this way humiliate himself in public. This sensitivity concerning the bishop's position might be related to the delicate position in which Lotharingian bishops found themselves in the later tenth and eleventh centuries. Lacking firm royal support, they were vulnerable on the local scene, but at the same time prime political actors. Their upright position in the ritual should emphasize their leading role in the community, while prostrating themselves might endanger their position.[66] Rituals of penance, therefore, were not only a means for sinners to be reconciled to the Christian community and to God, but also a means of self-representation for the clergy, in particular for the bishops presiding over the grand rituals of public penance. The varieties in ecclesiastical rituals can therefore be regarded as an indication of the differences in local status of individual bishops, although it remains difficult to relate particular liturgical texts and books to precise historical circumstances.

The evidence discussed so far has focussed on the Ottonian realm where Burchard wrote his imposing work and where the *Roman-Germanic Pontifical* was composed. Regino of Prüm wrote in the later days of the Carolingian rule in the same geographical region and his work is closely related to that of Burchard and the team in Mainz that worked on the pontifical. Their work reflects a lively interest in penitential matters in this Middle Rhine region and from there the texts radiated into southern Germany and Italy. This deep concern with penance may relate to the importance of penance in settling conflicts among the elite in Ottonian Germany, as will be discussed below. First we shall see how penitential books were being employed in England, Spain and Italy. As far as we know, no new texts of this kind were being composed in this period in the northern French regions. This might be a sign of a lack of interest in penance in this period. It is more plausible, however, that in this region which had seen so much productivity of penitential handbooks in the ninth century that the existing books of penance sufficed, making the composition of new texts unnecessary.

---

[65] Hamilton, *The Practice of Penance*, pp. 150–66.
[66] Hamilton, *The Practice of Penance*, pp. 162–6.

England

We have seen that in the seventh and eighth centuries at least some Irish penitentials were known in England and that Theodore of Canterbury taught penitential discipline in a way that was to influence Francia profoundly. From the ninth century, however, we have no evidence at all about penitential activity in England. We know no penitential text dating from this period coming from England, whereas in Francia many new texts were being put together. It is only from the tenth century that we have knowledge of the composition of new texts in England and it is remarkable that these new texts did not follow in the footsteps of the earlier English tradition, but looked for inspiration to Francia and particularly to works related to the Carolingian Reforms.[67] This is not only further evidence to suggest that in Francia in the tenth century churchmen still employed the Carolingian Reform books, but also that there was at best minimal continuity between the English tenth-century Church and the eighth-century one as far as the practice of penance was concerned. This sharp break has been explained by the Viking invasions that wrought havoc with ecclesiastical organization and monastic life.[68] How decisive the Viking invasions in England were is a matter of dispute, but in the field of penitential texts a great divide can certainly be established.[69] Allen Frantzen expressed this clearly when he wrote: 'In the tenth century, as in the eighth, penitentials and penance were new to the English.'[70] However, linguistic evidence demonstrates that we should not imagine a complete disappearance of penitential practice in the ninth century. In the late ninth century a well-developed technical vocabulary for penitential practice was in use, indicating that penitential practice had not been totally forgotten.[71]

The revival of the tenth-century English Church is closely related to the person and the court of King Alfred the Great († 899), who not only

---

[67] Frantzen, *Literature of Penance*, pp. 122–50.

[68] Frantzen, *Literature of Penance*, p. 126.

[69] For a more nuanced take on the influence of the Viking attacks on the English Church, see Blair, *The Church in Anglo-Saxon Society*, pp. 291–7, who observes however that particularly in the field of book production and manuscript copying, there is a sharp break between the period before and after 850; see also M. Lapidge, *The Anglo-Saxon Library* (Oxford 2006), pp. 44–5. For a reaction against too positive a view of the Viking invasions, see A. P. Smyth, 'The effect of the Scandinavian raiders on the English and Irish churches: a preliminary reassessment', in B. Smith, *Britain and Ireland 900–1300. Insular Reponses to Medieval European Change* (Cambridge 1999), pp. 1–38.

[70] Frantzen, *Literature of Penance*, p. 122.

[71] For the presence of a penitential terminology, see C. Cubitt, 'Bishops, priests and penance in late Anglo-Saxon England', *Early Medieval Europe* 14 (2006), pp. 41–63, at pp. 44–8.

organized the opposition against the Danes, but also initiated a reform programme for the English Church. His famous lament on the decline of Latin learning, in which he declared that very few men on either side of the Humber were able to understand the divine service in English or were able to translate from Latin into English, possibly presents too grim a picture of ecclesiastical culture in England at this time, but a survey of the manuscript tradition in the ninth century clearly supports such a bleak view.[72] Alfred must have known about penitential discipline, since he refers to it three times in the laws promulgated by him. Particularly in regard to the breaking of oaths and sureties, ecclesiastical penance formed in Alfred's view an important element in the punishment prescribed, surely because oaths were sworn in a highly charged religious context.[73]

Whether Alfred drew on existing English forms of penance here or was inspired by continental practice is hard to establish. We do know, however, that Alfred was in close contact with Fulk, the archbishop of Reims at that time. Fulk responded to Alfred's request for assistance by dispatching Grimbald, a priest from the northern French monastery of St Bertin, to England to instruct the English amongst other things in canonical matters.[74] We may presume that Grimbald was well versed in penitential matters and that he was one of the channels by which continental texts reached England. There are several indications that penitential texts travelled from the Continent to England, although it is not always easy to establish the precise date at which this happened. The earliest evidence we have of knowledge of the penitential of Halitgar consists of a few glosses in a manuscript written in St Augustine's Abbey in Canterbury in the second quarter of the tenth century, which translate a few technical terms from this work into Old English. The same scribe also had access to the penitential of Theodore of

[72] For Alfred's lament in the Preface to his translation of Gregory the Great's *Regula Pastoralis*, see *Alfred the Great. Asser's 'Life of King Alfred' and Other Contemporary Sources*, translated with an introduction and notes by Simon Keynes and Michael Lapidge (Harmondsworth 1983), p. 125; for the manuscript evidence see Lapidge, *The Anglo-Saxon Library*, p. 45.
[73] Alfred's Laws, 1, 2 and 1, 8, ed. F. Liebermann, *Die Gesetze der Angelsachsen I: Text und Überlieferung* (Halle 1903, repr. Aalen 1960), pp. 26–89, at pp. 48–9. Discussion in Frantzen, *Literature of Penance*, p. 125.
[74] Letter of Fulk to Alfred, ed. D. Whitelock, M. Brett and C. Brooke, *Councils and Synods with Other Documents Relating to the English Church* (Oxford 1981), vol. I, 1, pp. 6–12. See J. Nelson, '"... sicut olim gens Francorum ...": Fulk's letter to Alfred revisited', in J. Roberts, J. Nelson and M. Godden (eds.), *Alfred the Wise. Studies in Honour of Janet Bately on the Occasion of her Sixty-Fifth Birthday* (Cambridge 1997), pp. 135–44 and S. Vanderputten, 'Canterbury and Flanders in the late tenth century', *Anglo-Saxon England* 35 (2006), pp. 219–44.

Canterbury.[75] We also know of manuscripts written on the Continent and containing penitential handbooks that travelled to England in the tenth or early eleventh centuries. A manuscript written in the tenth century possibly in northern France, containing an intriguing well-organized collection of penitential canons, was in Exeter by the eleventh century at the latest, as is shown by an Old English gloss.[76] Another manuscript, containing a form of the penitential attributed to Bede and Egbert, the so-called *Paenitentiale additivum*, was written in the second half of the ninth century in Brittany, but was in England in the tenth century. In this case an Old English gloss forms again the tell-tale sign.[77]

There is also a group of manuscripts containing penitential handbooks which were written in England but copied from Frankish exemplars. A manuscript now in Oxford was written in southern England in the tenth century, possibly in the abbey of Christ Church in Canterbury, and contains the penitential attributed to Egbert, in combination with an early Carolingian episcopal statute (Gerbald I) and a penitential liturgical *ordo* with parallels in ninth-century Frankish sources.[78] These three texts are here combined in order to form a new text, which is attributed as a whole to Egbert, archbishop of York. The rest of the manuscript is formed by Books 2-4 of the *Quadripartitus*, a canonical handbook closely associated with the Carolingian Reforms.[79] The context in which the Egbert penitential occurs here suggests that it was derived from a Frankish exemplar.[80] Another manuscript, also written in tenth-century Canterbury, but this time in St Augustine's Abbey, contains two

---

[75] See the ingenious argument in P. Rusche, 'St Augustine's Abbey and the tradition of penance in early tenth-century England', *Anglia* 120 (2002), pp. 159–83.

[76] Ms. Oxford, Bodleian Library, Bodl. 311, see Frantzen, *Literature of Penance*, p. 130; for a thorough analysis of this manuscript, see Körntgen, *Studien zu den Quellen*, pp. 91–8. For the gloss, see N. Ker, *Catalogue of Manuscripts Containing Anglo-Saxon* (Oxford 1957), p. 360. See also H. Gneuss, *Handlist of Anglo-Saxon Manuscripts. A List of Manuscripts and Manuscript Fragments Written or Owned in England up to 1100*, Medieval and Renaissance Texts and Studies 241 (Tempe, Arizona 2001), nr. 565, p. 93.

[77] Ms. London, BL, Royal 5 E. XIII, see Frantzen, *Literature of Penance*, p. 130; the description of this manuscript in S. Ambrose, 'The codicology and palaeography of London, BL, Royal 5 E. XIII and its abridgment of the *Collectio Canonum Hibernensis*', *Codices Manuscripti* 54/55(2006), pp. 1–26, is not very helpful.

[78] For a detailed analysis of this penitential *ordo*, see Haggenmüller, *Die Überlieferung der Beda und Egbert zugeschriebenen Bußbücher*, pp. 167–70.

[79] For a careful description of this manuscript, Oxford, Bodleian Library, Bodl. 718, see Kerff, *Quadripartitus*, pp. 20–4. A Canterbury origin as opposed to the traditional attribution to Exeter has been argued in R. Gameson, 'The origin of the Exeter Book of Old English poetry', *Anglo-Saxon England* 25 (1995), pp. 135–85, at pp. 172–77.

[80] Frantzen, *Literature of Penance*, p. 131; the combination Egbert and Gerbald I is also found in the tenth-century English ms. Paris, BN lat. 943, the so-called *Sherborne Pontifical*.

penitential handbooks: Theodore's penitential and the so-called *Paeni-tentale Cantabrigiense*. The latter, formerly known as the *Paenitentiale Sangermanense*, is based exclusively on Frankish sources and might have been composed in Francia, although an English origin cannot be excluded.[81] Again the text shows how heavily English texts leaned on Frankish predecessors.

Wulfstan, the influential bishop occupying the (arch)episcopal sees of London, Worcester and York between the years 996 and 1023, is another case in point. His reliance on Carolingian models is becoming ever more apparent and a recent author characterized this aspect of his personality as 'Francophilia'. Wulfstan was not only an influential bishop but also the advisor of King Aethelred II and of his successor the Danish King Cnut in a period of great turmoil when the Anglo-Saxon nation was threatened once again by invaders coming from Scandinavia. He left an abundant literary record of sermons – among which is the famous *Sermo Lupi ad Anglos*, stressing the sinfulness of the English as a cause of the invasions from the north – treatises and secular laws, which has attracted a lot of attention in the twenty-first century.[82] His homiletical work is closely connected with his contributions to secular and canon law, which can be seen as a 'logical response to the position of Carolingian and sub-Carolingian bishops as God's servants and the king's too'.[83] Among his legacy, the so-called commonplace books are of eminent importance. Although most modern historians are not happy with this label, a group of closely related manuscripts has been identified in which Wulfstan or his associates assembled a variety of moral and legal precepts, which were employed by Wulfstan when preaching or formulating new laws: two activities which in his view were intimately connected. In these common-place books – or handbooks as they are sometimes called – penitential texts are of great importance, which does not come as a surprise since the topics of sin, penance and atonement are of such importance in Wulfstan's work. They have been compared to Regino's handbook and to Burchard's *Decretum*, and although Wulfstan's collection seems a more flexible text than those works, the stress on penance in all of them

---

[81] For the *P. Cantabrigiense*, see K. Delen, A. Gaastra, M. Saan and B. Schaap, 'The *Paenitentiale Cantabrigiense*. A witness of the Carolingian contribution to the tenth-century reforms in England', *Sacris Erudiri* 41 (2002), pp. 341–73.

[82] M. Townend (ed.), *Wulfstan, Archbishop of York. The Proceedings of the Second Alcuin Conference* (Turnhout 2004); for the use of the term 'Francophilia', see Matthew Townend's introduction, p. 4. and C. Jones, 'Wulfstan's liturgical interests', in Townend (ed.), *Wulfstan. Archbishop of York*, pp. 325–52, at p. 344.

[83] P. Wormald, 'Archbishop Wulfstan: eleventh-century state builder', in Townend (ed.), *Wulfstan, Archbishop of York*, pp. 9–27, at p. 21.

is surely remarkable.[84] Wulfstan's strong reliance on Carolingian sources is exemplified here, for example, by the inclusion of the ninth-century Carolingian penitential known as Pseudo-Theodore.[85] The fact that these handbooks include homilies, canon law material, secular law tracts, penitental canons and prayers should warn us not to examine these sources as neatly distinguished individual genres, but to be aware of the intricate ways in which these texts were closely related for a bishop like Wulfstan.

Apart from promoting Latin continental penitentials in England, Wulfstan contributed to a flourishing penitential culture in England in all sorts of ways. One of these was to promote penitential handbooks written no longer in Latin, but in the vernacular. In one of the copies of Wulfstan's commonplace book, now preserved in Cambridge, we find two penitentials written in the vernacular. From the tenth and eleventh centuries we know of four penitentials written in Old English. The preface attached to two of these is sometimes reckoned as an independent text, and named as the *Old English Introduction*.[86] These Old English texts rely heavily on continental Frankish sources. This may even be the case for the Old English translation of canons of Theodore of Canterbury. This translation is based on the *Capitula Dacheriana* and the *Discipulus Umbrensium* versions of Theodore's penitential, texts that we know only through continental manuscripts. The *scrift boc*, the language of which is mainly West Saxon, is probably the earliest of the full-grown Old English penitentials. Its main sources are Theodore's penitential, the penitentials attributed to Bede and Egbert and the *Excarpsus Cummeani*.[87] The '*Old English Penitential*', as the other vernacular penitential in Wulfstan's commonplace book is known, is more up to date as it relies mainly on Halitgar's reform penitential, but it also uses other sources, among them the *scrift boc*. In one manuscript, the fourth book of the 'Penitential' is abbreviated and replaced by the *scrift boc*.[88] The fourth

---

[84] For the comparison with Regino and Burchard, see P. Wormald, 'Archbishop Wulfstan and the holiness of society', in Wormald, *Legal Culture in the Early Medieval West. Law as Text, Image and Experience* (London / Rio Grande 1999), pp. 225–51, at pp. 239–40; see also P. Wormald, *The Making of English Law. King Alfred to the Twelfth Century*, vol. I: *Legislation and its Limits* (Oxford 1999), p. 218.

[85] J. Hill, 'Archbishop Wulfstan: Reformer?', in M. Townend, *Wulfstan, Archbishop of York*, pp. 309–24, at p. 315.

[86] See the instructive website www.anglo-saxon.net/penance/index.html.

[87] Frantzen, *Literature of Penance*, p. 137 (where his reference to 'the penitential of Cummean or pseudo-Cummean' is a bit misleading. The text is to be found in Cambridge, Corpus Christi College, Ms. 190 and in Oxford, Bodleian, Junius 121 and Laud Miscellaneous 482, see Frantzen, *Literature of Penance*, p. 133).

[88] Ms. Oxford, Bodleian, Junius 121, see Frantzen, *Literature of Penance*, p. 137.

vernacular penitential is known as the *Handbook*. It is based for a great part on the *Old English Penitential* and is the most concise of the three and more uniformly organized compared to the others. Of the vernacular texts this work was, according to Allen Frantzen, 'the easiest to consult'.[89] The *Handbook* is also closely related to Wulfstan and recently it has been suggested that it may have originated in close proximity to, or even been partly composed by the archbishop himself.[90]

The effort put into the translation of penitential texts from Latin into the vernacular is in the end a result of King Alfred's efforts to further ecclesiastical culture in England by a programme of translating important texts. Penance was also an important topic for preaching as the vernacular sermons in England demonstrate. In the rich sermon literature from this period, for example in the Blickling and Vercelli collections or in the homilies preached by Aelfric and Wulfstan, the theme of penance and confession appears in several ways. From these sermons penance emerges not solely as an instrument for church discipline, but also as a means for instruction. The same can be said of the rich variety of penitential prayers and instruction to be found in Old English and in Latin from this period.[91] Sermons also indicate that confessors were supposed to make use of penitential handbooks when hearing confession. The so-called Blickling homilist, named after the tenth-century collection of sermons known under this name, refers explicitly to the use of penitential handbooks when he discusses the ways in which a confessor should deal with penitents and Aelfric of Eynsham († *c.* 1025) listed the penitential among the books that a priest should possess in order to fulfil his pastoral duties.[92]

The linguistic, Latin and the vernacular evidence, therefore, indicates that penance was of great importance in late Anglo-Saxon England, yet the manuscript evidence does not really substantiate this view. The vernacular penitentials and a lot of instructive and devotional confessional texts are found in only a handful of manuscripts, many of them closely associated with Archbishop Wulfstan.[93] Another group of manuscripts is

---

[89] Frantzen, *Literature of Penance*, p. 140.
[90] M. Heyworth, 'The "Late Old English Handbook for the use of a Confessor": authorship and connections', *Notes and Queries* 54 (2007), pp. 218–22; cf. Cubitt, 'Bishops, priests and penance', p. 54.
[91] Frantzen, *Literature of Penance*, pp. 151–74.
[92] *Blickling Homilies* no. 4, ed. R. Morris, *The Blickling Homilies with a Translation and Index of Words together with the Blickling Glosses*, Early English Texts Society 58, 63, 73 (reprinted in one volume, London 1967), pp. 42–3; Aelfric's *First Old English Letter for Bishop Wulfsige, c.* 52, ed. Whitelock, Brett and Brooke, *Councils and Synods*, pp. 206–7.
[93] Cubitt, 'Bishops, priests and penance', pp. 59–60; see also Allen Frantzen's website, cited above, n. 86.

closely related to Canterbury, both St Augustine's Abbey and Christ Church, while there is also a link between penitential manuscripts and the episcopal see of Exeter.[94] This evidence suggests a rather narrow circle of clerics supporting a penitential system imported from Francia. Most of these clerics were closely connected to the bishops who played such a central role in the tenth-century reforms of the English Church. The role of bishops in this process would also explain the emphasis that we find in English texts on the function of public penance, an emphasis that can mainly be observed in liturgical manuscripts. The promotion of such rituals, particularly in circles around Wulfstan, should be connected to their views on episcopal authority.[95] For the question as to exactly when public penance was required and when a more informal penitential procedure would suffice, the English bishops relied on the solution invented by their ninth-century Carolingian colleagues: a notorious sin required public penance, a sin which had remained secret could be atoned for in an informal way.[96] It seems improbable that this solution worked neatly in England when it had been ambiguous in Francia. The liturgical evidence suggests that also in England the concept of public penance was neither clearly defined nor employed in a uniform way.[97]

Spain

In England reforming circles in the tenth and eleventh centuries clearly drew on Carolingian precedents in their efforts to attain a truly Christian society. In the reforming circles around Wulfstan penance was an important means that could be used to perfect society, and Carolingian handbooks of penance, particularly Halitgar's and the Pseudo-Theodorian penitential, contributed to the reform programme. Carolingian penitential texts also spread to other regions, although with some differences. Other texts were being used in Spain and Italy and the political circumstances in which penitential traditions were employed were different.

In Spain, as in England, there seems to have been a hiatus in the knowledge of penitential handbooks. Already in the sixth century, at the third council of Toledo (589), bishops criticized the custom of

[94] Cubitt, 'Bishops, priests and penance', pp. 59–61.
[95] S. Hamilton, 'Rites for public penance in Late Anglo-Saxon England', in H. Gittos and M. B. Bedingfield (eds.), *The Liturgy of the Late Anglo-Saxon Church*, Henry Bradshaw Society Subsidia 5 (London 2005), pp. 65–103; M. Bedingfield, 'Public penance in Anglo-Saxon England', *Anglo-Saxon England* 31 (2002), pp. 223–55; Jones, 'Wulfstan's liturgical interests', p. 350.
[96] Hamilton, 'Rites for public penance', pp. 65–6.
[97] Bedingfield, 'Public penance in Anglo-Saxon England', pp. 248–53.

frequent penance, which was not in line with the ancient practice of penance as a unique procedure to acquire absolution for sins.[98] It has been suggested that this canon was a reaction to the introduction of insular forms of penance introduced by British monks settling in northern Spain at that time. There is evidence that British monks settled in Spain, while further evidence suggests the existence of contacts between Spain and Ireland in this period. Yet insular monasticism had only a slight impact in Spain and the authority of the powerful Visigothic bishops was able to uphold the ancient customs of doing penance.[99] There is in Spain no trace of knowledge of penitential handbooks as they were composed in the insular world or in Francia until the middle of the ninth century, a fact which is, of course, related to the Muslim conquest of Spain.

The earliest known penitential handbook from the region of Spain is a short text known as the *Paenitentiale Vigilanum*, named after the scribe who wrote one of its manuscripts, or sometimes as the *P. Albeldense*, after the monastery where this Vigilanus was working, the monastery of St Martin in Albelda. It is preserved in two famous illuminated tenth-century manuscripts, both of them now kept at the Royal Library of the Escorial (see Figure 4).[100] These manuscripts are precisely dated to the years 994 and 976. The date of 976 is a firm *terminus ante quem* for the date of the composition of the text. A tenth-century origin of the *Vigilanum* is probable, although is is often dated earlier because of its uses of eighth- and early ninth-century penitential sources.[101] Its main source is the *Excarpsus Cummeani*, as we have seen, a text dating from the early years of the Carolingian Reforms. Furthermore the compiler made use of a Spanish canon law collection, the *Collectio Hispana*, while

---

[98] Third council of Toledo (589), c. 11, ed. J. Vives, *Concilios visigóticos e hispano-romanos* (Madrid / Barcelona 1963), p. 128.

[99] F. Bezler, *Les Pénitentiels Espagnols. Contribution à l'étude de la civilisation de l'Espagne chrétienne du haut Moyen Âge*, Spanische Forschungen der Görresgesellschaft, 2. Reihe, Bd. 30 (Münster 1994), pp. xxiv–xxv.

[100] Mss. El Escorial, Real Biblioteca de San Lorenzo, d.I.2 (Codex Vigilanus sive Albeldensis) and d.I.1 (Codex Aemilianensis); the Spanish penitentials discussed below were recently edited by F. Bezler (ed.), *Paenitentialia Hispaniae*, CC SL 156A (Turnhout 1998); for some corrections of Bezler's edition of the Spanish penitentials (mainly of a linguistic nature), see B. Löfstedt, 'Sprachliches zu den spanischen Bussbüchern', *Archivum Latinitatis Medii Aevi. Bulletin du Cange* 60 (2002), pp. 261–2; for a description of the two manuscripts, see Bezler, *Paenitentialia Hispaniae*, pp. xxxi–xxxviii.

[101] Bezler, *Paenitentialia Hispaniae*, p. xix: 'probablement de la deuxième moitié du IXe siècle'; Bezler, *Les Pénitentiels Espagnols*, p. 8: 'dans la première moitié du IXe siècle, vers la fin'; the traditional date 'vers 800', as mentioned by Vogel, *Les 'Libri Paenitentiales'*, p. 79, is clearly too early.

4. Ms. El Escorial, Real Biblioteca, Ms.d.I. 2 (Codex Vigilanus),
f. 428r: illustration containing representations of Visigothic kings and a
queen, with beneath them the scribe Vigilanus accompanied by a socius
and a disciple.

one canon derives from the monastic rule of Fructuosus of Braga. Contrary to many other penitentials, this text survives in two lavishly produced manuscripts, which are closely related. Both are not only richly illustrated, but also comprise an intriguing combination of texts.[102] They contain an array of ecclesiastical and secular legislation accompanied by related historical material and works of advice and exhortation, some of which seems to be meant for a royal audience.[103] These clearly are not manuscripts meant to be used in a pastoral context, as is further emphasized by the lack of any liturgical or catechetical introduction to the *Paenitentiale Vigilanum*. The manuscripts resemble in a way Wulfstan's collection of legal material, combining synodal decisions with papal decretals, penitential sentences and secular legislation, although the Spanish manuscripts show a more official, representative nature than Wulfstan's manuscripts. They have recently been characterized as belonging to a movement of 'ideological rearmament' under King Sancho III of Navarra.[104]

Another Spanish penitential, the *Paenitentiale Cordubense*, derives its name from the town of Cordoba where its sole manuscript witness is being preserved. The manuscript was written at the end of the tenth or in the first half of the eleventh century, probably in the region of Castile/León, and the text itself is probably of the same date as the manuscript.[105] It can hardly be a coincidence that this text uses the *Paenitentiale Remense* as its main source. This text is closely related to the *Excarpsus Cummeani*, the main source of the *Vigilanum* penitential. The use of two closely related sources indicates that the *Cordubense* and the *Vigilanum* penitentials are also intimately connected. Both, moreover, use the *Collectio Hispana* to enrich their main source. The *Cordubense*, however, contains much more material than the *Vigilanum*. It not only contains a greater number of penitential decisions, but it also includes a substantial preface to instruct the reader and provides liturgical directions. The text dates probably from the first half of the eleventh century. Two canons specify

---

[102] For their illustrations of ecclesiastical councils, see R. Reynolds, 'Rites and signs of conciliar decisions in the early Middle Ages', in *Segni e riti nella chiesa altomedievale occidentale*, Settimane di Studio 33 (Spoleto 1987), pp. 225–44.

[103] O. Eberhardt, *Via Regia. Der Fürstenspiegel Smaragds von St. Mihiel und seine literarische Gattung*, Münstersche Mittelalter-Schriften 28 (Munich 1977), pp. 96–7.

[104] A. J. Martin Duque, 'Sancho III el Mayor de Navarra, entre la leyenda y la historia', in *Ante el milenario del reinado de Sancho el Mayor. Un rey Navarro para España y Europa*, XXX Semana de Estudios Medievales, Estella (Pamplona 2004), pp. 19–42, at p. 34 speaks of a 'rearmo ideologico' of Sancho III the Great of Navara with help of these codices.

[105] Ms. Cordoba, Biblioteca del Cabildo, Cod. 1; see Bezler, *Paenitentialia Hispaniae*, p. xxx for the date of the ms. and p. xix for the date of the work.

the amount of money to be paid as alms. They refer to *sextarios gallicanes* which are equated with one *denarius*.[106] These monetary details make it possible to identify the place of origin of the *Paenitentiale Cordubense* as Galicia, in the northwestern part of the Iberian peninsula.[107]

Although the manuscript indicates that the Cordoba penitential was used in northern Christian Spain, there are indications that reveal that this text includes material that pertains specifically to a Mozarabic community. The last chapter consists of twenty-one canons. Some of these are derived from Spanish conciliar legislation, but others have no textual parallels. As a rule, the latter indicate the sinner as a 'christianus', something we normally only encounter in a context where Christians are living among a non-Christian population.[108] One canon censures a Christian for having two wives (*duas uxores*).[109] That this does not simply refer to cases of adultery or concubinage, but to a legally wedded wife, is not only clear from the usage of the word wife (*uxor*) here, but also from the following canon dealing with a married Christian keeping a concubine. The following canon assigns a death penalty to an adulterous woman, which is a sentence unheard of in penitential literature.[110] The fact that these peculiar canons censure polygamy, are particularly harsh on adulterous women and were written for Christians living among a non-Christian population indicates that they reflect attitudes in a community of Christians which ran the risk of going Muslim. The surrounding canons confirm this interpretation. They deal with entertaining sexual relations with Jews, non-Christians (probably Muslims, as glosses on the word *gentiles* show) or a Christian female slave, with participating in a non-Christian meal or with the case of a Christian who wanted to return to the Christian community after having abandoned the Christian religion. Handing over your children to heretics (read Muslims) or marrying your daughter out to them was also censured.[111] Interestingly, these canons sometimes simply assign a certain period of penance to the

[106] P. Cordubense, cc. 118–19, ed. Bezler, *Paenitentilia Hispaniae*, p. 62.
[107] Bezler, *Les Pénitentiels Espagnols*, pp. 33 and 95–9, for an analysis of the monetary situation; Bezler, *Paenitentialia Hispaniae*, p. xix: 'début du XIe siècle'. See also J. Andrade, 'Textos penitenciales y penitencia en el Noroeste de la peninsula Ibérica', in M. W. Herren, C. J. McDonough and R. Arthur (eds.), *Latin Culture in the Eleventh Century. Proceedings of the Third International Conference on Medieval Latin Studies. Cambridge, September 9–12–1998* (Turnhout 2002), pp. 29–38.
[108] As, for example, in the P. Oxoniense II, see Chapter 5.
[109] Canon 170, ed. Bezler, *Paenitentialia Hispaniae*, p. 68.
[110] Canon 171, ed. Bezler, *Paenitentialia Hispaniae*, p. 68.
[111] P. Cordubense, cc. 156–77, ed. Bezler, *Paenitentialia Hispaniae*, pp. 67–9; the Mozarabic character of this chapter has been identified by Bezler, *Les Pénitentiels Espagnols*, pp. 150–3.

sinner, but regularly impose public penance on them. This has been interpreted as the result of a recent introduction of the penitential tariffs from Frankish regions in a Spanish situation in which the ancient practice of public penance was still in use.[112] Most of the references to public penance, however, stem from the part which has been identified as deriving from a Mozarabic source. It is therefore perfectly possible that in those isolated Christian communities in Islamic Spain, Christians adhered to some form of public penance, but exactly how we should imagine such a ritual in a world where episcopal successions were often interrupted is hard to fathom.[113] The fact that these canons imposing public penance could be combined with canons from early Frankish penitential handbooks again suggests that in practice a strict distinction between public and secret forms of penance was not always recognized or upheld.

The third penitential handbook from the Iberian peninsula is named after the famous monastery of Santo Domingo at Silos, where one of the well-known Spanish illuminated Commentaries of Beatus of Liebana on the Apocalypse manuscripts was produced.[114] The sole manuscript of the *Silense* penitential was kept at this monastery during the Middle Ages until its library, stocked with mainly liturgical books, was dispersed in the nineteenth century and then was acquired by the British Library, where it is still being kept.[115] The manuscript contains a homiliary, to which the penitential was added, although it is unclear exactly when these two parts were combined into a single book. The penitential part has been dated to the second half of the eleventh century, a period for which there is no evidence for the existence of a scriptorium in the monastery of Silos.[116] It is written in Visigothic script, but the precise location of the place where it was produced has not yet been identified. In the second half of the eleventh century, Abbot Domingo commissioned books from the

---

[112] Bezler, *Les Pénitentiels Espagnols*, p. 136.

[113] For the interruption of episcopal succession in Spain, see T. Noble, 'The Christian church as an institution', in T. F. X. Noble and J. M. H. Smith (eds.), *The Cambridge History of Christianity*, vol. III: *Early Medieval Christianities c. 600–c. 1100* (Cambridge 2008), pp. 249–74, at pp. 253–4; for a general background, see R. Hitchcock, *Mozarabs in Medieval and Early Modern Spain. Identities and Influences* (Aldershot 2008): Hitchcock, however, does not discuss this penitential.

[114] The so-called Silos Beatus, ms. London, British Library, Add. 11695.

[115] Ms. London, British Library, Add 30853.

[116] For the date of the ms., see Bezler, *Paenitentialia Hispaniae*, p. xxxviii; for the scriptorium of Silos, see A. Boylan, 'The library at Santo Domingo de Silos and its catalogues (XIth–XVIIIth centuries)', *Revue Mabillon* 64 (1992), pp. 59–102, at p. 61; M. Diaz y Diaz, 'El escriptorio de Silos', *Revista de Musicologia* 15 (1992), pp. 389–401, is more optimistic about books being produced in Silos in this period and regards the London ms. as having been written in Silos (p. 396).

monastery of San Millán de la Cogolla to provide the necessary books for his monastery.[117] This Riojan monastery is also the location where one of the copies of the *Paenitentiale Vigilanum* was made, and it has been established that the compiler of the *Silense* penitential must have used one of manuscripts containing the *Vigilanum*.[118] The scriptorium where the *Silense* manuscript was written must therefore be identified as that of San Millán de la Cogolla.[119]

The close codicological affiliation affirms the thesis that the *Silense* penitential derives from the *Vigilanum*.[120] The former, however, is much richer than the latter. It adds not only a list of chapter headings and a catalogue of ways to atone for your sins that do not appear in its model, but also enriches the penitential canons with material taken from the *Collectio Hispana* as well as other penitential handbooks. The compiler seems to have had access to the main sources used in both the other Spanish penitentials: the *Excarpsus Cummeani* and the *P. Remense*.[121] The date of the penitential can be established by the list of commutations at the end. When the author lists the amount of money to be paid by a sinner who is not able to make amends for his sins by fasting, he arranges the amount to be paid according to social rank. At the top of this list the *imperator* is mentioned, a title used by the kings of León from the end of the tenth to the beginning of the twelfth centuries, but particularly important during the reign of Ferdinand I (1037–65).[122] This period fits with the numismatic peculiarities that are evident in the commutations as well. These presuppose the influx of Muslim money into the Christian kingdoms of northern Spain, which we can observe during Ferdinand I's reign when many taifas – the smaller political units into which the caliphate of Cordoba had dissolved – were forced to pay tribute to the kingdom of León. For these reasons, the penitential of Silos can be

---

[117] Boylan, 'The library at Santo Domingo', p. 61; for connections between these monasteries, see also R. Collins, 'Continuity and loss in medieval Spanish culture: the evidence of MS, Silos, Archivo Monástico 4', in R. Collins and A. Goodman (eds.), *Medieval Spain. Culture, Conflict, and Coexistence. Studies in Honour of Angus MacKay* (Basingstoke / New York 2002), pp. 1–22, at pp. 3–5.

[118] Bezler, *Les Pénitentiels Espagnols*, pp. 35–7.

[119] By other means the same conclusion has been reached by R. Wright, 'In what language are the glosses of San Millán and Silos?', in Wright, *A Sociophilological Study of Late Latin*, Utrecht Studies in Medieval Literacy 10 (Turnhout 2002), pp. 232–42 at p. 241, n. 23.

[120] Such a dependence has been argued by F. Bezler, *Paenitentialia Hispaniae*, p. xxix and F. Bezler, 'Chronologie relative des Pénitentiels d'Albelda et de Silos', *Sacris Erudiri* 23 (1991), pp. 163–9.

[121] Many of the other sources listed by Bezler, *Les Pénitentiels Espagnols*, p. 12, can in fact be found in these two works.

[122] Bezler, *Les Pénitentiels Espagnols*, p. 24.

dated to the first years of the second half of the eleventh century, years in which Ferdinand I convoked the council of Coyonza (1055) with which he sought to reform the Church in his kingdom. The care with which this text was composed has been related to the reforming efforts of Ferdinand I.[123] Another element demonstrating that this text was composed or at least read with care are its glosses. These glosses, which once were celebrated as attesting the 'birth of the Spanish language', but are now best regarded as reflecting a proto-Iberian language, or 'the oldest written appearance ... of something that is not Latin', were probably composed in San Millán and copied as such into the Silos manuscript from an earlier exemplar. The fact that these glosses were composed by the same glossator who wrote the related so-called San Millán glosses again supports the thesis that the *Silense* penitential originated at the nearby monastery of San Millán.[124]

The three Spanish penitentials discussed so far testify to a particular interest in penitential texts coming from north of the Alps into Spain in the tenth and eleventh centuries. They show that Carolingian texts such as the *Excarpsus Cummeani* or the *Remense* were known in northern Spain by that period, particularly in the kingdoms of Castile and León-Navarra. That the *Excarpsus Cummeani* was known in Catalonia in the eleventh century is evident from excerpts included in a manuscript that was copied there. The early eighth-century manuscript now in Copenhagen which was thought to be composed in Septimania is now regarded as having been written in northern French regions.[125] A tenth-century manuscript written in Visigothic script is said to contain a penitential attributed to Pope Gregory I, which possibly concerns the Pseudo-Gregory penitential, which was known in Spain since it was used for the creation of the *Silense* penitential.[126] Not all penitential texts in Spanish manuscripts have been analysed. The National Library in Madrid holds two more manuscripts written in Visigothic script dating

---

[123] Bezler, *Les Pénitentiels Espagnols*, pp. 99–107.

[124] See Wright, 'Glosses of San Millán and Silos', with ample references to the existing literature on these glosses; the citation is from Emilio Alarcos Llorach, referred by Wright on p. 234.

[125] Ms. New York, Library of the Hispanic Society of America, HC 380/819 (s. XI, Catalonia), see C. Faulhaber, *Medieval Manuscripts in the Library of the Hispanic Society of America* (New York 1983), p. 134 and R. Pokorny and M. Stratmann, *Capitula Episcoporum II*, MGH Cap. Ep. II (Hanover 1995), pp. 169–70; for the Copenhagen ms. see R. Meens, 'The oldest Manuscript witness of the *Collectio canonum Hibernensis*', *Peritia* 14 (2000), pp. 1–19.

[126] R. Reynolds, 'A Visigothic-script folio of a Carolingian collection of canon law', *Mediaeval Studies* 58 (1996), pp. 321–5, at p. 321. For the use of Pseudo-Gregory in the *Silense*, see Bezler, *Les Pénitentiels Espagnols*, pp. 11–12.

from the eleventh and early twelfth centuries, containing an unknown penitential and Burchard's *Decretum*.[127] Moreover, the Cistercian monastery of Alcobaça also contains penitential texts among its manuscript holdings.[128] Nonetheless, the three Spanish penitentials discussed above have attracted most scholarly attention. They seem closely related to one another and to the manuscripts produced in Spain, containing the *Excarpsus Cummeani* and the Pseudo-Gregory penitential. They bear a strong royal imprint and are best regarded as a reflection of a royally inspired movement of reform, rather than as witnesses to pastoral practice.[129] Yet the adaptations to Spanish circumstances, the inclusion of Spanish canonical and liturgical material as well as the intriguing inclusion of canons possibly stemming from Mozarabic communities, mark these texts as being of exceptional historical interest.

Italy

Whereas in England and Spain the textual and manuscript evidence suggests that penitential texts were newly introduced in the tenth and eleventh centuries, there was more continuity in the Italian peninsula. We may surmise that Columbanus introduced Irish texts and ways of doing penance in his foundation at Bobbio, while the appearance of the manuscript with the insular *Paenitentiale Ambrosianum* in Bobbio is probably also because of early Irish influence in this monastery.[130] The penitential handbook of Theodore of Canterbury was clearly known in Italy from the late eighth century onwards, particularly in the form of the *Canones Gregorii*. Frankish penitential material was also available in Italy, as an analysis of the *P. Merseburgense A* reveals. This later eighth- or early ninth-century penitential book was either composed in Italy on the basis of mainly Frankish sources or it was copied there in the first half of the ninth century from a Frankish original.[131] The definitely Italian *P. Vallicellianum I* reworked the *Merseburgense A* penitential, possibly in the northern Italian town of Vercelli.[132] Manuscript evidence further

---

[127] Madrid, Biblioteca Nacional, Mss. 10008 (s. XI) and Vitr. 5.5 (1105), for which see Reynolds, 'A Visigothic-script folio', p. 321. The latter ms. is, however, dated s. XIII in L. Kéry, *Canonical Collections of the Early Middle Ages*, p. 148.

[128] G. de Martel, 'Les textes pénitentiels du ms. Lisbonne 232', *Sacris Erudiri* 27 (1984), pp. 443–60.

[129] Bezler, *Les Pénitentiels Espagnols*, regards these texts too easily as witnesses to pastoral practice.

[130] For which see Chapter 3 above.

[131] Ms. Merseburg, Dombibliothek 103 (s. IX[1], northern Italy), for which see Hägele, *Das Paenitentiale Vallicellianum I*, pp. 34–6.

[132] See Chapter 5, pp. 136–7.

demonstrates the availability of a number of Frankish penitentials in northern Italy in the ninth century: the *P. Capitula Iudiciorum*, the penitentials attributed to Bede and Egbert and the reform penitential of Halitgar of Cambrai.[133] Northern Italy, therefore, seems to have conformed to Carolingian ecclesiastical developments, where penitential texts were quite a common feature in local churches. Rather of Verona, the troublesome tenth-century bishop of that northern Italian town, expected his priests to possess a penitential and assumed that they dealt with secret sins themselves, not according to their hearts but as it was written in their penitential. Penances for notorious sins, however, were for the bishop to decide.[134] This bishop of Verona, originally coming from the diocese of Liège, therefore accepted the Carolingian solution to public and secret forms of penance.

It has been suggested that the *P. Vallicellianum I* was composed in the north Italian town of Vercelli in the later ninth century or the first half of the tenth century. A manuscript containing this text and probably written in this town in the second half of the tenth century is still preserved in the chapter library there.[135] It was therefore possibly copied during the long episcopate of Atto of Vercelli (924 to *c.* 960), a bishop with a particular interest in canon law, who initiated a careful programme of reform in his diocese. In the episcopal capitulary that Atto wrote to buttress his reform progamme, however, he nowhere refers to penitential texts. When he speaks of 'leges penitentiae', he seems to have had sentences from canonical collections in mind such as the *Collectio Dionysiana aucta* or the *Collectio Anselmo dedicata*, two collections he employed when composing his capitulary.[136] Atto does not want to concede the treatment of sinners to local priests. These should enquire carefully into the sins of the flock committed to them, and should not eschew means such as interrogating the neighbours. They should inform the bishop in writing, who

---

[133] Italian mss. *P. Capitula Iudiciorum*: London, British Library, Add. 16413 (s. XI in., southern Italy); Paris, Bibliothèque Nationale de France, nouv. acq. lat. 281 (s. X/XI, northern Italy, south of France?); Vatican, Biblioteca Apostolica Vaticana, Vat. lat. 5751 (s. IX ex. or IX/X, Verona/Bobbio?); Vercelli, Biblioteca Capitolare, CCIII (32) (s. IX 4/4, possibly copied in northern Italy in a hand that is regarded as northern French, see above p. 112); for the Italian mss. of Halitgar's penitential and the penitentials attributed to Bede and Egbert, see Appendices 3 and 4.

[134] Rather of Verona, Letter 25, ed. F. Weigle, *Die Briefe des Bischofs Rather von Verona*, MGH, Briefe der deutschen Kaiserzeit I (Weimar 1949), pp. 133–7.

[135] Ms. Vercelli, Biblioteca Capitolare CXLIII (159), see Hägele, *Das Paenitentiale Vallicellianum*, pp. 29–30; for the possible origin of this penitential in Vercelli, see Hägele, *Das Paenitentiale Vallicellianum*, p. 98.

[136] See MGH Cap. Ep. 3, p. 251 and S. Wemple, 'The canonical resources of Atto of Vercelli (926–960)', *Traditio* 26 (1970), pp. 335–50; Hamilton, *The Practice of Penance*, p. 74 suggests that Atto refers to a penitential handbook here.

would then determine the appropriate penance for those penitents. Atto refers in this context to the entry of sinners on Ash Wednesday and their reconciliation on Maundy Thursday, and seems therefore to have thought of some kind of ecclesiastical ritual to accompany these moments. He nowhere mentions the Carolingian dichotomy of distinguishing secret from notorious sins and it is unclear, therefore, whether he was thinking solely of the latter when writing about how to deal with penitents. Atto refrains from using penitential handbooks and cites many prohibitions from early Christian councils dealing with the late antique forms of penance.[137] He therefore relies on the kind of authorities that the Carolingian Reformers promoted. The fact that the *Vallicellianum* penitential seeks to sanction traditional penitential clauses by looking for authoritative conciliar precedents suggests that this text may indeed have been produced in a similar context, in which the authority of proper canonical legislation was preferred over sentences adopted from penitential handbooks.[138] Atto's attitude therefore is clearly distinct from that of his fellow bishop Rather. Whereas Rather left room for priests hearing confession and assigning penances with the help of penitential books, Atto adopted a more strict policy, leaving less room for priests and penitential books and stressing the authority of the bishop and proper canon law. If the *Vallicellianum I* penitential really was composed in Vercelli during Atto's episcopacy, it was probably meant to assist the bishop rather than local priests in assigning penances. The fact that the Vercelli manuscript contains this work as Book 6 of Halitgar's reform penitential strengthens the reform context in which it was thought to function.[139]

Carolingian penitential material reached central and southern Italy through the channel of northern Italian texts and manuscripts.[140] The first reference by a pope to a penitential book comes from the letter Pope Nicholas I sent in 866 to the recently converted Bulgarians.[141] In this letter Nicholas refers to a penitential sentence (*iudicium poenitentiae*), which the bishops sent from Rome would carry with them. This book

---

[137] Atto of Vercelli, *Capitula Episcoporum*, cc. 90–3, ed. R. Pokorny, MGH Cap. Ep. 3, pp. 296–7. The comment in the MGH edition that the interrogation of neighbours demonstrates that this chapter deals with public penance for notorious deadly sins goes too far; see also Hamilton, *The Practice of Penance*, pp. 72–6.

[138] For the effort to provide penitential clauses with a proper canonical authority, see Chapter 5, pp. 136–7.

[139] Ms. Vercelli, Biblioteca Capitolare CXLIII (159), see the description in Hägele, *Das Paenitentiale Vallicellianum*, p. 29.

[140] A. Gaastra, 'Between liturgy and canon law. A study of books of confession and penance in eleventh- and twelfth-century Italy' (Dissertation, University of Utrecht, 2007), p. 10.

[141] Nicholas I, letter 99, ed. E. Perels, MGH Epp. VI (Berlin 1925), pp. 568–600, at p. 593.

should not fall into the hands of laymen. Apparently the Bulgarians knew about penitential books and had asked for such a text. Since they had received missionaries from Francia this is not surprising.[142] Nicholas's letter, however, suggests that the pope was also acquainted with penitential books, a fact which can be explained by his involvement with Frankish ecclesiastical politics, such as the debate over the divorce of the Frankish Emperor Lothar II, in which he was heavily implicated.[143] This problematic case engendered intense discussions within the Frankish Church, leading to the collection of canonical judgments concerning marriage and divorce, a topic that is generally addressed in penitential handbooks as well.[144] It is conceivable that Nicholas came to know penitential handbooks as a result of such activities. Although in the past historians have been trying to find earlier evidence for penitential books in Rome, there is no concrete evidence for their existence in those regions before the rule of Pope Nicholas I.[145]

The fact that Nicholas knew penitential books does not imply that these were used in Rome in a pastoral setting. Firm evidence for such a use dates only from the years around 1000, when the earliest manuscript evidence for the existence of a penitential handbook in Rome was produced, a manuscript containing the so-called *P. Vaticanum*.[146] This manuscript originated in the regions of Rome or Umbria and was probably written for a church in Rome where relics of St Eustratius were kept, possibly the Church of the Twelve Apostles or St Apollinare. Only later did it come into the possession of St Peter's.[147] The

[142] L. Heiser, *Die Responsa ad consulta Bulgarorum des Papstes Nikolaus (858–867)* (Trier 1979), p. 37.

[143] S. Airlie, 'Private bodies and the body politic in the divorce case of Lothar II', *Past and Present* 161 (1998), pp. 3–38 and K. Heidecker, *The Divorce of Lothar II. Christian Marriage and Political Power in the Carolingian World* (Ithaca 2010); in a letter in which he confirms the decisions of a council held in Mainz (861–3), Pope Nicholas refers to public forms of penance referring to late antique conciliar legislation; see Letter of Pope Nicholas, ed. W. Hartmann, MGH Concilia 4 (Hanover 1998), pp. 127–31.

[144] For an example of a collection of texts assembled in this context by Bishop Adventius of Metz, see N. Staubach, *Das Herrscherbild Karls des Kahlen* (Münster 1981), pp. 153–61.

[145] For the search for an elusive 'Roman penitential', see Meens, 'The historiography of early medieval penance', pp. 74–82.

[146] For this text, see L. Körntgen, 'Ein italienisches Bußbuch und seine fränkische Quellen. Das anonyme Paenitentiale der Handschrift Vatikan, Arch. S. Pietro H 58', in H. Mordek (ed.), *Aus Archiven und Bibliotheken. Festschrift für Raymund Kottje zum 65. Geburtstag* (Frankfurt a.M. / Bern / etc., 1992), pp. 189–205. It was named *P. Vaticanum* and analysed by Gaastra, 'Between liturgy and canon law', pp. 43–64, Reynolds named it after Körntgen, the *P. Körntgenianum*; see Reynolds, 'Penitentials in south and central Italian canon law manuscripts', p. 81.

[147] P. Salmon, 'Un "Libellus Officialis" du XIe siècle', *Revue Bénédictine* 87 (1977), pp. 257–88 opts for the Church of the Twelve Apostles; Kottje, *Die Bußbücher Halitgars*, pp. 65–9 for St Apollinare.

penitential it contains must be a bit older than its sole manuscript, dating probably to the tenth century.[148] It used a number of Frankish penitentials, mainly the *P. in duobus libris,* but also the penitential of Theodore of Canterbury (*Canones Gregorii*) and those attributed to Bede and Egbert. The Roman manuscript is clearly a liturgical book meant to be used by a priest. It has been characterized as the earliest *Rituale,* a book containing material to perform the necessary priestly duties.[149] Around the year 1000 therefore, when the Emperor Otto III visited Rome, Roman priests were familiar with penitential books and were using them in a pastoral setting.

This interest in penitential handbooks in Rome fits into a wider interest in such texts in middle and southern Italy, in the regions of Umbria, Spoleto and Benevento. In the period between the late tenth and the early twelfth centuries, four new penitential books were composed in this region. These are the *P. Casinense,* the *P. Vallicellianum E. 62,* the *P. Vallicellianum C. 6* and the *P. Lucense.* They were modelled upon texts such as the Carolingian *P. Capitula Iudiciorum,* with its neat division of sentences according to their origin, the *P. Vaticanum* and Burchard's penitential. They all survive only in a single manuscript and are somehow related to one another, as is clear from their use of the same set of sources. Moreover, all the texts can be linked to the influential collection of canon law material known as the *Collection in Five Books.* This collection was probably put together in Montecassino or a closely related monastery and demonstrates a remarkable interest in penitential matters.[150] The *Collection in Five Books* is in its turn closely related to another canonical collection from this region, again with a strong interest in penitential material, the *Collection in Nine Books.* The compilers of both collections were not slavishly copying their sources, but were constantly revising and editing them, forging new canons where necessary using parts of earlier regulations as building blocks. The penitential authors followed suit.[151]

The many links between these two Italian canonical collections suggest that they may have come into existence 'in a single canonistic

---

[148] Gaastra, 'Between liturgy and canon law', p. 61.

[149] S. Hamilton, 'The *Rituale*: the evolution of a new liturgical book', in R. Swanson (ed.), *The Church and the Book,* Studies in Church History 38 (Woodbridge 2004), pp. 74–86.

[150] R. Reynolds, 'Penitentials in south and central Italian canon law manuscripts', p. 72; for its influence on later Italian collections, see pp. 73–80 and R. Reynolds, 'The South-Italian canon law *Collection in Five Books* and its derivatives: new evidence on its origins, diffusion and use', *Mediaeval Studies* 52 (1990), pp. 278–95.

[151] As demonstrated for the *Collection in Nine Books* by A. Gaastra, 'Penance and the law: the penitential canons of the *Collection in Nine Books*', *Early Medieval Europe* 14 (2006), pp. 85–102.

"atelier"'.[152] The manuscripts come from places such as Montecassino, St Eutizio and Farfa and demonstrate that monasteries played an important part in the distribution of these texts. Such a pattern would fit the picture of a monastery such as Montecassino as an important ecclesiastical centre from where canonical material was distributed in many regions in southern Italy, material designed to direct the life of the laity as well as the clergy.[153] The many collections derived from the *Collection in Five Books* which have been identified testify to such a view. The size of the manuscripts containing the two collections and the order in which they present their material suggest that these were meant for the consultation or education of the clergy, while the manuscripts containing the related penitentials and the derivative collections strongly indicate a more practical pastoral use. These manuscripts are often smaller and present their material in combination with liturgical or canon law texts. Together this material suggests that the impressive manuscripts containing the *Collection in Five Books* and the *Collection in Nine Books* were kept in important monastic centres, where smaller more practical manuscripts were produced for everyday use in the smaller ecclesiastical centres, i.e. local monasteries and churches.[154] The rearrangement and reformulation of traditional penitential canons demonstrate that the compilers of these texts were working in a living and lively tradition.[155]

We have already observed in this chapter that Burchard's *Decretum* was widely disseminated in Italy, thus attesting the Italian interest in penance. Burchard's work was regularly combined with the *Collection in Five Books* because, as has been argued, of their mutual affinity and complementarity. Both texts emphasize the importance of penitence in ecclesiastical law and where Burchard drew on Frankish and insular texts which were not widely known in Italy, the *Collection in Five Books* added early Greek patristic material and a wide array of conciliar and other authoritative texts.[156] That in Italy a particular interest existed in canon law texts that were not very well known south of the Alps is also demonstrated by the many manuscripts from Italy containing the early eighth-century Irish collection of canon law material, the *Collectio Hibernensis*.[157] The Vatican manuscript of the *Collection in Five Books* included

---

[152] Gaastra, 'Between liturgy and canon law,' p. 210.

[153] H. Cowdrey, *The Age of Abbot Desiderius. Montecassino, the Papacy, and the Normans in the Eleventh and Early Twelfth Centuries* (Oxford 1983), pp. 43–4 and see F. Newton, *The Scriptorium and Library at Monte Cassino* (Cambridge 1999), p. 273, n. 126.

[154] Gaastra, 'Between liturgy and canon law', p. 209.

[155] As demonstrated by Gaastra, 'Between liturgy and canon law'.

[156] Reynolds, 'Penitentials in south and central canon law manuscripts', p. 76.

[157] R. Reynolds, 'The transmission of the *Hibernensis* in Italy: tenth to twelfth century', *Peritia* 14 (2000), pp. 20–50.

5. Ms. Vatican Library, Vat. lat. 1339, f. 12r, depiction of canonical authorities. In the middle is the Irish author Cummean.

St Patrick (under the name Paterius), Cummean and Theodore of Canterbury among the series of authorities with which an illuminator illustrated the canonical collection, portraits that reflect the interest in insular and penitential sources of this canonical collection (Figure 5).[158]

In the tenth and eleventh centuries, therefore, in the regions of Ottonian Germany, Italy, Spain and England we can observe a lively interest in penitential books. In these regions Frankish penitential books were being copied, adjusted and translated, whereas in the west-Frankish regions no new penitential books were being written. The choice of the specific Frankish penitentials used in these regions, however, varies remarkably. While in England Halitgar's penitential and the *P. Pseudo-Theodori* were best known, the Spanish penitentials based themselves almost exclusively on the eighth-century *Excarpsus Cummeani* and the

---

[158] For which see R. Gyug, 'The list of authorities in the illustrations of the Collection in Five Books (Ms. Vat. lat. 1339)', in K. Cushing and R. Gyug (eds.), *Ritual, Text and Law. Studies in Medieval Canon Law and Liturgy Presented to Roger E. Reynolds* (London 2004), pp. 241–54.

closely related *P. Remense*. In Italy the *P. Capitula Iudiciorum* was an influential source for later compilations. Although in earlier times penitentials were often used in close association with canonical collections, it is striking that in the period discussed in this chapter there is a particularly close relation between penitential books and canon law proper. Burchard of Worms assembled a mass of canonical material to be put at the service of the penitential process, in Wulfstan's commonplace books penitential sentences were included among secular and ecclesiastical legislation and the Spanish *P. Vigilanum* has survived in manuscripts with a mass of legal material. In Italy two important canonical collections, the *Collection in Five Books* and the *Collection in Nine Books* reveal a marked interest in penance, while many Italian penitentials of this period were composed with the help of these collections. Penitentials continue to appear in liturgical contexts, and the liturgy of penance is constantly being enriched in this period. This may suggest a more pastoral setting for penitential activities, but the greater visibility of the penitential process implied by elaborate liturgies can also point to a more 'public' use of penitential procedures. Regino's handbook for episcopal visitations is symptomatic of a more intrusive episcopate trying to discipline and educate local communities. Penance was clearly one of the ways available to a bishop for achieving this. This is also implied by Atto of Vercelli ordering his priests to enquire in local communities about sinning parishioners with the help of neighbours and to report about this in writing to the bishop, who should then take matters in hand. The central position of Wulfstan of York in England and the eminent importance of sin and atonement in his political programme also corroborate the impression of a close link between episcopal power on the one hand and the discipline of penance on the other. Yet penance does not seem to be solely an episcopal affair. In the monastery of Fulda a penitential rite for lay people was being developed, the monasteries of San Millán de la Cogolla and Silos were actively promoting penitential handbooks and the monasteries of Montecassino and Farfa played a comparable role in Italy. What catches the eye in all three cases – the dissemination of penitential texts from Francia to England, Spain and Italy – is, however, that the texts and manuscripts transmitting them that survive form a closely knit group centring around specific persons like Wulfstan in England, or specific ecclesiastical centres like Montecassino or San Millán de la Cogolla. We must probably assume that many of the simple and unadorned manuscripts used in local centres will have perished through the ages. Be that as it may, the fact that a small group of closely related texts and manuscripts survives does not seem to be a matter of chance or the result of better chances of survival in specific ecclesiastical centres.

It rather suggests that in England, Spain and Italy we are dealing with a conscious effort emanating from specific circles – ecclesiastical, but possibly also lay ones – to introduce Carolingian penitential texts, and, we may assume, Carolingian penitential practices.

Aristocrats and kings: *deditio* and penance

What exactly constituted the Carolingian penitential practices that the clerical elite wanted to emulate is harder to establish than the texts that they were using. Was it Carolingian-style episcopal authority, ecclesiastical power to influence lay behaviour, that churchmen tried to imitate? Or perhaps the demand from laymen for penance and the absolution of sins? Was penance an effective means to settle particular kinds of conflict? Or should we rather think of a combination of such factors? In Ottonian Germany disputes between aristocrats were often settled by the ritual of *deditio*, the formal submission of one party to another in cases of conflict.[159] It has been argued that this ritual borrowed many elements of its vocabulary from ecclesiastical penance.[160] It is clear that certain aspects of this ritual have a parallel in penitential liturgy. Very often the party submitting itself is wearing a hair shirt and walks barefoot. Tears are also often part of the required ritual vocabulary.[161] All these elements were also prominent in penitential rituals. Yet we may question the view of *deditio* as a purely secular ritual that merely uses ecclesiastical forms. In many cases ecclesiastical penance rather formed a central component of the whole process of conflict settlement. This can be illustrated by a famous case that has been used in the past to describe the ritual of *deditio*. The chronicler Thietmar, bishop of Merseburg from 1009 to 1018, describes how margrave Henry of Schweinfurt, after his support for the Polish king Boleslav Chrobry against Henry II during the dynastic troubles following Henry's succession to the throne in 1002, sought reconciliation with the Ottonian king.

---

[159] For the ritual of *deditio*, see the classic study by G. Althoff, 'Das Privileg der deditio. Formen gütlicher Konfliktbeendung in der mittelalterlichen Adelsgesellschaft', in Althoff, *Spielregeln der Politik im Mittelalter. Kommunikation in Frieden und Fehde* (Darmstadt 1997), pp. 99–125.

[160] Koziol, *Begging Pardon and Favor*, p. 187; Althoff, 'Das Privileg der deditio', p. 121; Althoff, *Die Macht der Rituale*, p. 69.

[161] G. Althoff, 'Empörung, Tränen, Zerknirschung. Emotionen in der öffentlichen Kommunikation des Mittelalters', in Althoff, *Spielregeln der Politik*, pp. 258–81; M. Becher, '*Cum lacrimis et gemitu*. Vom Weinen der Sieger und der Besiegten im frühen und hohen Mittelalter', in G. Althoff (ed.), *Formen und Funktionen öffentlicher Kommunikation im Mittelalter*, Vorträge und Forschungen. Konstanzer Arbeitskreis für Mittelalterliche Geschichte 51 (Stuttgart 2001), pp. 25–52.

The margrave expressed remorse over his actions and with the help of intercessors informed the king of his willingness to do penance. Among the intercessors were an important duke, Bernhard of Saxony, and an archbishop, Tagino of Magdeburg. When Henry met the king in person he came before him *more et habitu penitentis*, in a penitential mode and wearing penitential garb, and confessed his guilt in tears. On the orders of the king the archbishop then imprisoned the margrave in the castle of Giebichenstein, where he performed many good deeds, such as praying the psalter with 150 genuflections. When in 1004 on the feast of St Mary the king visited Prague, Bishop Gottschalk of Freising preached a sermon on the importance of mercy and at the end of the sermon reminded the king of margrave Henry of Schweinfurt, who was doing penance in a sincere way. He called on the king to be merciful, to release the prisoner and to accept him again as a royal servant.[162] In this case, which has been characterized as paradigmatic for the ritual of *deditio*, the ecclesiastical elements are so manifold and obvious that it is hard to speak of it as a purely secular ritual. That bishops and archbishops mediated in such highly politicized conflicts should not surprise us, but the language of penance used by Thietmar, the ritual vocabulary employed here (penitential dress and behaviour, the praying of psalms with genuflections as penitential satisfaction) and the importance of sacred time and place should caution us not to see this process of reconciliation between the king and his rebellious follower as a purely secular affair. Rather this case demonstrates nicely how ecclesiastical rituals of penance could be used in the complex process of settling conflicts among the higher echelons of the German aristocracy.[163] Whether such uses of penance were also exported to other regions is still unclear. In late Anglo-Saxon England a tendency to introduce demonstrative rituals from the Continent has been observed and penitential rituals may well be connected to these.[164]

Another area where Carolingian ideals can be seen to have influenced other regions is the field of royal penance. The Ottonian kings continued the Carolingian ideological traditions linking the moral behaviour of

---

[162] The episode is treated in two places: Thietmar of Merseburg, *Chronicle* VI, 2 and VI, 13, ed. W. Trillmich, *Thietmar von Merseburg, Chronik*, Ausgewählte Quellen zur deutschen Geschichte des Mittelalters 9 (Darmstadt 1985), pp. 244 and 256–8; the case is discussed in G. Althoff, 'Königsherrschaft und Konfliktführung im 10. und 11. Jahrhundert', in Althoff, *Spielregeln der Politik*, pp. 21–56, at pp. 24–31.

[163] R. Meens, 'Kirchliche Buße und Konfliktbewältigung. Thietmar von Merseburg näher betrachtet', *Frühmittelalterliche Studien* 41 (2007), pp. 317–30.

[164] J. Barrow, 'Demonstrative behaviour and political communication in later Anglo-Saxon England', *Anglo-Saxon England* 36 (2007), pp. 127–50.

kings to the well-being of the kingdom. Thietmar of Merseburg adds some details to the story of the victorious battle of Otto the Great over Hungarian forces at the Lech in 955, which stress the religious attitude of the victorious ruler. Before joining battle, the king prostrated himself, confessed that he was a sinful creature, promised to found a new bishopric at Merseburg – something that Thietmar as bishop of Merseburg of course wanted to remember – celebrated Mass and received communion from the hand of his confessor, the saintly bishop Ulrich of Augsburg. Then armed with his shield and the Holy Lance, the major royal relic, he went into battle.[165] According to Thietmar, therefore, confession by the king was one of the proper ways to prepare for battle. Thietmar also relates how Otto's successor, Otto II, confessed his sins in Latin before the pope, the bishops and priests present, before he passed away in Rome on 7 December 983.[166] For Thietmar a good death was important and this included confession and forgiveness of sins. In the case of Otto III, he even went so far as to describe a kind of posthumous public penance. When the emperor had died in Italy, his body was transferred to Cologne where during Holy Week it was solemnly carried through the most important churches to arrive at the cathedral on Maundy Thursday, where at that moment, Thietmar tells us, the penitents were let into the church to receive absolution. The dead body of Otto somehow participated in the ritual whereby sinners were absolved, because Archbishop Heribert of Cologne also gave Otto's soul absolution for his sins. Thereafter the royal body was brought to Aachen where on Easter Sunday it was buried in the Church of St Mary, that is in the famous church where Charlemagne was buried.[167]

The best-known case of royal penance is of course the submission of Henry IV in Canossa in January 1077. When Pope Gregory VII had excommunicated him, the king found himself in a difficult situation. The German princes were no longer obliged to keep their oath of fealty to the king and threatened to depose Henry and to choose a new king. The decision over a deposition would take place at Augsburg and the pope was already on his way to southern Germany when Henry travelled over the Mount Cenis pass to Italy, where the Lombard bishops provided him with a warm welcome. Gregory felt threatened and did not wish to leave Italy, particularly since the German princes had failed

---

[165] Thietmar of Merseburg, *Chronicle*, II, 10, ed. Trillmich, p. 44; see Bachrach, *Religion and the Conduct of War*, p. 80, although I do not think that the texts warrant the conclusion that Otto confessed his sins directly to God.

[166] Thietmar, *Chronicle* III, 25, ed. Trillmich, p. 112.

[167] Thietmar, *Chronicle* IV, 53, ed. Trillmich, p. 168; see Meens, 'Kirchliche Buße und Konfliktbewältigung', pp. 324–5.

to provide an escort to accompany him to Augsburg, as Gregory explained.[168] The pope went to Canossa where Countess Matilda of Tuscany welcomed him. What precisely happened in these eventful days in which the king and the pope finally came to an agreement is extremely difficult to establish since the sources informing us about this crucial event were all written to support one or the other party and their view cannot therefore be accepted without any reservation.[169] What is clear is that Gregory accepted Henry again as a full member of the Christian community after the king had stood barefoot for three days before the doors of the castle stripped of all his *regalia* and wearing only a hair shirt. Gregory wrote later that the king had in tears beseeched the pope to come to his assistance and solace.[170] Such elements as these formed part of penitential ritual, but were also used in *deditiones*, rituals of submission. The episode at Canossa has traditionally been regarded as an example of public penance, but lately it has been interpreted in terms of a secular *deditio*.[171] As may be clear by the discussion of the ritual of *deditio* above, such a distinction between a purely religious and a purely secular ritual does not seem to be very useful.[172]

Such an observation, however, does not solve the problem of what actually happened at Canossa. Henry had been excommunicated

---

[168] Letter of Gregory included in his *Register*, IV, 12, ed. E. Caspar, *Das Register Gregors VII*, MGH Epistolae selectae 2.1 (Berlin 1920), p. 312.

[169] The literature on Canossa is vast, see e.g. I. S. Robinson, *Henry IV of Germany 1056–1106* (Cambridge 1999), pp. 161–4; G. Althoff, *Heinrich IV* (Darmstadt 2006), pp. 150–60; S. Weinfurter, *Canossa. Der Entzauberung der Welt* (Munich 2006); T. Reuter, 'Contextualising Canossa: excommunication, penance, surrender, reconciliation', in T. Reuter, *Medieval Polities and Modern Mentalities* (Cambridge 2006), pp. 147–66; J. Fried, 'Der Pakt von Canossa. Schritte zur Wirklichkeit durch Erinnerungsanalyse', in W. Hartmann and K. Herbers (eds.), *Die Faszination der Papstgeschichte. Neue Zugänge zum frühen und hohen Mittelalter* (Cologne / Weimar/ Vienna 2008), pp. 133–97.

[170] Gregory, Register, IV, 12, ed. Caspar, p. 313; translation in E. Emerton (tr.), *The Correspondence of Pope Gregory VII. Selected Letters from the Registrum* (New York 1932), pp. 111–12. For a more recent translation see H. E. J. Cowdrey (tr.), *The Register of Pope Gregory VII, 1073–1085. An English Translation* (Oxford 2002).

[171] T. Reuter, 'Peace-breaking, feud, rebellion, resistance', p. 384: 'Henry's own submission at Canossa was, in fact, less a remodelled public penance, of the kind practised already in the Carolingian period and again by Henry III, than a *deditio*. Henry stood before the gates of Canossa as a rebel brought low' (originally appeared as 'Unruhestiftung, Fehde, Rebellion, Widerstand: Gewalt und Frieden in der Politik der Salierzeit', in S. Weinfurter in collaboration with Hubertus Seibert (eds.), *Die Salier und das Reich*, vol. III: *Gesellschaftlicher und ideengeschichtlicher Wandel im Reich der Salier* (Sigmaringen 1991), pp. 297–325); see the reaction by W. Goez, 'Canossa als deditio?', in M. Thumser (ed.), *Studien zur Geschichte des Mittelalters. Jürgen Petersohn zum 65. Geburtstag* (Stuttgart 2000), pp. 92–9 and Althoff, *Die Macht der Rituale*, pp. 117–18.

[172] Well observed by Weinfurter, *Canossa*, p. 21; in a similar vein Althoff, *Heinrich IV*, p. 156.

and this was the main reason for his problems in Germany, since excommunication entailed that his followers should avoid any contact with the king and were thus obliged to break any existing bonds, including the oaths of fidelity. This meant that Henry's followers had every right – or even the obligation – to revolt and to choose a new king, an event for which preparations had been made at the meeting of Tribur in the preceding year. Such a form of excommunication was generally used as a final resort to put pressure on sinners to make them repent and do penance for their misdeeds. It is clear that Henry's excommunication was lifted by Gregory in Canossa.[173] The question is, however, whether Henry also did penance and was thereby completely absolved of his sins. This is suggested by Gregory's letter asserting that Henry did penance and received absolution.[174] The idea that Henry was formally absolved is strengthened by the fact that Gregory provided Henry access to communion. Gregory conceded that he had given the king the Eucharist and Lampert of Hersfeld depicted this episode as an ordeal rather than as a fitting conclusion to a ritual of reconciliation. Lampert's depiction might be a ploy to challenge its interpretation as a final end to a procedure of reconciliation.[175] Instead of lifting Henry's excommunicaton in order to admit him to a form of penance and postponing absolution to a moment when the sinner had completed the appropriate penance, Gregory seems to have taken recourse to a 'one-stop procedure', in which the three steps were integrated into a single ritual, culminating in the formal taking of communion by the reconciled penitent. Such a procedure was not uncommon in Italy in the eleventh century, but the particular circumstances in this case resulted in an unfamiliar place for the ritual to take place.[176] Henry was standing in penitential garb not in front of the church doors, but in front of the entry to a castle, while the concluding Mass was probably celebrated in the tiny chapel located in the southeastern part of the fortress.[177] Again this shows the flexibility of the instrument of penitence. Such a flexibility contributed to the many

---

[173] Gregory, *Registrum*, IV, 12, ed. Caspar, MGH Epp. Sel. 2.1, p. 313: 'tandem eum [scil. Henry] relaxato anathematis vinculo in communionis gratiam et sinum sanctae matris ecclesiae recepimus'.

[174] Translation Emerton, *Correspondence*, p. 111; translating 'rex humiliatus ad paenitentiam absolutionis veniam impetraverit'.

[175] Gregory, *Registrum*, VII, 14a, ed. Caspar, MGH Epp. Sel. 2.2, p. 48; Lampert of Hersfeld, *Annales*, s.a. 1077, ed. O. Holder-Egger, AQ 13 (4th edn Darmstadt 2011), pp. 410–12; cf. Althoff, *Heinrich IV*, p. 159.

[176] Gaastra, 'Between liturgy and canon law', p. 148; Hamilton, *The Practice of Penance*, pp. 166–7.

[177] Weinfurter, *Canossa*, p. 16.

different ways in which the ritual could then be interpreted, used and manipulated by the different parties involved.

Not only Ottonian kings were submitting themselves to penitential rituals. Khan Boris of the Bulgarians, the first Bulgarian khan to convert to Christianity in the second half of the ninth century, went dressed in royal attire during the day, so Regino of Prüm informs us, but at night he went into church dressed in penitential garb to prostrate himself there.[178] Clearly there is no way of checking the historical validity of Regino's description, but it shows how this late Carolingian chronicler imagined exemplary royal conduct, where kings did penance during the night and played their royal part during the day. Ferdinand I of León ended his days in December 1065 in penance, at least that is the way the *Historia Silense* chose to present the final days of the king, describing the penitential end of the king's life as a grand finale of this early twelfth-century chronicle. Here the king subjected himself to a ritual of public penance in the basilica of Isidore of Seville in León, in imitation of this sixth-century bishop, whose relics he had translated from Seville to León.[179] Hugh abbot of Cluny invited King Philip I of France at the end of his life to enter the monastery of Cluny, which he referred to as an asylum for penitents, in order to atone for his sins.[180]

But while some kings received praise for their penitential efforts, others were criticized for their insincerity. Thietmar of Merseburg, for example, who stressed the willingness of Ottonian kings to do penance, wrote differently about the penitential attitude of the Polish king Boleslav Chrobry, in his eyes the arch-enemy of Henry II. When Boleslav knew he had sinned a lot or when he had been castigated about his sins by someone else, he ordered that the canons of the Church were brought in in order to establish how to make amends. He then ordered that his sins should be remedied according to the book, but, Thietmar stresses, his tendency to sin proved stronger than his endurance in salutary

---

[178] Regino of Prüm, *Chronicle*, ed. R. Rau, *Quellen zur karolingischen Reichsgeschichte* III. AQ 7 (4th edn Darmstadt 2002), s.a. 868, p. 222; English translation by S. MacLean, *History and Politics in Late Carolingian and Ottonian Europe. The Chronicle of Regino of Prüm and Adalbert of Magdeburg* (Manchester / New York 2009), pp. 157–8.

[179] J. Pérez de Urbel and A. González Ruiz-Zorilla (eds.), *Historia Silense* (Madrid 1959), pp. 208–9; for discussion see C. J. Bishko, 'The liturgical context of Ferdinand I's last days', *Hispania Sacra. Revista de Historia Eclesiástica* 17 (1964), pp. 47–59 (reprinted in: C. J. Bishko, *Spanish and Portuguese Monastic History 600–1300*, Variorum Reprints (London 1984), no. VII).

[180] Hugh, *Epistola* VIII, PL 159, 930–2; see H. Cowdrey, *The Cluniacs and the Gregorian Reform* (Oxford 1970), p. 128 and S. Hamilton, 'Penance in the age of the Gregorian Reform', in K. Cooper and J. Gregory (eds.), *Retribution, Repentance, and Reconciliation*, Studies in Church History 40 (Woodbridge 2004), pp. 47–73, at p. 54.

penance.[181] Thietmar's criticism of Boleslav's attitude touches upon two points. First of all the Polish king did not endure in his penance. This is a bit strange as Thietmar confessed elsewhere that he himself was guilty of the same fault.[182] The other point is perhaps more serious as it touches upon the king's lack of sincerity. Thietmar criticizes Boleslav's 'calculated piety' (*gezählte Frömmigkeit*), or 'bookkeeping for the beyond' (*la comptabilité de l'au-delà*) as Jacques Chiffoleau formulated it. With the help of penitential tariffs the king established the right amount of penance to make amends, without true feelings of remorse.[183]

That insincerity was regarded as an obstacle for true confession and absolution particularly by the mighty and powerful is illustrated by a prayer written possibly by Rather of Verona for the occasion of a powerful man seeking penance.[184] The rubric makes a distinction between a situation in which the powerful man wants to do heartfelt penance (*corde*) or only as a pretext (*pretextu*) and the prayer itself distinguishes between what the sinner pretends to do in the body as contrasted to what he does in his heart. The penance is intended to take place at the beginning of Lent and to be concluded at Easter when the body and blood of Christ are to be eaten by worthy lips and with a pure heart. The Eucharist is intended here as a kind of ordeal since the prayer threatens that whoever takes the Eucharist unworthily will be judged and damned. This prayer, therefore, demonstrates that contrary to the view of some historians, ideas of true penance were of importance in the tenth century. Thietmar's description of Boleslav Chrobry's insincere penance suggests the same. In the years after Canossa Gregory VII expressed concerns about the sincerity of penitents which could lead to 'false penances' in cases where outward penance was not accompanied by inner conversion. Partly Gregory's views were influenced by his continuing struggle with Henry IV, leading to the latter's renewed excommunication and deposition at the Lent council held in Rome in 1080. But it was not solely because of this affair that Gregory was concerned about the sincerity of

---

[181] Thietmar, *Chronicle*, VI, 92, ed. Trillmich, p. 340.

[182] Thietmar, *Chronicle*, VI, 45–6, ed. Trillmich, pp. 292–4.

[183] For the concept of calculated piety, see J. Chiffoleau, *La comptabilité de l'au-delà: Les hommes, la mort et la religion dans la région d'Avignon à la fin du moyen âge* (Rome 1980) and A. Angenendt, T. Braucks and R. Busch, 'Gezählte Frömmigkeit', *Frühmittelalterliche Studien* 29 (1995), pp. 1–71. See also A. Angenendt, *Grundformen der Frömmigkeit im Mittelalter* (Munich 2004), pp. 98–9.

[184] According to the editor of this prayer it was composed by Rather since it was written in his hand, see Weigle (ed.), *Die Briefe des Bischofs Rather von Verona*, pp. 189–92. It is to be found in a manuscript from the tenth century which was once owned by Rather, Leiden, Universiteitsbibliotheek, Vossius lat. f. 48.

atonement. The concerns of Gregory VII over the sincerity of Henry IV's contrition, therefore, is not something entirely novel.[185]

At the end of the eleventh century, in the year 1095, Pope Urban II preached in Clermont and summoned Christian believers to march to the Holy Land. This campaign resulted in something spectacularly new: the First Crusade, which arrived in Jerusalem four years later and succeeded in conquering huge chunks of the Near Eastern Muslim world. This movement was conceived as a holy war. As a consequence, killing the unbelieving enemy was regarded as an act of salvation. The reforming papacies of Leo IX, Gregory VII and Urban II had increasingly been combining penance and violence, thus offering salvation for whoever fought in their cause. The crusade was the culmination of such attitudes towards violence and can therefore be seen as 'a penitential holy war'.[186] The participants of the First Crusade probably did not perceive the novelty of the movement and interpreted it in traditional terms of penance and pilgrimage. The charters made up on behalf of departing crusaders reveal that penance was a powerful motivation for their undertaking, indicating real concerns about the fate of the souls of those who went on crusade, and that of their relatives.[187]

During their hazardous journey to Jerusalem sin and its atonement remained central motives in the crusader armies. The sources not only report that individual crusaders confessed their sins before going into battle, but also describe communal penitential rituals staged by the crusading army. The papal legate leading the campaign, Bishop Adhémar of Le Puy, organized penitential fasting and processions before the wall of Antioch when the crusaders were in dire straits because they were threatened by Muslim forces. Their concern for purity was not only expressed by confessing their sins, but also by sending away women from the camp.[188] In order to secure divine assistance before storming the walls of Jerusalem the army, moreover, prepared itself by a three days'

---

[185] S. Hamilton, 'Penance in the Gregorian Reform', arguing against H. Cowdrey, 'The spirituality of Gregory VII', in J. Hogg (ed.), *The Mystical Tradition and the Carthusians* (Salzburg 1995), vol. I, pp. 1–22 (reprinted in H. Cowdrey, *Popes and Church Reform in the Eleventh Century* (Aldershot 2000)).

[186] C. Tyerman, *God's War. A New History of the Crusades* (Cambridge MA, 2006), p. 72.

[187] G. Constable, 'Medieval charters as sources for the history of the crusades', in P. Edbury (ed.), *Crusade and Settlement. Papers read at the First Conference of the Society for the Study of the Crusades and the Latin East Presented to R. C. Smail* (Cardiff 1985), pp. 73–89; M. Bull, *Knightly Piety and the Lay Response to the First Crusade. The Limousin and Gascony, c. 970–c. 1130* (Oxford 1993), pp. 157–91.

[188] Tyerman, *God's War*, p. 138; Bachrach, *Religion and the Conduct of War*, pp. 113–14; and J. Brundage, 'Prostitution, miscegenation and sexual purity in the First Crusade', in P. Edbury (ed.), *Crusade and Settlement* (Cardiff 1985), pp. 57–65.

fast before going round the town in a procession.[189] The penitential nature of the whole enterprise demonstrates how deeply ideas of sin and repentance had penetrated into many parts of Western society. That so many knights, nobles and commoners responded to Urban II's call reveals the widespread acceptance of ideas of sin and repentance as they had been preached in the period discussed in this chapter.[190] The close relation established between violence and penance in the First Crusade provided a means to attain salvation for the group of knights which their violent means of living hitherto had made almost impossible.

The length of this chapter already suggests that during the tenth and eleventh centuries penance was an important element of Christian life in the Latin Church. Particularly in the eleventh century we can observe an increase in sources of various kinds, enabling us to study penitential practice in greater detail. Whether the increasing number of sources relating to penance reflects a greater frequency of the practice of confession or an increase in documentation as a consequence of the growing impact of the written word in these centuries is a moot point.[191] We have already seen how Atto of Vercelli demanded that the priests in his diocese report in writing to the bishop the sins of the people.[192] Thietmar of Merseburg relates how a priest named Bernar showed him a long document (*volumen longum*) in which he had recorded all his sins. Bemoaning his sins, he read this document to Thietmar and begged for absolution. Thietmar, whose history also chronicles his own sins, forgave Bernar his sins 'by divine power with which he had been commissioned', but he also put the written document on the relic holder to obtain the intercession of the saints whose relics were preserved in that little container. Thietmar admits that he is experimenting here, since he acknowledges that he has never seen anyone doing this before, nor has he heard of such behaviour.[193]

[189] Tyerman, *God's War*, p. 156; Bachrach, *Religion and the Conduct of War*, p. 120.
[190] Bull, *Knightly Piety*.
[191] The compilation and rapid distribution of Burchard's *Decretum* or of the *Pontificale Romano-Germanicum* illustrate the growing importance of the written word in the eleventh centry.
[192] Atto of Vercelli, *Capitula Episcoporum*, c. 90, ed. R. Pokorny, MGH Cap. Ep. III, pp. 297; see above, pp. 173–4.
[193] Thietmar, *Chronicle* VIII, 10, ed. Trillmich, pp. 450–2. For Thietmar's history as a chronicle of his own sins, see Meens, 'Kirchliche Buße', pp. 322–3 and H.-W. Goetz, 'Die Chronik Thietmars von Merseburg als Ego-Dokument. Ein Bischof mit gespaltenem Selbstverständnis', in R. McKitterick, I. van Renswoude and M. Gillis (eds.), *Ego Trouble. Authors and Their Identities in the Early Middle Ages* (Vienna 2009), pp. 259–70.

This chapter demonstrates that Carolingian texts were spread to England, Spain and Italy in this period and that they had a specific impact on penitential ideas and practice. Regino of Prüm and Burchard contributed to their continuing influence by incorporating much of the existing penitential tradition. The work of Regino and Burchard, much like that of Wulfstan of York, indicates that bishops could acquire considerable control over penitential processes and thereby over what was going on within their parishes. In Italy a monastery like Monte Cassino seems to have played a comparable role, whereas in Spain penitential texts seem more closely linked to royal representation. The frequent use of penance and penitential procedures as a way to settle conflicts with aristocrats raised the issue of sincerity and thereby laid greater emphasis on the question of the inner motivation of penitents. While not absent in the centuries discussed in this chapter, such questions were probed with greater acuity in the twelfth century in the nascent universities. It is to these developments that we now turn.

7   The twelfth century

The twelfth century is often seen as a revolutionary age in which a static archaic society changed into a dynamic one laying the foundations for modern society. There has been ample discussion about the exact moment when these revolutionary changes began as well as about the causes for this development, but that demographic and economic growth, urbanization, the development of new institutions such as universities and new religious orders had a great impact on medieval society is generally accepted.[1] The clarity of the divide between the earlier period and the later one, however, has recently become subject to debate. A lot of work on the early Middle Ages stresses the dynamics of this period, thus adding nuance to the notion of a sharp break between the early Middle Ages and the later ones.[2] Nevertheless, the twelfth century is deservedly known as an 'age of renaissance and renewal' and this is also true for the history of penance in this period. This chapter tries to outline the new developments in the field of penance and confession and to assess the impact of these changes on religious experience in this century and beyond. Because of the multitude of sources from this period, which is a reflection of the growing use of the written word accompanying the major changes in society, this chapter cannot be as comprehensive as

---

[1] Seminal for modern views on the twelfth century is C. H. Haskins, *The Renaissance of the Twelfth Century* (Cambridge MA 1927); another influential book propagating the idea of profound change in the twelfth century is R. Southern, *The Making of the Middle Ages* (New Haven 1953); see also R. L. Benson and G. Constable (eds.), *Renaissance and Renewal in the Twelfth Century* (Oxford 1982); R. Bartlett, *The Making of Europe. Conquest, Colonization and Cultural Change 950–1350* (Harmondsworth 1994); G. Constable, *The Reformation of the Twelfth Century* (Cambridge 1996); and R. I. Moore, *The First European Revolution, c. 970–1215* (Oxford 2000). For the application of a different basic concept, see T. Bisson, *The Crisis of the Twelfth Century. Power, Lordship, and the Origins of European Government* (Princeton / Oxford 2009).

[2] For an overview of this new trend see J. Smith, *Europe after Rome*; M. Innes, *Introduction to Early Medieval Western Europe, 300–900. The Sword, the Plough and the Book* (London / New York 2007); C. Wickham, *The Inheritance of Rome. A History of Europe from 400 to 1000* (London 2009). Wickham explicitly sees his book as a refutation of the grand narrative of modernity with regard to the early Middle Ages, see pp. 5–6.

earlier chapters. It will necessarily probe into some topics more than others and rely more on secondary sources than on a fresh analysis of the primary sources.

Following the trail of penitential books, there are indications that things changed in the twelfth century. The traditional penitential books apparently were no longer copied, indicating that they were no longer regarded as useful.[3] Even Burchard's *Decretum*, of which we have only a handful of twelfth-century manuscripts, was no longer copied after the year 1200.[4] We have to be careful, however, in jumping to conclusions because the later copies of early medieval penitentials generally attract a lot less scholarly interest than the new forms of penitential writings that were composed from the twelfth century onwards, often in academic circles. Abelard's thinking on the subject of penance and atonement is frequently presented as a major turning point, but the influence of his thinking has never been charted. It may give pause for thought to realize that his most important work in this field, his *Scito te ipsum*, is known from only five medieval manuscripts, of which only two stem from the twelfth century and the others from the fourteenth and fifteenth centuries.[5]

Two major changes affected the ways in which people thought and wrote about penance and confession. The first of these is the growing sophistication and complexity of legal thinking. In the earlier Middle Ages penitential texts and canon law collections were often closely related, but the distinction between the two genres was not a matter of discussion or thought. This changed when Burchard of Worms carefully integrated canon law and penitential practice.[6] Canonists began to think harder about the nature of their sources, their sometimes conflicting sentences and ways to deal with these in a systematic way.[7] The second major development, associated with the first, is the rise of cathedral

---

[3] Kottje, *Die Bußbücher Halitgars*, p. 254; Haggenmüller, *Die Überlieferung der Beda und Egbert zugeschriebenen Bußbücher*, p. 298.

[4] Based on the list of manuscripts in Kéry, *Canonical Collections of the Early Middle Ages*, pp. 134–45

[5] Peter Abelard, *Scito te ipsum*, ed. D. Luscombe, *Peter Abelard's 'Ethics'*, Oxford Medieval Texts (Oxford 1971), pp. xxxviii–lx; see n. 53 below.

[6] See Chapter 6 above.

[7] See P. Fournier, 'Un tournant de l'histoire du droit 1060–1140', *Nouvelle revue historique de droit français et étranger* 41 (1917), pp. 129–80; reprinted in P. Fournier, *Mélanges de droit canonique*, ed. T. Kölzer (Aalen 1983), vol. II, pp. 373–424; M. Brett, 'Finding the law: the sources of canonical authority before Gratian', in P. Andersen, M. Münster-Swendsen and H. Vogt (eds.), *Law before Gratian. Law in Western Europe, c. 500–1100. Proceedings of the Third Carlsberg Academy Conference on Legal History* (Copenhagen 2007), pp. 51–72; for Burchard of Worms and Ivo of Chartres, see G. Austin, 'Authority and the canons in Burchard's *Decretum* and Ivo's *Decretum*', in M. Brett and K. Cushing (eds.),

schools and universities. When more and more intellectuals were able to engage with questions of the right ordering of Christian life and Christian society, ethical treatises were composed touching upon the ways to correct sinful behaviour. Thinking about sin and its correction became ever more refined and advanced. These new forms of learning, in the field of canon law and in the field of ethics, led to new texts instructing confessors on how to deal with sins and their remedies.

Penance and the law

Burchard of Worms had organized his collection of canon law in order to establish the proper ways of doing penance for specific sins. The nineteenth book on penance should not be seen as an appendix to his collection, but rather as its fulfilment. For him canon law was to be put 'in the service of pastoral care'.[8] In a number of canon law collections from the eleventh century, penance was a central theme. This is true, for example, for the Italian collections known as the *Collection in Five Books* and the *Collection in Nine Books*. It has been argued that their continuing influence in the eleventh and twelfth centuries, mainly through derivative collections, was a result of the attention these collections paid to penance and traditional penitential texts.[9] As mentioned above the *Collection in Five Books* in manuscript Vat. lat. 1339 contains an intriguing programme of illustrations depicting the authorities cited in the text, among which we find several penitential authors, such as Theodorus episcopus (for Theodore of Canterbury), Commeanus (for Commean) and Paterius (for Patrick).[10]

Anselm of Lucca, writing in the turbulent period of the 'Gregorian Reform', added a separate book to his canonical collection dealing with the topic of penance, in which he also drew heavily upon penitential handbooks, mainly Burchard of Worms's *Decretum* and the *Paenitentiale Capitula Iudiciorum*.[11] For him the theme of penance was closely linked

---

Readers, Texts and Compilers in the Earlier Middle Ages. Studies in Medieval Canon Law in Honour of Linda Fowler-Magerl (Farnham 2009), pp. 35–58.

[8] G. Austin, 'Jurisprudence in the service of pastoral care'; see the discussion in Chapter 6.

[9] See Gaastra, 'Between liturgy and canon law'; and Gyug, 'The list of authorities in the illustrations of the Collection in Five Books', p. 243.

[10] See Chapter 6, pp. 177–8; for the pictorial programme, see R. Gyug, 'The list of authorities in the illustrations of the Collection in Five Books'.

[11] For Anselm and his collection, see K. Cushing, *Papacy and Law in the Gregorian Revolution. The Canonistic Work of Anselm of Lucca* (Oxford 1998). The collection is edited in 2 vols. by F. Thaner, *Anselmi Episcopi Lucensis Collectio Canonum una cum Collectione Minore* (Innsbruck 1906 and 1915). This edition is unfortunately incomplete, breaking off at Book XI, 15, thereby leaving out much of the penitential material.

to a canon law collection in which he strove to strengthen the case of the Gregorian party, and traditional penitential rulings were clearly of use. It is striking, though, that Anselm chose from the *Capitula Iudicorum*, with its neat division of authorities, mostly the canonical sentences and those from Theodore of Canterbury.[12] He seems to have regarded Cummean's rulings as less authoritative and therefore suspect, although in the *Collection in Five Books* the Irish abbot was depicted as one of the authorities of canon law. In later recensions of Anselm's collection, the penitential Book 11 has been left out, possibly because of some opposition to this penitential book.[13]

As we have seen, such a concern for the proper authorities used in penitentials and canonical rulings was already very much alive in the Carolingian period. The movement for Church reform known as the Gregorian Reform made such concerns even more acute. The papal reform movement tried to enhance the authority of the papacy in many different fields, such as its relations to local monasteries, to bishops and to the emperor. This emphatic struggle for papal influence throughout Europe led to a growth of legal disputes and therefore to a greater interest in legal matters. A number of canon law collections have been identified as closely related to the papal reform movement and as fostering papal authority.[14] The interest in legal issues furthered the development of canonical legal thinking about the proper sources of ecclesiastical authority and the ways in which texts were to be interpreted particularly in cases when existing regulations seemed to conflict with one another.[15] The growth of towns and the establishment of cathedral schools in this period also contributed to a deepening of the study of law. In the field of canon

---

[12] K. Cushing, 'Anselm of Lucca and Burchard of Worms: re-thinking the sources of Anselm 11, *De Penitentia*', in K. Cushing and R. Gyug (eds.), *Ritual, Text and Law. Studies in Medieval Canon Law and Liturgy Presented to Roger E. Reynolds* (Aldershot 2004), pp. 225–39, for its avoidance of Cummean, see p. 232 and P. Payer, *Sex and the Penitentials*, p. 85.

[13] Cushing, 'Anselm of Lucca and Burchard', pp. 225–6 and Payer, *Sex and the Penitentials*, p. 84.

[14] For example those of Anselm of Lucca or Cardinal Deusdedit; see Cushing, *Papacy and Law* on Anselm; the *Collection in Seventy-four Titles* which was also identified as a reform collection is now regarded as a monastic collection, see C. Rolker, 'The collection in seventy-four titles', in Brett and Cushing (eds.), *Readers, Texts and Compilers*, pp. 59–72. For a reappraisal of the connection between papally led reform and canon law collections, see Rolker, *Canon Law and the Letters of Ivo of Chartres*, pp. 292–7.

[15] For an intriguing case of papal interference in a local diocese, see B. Meijns, 'Within were fightings, within were fears. Pope Gregory VII, the canons regular of Watten and the reform of the Church in the diocese of Thérouanne (*c.* 1075–c. 1100)', in P. Andersen, M. Münster-Swendsen and H. Voght (eds.), *Law and Power in the Middle Ages. Proceedings of the Fourth Carlsberg Academy Conference on Medieval Legal History* (Copenhagen 2008), pp. 73–96.

law, an influential treatise was written by Ivo of Chartres, bishop of that town from 1090 to 1115 and 'one of the finest legal scholars' of his age.[16] Ivo, closely attached to the Reform movement and particularly to Pope Urban II, added this treatise as a prologue to his collection of canon law, the *Decretum*. Later it was added to the *Panormia*, a collection that was traditionally attributed to Ivo. Recently Christoph Rolker has been able to demonstrate, however, that the *Panormia* was not composed by Ivo, but must have originated in northern France in the early years of the twelfth century.[17] To judge from the number of surviving manuscripts – more than 150 – the *Panormia* must have been an extremely influential text.[18]

In his prologue Ivo instructed his readers on how to deal with cases in which they found parts of the canonical tradition difficult to understand or even judged them to be contradictory.[19] Ivo distinguished between the rigour of the law (*rigor, iudicium*) on the one hand and merciful moderation (*moderatio, misericordia*) on the other and used a medical metaphor cherished by penitential authors, that doctors sometimes apply harsh remedies and sometimes gentle ones according to the patient's sickness. In a similar manner, the doctors of the Church had prescribed sometimes strict, sometimes lenient treatment, without deviating from the final goal: curing the sinner. Ivo goes on to distinguish between the character of existing rulings, whether we are dealing with admonitions, indulgences, precepts or prohibitions. He also introduces the distinction between mutable precepts and immutable ones, the latter immediately affecting one's salvation. In such cases no dispensations were admitted, while in the case of mutable precepts dispensation could be allowed if they were accompanied by an honest and suitable compensation. Ivo's prologue can be seen as an early scholarly, or perhaps even scholastic, treatise on canon law and is now generally considered to have originated as an independent text.[20] What is clear is that the author is dealing in a very

---

[16] Somerville and Brasington, *Prefaces to Canon Law Books in Latin Christianity*, p. 111.

[17] Rolker, *Canon Law and the Letters of Ivo of Chartres*.

[18] For a list of mss. of Ivo's work, see Kéry, *Canonical Collections in the Early Middle Ages*, pp. 244–60; the manuscripts of the *Panormia* are listed by Martin Brett on the website: http://wtfaculty.wtamu.edu/~bbrasington/panormia.html (visited 4 November 2009).

[19] The *Prologue* has been edited twice in recent years by J.-M. Werckmeister, *Yves de Chartres. Prologue*, Sources Canoniques (Paris 1997) and B. Brasington, *Ways of Mercy. The Prologue of Ivo of Chartres. Edition and Analysis* (Münster 2004). I use the most recent edition. For Brasington's critique of Werckmeister's edition, see *Ways of Mercy*, pp. 11–12. A translation is available in Somerville and Brasington, *Prefaces*, pp. 132–58. S. Violi, *Il Prologo di Ivo di Chartres. Paradigmi e prospettive per la teologia e l'interpretazione del diritto canonica* (Lugano 2006) reproduces Brasington's edition and offers an Italian translation.

[20] Brasington, *Ways of Mercy*, p. 105.

sophisticated way with the frictions between canonical texts passed on to him from the wide range of Christian backgrounds in which these ecclesiastical rules had been formulated. He did not try to solve the apparent contradictions between the canons. Instead he provided those who had to work with such texts with the necessary tools to solve pastoral and legal problems raised by their application.[21]

Whereas Burchard of Worms had acknowledged the importance of penitential sentences as sources of canon law and Anselm of Lucca had used them quite extensively, Ivo's prologue did not refer explicitly to such texts as sources of canon law. He only mentioned papal letters, decisions of councils, treatises of orthodox Church Fathers and secular legislation as acceptable sources for canon law.[22] The *Decretum*, a work highly influenced by Burchard's collection, did use penitential canons, however, particularly in Book 15, which is concerned with penance.[23] It includes the penitential attributed to Ivo's predecessor, Fulbert of Chartres, referred to as a *paenitentiale laicorum*, and furthermore refers to the triad of penitentials that Burchard also mentioned: the Roman penitential and those attributed to Bede and Theodore. Ivo adopted his penitential canons mostly through Burchard's *Decretum*.[24] That the penitential *iudicia* of Theodore of Canterbury are cited explicitly by Ivo accords with his positive statement that 'Archbishop Theodore and abbot Adrian, a man equally learned, were sent by Pope Vitalian to Britain and nourished many churches of the English with the fruit of ecclesiastical teaching. From his teaching Theodore wrote wonderful judgments for sinners, that is, for how many years anyone would have to do penance for each sin.'[25]

While Book 15 of Ivo's *Decretum* used traditional penitential canons, the *Panormia*, composed a little later possibly by a pupil of Ivo, was a much more selective compilation and it seems a more useful one.[26] The

---

[21] Brasington, *Ways of Mercy*, p. 30; Rolker, *Canon Law and the Letters of Ivo of Chartres*, pp. 300–2.

[22] *Prologue*, ed. Brasington, p. 115, tr. Somerville and Brasington, *Prefaces*, p. 133.

[23] Payer, *Sex and the Penitentials*, p. 85 describes Ivo's rather restricted use of traditional penitential sentences related to sexual behaviour in the *Decretum*.

[24] See the table of sources compiled by Martin Brett on http://knowledgeforge.net/ivo/decretum/idsort_1p3.pdf (visited 9 November 2009). For the penitential attributed to Fulbert of Chartres, see F. Kerff, 'Das sogenannte Paenitentiale Fulberti. Überlieferung, Verfasserfrage, Edition', *ZRG Kan. Abt.* 73 (1987), pp. 1–40. There is reason to doubt the attribution to Fulbert.

[25] Ivo of Chartres, *Decretum* 4.146, ed. PL 161, col. 299; translation in Payer, *Sex and the Penitentials*, p. 85. Ivo relies here on a description in Paul the Deacon, *Historia Langobardorum* V, 30, p. 154 (cf. p. 96 above).

[26] C. Rolker, 'The earliest work of Ivo of Chartres: the case of Ivo's Eucharist florilegium and the canon law collections attributed to him', *ZRG Kan.* 93 (2007), pp. 109–27; on p. 113 he elucidates the selective approach of the *Panormia*: the *Panormia* 'dropped most

Panormia left out Book 15 of the *Decretum*, the book concerned specific-ally with penance. The immense success of the *Panormia* is indicated by its abundant manuscript diffusion, whereas Ivo's *Decretum* is only known from some ten manuscripts and fragments. This indicates that with the increasing development of legal thinking, purely penitential matters may have received less attention, not solely for the reason that penitential handbooks lacked sufficient authority, but also because legal matters were more and more separated from the practice of hearing confession and imposing a proper penance. For Ivo these two processes were closely connected; for the author of the *Panormia*, possibly one of Ivo's pupils, this apparently was no longer the case.

The close connection between penance and canon law diminished even further with the composition of the text that would for centuries to come dominate the field of the study of canon law: Gratian's *Decretum*. Gratian is generally regarded as the 'father of the science of canon law'.[27] The text that until recently was regarded as Gratian's *Decretum*, however, has now been proven to be a second recension of an earlier more compact work.[28] Gratian is probably responsible for the first recension and an anonymous author (or authors) for the revision of this work.[29] The earliest version of the *Decretum* might predate the traditional date of around 1140; the vulgate text surely existed in the year 1158.[30] Both recensions must have been composed between 1139 and 1158 in the city of Bologna, which at that moment was a thriving legal centre where canon law and Roman law were intensively studied.[31] About the person of Gratian we know hardly anything.[32] Recently Anders Winroth has

---

material found in the last three books of the Decretum'. See now Rolker, *Canon Law and the Letters*, pp. 148–9.

[27] S. Kuttner, 'The father of the science of canon law', *Jurist* 1 (1941), pp. 2–19; See also P. Landau, 'Gratian and the *Decretum Gratiani*', in W. Hartmann and K. Pennington (eds.), *The History of Medieval Canon Law in the Classical Period. From Gratian to the Decretals of Pope Gregory IX* (Washington 2008), pp. 22–54, at p. 53: 'the father of the discipline of canon law'.

[28] A. Winroth, *The Making of Gratian's 'Decretum'* (Cambridge 2000). Atria Larson argued for a more organic development of the vulgate text out of the earliest version, see her 'The evolution of Gratian's *Tractatus de penitentia*', *Bulletin of Medieval Canon Law* n.s. 26 (2004–6), pp. 59–123.

[29] Winroth, *The Making*, pp. 193–5.

[30] Winroth, *The Making*, argued for a post-1139 date for the first recension; Atria Larson holds an origin in the 1130s possible, see her 'The evolution of Gratian's *Tractatus de penitentia*' and her dissertation: 'Gratian's *Tractatus de penitentia*. A textual study and intellectual history' (PhD thesis, Catholic University of America, at Washington DC 2010).

[31] Winroth, *The Making*, pp. 136–44.

[32] J. T. Noonan, 'Gratian slept here: the changing identity of the father of the systematic study of canon law', *Traditio* 35 (1979), pp. 145–72.

demonstrated that there are good reasons to suppose that he ended his life as bishop of Chiusi.[33] Parallels with texts and concepts used in the school of Anselm of Laon have been interpreted to indicate that Gratian, like other north-Italian scholars before and after, studied in the cathedral schools of northern France, particularly with Anselm in Laon.[34] Although it has been stated that Gratian must have worked mainly as a lawyer in Bologna, his canon law collection seems first and foremost to be the result of a process of teaching.[35] We have no firm evidence that Gratian taught canon law himself, but it seems certain that his work was used very quickly in teaching, as a result of which his text was developed leading to 'the second recension' of the work. Anders Winroth argues convincingly that this happened at the same time as Roman law was starting to be taught in Bologna by masters such as Bulgarus. This would explain the advanced treatment of Roman law in the second recension compared with Gratian's rather poor grasp thereof in the first.[36]

So we can say that in the period between the composition of the first and the second recensions of Gratian's *Decretum*, that is between the 1130s and 1158, the scholarly study of canon law originated in the town of Bologna. Whereas Burchard had implicitly tried to iron out differences that he observed in his sources, Gratian dealt with such issues in an explicit way. The title that he gave his work, *Concordia discordantium canonum* ('A concord of discordant canons') already reveals his method. Gratian signalled those places where canon law regulations were not in harmony and tried to harmonize them with the help of logical arguments that he presented in his *Dicta*. The prologue of Ivo of Chartres's canonical collections proved to be a helpful tool in dealing with these differences. The study of Roman law developed alongside that of canon law and the second recension of Gratian bears ample proof of the more scholarly approach to Roman law. Gratian did have a particular interest in penance, as is demonstrated by the inclusion of a long discussion on

---

[33] In a paper delivered at the Fourteenth International Congress of Medieval Canon Law (Toronto, August 2012).

[34] Larson, 'Gratian's *Tractatus de penitentia*'.

[35] For the view of Gratian as a lawyer, see R. Southern, *Scholastic Humanism and the Unification of Europe*, vol. I: *Foundations* (Oxford 1995), pp. 301–4. The educational character of the *Decretum* has been emphasized by Landau, 'Gratian and the *Decretum Gratiani*', p. 24 and J. Brundage, 'The teaching of canon law in the schools', in W. Hartmann and K. Pennington (eds.), *The History of Medieval Canon Law in the Classical Period. From Gratian to the Decretals of Pope Gregory IX* (Washington 2008), pp. 98–120, at p. 99: 'the *Decretum* itself seems unmistakably designed for, and may well have been the product of, the classroom'. Compare Winroth, *The Making*, pp. 146–74 for an assessment of the teaching of Roman and canon law in Bologna in the first half of the twelfth century.

[36] Winroth, *The Making*, pp. 146–74.

the topic, which is known as the *Tractatus de penitentia*. Since this treatise is found in the first recension and since the argument fits in with Gratian's approach in other questions, it seems beyond doubt that this treatise was composed by Gratian himself. The first recension reveals a more tightly organized argument than the vulgate version, dealing with the question of what exactly leads to the forgiveness of sin: contrition or confession?[37] This question does not mean that Gratian somehow doubted the necessity of confession to a priest, but he was interested in locating exactly when remission of sins took place.[38] The fact that Gratian nowhere offers his reader a set of penitential tariffs does not mean that he rejected such tariffs, but rather that he 'assumed their continued usage' and 'trusted the old penitentials to serve their purpose'.[39] When discussing the education of priests, he numbered penitential books among those books a priest should know.[40] Gratian went further than this, however. His *Tractatus de penitentia* tried to train priests to think about penance in a new theological way.[41]

Gratian's work was to form the basis of every education in medieval canon law during the whole period of the Middle Ages and beyond. With him originated a curriculum in canon law that every student had to absorb. A further consequence was that canon lawyers were now properly trained and started to form a legal profession. Canon law was no longer a matter for bishops and priests who were involved in pastoral care, but became more and more the domain of legal professionals.[42] They received a formal legal training where they were taught to deal with the complicated stucture of Gratian's work and, in discussing the ways in which Gratian harmonized seemingly conflicting canons, with the principles of legal reasoning. The structure of the *Decretum* is not easy and it can be hard to find exactly what you are looking for, but 'it was easier to

---

[37] Cf. J. Gaudemet, 'Le débat sur la confession dans la Distinction I du "De penitentia" (Décret de Gratien C.33, q.3)', *ZRG KA* 71 (1985), pp. 52–75, at p. 53 speaking of 'la démarche sinueuse et parfois hésitante de son auteur' when discussing the vulgate version.

[38] Larson, 'Gratian's *Tractatus de penitentia*. A textual study and intellectual history'.

[39] Larson, 'Gratian's *Tractatus de penitentia*. A textual study and intellectual history', pp. 294–5.

[40] D 38, c. 5, ed. E. Friedberg, *Corpus iuris canonici I. Decretum magistri Gratiani* (Leipzig 1879), pp. 141–2, a text ultimately deriving from Haito of Basel.

[41] Larson, 'Gratian's *Tractatus de penitentia*. A textual study and intellectual history', p. 340.

[42] J. Brundage, 'The rise of professional canonists and the development of the Ius Commune', *ZRG Kan.* 81 (1995), pp. 26–63; Brundage, 'Legal learning and the professionalization of canon law', in H. Vogt (ed.), *Law and Learning in the Middle Ages. Proceedings of the Second Carlsberg Academy Conference on Medieval Legal History 2005* (Copenhagen 2006), pp. 5–27.

adjust the student to the book than to alter a text which had become the foundation of a new science'.[43] Because of this process of professionalization and the development of a scholarly discipline of canon law, canon law from the middle of the twelfth century became more and more divorced from pastoral care and the practice of confession. This separation was reflected in the development of a distinction that now made its entry into canon law: that between the *forum internum* and the *forum externum*. The former dealt with individuals seeking spiritual counsel by confessing their sins, the latter existed in the form of ecclesiastical tribunals in which professional canon lawyers made their living.[44]

Sin and guilt

The development of the study of law at centres like Bologna led to a growing separation between canon law and pastoral care. A similar process can be observed in the field of theology, where the rise of the cathedral schools and universities made penance increasingly into a topic for theological discourse. In Laon the masters Anselm of Laon and William of Champeaux thought about the ontological status of sin. Was it part of creation or a mere negation of something created? They also discussed the exact moment at which sin occurred. Was it the moment when something forbidden entered the mind, the moment the mind savoured this thought, when it decided to act or when the thought was finally put into action? From this 'stages theory' it did not follow that the sinful deed itself was no longer of any importance, but the careful investigation of the process by which the initial temptation was finally put into action (or not), steered the attention more and more towards the 'interior aspects' of sin. Yet for the masters teaching in Laon questions of sin and guilt were only peripheral to their teachings.[45]

It was different for Peter Abelard, who through his book titled 'Know thyself' is one of the first authors and teachers who discussed questions of sin, guilt and penance in great detail.[46] As a sometimes rather insolent pupil of both Anselm and William, Abelard was probably well acquainted

---

[43] Southern, *Scholastic Humanism*, p. 306.

[44] J. Goering, 'The internal forum and the literature of penance and confession', in Hartmann and Pennington, *History of Medieval Canon Law in the Classical Period*, pp. 379–428, at pp. 379–80.

[45] R. Blomme, *La doctrine du péché dans les écoles théologiques de la première moitié du XII siècle* (Louvain 1958), pp. 21–53.

[46] I here refer to D. E. Luscombe (ed.), *Peter Abelard's 'Ethics'. An Edition with Introduction, English Translation and Notes* (Oxford 1971); there is a more recent edition by R. M. Ilgner (ed.), *Petri Abaelardi opera theologica IV: Scito te ipsum*, CC CM 190 (Turnhout 2001).

with his masters' thinking on the subject, yet there may be very personal motives for his engagement with this topic. Abelard's lover, Héloise, whom he had made pregnant when acting as her teacher, was struggling with the conviction that she constantly sinned in thought, although she did not put her thoughts into practice. She made it known to Abelard that she felt at the same time guilty and innocent about this.[47] Abelard may have written his *Scito te ipsum* shortly before 1140 to help his former mistress deal with such problems, as he assisted her and her monastic community of the Paraclete in many other ways.

Abelard is often represented as the historical person who finally closed the era of penitential tariffs by shifting the attention from the outward deed to the interior motivation behind it.[48] This is a somewhat simplifying representation of a complex phenomenon. We have already noticed that Abelard was not the first teacher discussing the role of intention in sinning. Moreover, while penitential handbooks may suggest a mechanical interpretation of their tariffs, the prologues and epilogues of these texts stress that the confessor should weigh the circumstances of an act, the person of the sinner as well as his or her intention when committing the sinful act.[49] Penitential books did their best to distinguish between similar cases arising from different motives, for example in the case of killing. Was the homicidal act committed on premeditation, did the killer act from anger or to avenge the killing of relatives, did it happen on somebody else's order – the king, for example – or in a public war?[50] We also saw that in the tenth century people were worrying about insincere

[47] Héloise, Letter 1, ed. J. Monfrin, *Historia Calamitatum* (4th edn, Paris 1978), p. 116; cf. M. Clanchy, *Abelard. A Medieval Life* (Oxford 1997), p. 279; for Héloise's influence on Abelard, see C. Mews, *Abelard and Heloise* (Oxford 2005); see also the more sceptical approach of M. Cameron, 'Abelard (and Héloise?) on intention', *American Catholic Philosophical Quarterly* 81 (2007), pp. 323–38.

[48] See e.g. C. Morris, *The Discovery of the Individual 1050–1200* (New York 1972), p. 74 or H. Lutterbach, 'Die mittelalterlichen Bußbücher – Trägermedien von Einfachreligiosität?', *Zeitschrift für Kirchengeschichte* 114 (2003), pp. 227–44; Lutterbach, *Sexualität im Mittelalter*, pp. 240–7; A. Vauchez, 'The Church and the laity', in D. Abulafia (ed.), *The New Cambridge Medieval History*, vol. v: *c. 1198 – c. 1300* (Cambridge 2008), pp. 182–203, at p. 186; for a nuanced revision of such views, see Goering, 'The internal forum and the literature of penance and confession', pp. 401–2.

[49] P. Payer, 'The humanism of the penitentials and the continuity of the penitential tradition', *Mediaeval Studies* 46 (1984), pp. 340–54.

[50] Discussed for example in Theodore's penitential, see *P. Theodori U* I, 4, ed. Finsterwalder, *Die Canones Theodori Cantuariensis*, pp. 294–5; for some discussion regarding the differences in approach to moral questions of killing in the early Middle Ages, see R. Kottje, 'Tötung im Krieg als rechtliches und moralisches Problem im früheren und hohen Mittelalter', in H. Hecker, *Krieg in Mittelalter und Renaissance* (Düsseldorf 2005), pp. 17–39.

forms of penance, a problem that would not arise if penance had been purely outward.[51] Moreover, Abelard in his ethical work argued against the view that intention was all that mattered. Héloise had been troubled by the fact that although she did not put her erotic thoughts into action, she nevertheless sinned in intention, for in her view, which accorded with the teachings of Anselm of Laon, intention alone could be sinful, even if not followed upon by an act.[52] Abelard argued that it was not the intention to act that was sinful, but the will to put a bad intention into practice, thus exonerating Héloise's sinful thoughts that she had not put into practice. In his views on sin and guilt Abelard ostensibly builds upon existing views, although it is not always clear exactly to what extent, because the teachings of Anselm and William of Champeaux only survive in a piecemeal manner.[53] To claim that Abelard caused a major shift in the treatment of sins by putting the emphasis no longer on the exterior act, but on the intention of the actor, is surely beside the point. His *Scito te ipsum* is without doubt an intriguing work of great acuity, but it did not single-handedly change the prevailing attitudes towards penance, sin and guilt. Abelard's work should, first and foremost, be regarded as representing a detailed analysis of the workings of the human mind and will as it had developed in the cathedral schools of northern France.

To exemplify the continuities, it may be helpful to compare Abelard's treatment of a specific case with that of the early eighth-century penitential known as the *Paenitentiale Oxoniense II*, possibly composed by Willibrord.[54] Abelard considered a case in which a woman suffocated her child after taking it into bed to keep it warm.[55] In penitential handbooks such a sad state of affairs was regularly mentioned, while Rathramnus of Corbie in the ninth century devoted a small treatise to a discussion of such an event.[56] Abelard's discussion of the case has by some been regarded as a reaction to its treatment in existing penitential texts.[57] In fact, his discussion is remarkably consistent with penitential literature.[58] Abelard focusses on the question of why a mother appearing before the bishop should be punished, since the death of her child was

[51] See the prayer by Rather of Verona discussed in Chapter 6.
[52] See Blomme, *Doctrine*, p. 81 and J. Marenbon, *The Philosophy of Peter Abelard* (Cambridge 1997), p. 254.
[53] For Abelard's use of Anselm and William, see Clanchy, *Abelard*, p. 84 and Marenbon, *Philosophy*, pp. 252–5.
[54] Discussed in Chapter 5 above.
[55] *Scito te ipsum*, ed. D. Luscombe, *Peter Abelard's 'Ethics'*, pp. 38–40.
[56] G. Schmitz, 'Schuld und Strafe. Eine unbekannte Stellungnahme des Rathramnus von Corbie zur Kindestötung', *Deutsches Archiv* 38 (1982), pp. 363–87.
[57] Blomme, *Doctrine*, p. 202, fn. 1.
[58] See Luscombe's comment *Peter Abelard's 'Ethics'*, p. 39, fn. 3.

clearly not intended. Abelard states that such a woman is punished not because of her guilt, but to set an example in order to instruct others. According to him, only God is able to judge the secrets of the heart, while men can only judge things that are manifest, and therefore the deed of the mother has to be judged and punished, while in her heart she may very well be innocent. If we compare Abelard's views with the way the *Paenitentiale Oxoniense II* treats the same case, it turns out that the penitential author is completely in line with Abelard. The penitential states that when a child is found dead in a cradle or in another place where a mother had put it to rest, the mother is without guilt. When a mother finds a child dead beside her in bed and it is unsure whether the child died because of her, she is to fast for four weeks in order to purify her soul. If she is sure that the child died because of her, but the mother did not do so intentionally, she is to fast for fourteen weeks. When the child has not yet been baptized, the period of fasting is increased to twenty-eight weeks. If the mother suffocated her child when drunk, she has to fast twenty weeks, but in a case when the child had not yet been baptized, penance is increased to thirty-five weeks. The most serious case is when a woman suffocated her unbaptized child intentionally. In that case she has to do penance for forty weeks, in tears and sighs.[59] Abelard's treatment of the exact location of the will to sin and its relation to acts is of course much more detailed than the one found in the Oxford penitential, but it is clear that the author of the *Oxoniense II* distinguishes between the act itself, the intention of the actor and the influence of attenuating or aggravating circumstances in order to find the appropriate penance for the mother. Prescribing a penance to purify the soul in the case where a mother finds her child dead, but is unsure whether she smothered it or the child died of some other cause, seems a humane strategy, perhaps more refined than Abelard's, who after all saw the punishment only as a deterring device for others. Fulfilling a penance in such a case might also help a mother in coming to terms with her own possible role in her child's demise. Such a careful treatment of this case is not found in other penitential texts, but the frequent consideration of this case demonstrates that questions of sin, guilt and penance were a topic for discussion well before Abelard's time.[60] What Abelard and his colleagues brought to the debate was not a greater sensitivity to the topic of intention, but rather the development of a scholastic discourse centring

[59] *P. Oxoniense II*, cc. 25–30, ed. Kottje, *Paenitentialia minora*, pp. 195–6; see also the discussion in Meens, 'Children and confession', p. 58.
[60] See the careful discussion in Schmitz, 'Schuld und Strafe'.

around the question where the exact location of sin was to be found: in desire, the fruition of desire, the will to act or the act itself.

Abelard's discussion of such questions laid the basis of scholastic thought in the field of ethics. His disciples developed his ideas and historians have talked about Abelard's followers as 'a school'.[61] That Abelard had followers who discussed and developed his ideas seems clear, while the emphatic opposition that he inspired also contributed to the dissemination and discussion of his concepts. Whether Abelard caused a major shift in the practice of penance is, however, another matter. His *Scito te ipsum* apparently was not a well-known text. It survives in only five medieval manuscripts. Two of these are from the twelfth century; the remaining three stem from the fourteenth and fifteenth centuries.[62] William of St-Thierry noticed in 1139 that the work was hard to come by, and its most recent editor contrasts the importance of the work with the disappointingly low number of surviving manuscripts.[63] Two of the fifteenth-century manuscripts contain warnings that the author was a condemned heretic, a fact that may have contributed to the apparent shortage of manuscripts.[64] Nevertheless, the immediate influence of Abelard's writing on the theme of ethics, sin and penance seems to have been rather meagre. To think of him as a person who played a central role in the development of new penitential concepts and practices is therefore misleading. Abelard should first of all be seen as someone who contributed to the development of an intellectual ethical discourse that came to fruition in scholastic circles. Only through the emerging world of cathedral schools and universities and the accompanying education of the clergy were such ideas gradually introduced in pastoral practice. Although in past decades a lot of research has been

[61] See D. Luscombe, *The School of Peter Abelard: The Influence of Abelard's Thought in the Early Scholastic Period* (Cambridge 1970) and Luscombe, 'The school of Peter Abelard revisited', *Vivarium* 30 (1992), pp. 127–38.

[62] The surviving manuscripts are: Munich, Bayerische Staatsbibliothek, Clm 14160 (s. XII, Regensburg/Prüfening?); Munich, Bayerische Staatsbibliothek, Clm 28363 (s. XII ex., France); Munich, Bayerische Staatsbibliothek, Clm 18597 (1469, Tegernsee?); Mainz, Stadtbibliothek, lat. 76 (1458, Heidelberg) and Oxford, Baillol College, Ms. 296 (s. XV med., England?); for a description of these manuscripts, see Luscombe, *Peter Abelard's 'Ethics'*, pp. xli–liii. The ms. clm 14160 is dated to s. XII 3/3 and the Prüfening origin is rejected in E. Klemm, *Die romanischen Handschriften der Bayerischen Staatsbibliothek*, vol. I: *Die Bistümer Regensburg, Passau und Salzburg* (Wiesbaden 1980), pp. 41–2; the origin of Clm 28363 should be Italian, as indicated in G. Glauche, *Katalog der lateinischen Handschriften der Bayerischen Staatsbibliothek München: Clm 28255–28460* (Wiesbaden 1984), pp. 154–6. Ilgner's edition is based on the same five manuscripts, Ilgner (ed.), *Petri Abaelardi opera theologica IV: Scito te ipsum*, p. x.

[63] Luscombe, *Peter Abelard's 'Ethics'*, p. liv, citing William of St-Thierry, Epistola 326, PL 182, 532 D-533 A.

[64] Luscombe, *Peter Abelard's 'Ethics'*, p. xliv–v and xlviii.

devoted to the question of exactly how this happened, one of the experts in this field recently stated that the study of the literature in which we find the most detailed information about this process – the literature of pastoral care, in particular the manuals and *summae* composed as a tool for the priest hearing confessions – still needs a lot of research and is an area of study that 'remains in its infancy'.[65]

Practical literature

The teachings of Gratian and Abelard demonstrate the growing importance of academic teaching in the field of penance. After Gratian canon law developed into a full academic subject in the university of Bologna, while in Paris theology became the dominant subject in the early years of the university in the aftermath of Abelard's turbulent career. In the twelfth century and beyond new practical handbooks were developed which were meant to instruct priests in the art of confession. This literature is characterized by a tension between academic interest and practical use, as exemplified, for example, by Thomas of Chobham who proposed to do away with all theoretical subtleties and discussions in order to concentrate on the practical issues that are of use to priests when hearing confession and assigning the proper form of penance.[66] Historians have been trying to classify this wealth of pastoral literature according to its theoretical nature or practical suitability.[67] To deal fully with this extensive literature would require another book; therefore I shall briefly discuss only two of these texts, both from the later twelfth century: the penitential handbook written by Bartholomew of Exeter and the anonymous work known as *Homo quidam*.

Bartholomew, bishop of Exeter (died 1184), was a well-known canonist, although his work is not widely known or studied. As the latest editor of one of his works put it: 'it is curious that this renowned and respected prelate so rarely escapes the confines of learned footnotes'.[68] He taught

---

[65] Goering, 'The internal forum', p. 411.

[66] Thomas of Chobham, *Summa Confessorum*, ed. F. Broomfield, Analecta Mediaevalia Namurcensia 25 (Louvain / Paris 1968), p. 3; see P. Payer, *Sex and the New Medieval Literature of Confession, 1150–1300* (Toronto 2009), p. 24.

[67] Payer, *Sex and the New Medieval Literature of Confession*, pp. 24–7; L. E. Boyle, 'Summae Confessorum', in *Les genres littéraires dans les sources théologiques et philosophiques médiévales: Définition, critique et exploitation: Actes du Colloque International de Louvain-la-Neuve, 25–27 mai 1981* (Louvain-la-Neuve 1982), pp. 227–37.

[68] For Bartholomew, see A. Morey, *Bartholomew of Exeter, Bishop and Canonist. A Study in the Twelfth Century* (Cambridge 1937) and the introduction in D. N. Bell (ed.), *Bartholomaei Exoniensis Contra Fatalitatis Errorem*, CC CM 157 (Turnhout 1996), pp. v–xxii; citation from p. v.; his penitential handbook is briefly discussed in A. Diem,

in Paris and served as a legate and sometimes mediator in the conflict between the English King Henry II and the archbishop of Canterbury, Thomas Becket. When late in 1170 the archbishop had been murdered by five of the king's men in the sacred space of Canterbury cathedral, Bartholomew was in several ways involved in the complicated process of reconciliation. Not only was he leading the ceremony by which the cathedral, polluted by the spilling of blood, was to be purified, but he also acted as confessor to the murderers of the rapidly canonized archbishop. To this end, he received a letter from Pope Alexander III with advice on how to deal with the murderers in proportion to their degree of participation.[69] He seems therefore to have had a reputation as a confessor, while he also acted frequently as papal judge delegate, which can be regarded as a sign of his competence in canon law.

At some point in his career, possibly shortly after his episcopal election in 1161, Bartholomew composed a finely tuned handbook for confessors which one manuscript copy titled: *liber pastoralis sive poenitentialis*.[70] A full investigation of the sources that Bartholomew used is still wanting, but the main sources that he built upon when composing this work were Burchard's *Decretum*, the *Decretum* of Ivo of Chartres, Gratian's *Decretum* and the *Sentences* of Peter the Lombard. He employed these texts in such a way as to build a nicely structured informative text in which he first dealt with the good things that help a Christian on his road to salvation: faith, hope and love. A sinner who wants to confess his sins needs first of all faith, that is he needs to be able to recite the creed and the Lord's Prayer. Essential elements of a confession were, according to Bartholomew, these: true penitence, a pure confession, the willingness to provide satisfaction to the offended party and finally the willingness to forgive others. He proceeds to discuss the merits of specific ways to atone for

---

'Virtues and vices in early texts on pastoral care', *Franciscan Studies* 62 (2004), pp. 193–223, at pp. 207–9 and more thoroughly in J. Taliadoros, 'Bartholomew of Exeter's penitential: some original observations on his personal dicta', in P. Erdö and S. A. Szuromi (eds.), *Proceedings of the Thirteenth International Congress of Medieval Canon Law: Esztergom, 3–8 August 2008* (Vatican 2010), pp. 457–76 (I thank the author for providing me with the article before publication).

[69] Morey, *Bartholomew of Exeter*, pp. 31–3.

[70] For the date of his penitential book, see Morey, *Bartholomew of Exeter*, p. 174; Bell (ed.), *Bartholomaei Exoniensis*, p. xviii: 'perhaps ... from the early 1160s' and Goering, 'Internal Forum', p. 413: 'between 1155 and 1170'; the latest source being used in this text is Peter the Lombard's *Sentences*, finished in 1155–7, which must be regarded as the *terminus post quem* for this work; for its title in Ms. London, BL, Royal 5 E. VIII, see Morey, *Bartholomew of Exeter*, p. 164; in Ms. Biblioteca Apostolica Vaticana, Vat. lat. 152, it reads: 'paenitentialis sive pastoralis liber', Morey, *Bartholomew of Exeter*, p. 166.

your sins: alms, prayer, fasting, weeping, manual labour, vigils, genuflections, bodily afflictions, penitential garb and finally pilgrimage.

Bartholomew then started his discussion of the knowledge that a confessor should have by listing the books that he should know. He produced a traditional list of mostly liturgical books deriving originally from the early ninth-century episcopal capitulary of Haito of Basel, comprising works such as a sacramentary or a lectionary. Bartholomew took Haito's text from Burchard, Ivo or Gratian, who all adopted it in their work. This list required knowledge of a *canon penitentialis*.[71] Exactly how Bartholomew understood this term is uncertain, but as he mostly used Burchard and Ivo for the part of his work in which he determined the amount of penance for specific sins, we may assume that he was thinking of such texts. Bartholomew advised confessors to use the canons found in these texts, but not blindly. They had to use their discretion in order to identify the right sort of penance to assign to the sinner and should be careful not to let their judgment be influenced by feelings of hatred or sympathy. Bartholomew then went on to discuss the way in which the confessor should weigh sin. He had to consider the person of the sinner, whether he was free or unfree, whether he was a layperson or a cleric, a man or a woman, married or single, poor or rich, young, adult or old, and so on. He also had to consider the character of the sin committed: was it a mortal sin or a venial one, had it become public or remained secret (*occultum*), had it been committed knowingly or unknowingly, deliberately or by accident? Bartholomew demonstrated his acquaintance with the new scholastic theology when he distinguished between the stages (*gradus*) of sin in scholastic terms, distinguishing suggestion from delectation, entertaining a particular sin from putting the thought into action, making sin into customary behaviour, being blinded by excuses and persisting in sin out of obstinate impenitence.[72]

Bartholomew dealt with the danger of assigning a penance that was too light or too heavy. He also discussed the problems a confessor might encounter when he was unable to find the sin he was confronted with in his documentation or when he found more than one solution to his specific problem. In the first case the priest had to deduce general principles from similar cases and should use these to judge the penitent. In the latter case he should try to relate the plurality of penances to the neat distinctions applicable to individual cases that Bartholomew had just

---

[71] Bartholomew, *Penitential*, c. 23, ed. Morey, p. 192; Haito, *Capitula Episcoporum*, c. 6, ed. P. Brommer, MGH Cap. Ep. I, p. 211: for a discussion of the term, see Payer, 'The humanism of the penitentials', pp. 350–1.

[72] Bartholomew, *Penitential*, c. 26, ed. Morey, *Bartholomew of Exeter*, p. 195.

discussed, such as the age of the penitent, the precise nature of the sin or the particular circumstances.[73] Bartholomew also provided liturgical guidance as to how to receive a penitent. Bartholomew considered three occasions: the hearing of confession, the case of a dying penitent and finally the rite of public penitence (*puplica penitentia*).[74] In the process of confession the priest should examine the penitent with the help of the scheme of the seven deadly sins (*vii principalia vitia*), but he should be careful to avoid being too explicit in questioning, for Bartholomew had heard, so he informs his reader, of men and women who fell into sins they had only got to know about during confession.[75] Before starting his discussion of individual sins, Bartholomew stressed the elementary importance of three distinctions in determining the amount of penance: the confessor should always keep in mind whether a penitent was healthy or not, whether the sin was venial or mortal and finally whether it had become public or remained secret.[76]

Bartholomew then proceeded with a catalogue of sins and their proper penance. The order he follows here is familiar, starting with the topic of murder, then proceeding with sins of a sexual nature, perjury, lying, theft and bearing false witness. A particular concern for the position of the church and its possessions is conspicuous, as well as a striking interest in matters of heresy and simony. Bartholomew seems to discuss what looks like an embryological theory of the sacraments, when he treats baptism, confirmation, the Eucharist and the last rites in that chronological order. Remarkable is also the long chapter on different kinds of divination, a subject that Bartholomew would return to at the end of his life when writing his book *Contra fatalitatis errorem*.[77] At the end of his catalogue he turned to rules and sins related to last things, as he discussed burial, bequests to the church and the question of whether people hanged for legal reasons deserve a Christian burial. He concluded with the topic of penitents who returned to their former sins, a long discussion of the different forms of excommunication including posthumous ones – curiously, but perhaps significantly in this context, violence against clerics, apostasy and a discussion of the reconciliation of sinners. Before ending with a list of commutations taken from the *Decretum* of Ivo of Chartres, he considered the most serious offences of all: sins against the

---

[73] Bartholomew, *Penitential*, c. 37, ed. Morey, *Bartholomew of Exeter*, p. 203.
[74] Bartholomew, *Penitential*, cc. 38–40, ed. Morey, *Bartholomew of Exeter*, pp. 204–210.
[75] Bartholomew, *Penitential*, c. 38, ed. Morey, *Bartholomew of Exeter*, p. 205; see the discussion of this issue by Payer, *Sex and the New Medieval Literature*, p. 60.
[76] Bartholomew, *Penitential*, c. 38, ed. Morey, *Bartholomew of Exeter*, p. 205.
[77] Bartholomew, *Penitential*, c. 104, ed. Morey, *Bartholomew of Exeter*, pp. 271–3; cf. Bell (ed.), *Bartholomaei Exoniensis Contra Fatalitatis Errorem*.

Holy Ghost. As Bartholomew affirms, the discussion of sins had led him from the smallest to the most heinous sin: *a minimis ad hoc maximum perveniatur.*[78]

Bartholomew's penitential seems particularly well suited to guide a priest confessor through the process of hearing confession, assigning a proper penance and finally reconciling the sinner.[79] Bartholomew supplies the confessor with general knowledge about sin, provides him with the necessary liturgical instruction and includes a list of canons dealing with specific sins. He gives guidance on how to deal with impenitent sinners (excommunication) and finally discusses penitential computistics in the form of commutations. His work shows knowledge of the latest forms of scholarship when he uses Gratian's *Decretum* and the *Sentences* of Peter the Lombard. His use of both the *Decretum* of Ivo of Chartres and that of Burchard of Worms demonstrates that these works were still being used in spite of the availability of the works of Gratian and Peter Lombard. In general, Bartholomew referred explicitly to authorities such as councils and papal decisions, but occasionally he also refers to the penitentials that Regino already regarded as authoritative: the Roman penitential and those attributed to Theodore of Canterbury and Bede the Venerable. The suitability of Bartholomew's penitential for pastoral practice is demonstrated by its relatively rich manuscript tradition. At least twenty-two manuscripts containing this work have been identified, while it is also frequently mentioned in medieval booklists. Later authors such as Robert of Flamborough and magister Serlo used it when composing their confessors' manuals.[80] Many of the manuscripts of this work are linked to monastic institutions, which might suggest that it was more useful for teaching purposes than for parochial uses.[81] Since the editor of the text published it from one manuscript, it is, unfortunately, impossible to see how readers of Bartholomew's book chose to adapt it to their own purposes. The editor's remarks concerning a different order at the end of

---

[78] Bartholomew, *Penitential*, c. 134, ed. Morey, *Bartholomew of Exeter*, p. 296.

[79] Taliadoros, 'Bartholomew', also stresses the practical character of the work.

[80] Diem, 'Virtues and vices in early texts,' pp. 207 and 219.

[81] For its manuscript tradition, see Morey, *Bartholomew of Exeter*, pp. 164–6, who knew eighteen manuscripts; three more mss. are mentioned in Bell, *Bartholomaei Exoniensis*, p. xviii, fn. 93; for its inclusion in booklists, Morey, *Bartholomew of Exeter*, and Bell, *Bartholomaei Exoniensis*, p. xix. The copy in Uppsala, Universitätsbibliothek, Ms. C 60 (England, s. XIII) was not known to Morey or Bell; see M. Andersson-Schmitt and M. Hedlund, *Mittelalterliche Handschriften der Universitätsbibliothek Uppsala. Katalog über die C-Sammlung*, vol. II (C 51–200) (Stockholm 1989), pp. 25–30, although it was already known to S. Kuttner, see his 'Retractationes', in S. Kuttner, *Gratian and the Schools of Law 1140–1234* (London 1983), VIII, 29, as noted by Taliadoros, 'Bartholomew', p. 457, fn. 9.

the text in some manuscripts suggest that it was not always used in the way that Bartholomew had intended.[82]

Bartholomew's *Penitential* is clearly a work stemming from the early phases of what is sometimes called a pastoral revolution.[83] One important impetus behind these developments is formed by the changes in educational institutions. The establishment of cathedral schools and universities in the eleventh and twelfth centuries led to a greater attention on logical consistency and to the creation of works like the *Decretum* of Gratian, which tried to evaluate apparent inconsistencies. Such grand systematizing works in turn influenced the production of texts meant to translate this general knowledge into useful tools for their implementation into everyday practice. How far this process was really successful is still to be investigated. Another text dated to the early years of the second half of the twelfth century, a text generally referred to by the two words with which it begins, *Homo quidam*, also shows clear signs of the learning taught in schools in France.[84] Its author has a clear didactic interest as is demonstrated, for example, by the chapter on the learning required of a priest ('De scientia sacerdotis') or by his ample use of definitions.[85] Occasionally he refers to French schoolmasters, when he criticizes 'magister Abailardus' or follows 'magister Gislebertus', probably Gilbert de la Porrée, who taught in Chartres and Paris in the second quarter of the twelfth century.[86] The uses of mythological knowledge in *Homo quidam*, for example when it refers to Parsiphae in discussing female sexual aberrances, or citing the *amorographus* Ovid, clearly reveals a certain degree of scholarly education.[87]

---

[82] Cf. the liberty scribes took when copying the penitential writings of Robert Grosseteste, see J. Goering and F. Mantello, 'The early penitential writings of Robert Grosseteste', *Recherches de Théologie Ancienne et Médiévale* 54 (1987), pp. 52–112, at pp. 59–61.

[83] For example, see H. Leyser, 'Clerical purity and the reordered world', in M. Rubin and W. Simons (eds.), *The Cambridge History of Christianity*, vol. IV: *Christianity in Western Europe c. 1100–1500* (Cambridge 2009), pp. 11–21, at p. 14.

[84] For this text, see P. Michaud-Quantin, 'Un manuel de confession archaïque dans le manuscrit Avranches 136', *Sacris Erudiri* 17 (1966), pp. 5–54. It is dated to the years 1155–65 by its editor because of its archaic character. It would be worthwhile to investigate this text and its date in more detail.

[85] Chapter 14: 'De scientia sacerdotis', ed. Michaud-Quantin, 'Un manuel', pp. 36–8; for definitions, see e.g. chapter 24 (p. 48) 'crapula, quae dicitur cruda epula', from Isidore of Seville, *Etymologiae* XX, 2, ed. W. Lindsay, *Isidori Hispalensis Episcopi Etymologiarum sive Originum Libri XX* (Oxford 1911); or 'nigromantia ... a nigros, quod est mors, et mantia, quod est divinatio', cf. Isidore. *Etymologiae* VIII, 9, 11.

[86] Chapter 10, ed. Michaud-Quantin, 'Un manuel', p. 31 and chapter 15, p. 38.

[87] 'Parsiphae', chapter 18, ed. Michaud-Quantin, p. 40; *amorographus* referring to Ovid and not to Horace as the editor indicates, chapter 10, p. 31. I have found no other instances of the term *amorographus* to indicate Ovid.

Homo quidam is therefore clearly influenced by the twelfth-century schools, but remarkably it nowhere reveals any use of Gratian's *Decretum*, a fact which has been used as a major argument to date it to the early years of the second half of the twelfth century. The author based himself mainly on Burchard's *Decretum*, and he counsels priests to read frequently in the choir of the church 'the Roman penitential, or that of Theodore of Canterbury or Bede or Burchard, or excerpts from these'.[88] The specification of the place where the priest has to read these books gives us an indication that these were generally preserved among the liturgical books in church. The author of *Homo quidam* clearly envisaged priests continuing to use the earlier penitential handbooks in conjunction with his own work. This corroborates the continuous employment of these texts, as is also suggested by the explicit use Bartholomew of Exeter made of these works. *Homo quidam* is a work that clearly combines an interest in the proper education of priest confessors with the earlier tradition of providing penitential tariffs. It discusses for example the question of what constitutes penance, where it originated (in paradise), or who created it; questions which reflect knowledge from the schools.[89] It also discusses more practical issues, such as the question of how often people are to come to confession. The text states that clerics should confess every Saturday, lay people at least three times a year with Easter, Pentecost and Christmas, a frequency that seems related to receiving the Eucharist.[90] Furthermore the confessor priest is instructed that when he establishes the proper penance for a sinner, he should discriminate according to the sinner's age, sex, wealth, health, legal and religious status, and should also take the precise nature of the offence into account; he should determine whether it concerned a sin out of volition, whether it was put into practice or not, whether it had become a habit, whether it became public, was done knowingly, spontaneously or under duress.[91]

Homo quidam also contains more practical information for the confessor, particularly in the second part, which the author explicitly introduces by expressing his intention to turn to more practical matters.[92] Here the author, for example, explains that someone who had publicly confessed

---

[88] *Homo quidam*, chapter 14, ed. Michaud-Quantin, 'Un manuel', p. 36: 'Legat ergo sacerdos frequenter in abside ecclesiae poenitentiale romanum vel Theodori Cantuariensis vel Bede vel Brocardi vel ex eis excerpta'.

[89] Chapter 1: 'De poenitentia', ed. Michaud-Quantin, 'Un manuel', p. 14.

[90] *Homo quidam*, chapter 2, ed. Michaud-Quantin, 'Un manuel', p. 15.

[91] *Homo quidam*, chapter 4, ed. Michaud-Quantin, 'Un manuel', pp. 19–20.

[92] *Homo quidam*, chapter 8: 'Nunc ea quae pertinent ad practicam dicamus', ed. Michaud-Quantin, 'Un manuel', p. 27.

to murder had to be guarded in a safe place by the priest in order that his life would not be threatened by a relative of the murdered person. He also gives the advice that the husband is to come to confession before his wife and that the penance assigned to the wife should conform to that of her husband, so as to avoid any suspicion on the husband's part that the woman in question had committed a serious offence.[93] In this part the author not only deals with the practical matter of how to receive a penitent, but also discusses the main characteristics and problems of major sins such as murder, fornication, theft and perjury as well as lesser sins such as flattery and sinful thoughts. At the end of the treatise the author deals with forms of penance: fasting, praying, alms and physical chastisement (*corporalis disciplina*). Among the latter we find the peculiar and original recommendation to order someone who liked kissing women to kiss the hand of a leper.[94] A sinner should hold back from inflicting such physical correction upon himself by his own initiative, for when it is imposed by someone else it provokes shame and this shame, so this text argues, forms part of the penance.[95]

Homo quidam contains penitential tariffs, but only when discussing specific cases. There is no attempt to provide a full catalogue of such tariffs, as in the earlier traditional penitentials. The author rather seems to anticipate that his work would be used in combination with the earlier texts, the reading of which he advocates in his work. The canons that he does include are sometimes rather peculiar. He censures, for example, sexual pollution in churches, negligence of the host or the breaking of dietary rules, which motivated its editor to conclude that the survival of such 'very primitive penitential practices' indicates that *Homo quidam* is an 'archaic text'. Together with the lack of any reference to Gratian's *Decretum*, this led him to date this work to the early years of the second half of the twelfth century.[96] Nevertheless, the text survives in two manuscripts which are dated to the period around the year 1200, indicating that at this date there still was an interest in such an allegedly archaic manual. The existence of only two manuscripts containing the work indicates, however, that it was not as popular as the penitential written by Bartholomew of Exeter.[97]

---

[93] *Homo quidam*, chapters 8 and 27, ed. Michaud-Quantin, 'Un manuel', pp. 27 and 54; for the latter case see the discussion in Payer, *Sex and the New Medieval Literature*, p. 70.

[94] For the importance of this theme mainly in hagiographical texts, see C. Peyroux, 'The leper's kiss', in S. Farmer and B. H. Rosenwein (eds.), *Monks & Nuns, Saints and Outcasts. Religion in Medieval Society* (Ithaca / London 2000), pp. 172–88.

[95] Chapter 26, 'De satisfactione', ed. Michaud-Quantin, 'Un manuel', p. 51.

[96] Michaud-Quantin, 'Un manuel', p. 6.

[97] Mss. Avranches, Bibliothèque municipale, 136 and Paris, Bibliothèque Nationale de France, Ms. lat. 13582.

If we look at the two texts discussed above, it becomes clear that the schools certainly had an influence on the genesis of new penitential handbooks. They testify to the existence of a more general discussion of a theoretical kind, regarding several aspects of penance. The texts deal with the nature of penance, its origin and its components, as well as the nature of sins. At the same time these texts demonstrate that the existing penitential tariffs were not done away with. On the contrary, both texts presuppose that a priest when hearing confession would be looking to penitential tariffs for guidance when deciding what kind of penance to impose. The penitentials referred to in *Homo quidam*, i.e. the Roman penitential or those attributed to Theodore of Canterbury, Bede or Burchard, however, are no longer being copied after the twelfth century. This does not mean that there was no longer a need for penitential tariffs. A confessional treatise attributed to Robert Grosseteste, bishop of Lincoln from 1235 to 1253, includes a long list of rather traditional canons prescribing precise tariffs for specific sins, many of them stemming from the *Corrector sive Medicus* of Burchard of Worms.[98] The Bolognese canonist John of God (Johannes de Deo) composed around the middle of the thirteenth century a penitential manual in seven books. The second book contains a simple list of 112 penitential canons determining specific penances for specific sins, but always indicating the authoritative canonical sources, such as Gratian's *Decretum* or the collection of decretals made by Gregory IX known as the *Liber Extra*, on which the individual judgments were based.[99] In the thirteenth century this list collected by John probably took over the function of earlier penitential tariffs. It was widely known not only through John's work but also through numerous later handbooks for confessors that adopted John's list.[100]

The twelfth century, therefore, certainly brought changes in the way people thought about penance and confession. This was mostly evident in the schools where teachers and students discussed the nature of sin and the proper forms of atonement in a sophisticated way. The development of canon law as a proper academic subject led to a greater stress on the demarcations between the fields of canon law and pastoral literature treating penance and confession. The pastoral literature from the twelfth century dealing with penance shows clear signs of the education in the schools, but there is not a sharp break with the earlier tradition. Tariffs as

---

[98] Goering and Mantello, 'The early penitential writings of Robert Grosseteste'; for his uses of Burchard, see pp. 69–70.

[99] P. Payer, 'The origins and development of the later *canones penitentiales*', *Mediaeval Studies* 61 (1999), pp. 81–105.

[100] See Payer, 'The origins and development of the later *canones penitentiales*'.

they are found in earlier penitential handbooks did not disappear but continued to be used in pastoral care. Historians sometimes see such tariffs as indicators for a formalistic, purely 'outward' approach of morality, contrasting it with the greater interiority that was advocated in the twelfth century.[101] This seems too simplistic a view. It not only presupposes a very specific, mechanical use of penitential canons that is not corroborated by the sources, it also underestimates the importance of penitential tariffs in the twelfth century and beyond. The growing complexity of society and the fact that intellectuals in cathedral schools and the incipient universities spent time, reason and energy in their endeavour to understand and define sin, contrition and atonement surely had consequences for the way people dealt with confession, but to interpret such changes as a fundamental revolution in moral behaviour, a turnabout from a purely formalistic perception of sin to a purely moral one, is not an interpretation that is supported by the evidence. As we have seen, Abelard's treatment of penance in his *Scito te ipsum* is not radically different from earlier conceptions, while on the ground didactic confessional treatises, if they do not incorporate earlier penitential texts, often recommend their use. Instead of a moral revolution, there seems to have been much more continuity in pastoral practice than some historians in the past have concluded. In this respect the closer study of penitential attitudes supports recent historical studies that add nuance to the divide between the early Middle Ages and the twelfth century.

---

[101] Angenendt, *Geschichte der Religiosität im Mittelalter*, pp. 634–41; Lutterbach, 'Intentions- oder Tathaftung?' and Angenendt, 'Die mittelalterlichen Bußbücher – Trägermedien von Einfachreligiosität?'.

Conclusion

In 1215 the Fourth Lateran Council decreed that every Christian who had come to the age of discretion should confess his sins at least once a year individually in front of his own priest.[1] This decree is sometimes regarded as innovative for introducing regular lay confession, but it should rather be seen as the first general regulation on this topic in a centralizing Christian Church. There had been earlier rules concerning the frequency of confession, which was mostly closely related to receiving the Eucharist, sometimes requiring a higher rate of three times a year.[2] Regino of Prüm had included among his demands for the laity that they should confess their sins at the beginning of Lent and fulfil their penitential obligations at least once a year.[3] What was new was the way in which Innocent III now called together this enormous gathering of prelates and secular lords in order to formulate a truly formidable programme of reform that was to be applicable for all Christendom. The Fourth Lateran Council has been called 'the most important statement of the nature and structure of the Catholic faith since the great ecumenical councils of late antiquity', as well as 'the most pastoral of all the general church councils of the Middle Ages'.[4] Inspired by ideas about a much more active role of the church in society as they had been developing in Parisian circles, Lateran IV inaugurated a remarkable increase in the composition of pastoral works, a development that is sometimes referred

---

[1] This is the famous c. 21 'Omnis utriusque sexus fidelis postquam ad annos discretionis pervenerit, omnia sua solus peccata saltem semel in anno fideliter confiteatur proprio sacerdoti', ed. A. García y García, *Constitutiones Concilii quarti Lateranensis una cum Commentariis glossatorum*, Monumenta Iuris Canonici, Series A: Corpus Glossatorum 2 (Vatican 1981), pp. 67–8.

[2] Meens, 'Frequency and nature', pp. 37–8.

[3] Regino, *Libri duo*, II, 5, 65, ed. Wasserschleben, *Reginonis libri*, p. 214; the attempt by M. Ohst, *Pflichtbeichte. Untersuchungen zum Bußwesen im Hohen und Späten Mittelalter* (Tübingen 1995), pp. 21–2 to explain this text away is unconvincing.

[4] W. C. Jordan, *Europe in the High Middle Ages* (London 2001), p. 212 and L. Boyle, 'The Fourth Lateran Council and manuals of popular theology', in T. J. Heffernan (ed.), *The Popular Literature of Medieval England* (Knoxville TN 1985), pp. 30–43, at p. 30.

to as a pastoral revolution.[5] These works, many of which still need careful study, were meant to propagate the new ideas about penance and confession as they had developed in the twelfth-century schools to the priests and monks hearing confession and through them to communicate these to the laity. Penance, vices and virtues became the main subjects of a wealth of pastoral literature that was being produced in this period. Many of these works are concerned with the proper way in which a confessor should deal with a confessing sinner: by carefully probing and questioning him or her, the confessor should not only extract a full confession, but also assess whether the sinner was moved by real contrition and at the same time assess the personal qualities and social position of the sinner in order to establish the proper form of satisfaction for this person.

This interest in the inner life of the sinner is often regarded as something radically new, reflecting a focus on the interior, which is contrasted with the focus on the exterior in the earlier period. This book argues that this is too simplistic a distinction. Not only do earlier handbooks for confessors demonstrate that the motivation of the sinner, the sincerity of his conversion and his personal and social predispositions were already of great importance for assessing the correct forms of satisfaction, but we also know that in the twelfth century and later penitential tariffs – the main reason for assuming that penance before the twelfth century had been exterior – continued to be used by confessors. Of course one could argue that in the earlier period the penitential handbooks were used in ways that were contrary to the intentions of the composers of such texts, but why should this be different for the later period? What is new, however, in the handbooks for confessors is the focus on the proper way to interrogate the sinner, we could say the pastoral aspects of penitential practice. This technique of questioning is closely related to the development in schools and later in the universities, where many of the authors of these manuals had been educated. And it is surely no coincidence that religious orders that were specializing in hearing confession were also very active in the Inquisition.

It is now generally accepted that public penance, which, as we have seen, never completely disappeared in the earlier period, continued to be practised throughout the thirteenth, fourteenth and fifteenth centuries. We saw that from the Carolingian period onwards public penance was employed in highly politicized settings. From the thirteenth century on,

---

[5] For the influence of Parisian scholastics, see J. Baldwin, *Masters, Princes and Merchants. The Social Views of Peter the Chanter & His Circle*, 2 vols. (Princeton 1970), vol. I, pp. 315–43; for the central importance of the *cura animarum* at this council and the consequent effusion of pastoral texts, see Boyle, 'The Fourth Lateran Council'.

public penance was a regular feature of the liturgical life of towns in northern France, as Mary Mansfield was able to establish.[6] In Konstanz in the fifteenth century large groups of several hundred public penitents were being readmitted to the church on Maundy Thursday.[7] Despite all discussions about the importance of the inner life, there remained the need to shame sinners publicly as well as, so it seems, the need of sinners to be humiliated. During the later medieval period the tension that we observed for the earlier period, the tension between the inward and the outward, between the personal and the social aspects of penance, continued to be a central feature of the penitential process. Because penance was meant to reconcile the sinner with God as well as with the Christian community, interior feelings of remorse and outward signs of humility were necessarily part of this process. There may have been differences in the emphasis that was put on the personal or the social aspects, but there is no clear evidence to show that in the earlier period there was generally more stress on the social and outward aspects than on the personal or interior ones.

The evolution from an outward ritualistic penitential process towards an interior personal one seems to be more the result of historiographical concerns than suggested by the sources themselves. Does this mean that there were no important developments in the history of penance at all during the period under discussion? This study has argued that there were important developments, but that the long-cherished narrative of an evolution from a late antique public form of penance to a private one, through the intermediate stages of a tariffed insular penance that in its turn was combined with the ancient public one in the Carolingian era, is too simplistic. Following the trail of the books intended to help a confessor in his task, we have observed several important moments in the history of penance.

First it is clear that sixth-century Gaul was no penitential wasteland, but rather a period in which ecclesiastical councils were discussing penance in many aspects. The focus on institutional forms of penance (public or private) has clouded the rich variation of penitential procedures that existed on the ground. Contemporaries apparently saw no fundamental differences where twentieth-century historians spoke of clearly distinguishable forms of penance. Penance was a means of repairing disturbed relations not only with God, but also with the social

---

[6] Mansfield, *The Humiliation of Sinners*.

[7] F. Neumann, *Öffentliche Sünder in der Kirche des späten Mittelalters. Verfahren – Sanktionen – Rituale* (Cologne / Weimar / Vienna 2008), p. 28 referring to the chronicle written by Christoph Schulhaiß.

environment. Particularly in the earlier period that has been discussed here, that is up to the late eighth and early ninth century, we see that penitential procedures were applied for lay people in cases where they had caused major social disturbance by their behaviour. By committing acts of violence or sexual licence, they had besmirched the honour of the victim and/or his family, and this loss of honour had to be redressed. In order to be able to give proper satisfaction for such a loss of honour, clerical mediation and penitential procedures could be applied. As such penance probably was often the result of a process of negotiation, and the use of the term private in this context must be regarded as misleading.

In Ireland monasteries, monks and nuns played an important role in the church as well as in society, and therefore were eminently suitable for acting as intermediaries in conflicts. It is in this context that we first encounter penitential handbooks, and these were written in a group of closely related monastic centres in Ireland. These texts helped to establish some standards for such mediation. Whether such books were in general use in Ireland is doubtful, while there is also a lot of uncertainty about how general the practices of confession and penance were. There are indications that they were confined to those families closely related to monastic centres, the dependent farmers (*manaig*) and the benefactors of such institutions. Penitential books speak of compensation for the offended parties, while the periods of fasting prescribed in them probably also helped to satisfy existing desires for revenge. For the offender penance was not only a means of settling a conflict, but the close association with monks and holy men and women could also be honourable. Precisely because of the ambiguity inherent in the concept of humiliation, an ambiguity fed by the very positive connotations of the virtue of humility in Christian morality, penance could also be a source of honour. Much depended, however, on the perception of what actually transpired.

In the wake of the Irish and Anglo-Saxon missionaries travelling on the European mainland, penitential handbooks were introduced in the Frankish kingdoms. We find evidence of them in the monasteries founded by the Irish monk Columbanus and his followers. The Irish concept of penance as a form of conflict mediation was used in combination with existing regulations concerning the right of sanctuary in churches. The Columbanian monasteries became holy places *par excellence* and were therefore ideal places of refuge for aristocrats when they ran into trouble with more powerful groups.

In the seventh century we can see that penitential decisions for the laity are no longer geared only towards socially upsetting sorts of behaviour. Theodore of Canterbury provided, for instance, proper penances for improper forms of sexual behaviour among spouses. This indicates that confession and penance were used more as a pastoral tool meant to foster compliance with ecclesiastically regulated moral behaviour. Other Anglo-Saxon works followed suit, but with less stress on ecclesiastical rules and legislation than in the work of Theodore. In the eighth-century penitential attributed to Archbishop Egbert of York, which was possibly composed in England, we can observe a greater sensitivity for the needs of lay sinners coming to confession. The penitential associated here with the famous Anglo-Saxon missionary Willibrord was written in the same mood. It also distinguishes itself by a remarkable attention for the needs of lay people who wanted to make atonement for their sins. Both works, associated with Egbert of York and Willibrord, were employed in missionary fields on the Continent. Another famous missionary and church reformer, the West-Saxon monk Boniface, who later became archbishop of Mainz, probably had a hand in the composition of a very influential penitential, the *Excarpsus Cummeani*. Boniface did not shy away from imposing penance on reluctant sinners, and the themes expressed in the *Excarpsus* do not only seem to reflect Bonifatian concerns: the fact that the composers of the text always selected only one sentence dealing with a specific issue instead of offering a plurality of choices seems to concord well with Boniface's anxiety for clear rulings. These texts associated with Anglo-Saxon clerical authorities demonstrate more of a pastoral concern than the earlier Irish ones.

These still very tender Anglo-Saxon traditions received an enormous impetus by their contact and cooperation with the family of the Carolingians who took over royal authority from the Merovingian dynasty in 751. Willibrord and Boniface were both closely allied with the Carolingian family. In the second half of the eighth century and into the ninth, we can observe an increase in the production of new penitential handbooks as well as of manuscripts containing such texts, particularly from the northern and eastern parts of the Frankish empire, regions where the Carolingian family owned most of their landed possessions. Such proliferation of texts and manuscripts must be related to Carolingian efforts to forge a truly Christian empire, a venture also known as the Carolingian Reforms. To retain divine favour it was important that the Franks lived a genuinely Christian life, and sins were seen as endangering their favourable relationship with the Deity. The increase in the production of penitential texts and manuscripts was also part of the greater effort to train and to educate the priesthood and the laity, an effort in which the Carolingian Church invested heavily, assisted by the secular rulers.

Such a proliferation of penitential texts led in the early ninth century to fierce discussions among ecclesiastical rulers, who were clearly inspired by conceptions of uniformity that did not correspond with the diversity of penitential rulings that were circulating in the Frankish empire. At the five great reform councils assembled by the aging Emperor Charlemagne in the year 813, penance and the proper use of penitential texts were important issues. The councils demonstrate, however, the great scope of variation in dealing with sins that existed in the Carolingian realms, and the bishops of the empire were incapable of solving the issue conclusively. During those councils penance seems to have been a major topic of discussion in which particularly at the council of Chalon-sur-Saône stress was being laid on the venerable ancient tradition as well as on the public nature of the ritual of penance. The councils, moreover, reveal the wide variety of penitential means that were being employed in the wide geographical region under Carolingian political dominance. What is clear, however, is that in this period not only were penitential texts widely distributed but also penance in its manifold manifestations was an eagerly discussed phenomenon. This demonstrates that penance was no longer something that reached only a minority of the lay world, but it had become a central aspect of Christian religiosity. The greater control of Carolingian bishops over their diocesan priests, as manifested for example in the episcopal statutes that were composed in this period, and the development of parochial structures in many parts of the Carolingian empire were doubtless important elements contributing to the increasing importance of penitential practices in the Carolingian world.

The central importance of penance in the Carolingian world is further stressed by the ways in which in times of turmoil empire-wide penitential rituals were organized, radiating from the court. Penitential fasts and litanies had to appease an enraged Deity, or should secure divine favour for the army during dangerous campaigns. The close connections between the court and the Frankish people also prompted a special interest in sins occurring in the immediate entourage of the emperor, for these could endanger the whole realm. Louis the Pious removed Charlemagne's daughters from the court when he took the throne after his father's demise in 814 because of their sinful and scandalous behaviour.[8] In 822 Louis did public penance for his treatment of his brothers and in 833 he was forcefully submitted to a penitential ritual by his revolting sons in Soissons. This was a thoroughly orchestrated ecclesiastical ritual by which the sons removed their father from political office. Because of the crucial political consequences involved, the bishops in charge were carefully stressing that they were following authoritative and

---

[8] J. Nelson, 'Women at the court of Charlemagne. A case of monstrous regiment?', in J. Parsons (ed.), *Medieval Queenship* (New York 1993), pp. 43–62 and 203–6. De Jong, *The Penitential State*, p. 21.

legal traditions, but the ways in which they twisted existing rituals demonstrates the flexibility and therefore the variety of penitential ritual in the Carolingian world.

In the period that saw the public penance of Louis the Pious, we can see the traces of a fierce discussion regarding the authority of the existing penitential handbooks. The authority of such texts and the variety of traditions that were available led to the composition of penitential books which addressed these problems in different ways. The council of Paris of 829, a council closely related to the political troubles that would lead to Louis's penance in Soissons, pronounced sharp criticism of traditional penitentials and their lack of canonical authority. At the behest of Ebo of Reims, one of the key players in Louis's downfall, Halitgar of Cambrai produced the first penitential in a new style, trying as much as possible to keep to the authority of well-established sources of canon law. Hrabanus Maurus and others followed in his wake. These reform penitentials were clearly successful if the number of remaining manuscripts containing such works form an appropriate yardstick to measure their success. We can observe, however, that those reform penitentials that did not solely stick to the narrowly defined sources of canon law, but were willing to include sentences from traditional penitential handbooks, survive in more manuscript copies than the stricter ones. The fact that the reform penitentials were often copied together with more traditional texts of the genre is a further indication that earlier ways of dealing with sins and sinners remained important. The whole discussion about the importance of the proper authority of penitential sentences that we see revealed in the texts composed in the late eighth and first half of the ninth centuries does indicate that bishops were trying to get a better grip on penitential practice. Given the central importance of the concept of penance in Carolingian society, this need not come as a surprise.

The issues of episcopal control of penitential procedures and the close relation between penitential rulings and canon law were central to the handbook for pastoral visitations that Regino of Prüm wrote shortly after the year 900 and to the impressive collection of canon law that Burchard of Worms composed a hundred years later. Regino's handbook provided a bishop with the necessary canonical tools to correct local abuses when touring his diocese and visiting local communities. Burchard assembled twenty books of canon law to assist confessors in hearing confession. Both works contain long lists of questions that a confessor could use when interrogating a repentant sinner. Regino and Burchard both worked in the Rhineland where episcopal control might have been more pervasive than elsewhere, but particularly Burchard's *Decretum* had a huge influence and spread rapidly within the Ottonian kingdom and beyond.

In the tenth and eleventh centuries we see a decrease in penitential activity in the early Capetian kingdom. After the abundant productivity of the Carolingian period with its many new compilations and a generous copying of penitential books, demand seems to have been met. Lack of support for the royal dynasty may also explain part of this decrease in scribal and compilatory activity. In other regions, however, Frankish texts were being copied and used for composing new texts in this field. In England Archbishop Wulfstan played a pivotal role in promoting penance with the help of Carolingian material. The emphasis on instructing the clergy with the help of the vernacular, however, went back to royal initiative, as it can be related to the translation programme of Alfred the Great. In Spain royal initiative was also crucial for the introduction and employment of Carolingian penitential books. There the *Excarpsus Cummeani* and the *P. Remense* were being excerpted to compose three new texts, the *P. Vigilanum*, the *Cordubense* and the *Silense*. These three texts are closely related and are better regarded as reflections of a royally inspired movement of reform than as witnesses to pastoral care, as the two impressive manuscripts preserving the *Vigilanum* clearly illustrate. The *Cordubense* is unique in that it preserves regulations for Christians living among a Muslim majority. In central and southern Italy Carolingian penitential books were only introduced in the tenth century and later, but here this did not seem to have been the result of royal ambitions. It was the monastery of Montecassino or a closely affiliated institution that played a crucial role in this process. It was there that the influential canon law collections in five and nine books were being composed and preserved which shaped those modest penitential texts that are found in rather small manuscripts in combination with liturgical and pastoral material. This suggests that in central and southern Italy penance was organized from central monastic institutions thus influencing local communities, with only a limited role being preserved for bishops.

The dissemination of Frankish penitential books in regions bordering on the former Carolingian empire in the tenth and eleventh centuries does not seem to have been the result of a spontaneous expansion of penitential Frankish traditions and texts, but rather of conscious efforts in specific circles, such as that of Archbishop Wulfstan, King Ferdinand I of León or the monastery of Montecassino. Although we can observe which texts were being employed in these border regions, it is hard to pin down what exactly constituted the penitential traditions that were borrowed from the Carolingians. Was it a greater grip on local communities that penitential discipline and ritual allowed? Was it the idea of divine support in battle that demanded a particular Christian way of life for a king's subjects? The ritual of *deditio* by which conflicts could be settled without recourse to violent means, which is closely associated with penitential ritual, could be another attraction of Carolingian penitential traditions. The ritual is well studied for the Ottonian and Salian period and regions, and there are some indications for its wider diffusion. Royal penance also seems to be a Carolingian tradition that was adopted in neighbouring regions.

The importance of penance and beliefs about salvation in medieval Christianity is clearly revealed by the immediate and impressive response to Urban II's call to liberate the Holy Land from Muslim hands. For most participants in the First Crusade penance and redemption were central in their motives to undertake such an arduous and demanding journey. This suggests that penance was not only a tool for the ecclesiastical elite to better control and monitor the laity, but that the laity truly experienced an urgent need to obtain absolution for their sins.

The twelfth century brought change, but not as radical a change as has sometimes been supposed. There is not enough ground for the supposition that Christians in the earlier period were driven by external motives to comply to rigorous penitential rules while in the twelfth century we would meet confessing individuals searching their souls for true repentance. What was new, however, was the development of new modes of discourse. In the cathedral schools teachers were clearly thinking hard about the nature of sin and of true repentance. Abelard was one of those teachers, although his influence in the twelfth century remained rather limited. The other form of discourse that was developed pertains to the field of the scholarly study of canon law that we see truly developing in this period. Gratian's *Decretum*, in its first and its second recensions, forms the apogee of this process. In this process pastoral and penitential themes were ever more clearly separated from legal procedures. This is exemplified in the northern French canonical collection known as the *Panormia*, a work formerly attributed to Ivo of Chartres. The *Panormia* is based on the much more comprehensive authentic collection of Ivo, the *Decretum*, but leaves out all penitential material. Where, for example, Burchard of Worms had organized an impressive body of canon law in order to assist priests in hearing confession, the canon lawyers of the twelfth century were growing into an ever more specialized profession, members of which hardly if ever heard confessions themselves.

Two twelfth-century penitential handbooks, that written by Bartholomew of Exeter probably in the 1160s and the anonymous work known as *Homo quidam*, traditionally dated in the early second half of the twelfth century, demonstrate that the knowledge of the cathedral schools did reach the practical literature that was intended to be used by confessors.

They use or refer to the famous masters such as Gratian and Abelard and contain advanced discussions of the nature of sin or of the origin of penance. Both emphasize that they were first of all designed to be of practical assistance to confessors. Both moreover contain traditional lists of tariffs and are clearly designed to be used in conjunction with more traditional handbooks. These works testify to the seeping in of knowledge from the schools into the practice of penance, which is also manifest in their clear concern for the proper instruction of confessors, but the footing that the lists of sins with their accompanying penances gave to confessors was not done away with. There is therefore no sign that in practice penance changed as drastically in the twelfth century as has sometimes been supposed. The *canones penitentiales* as developed by John of God around the middle of the thirteenth century were widely adopted and continued to fulfil the role of the earlier traditional penitential manuals with their tariffs well into the later Middle Ages. How exactly they functioned in the changing world of the thirteenth century and later cannot be treated here.

Penance, therefore, clearly changed in the years between 600 and 1200. Yet it is hard to fit these changes into a simple scheme. Even by concentrating on the tradition of penitential handbooks and thereby excluding several less formal forms of penitential procedures, it is clear that there was rich variety on the ground. This is the more striking since the handbooks for confessors were closely interrelated as they frequently borrowed material from earlier texts of this kind. Yet the distribution of these texts, the way they arranged their material as well as the combination of texts in which they are preserved in their codicological context all suggest development, diversity and change. Such change was not one-directional. Instead we see a lot of diversity and experiments. Nonetheless, it is possible to see some general developments. In concluding this book I want to highlight a few of those with due caution. First, we see that formal ways of dealing with sins in the earlier period discussed in this book concentrated on sins of a socially disruptive kind. Other sins were dealt with in a much more informal way. Gradually more segments of human behaviour were being drawn to formal ways of atonement that were directed and controlled by the clergy. Whether we are dealing here with a topdown policy or with a more demand-driven development is hard to decide. Some ecclesiastical authorities, such as Regino of Prüm or Wulfstan of York, seem to have been advocating a topdown approach, but we should not rule out the possibility that sinners were really concerned about their salvation and actively sought confession and penance. Sinners might have been attracted by three major factors. First by the religious prestige that performing penance could bring, second by the possibility to substitute secular punishments or forms of satisfaction with ecclesiastical penance and lastly by the social prestige that a close association with an authoritative ecclesiastical personality or institution might provide.

How pervasive penance was is hard to decide. If the numbers of penitential books provide some guidance here, it seems safe to conclude that from the ninth century onwards confessing one's sins was a well-known practice in many regions of the Carolingian empire. Moreover, in that period we see penance forming a crucial aspect of political discourse, we observe a notable increase in texts and manuscripts for priests regarding confession, we have inventories of local churches which reveal that penitential books were part of the personal library of a priest and we have provisions which decree that every Christian should receive communion at least three times a year. Since confession was closely linked to receiving the Eucharist, this provides a clear indication of the frequency of confession in this period. Whether we can infer from this evidence that confession was a regular feature of Christian life in the whole Carolingian realm, let alone in other regions, remains difficult. It seems, however, that the Fourth Lateran Council did not decree something revolutionary and new when it demanded that every Christian should confess his or her sins at least once a year.

In many regions we see a concern on behalf of ecclesiastical authorities to gain control of the remedies for sin. We must assume that quite a few laymen and women managed to deal with their sins without ecclesiastical mediation, but we see the role of clerics increasing over time. In the early stages charismatic men and women could hear confession and help to absolve sins, but from the seventh century onwards the role of priests in this process was ever more emphasized. In the ninth century and later our sources reveal that bishops were trying to get a better grip on the whole process of confession and penance. Confessors not only mediated between the sinner and God or the Church, but as has been argued here often also between conflicting parties. In this process of increasing ecclesiastical control, texts were composed in order to assist priests in their task of hearing confession, which not only helped them to assign the appropriate form of penance, but also gave direction on how to receive and absolve sinners. Books for penitential guidance moreover contained quite a few ecclesiastical regulations that we would now regard as being part of canon law. The fields of canon law and penance were closely connected during the period under study here and only grew apart in the twelfth century with the birth of the science of canon law.

Whether we can use the frequency of confession as a yardstick with which to measure the nature of medieval religion is questionable. The same should be said about the range of sins that penitential books describe or the way that people dealt with such sins. To infer from such observations that medieval people were still essentially pagan or stuck in a kind of archaic religiosity seems hazardous, at least. Christianity is not an ahistorical phenomenon, but can take many different forms and changed and still changes over time. A genuinely historical question is not whether we regard medieval men and women as really Christian, but how they regarded themselves and how they saw others. What they regarded as truly Christian may differ from our perception of true Christianity, but is therefore no less true, if we look at this question from a historical perspective. This book argues that conceptions of sin and atonement were a crucial part of medieval Christianity for the period 600–1200. Like Christianity itself, however, ideas and practices concerning sins and their remedies were neither uniform nor unchanging. The sources discussed in this book clearly demonstrate this. They also demonstrate that it is hardly justifiable to characterize early medieval penance as purely outward and mechanical.

There still are many other sources that one could study fruitfully to get a fuller picture of penance and confession in this age and regretfully quite a lot of regions have remained underexplored in this study. Nonetheless, if this book has succeeded in getting across some idea of the variety and of the experiments and new directions that medieval people were developing with regard to their feelings of guilt and the ways they could make up for their faults, it will have done its job.

Appendix 1: The manuscripts of Theodore's penitential

VERSION G (*CANONES GREGORII*)

Kynžvart, Zámecká knihovna, 20 K 20 (s. XII/1, St Blasien)

London, British Library, Add. 8873 (s. XII/1, Italy)

London, British Library, Add. 16413 (s. XI in., southern Italy)

Merseburg, Dombibliothek, Ms. 103 (s. IX/1, northern Italy)

Monte Cassino, Archivio dell'Abbazia, Cod. 372 (s. XI in., S. Nicola della Cicogna, near Monte Cassino)

Munich, Bayerische Staatsbibliothek, Clm 3852 (s. XI, southern Germany)

Munich, Bayerische Staatsbibliothek, Clm 6241 (s. X/2, Freising)

Munich, Bayerische Staatsbibliothek, Clm 6245 (s. IX/2, Freising)[1]

Munich, Bayerische Staatsbibliothek, Clm 14789 (s. VIII/IX, France)

Oxford, Bodleian Library, Bodl. 311 (s. X, northern–northwestern France)[2]

Paris, Bibliothèque Nationale de France, lat. 2123 (814–16, Flavigny)

Paris, Bibliothèque Nationale de France, lat. 3848 B (s. VIII–IX, Flavigny)

Paris, Bibliothèque Nationale de France, n.a.l. 281 (s. X/XI, northern Italy/southern France)

Prague, Knihovna pražké kapituly, O. LXXXIII (short before 794, Bavaria?)[3]

Vatican, Biblioteca Apostolica Vaticana, lat. 5751 (s. IX ex., northern Italy)

---

[1] A short excerpt on f. 2v.   [2] Körntgen, *Studien zu den Quellen*, p. 91.
[3] For a Bavarian origin of this ms., see R. McKitterick, 'The scripts of the Prague Sacramentary, Prague Archivo O 83', *Early Medieval Europe* 20 (2012), pp. 407–27.

VERSION U (*DISCIPULUS UMBRENSIUM*)

Berlin, Staatsbibliothek Preußischer Kulturbesitz, Hamilton 132 (H) (s. IX in., Corbie)

Brussels, Koninklijke Bibliotheek, 10127–44 (s. VIII/IX, northeastern France, Belgium?)

Cambridge, Corpus Christi College, 320 (s. XI–XII, England)

Cologne, Dombibliothek, 91 (s. VIII/IX, Burgundy or Corbie)

Cologne, Dombibliothek, 210 (s. VIII/2, northeastern France)[4]

Eton College Library, Bp 5.16 (eighteenth-century copy made by Muriall)

London, British Library, Add. 16413 (s. XI in., southern Italy)

Munich, Bayerische Staatsbibliothek, Clm 22288 (s. XII/1, Windberg, bei Straubing)

Paris, Bibliothèque Nationale de France, lat. 1454 (s. IX 3/4, near Paris)

Paris, Bibliothèque Nationale de France, lat. 1455 (s. IX/2, northern France)

Paris, Bibliothèque Nationale de France, lat. 1603 (s. VIII/IX, northern France)

Paris, Bibliothèque Nationale de France, lat. 3842A (s. IX med. or 3/4, Paris?)

Paris, Bibliothèque Nationale de France, lat. 3846 (s. IX in., northern France)

Paris, Bibliothèque Nationale de France, lat. 12444 (s. VIII/IX, probably Fleury)[5]

Paris, Bibliothèque Nationale de France, lat. 12445 (s. IX 3/4, Reims)

Paris, Bibliothèque Nationale de France, lat. 13452 (s. XVII made on behalf of the Maurists)

St Gall, Stiftsbibliothek, Cod. 150 (820–40, St Gall)

Stuttgart, Württembergische Landesbibliothek, HB VI 107 (s. XI ex., near Lake Constance)

Stuttgart, Württembergische Landesbibliothek, HB VI 109 (s. IX 1/3, southwest Germany, Constance?)

---

[4] Actually a comprehensive reception of Theodore's work in a canon law collection, see Zechiel-Eckes, 'Zur kirchlichen Rechtspraxis'.

[5] See M. Stadelmaier, *Die Collectio Sangermanensis XXI titulorum. Eine systematische Kanonessammlung der frühen Karolingerzeit. Studien und Edition* (Frankfurt a.M. 2004), pp. 97–100.

Stuttgart, Württembergische Landesbibliothek, HB VI 112 (s. X, near Lake Constance)

Vatican, Biblioteca Apostolica Vaticana, Pal. lat. 485 (s. IX 3/4, Lorsch)

Vatican, Biblioteca Apostolica Vaticana, Pal. lat. 554 (s. IX/1, Lorsch?)

Vesoul, Bibliothèque Municipale, Ms. 79 (73) (s. XI, France)[6]

Vienna, Österreichische Nationalbibliothek, lat. 2195 (s. VIII ex., Salzburg)

Vienna, Österreichische Nationalbibliothek, 2223 (s. IX 1/3, Main region)

Würzburg, Universitätsbibliothek, M. p. th. q. 32 (s. IX/1, Würzburg/ Fulda)

[6] Mordek, *Bibliotheca*, pp. 894–8

Appendix 2: The manuscripts of the *Excarpsus Cummeani*

Aschaffenburg, Stiftsbibliothek, Ms. Perg. 37 (s. XII, Aschaffenburg)

Avignon, Bibliothèque municipale, Cod. 175 (s. IX 2/4, Gellone)

Basel, Universitätsbibliothek, Fragm. N I 4 (s. IX, 2/4)

Berlin, Staatsbibliothek Preußischer Kulturbesitz, Phillipps 1667 (s. VIII/IX, France, Autun)[1]

Cologne, Dombibliothek, 91 (s. VIII/IX, Burgundy or Corbie)

Copenhagen, Kongelige Bibliotek, Ny. Kgl. S. 58 8° (s. VIII in., northern France)[2]

Darmstadt, Hessische Landesbibliothek, Hs. 895 Fragm. (s. VIII ex., northern Italy)[3]

Einsiedeln, Stiftsbibliothek, Cod. 326 (s. IX ex., Germany)

Karlsruhe, Badische Landesbibliothek, Aug. IC (s. IX/2, western Germany)

Leiden, Bibliotheek der Rijksuniversiteit, Cod. Vulc. 108 nr. 12 (s. IX)[4]

Munich, Bayerische Staatsbibliothek, Clm 6243 (s. VIII ex., near Lake Constance)

Munich, Bayerische Staatsbibliothek, Clm 22288 (s. XII, Bamberg)

Munich, Bayerische Staatsbibliothek, Clm 29505/1 (s. IX med.-2, Bavaria?) (fragment)[5]

---

[1] O. Heiming argued for an Autun origin on the basis of the baptismal litany in the sacramentary included in the manuscript, see Heiming, *Liber Sacramentorum Augustodunensis*, pp. xii–xvii.

[2] For its origin in northern France, see Meens, 'The oldest Manuscript witness of the *Collectio canonum Hibernensis*', pp. 9–12.

[3] See Haggenmüller, *Die Überlieferung der Beda und Egbert zugeschriebenen Bußbücher*, pp. 58–9.

[4] See Haggenmüller, *Die Überlieferung der Beda und Egbert zugeschriebenen Bußbücher*, pp. 68–9.

[5] H. Hauke, *Katalog der lateinischen Fragmente der Bayerischen Staatsbibliothek München*, vol. II: *Clm 29315–29520* (Wiesbaden 2002), p. 482.

New York, Library of the Hispanic Society of America, HC 380/819 (s. XI, Catalonia)

Oxford, Bodleian Library, Bodl. 572 (s. IX 1/3, northern France)

Oxford, Bodleian Library, Laud. Misc. 263 (s. IX in., Mainz)

Paris, Bibliothèque Nationale de France, lat. 2296 (s. IX 2/4, St Amand)

Paris, Bibliothèque Nationale de France, lat. 10588 (s. IX/1-med., Burgundy/southern France)

Sélestat, Bibliothèque Humaniste, Ms. 132 (s. IX 2/3, Mainz?)

St Gall, Stiftsbibliothek, Cod. 550 (s. IX med., Switzerland)

St Gall, Stiftsbibliothek, Cod. 675 (s. IX/1, Bavaria)

Stuttgart, Württembergische Landesbibliothek, HB VI 113 (s. VIII ex. Rhaetia)

Vatican, Biblioteca Apostolica Vaticana, Pal. lat. 485 (s. IX 3/4, Lorsch)

Vesoul, Bibliothèque Municipale, Ms. 79 (73) (s. XI, France)

Vienna, Österreichische Nationalbibliothek, lat. 2171 (s. IX 3/4, southwest Germany)

Vienna, Österreichische Nationalbibliothek, lat. 2195 (s. VIII ex., Salzburg)

Vienna, Österreichische Nationalbibliothek, lat. 2225 (s. IX/X, southern Germany)

Zürich, Zentralbibliothek, Rh. XXX (s. VIII ex., Switzerland)

Appendix 3: The manuscripts of the Bede and Egbert penitentials

P. PSEUDO-EGBERTI

Cambridge, Corpus Christi College, 265 (s. XI/1, England?)[1]

Munich, Bayerische Staatsbibliothek, Clm 22288 (s. XII 1, Bamberg?)

Oxford, Bodleian Library, Barlow 37 (s. XIII in., England)

Oxford, Bodleian Library, Bodl. 718 (s. X/XI, England, possibly Exeter)

Sélestat, Bibliothèque Humaniste, 132 (s. IX 2/3, Mainz?)

St Gall, Stiftsbibliothek, Cod. 677 (s. X med., St Gall)

Vatican, Biblioteca Apostolica Vaticana, Pal. lat. 294 (s. X /XI, probably Lorsch)

Vatican, Biblioteca Apostolica Vaticana, Pal. lat. 485 (860–75, Lorsch)

Vatican, Biblioteca Apostolica Vaticana, Pal. lat. 554 (s. VIII/IX, England / insular circles on the Continent?)

Vienna, Österreichische Nationalbibiothek, lat. 2223 (s. VIII/IX, Main region)

P. PSEUDO-BEDAE

Montpellier, Bibliothèque Interuniversitaire, Médecine H. 387 (s. IX med., northeastern France?)

Sélestat, Bibliothèque Humaniste, Ms. 132 (s. IX 2/3, Mainz?)

Vienna, Österreichische Nationalbibliothek, lat. 2223 (s. VIII/IX, Main region)

Zürich, Zentralbibliothek, Car. C. 176 (s. IX med.-IX 3/4, eastern France, Alsace?)

---

[1] s. XI/2 according to H. Mordek, *Bibliotheca capitularium regum Francorum manuscripta. Überlieferung und Traditionszusammenhang der fränkischen Herrschererlasse*, MGH Hilfsmittel 15 (Munich 1995), pp. 95–7.

PRELIMINARY VERSION OF THE *P. ADDITIVUM*

Kassel, Landesbibliothek und Murhardsche Bibliothek der Stadt Kassel, Theol. Q 24 (s. IX 1/4, Bavaria, possibly Regensburg)

Milan, Biblioteca Ambrosiana, G. 58 sup. (s. IX ex. or X/1, Bobbio)

Munich, Bayerisch Staatsbibliothek, Clm 6311 (s. IX in., northeastern France, possibly St Amand)

Munich, Bayerisch Staatsbibliothek, Clm 12673 (s. X, Salzburg?)

Vatican, Biblioteca Apostolica Vaticana, Pal. lat. 294 (s. X/XI, Lorsch)

Vatican, Biblioteca Apostolica Vaticana, Pal. lat. 485 (860–75, Lorsch)

Verdun, Bibliothèque Municipale, 69 (s. IX 2/4, eastern France, Lotharingia)

Vienna, Österreichische Nationalbibliothek, lat. 2171 (s. IX 3/4, southwestern Germany)

Würzburg, Universitätsbibliothek, M.p.j.q. 2 (s. XI/XII, western parts of France).[2]

P. ADDITIVUM

Albi, Bibliothèque municipale, 38 (59), (s. X/1, southern France)

Albi, Bibliothèque municipale, 38 bis (61) (s. IX med., southern France, Albi?)

Escorial, Real Biblioteca, L III 8 (s. IX 3/4, Senlis)

Karlsruhe, Badische Landesbibliothek, Aug. CCLV (s. IX/1, probably Reichenau)

London, British Library, Royal 5 E. XII (s. IX med., Brittany?)

London, British Library, Add. 19725 (s. IX ex., eastern France, near Reims?)

Merseburg, Dombibliothek, Ms. 103 (s. IX/1, northern Italy)

Paris, Bibliothèque Nationale de France, lat. 2341 (s. IX 2/4, near Orléans)

Paris, Bibliothèque Nationale de France, lat. 2998 (s. X/XI, southern France, possibly Moissac)

Prague, Státni Knihova, Tepla 1 (s. IX med., near Regensburg)

St Gall, Stiftsbibliothek, Cod. 682 (s. IX 2/4, Germany)

---

[2] R. Haggenmüller, 'Die Überlieferung Ps.-Beda *De Remediis Peccatorum* in der Würzburger Hs. M.p.j.q. 2. Ein weiteres Zeugnis der Vorstufe des *Paenitentiale Additivum* Ps.-Beda-Egberti', *Bulletin of Medieval Canon Law* N.S. 23 (1999), pp. 66–76.

Vatican, Biblioteca Apostolica Vaticana, Barb. lat. 477 (s. XI in., southern France, possibly Avignon)

Verona, Biblioteca Capitolare, Ms. LXIII (61) (s. X med-X/2, northern Italy, possibly Verona)

Vesoul, Bibliothèque municipale, Ms. 79 (73) (s. XI, France)

P. MIXTUM

Châlons-en-Champagne, Bibliothèque municipale, Ms. 32 (s. XI/2, western parts of Germany / Lotharingia?)

Cologne, Dombibliothek, 118 (Darmst. 2117) (s. IX ex., near Reims)

Düsseldorf, Universitätsbibliothek, B 113 (s. IX 3/4, Lower Rhine region)

Heiligenkreuz, Stiftsbibliothek, Hs. 217 (s. X ex., southern Germany or Bohemia)

Munich, Bayerische Staatsbibliothek, Clm 3851 (s. IX ex., eastern France, Lotharingia?)

Munich, Bayerische Staatsbibliothek, Clm 3853 (s. X/2, southern Germany, Augsburg?)[3]

Munich, Bayerische Staatsbibliothek, Clm 14531 (s. IX ex., northeastern France, Lotharingia?)

Munich, Bayerische Staatsbibliothek, Clm 17068 (1152-8, written for or in the monastery of Schäftlarn)

Münster, Staatsarchiv, VII 5201 (c. 945, Corvey)

Paris, Bibliothèque Nationale de France, lat. 3878 (s. X ex., northeastern France, near Liège?)

---

[3] See the detailed description in Mordek, *Bibliotheca*, pp. 287-305.

Appendix 4: The manuscripts of Halitgar's penitential

Arezzo, Biblioteca Consorziale, Ms. 312 (s. XII/1)

Bamberg, Staatliche Bibliothek, Ms. Can.2 (A.I.35) (s. IX med., northeastern France)

Barcelona, Biblioteca de la Universidad, Ms. 228 (s. X/2, northern Italy)

Berlin, Staatsbibliothek Preußischer Kulturbesitz, Hamilton 290 (s. X/2, northern Italy)

Brussels, Koninklijke Bibliotheek, 10034–7 (s. IX med., northeastern France)

Cambridge, Corpus Christi College, 265 (s. XI/1, England)

Châlons-en-Champagne, Bibliothèque municipale, Ms. 32 (s. XI/2, western parts of Germany/Lotharingia?)

Cologne, Dombibliothek, 117 (Darmst. 2116) (s. IX med.-IX/2, eastern France?)

Einsiedeln, Stiftsbibliothek, 281 (886) (s. IX 2/4, France)

Florence, Biblioteca Medicea Laurenziana, Ashburnham 1814 (s. IX/2, France)

Gent, Bibliotheek der Rijksuniversiteit, Ms. 506 (551) (s. IX 3/4, west of the Rhine)

Heiligenkreuz, Stiftsbibliothek, Hs. 217 (s. X ex., southern Germany or Bohemia)

Koblenz, Landeshauptarchiv, Best. 701 Nr.759,7 (s. XI/XII)

Kynžvart, Zámecká knihovna, 20 K 20 (s.XII/1, St Blasien)

Milan, Biblioteca Ambrosiana, Ms. L 28 sup. (s. IX 3/3, northern Italy)[1]

Milan, Biblioteca Ambrosiana, Ms. Trotti 440 (s. XII/1, northern Italy, possibly Milan)

Monte Cassino, Archivio dell'Abbazia, Cod. 557 bis 0 (s. XI/1, Monte Cassino)

---

[1] S. Keefe, *Water and the Word: Baptism and the Education of the Clergy in the Carolingian Empire* (Notre Dame 2002).

Montpellier, Bibliothèque Interuniversitaire, Médecine 304 (s. XII med., Normandy)

Munich, Bayerische Staatsbibliothek, Clm 3851 (s. IX ex., eastern France, Lotharingia?)

Munich, Bayerische Staatsbibliothek, Clm 3853 (s. X/2, southern Germany, Augsburg?)

Munich, Bayerische Staatsbibliothek, Clm 3909 (1138–43, Augsburg)

Munich, Bayerische Staatsbibliothek, Clm 12673 (s. X, Salzburg?)

Munich, Bayerische Staatsbibliothek, Clm 14532 (s. IX ex., northeastern France, Lotharingia?)

Munich, Bayerische Staatsbibliothek, Clm 17068 (1152–8, written for or in the monastery of Schäftlarn)

Munich, Bayerische Staatsbibliothek, Clm 17195 (s. XII med., in or for Schäftlarn)

Münster, Staatsarchiv, VII 5201 (*c.* 945, Corvey)

Novara, Biblioteca Capitolare, 18 (LXXI) (s. IX med.-IX 3/4, northern Italy)

Orléans, Bibliothèque municipale, Ms. 216 (188) (s. IX/2, northeastern France)

Oxford, Bodleian Library, Bodl. 516 (2570) (s. IX 3/4, northern Italy)

Oxford, Bodleian Library, Ms. Can. Patr. lat. 49 (s. XII med., northern Italy)

Paris, Bibliothèque Nationale de France, lat. 614 a (s. X in., southern France)

Paris, Bibliothèque Nationale de France, lat. 2077 (s. X/2, Moissac)

Paris, Bibliothèque Nationale de France, lat. 2341 (s. IX 2/4, Orléans)

Paris, Bibliothèque Nationale de France, lat. 2373 (s. IX 3/4, northeastern France, near the court of Charles the Bald)

Paris, Bibliothèque Nationale de France, lat. 2843 (s. XI, Limoges?)

Paris, Bibliothèque Nationale de France, lat. 2998 (s. X/XI, Moissac)

Paris, Bibliothèque Nationale de France, lat. 2999 (s. IX med., St Amand)

Paris, Bibliothèque Nationale de France, lat. 3878 (s. X ex., northeastern France, near Liège?)

Paris, Bibliothèque Nationale de France, lat. 8508 (s. IX ex., southern France)

Paris, Bibliothèque Nationale de France, lat. 12315 (s. XII/2, northern France, Corbie?)

Paris, Bibliothèque Nationale de France, lat. 18220 (s. X/2)

Rome, Biblioteca Vallicelliana, T. XVIII (s. XI, southern Italy)[2]

---

[2] See Reynolds, 'Penitential material in Italian canon law manuscripts', p. 68.

St Gall, Stiftsbibliothek, Cod. 184 (856, closely connected to Grimald, Weissenburg, St Gall?)

St Gall, Stiftsbibliothek, Cod. 277 (s. IX 2/4, Weissenburg)

St Gall, Stiftsbibliothek, Cod. 570 (s. IX med., eastern France, Lotharingia)

St Gall, Stiftsbibliothek, Cod. 676 (s. XI ex., St Blasien/Schaffhausen)

St Gall, Stiftsbibliothek, Cod. 679 (s. IX/X, St Gall?)

St Petersburg, Publicnaja Biblioteka im. M.E. Saltykova –Ščedrina, Cod. Q. v. I. nr. 34 (Corbie 230) (s. IX ex., Corbie)

Stuttgart, Württembergische Landesbibliothek, Cod. HB VI 107 (s. XI ex., near Lake Constance)

Troyes, Bibliothèque municipale, Ms. 1349 (s. XII med., Liège)

Troyes, Bibliothèque municipale, Ms. 1979 (s. X/XI, eastern France/ western parts of Germany?)

Vatican, Arch. S. Pietro, H 58 (s. X ex/XI in., Rome)[3]

Vatican, Biblioteca Apostolica Vaticana, Ottob. lat. 3295 (s. IX 3/4, Rhine-Main region)

Vatican, Biblioteca Apostolica Vaticana, Reg. lat. 191 (s. IX/2, near Reims)

Vatican, Biblioteca Apostolica Vaticana, Reg. lat. 207 (s. IX 2/4, north-eastern France, Reims?)

Vatican, Biblioteca Apostolica Vaticana, Reg. lat. 215 (s. IX/2, Tours)

Vatican, Biblioteca Apostolica Vaticana, Reg lat. 263 (s. XII med.-XII/2, France or northern Italy)

Vatican, Biblioteca Apostolica Vaticana, Reg lat. 407 (s. IX med.-IX 3/4, southern Germany, near Lake Constance)

Vatican, Biblioteca Apostolica Vaticana, lat. 5751 (S. IX ex., Bobbio)[4]

Vercelli, Biblioteca Capitolare, Ms. CXLIII (159) (s. X/2, northern Italy)

Vercelli, Biblioteca Capitolare, Ms. CCIII (32) (s. IX 4/4, northern France?)

Verona, Biblioteca Capitolare, Ms. LXIII (61) (s. X med.-X/2, northern Italy, possibly Verona)

Vienna, Österreichische Nationalbibliothek, lat. 956 (Theol.320) (s. X ex., western Germany)[5]

---

[3] For a thorough analysis, see Gaastra, 'Between liturgy and canon law', pp. 49–55.

[4] See W. Kaiser, 'Zur Rekonstruktion einer vornehmlich Bußrechtlichen Handschrift aus Bobbio (Hs. Vat. lat. 5751 ff. 1–54v + Hs. Mailand, Bibl. Ambr. G. 58 sup. ff. 41r–64v)', *ZRG Kan. Abt.* 86 (2000), pp. 538–53.

[5] O. Eberhardt, *Via Regia. Der Fürstenspiegel Smaragds von St. Mihiel und seine literarische Gattung*, Münstersche Mittelalter-Schriften 28 (Munich 1977), p. 93.

Wolfenbüttel, Herzog August Bibliothek, 656 (Helmsted.) (s. IX med., Mainz)

Würzburg, Priesterseminar, Ms. Membr. 1 (lost in a fire in 1944) (s. IX?)

Zürich, Zentralbibliothek, Ms. Car. C 123 (s. X, Zürich?)

Zürich, Zentralbibliothek, Ms. Car. C 176 (s. IX med-IX 3/4, eastern parts of France, Alsace?)

Zürich, Zentralbibliothek, Ms. Rh. 102 (s. X in., Rheinau)

Sources

Admonitio Generalis, ed. H. Mordek, K. Zechiel-Eckes and M. Glatthaar, *Die Admonitio generalis Karls des Großen*, MGH Fontes Iuris Germanici Antiqui in usum scholarum separatim editi 16 (Hanover 2012).

Aelfric, *First Old English Letter for Bishop Wulfsige*, ed. D. Whitelock, M. Brett and C. Brooke, *Councils and Synods with Other Documents Relating to the English Church*, vol. ɪ,1 (Oxford 1981), pp. 191–226.

Agobard of Lyon *Liber apologeticus I*, ed. L. van Acker, *Agobardi Lugdunensi Opera Omnia*, CC CM 52 (Turnhout 1981), pp. 309–12.

Liber contra insulsam vulgi opinionem de grandine et tonitruis, ed. L. van Acker, CC CM 52 (Turnhout 1981), pp. 3–15.

Alcuin *Epistolae*, ed. E. Dümmler, MGH Epistolae IV (Berlin 1895), pp. 1–481.

Vita Willibrordi, ed. W. Levison, MGH SS rer. mer. VII (Hanover / Leipzig 1920), pp. 81–141.

Alfred the Great *Laws*, ed. F. Liebermann, *Die Gesetze der Angelsachsen I: Text und Überlieferung* (Halle 1903, repr. Aalen 1960), pp. 26–89.

Preface to the translation of Gregory the Great's *Regula Pastoralis*, in *Alfred the Great. Asser's Life of King Alfred and Other Contemporary Sources*, translated with an introduction and notes by Simon Keynes and Michael Lapidge (Harmondsworth 1983), pp. 124–7.

Ambrose of Milan *De obitu Theodosii*, ed. O. Faller, *Sancti Ambrosii Opera. Pars Septima: Explanatio symboli, De sacramentis, De mysteriis, De paenitentia, De excessu fratris, De obitu Valentiniani, De obitu Theodosii*, CSEL 73 (Vienna 1955), pp. 369–401 [translated in Ambrose of Milan, *Political Letters and Speeches*, pp. 174–203].

Epistola extra collectionem 11 [51], ed. M. Zelzer, *Sancti Ambrosi Opera. Pars Decima. Epistularum liber decimus, epistulae extra collectionem, Gesta concili Aquileiensis*, CSEL 82, 3, pp. 212–18 [translated in Ambrose of Milan, *Political Letters and Speeches*, translated by J. H. W. G. Liebeschuetz, Translated Texts for Historians 43 (Liverpool 2005), pp. 262–9].

Sermo contra Auxentium, 36, PL 16, cols. 1007–18.

Annales Fuldenses, ed. G. H. Pertz and F. Kurze, MGH SS rer. Germ. 7 (Hanover 1891).

Annales regni Francorum, ed. G. H. Pertz and F. Kurze, MGH SS rer. Germ. 6 (Hanover 1895).

Annales Sithienses, ed. G. Waitz, MGH SS 13 (Hanover 1881), pp. 34–8.

Annals of Ulster, ed. S. MacAirt and G. Mac Niocaill, *Annals of Ulster (to AD 1131). Part I. Text and Translation* (Dublin 1983).

Ansegisus, *Collectio Capitularium Ansegisi*, ed. G. Schmitz, *Die Kapitulariensammlung des Ansegis*, MGH Cap. N.S. I (Hanover 1996).

Anselm of Lucca, *Collectio Canonum*, ed. F. Thaner, *Anselmi Episcopi Lucensis Collectio Canonum una cum Collectione Minore* (Innsbruck 1906 and 1915).

Astronomer, *Vita Hludowici imperatoris*, ed. F. Tremp, MGH SS rer. Germ. 64 (Hanover 1995), pp. 279–555.

Atto of Vercelli, *Capitula Episcoporum*, ed. R. Pokorny, MGH Cap. Ep. 3 (Hanover 1995), pp. 243–304.

Augsburger Sendordnung, ed. A. Koeniger, *Die Sendgerichte in Deutschland* (Munich 1907), pp. 191–4.

Augustine, *Tractatus habitus tertia feria*, ed. S. Poque, *Augustin d'Hippone, Sermons pour la Pâque. Introduction, texte critique, traduction et notes*, Sources Chrétiennes 116 (Paris 1966), pp. 260–79.

Avitus of Vienna, *Epistula ad Gundobadum regem de subita paenitentia*, ed. R. Peiper, MGH AA 6,2 (Berlin 1882), pp. 29–32 [tr. Shanzer and Wood, *Avitus of Vienne*, pp. 193–21].

  Homilia in rogationibus, ed. R. Peiper, MGH AA 6.2 (Berlin 1883), pp. 108–12 [translated in D. Shanzer and I. Wood, *Avitus of Vienne. Letters and Selected Prose* (Liverpool 2002), pp. 381–8].

Bartholomew of Exeter, *Contra Fatalitatis Errorem*, ed. D. N. Bell, *Bartholomaei Exoniensis Contra Fatalitatis Errorem*, CC CM 157 (Turnhout 1996).

  Liber pastoralis sive poenitentialis, ed. A. Morey, *Bartholomew of Exeter, Bishop and Canonist. A Study in the Twelfth Century* (Cambridge 1937), pp. 161–300.

Bede, *Historia Ecclesiastica Gentis Anglorum*, ed. B. Colgrave and R. Mynors, *Bede's Ecclesiastical History of the English People* (Oxford 1992, 2nd rev. edn).

  Vita Cuthberti, ed. B. Colgrave, *Two Lives of St. Cuthbert* (Cambridge 1940), pp. 141–307.

Blickling Homilies, ed. R. Morris, *The Blickling Homilies with a Translation and Index of Words together with the Blickling Glosses*, Early English Texts Society 58, 63, 73 [reprinted in one volume, London 1967].

Bobbio Missal, ed. E. Lowe, *The Bobbio Missal. A Gallican Mass-Book*. Henry Bradshaw Society 58 (London 1920).

Burchard of Worms, *Decretum*, ed. G. Fransen and T. Kölzer, *Burchard von Worms. Decretorum libri XX* (Aalen 1992).

Caesarius of Arles, *Sermones*, ed. G. Morin, *Sancti Caesarii Arelatensis Sermones nunc primum in unum collecti et ad leges artis criticae ex innumeris Mss. recogniti*, 2 vols. CC SL 103 and 104 (Turnhout 1953).

Canones Hibernenses, ed. L. Bieler, *The Irish Penitentials*, Scriptores Latini Hiberniae 5 (Dublin 1963), pp. 160–75.

Capitula de examinandis ecclesiasticis, from 802, ed. A. Boretius, MGH Cap. reg. Franc. I (Hanover 1883), p. 109–11.

Capitula de examinandis ecclesiasticis, ed. R. Pokorny, MGH Cap. Ep. 3 (Hanover 1995), pp. 206–11.

Capitula Helmstadensia, ed. R. Pokorny, MGH Cap. Ep. 3 (Hanover 1995), pp. 181–6.

240   Sources

Capitula Neustrica tertia, ed. R. Pokorny, MGH Cap. Ep. 3 (Hanover 1995), pp. 62–7.

Capitulare de disciplina palatii Aquisgranensis, ed. A. Boretius, MGH Cap. I, pp. 297–8.

Capitulare Haristallense secundum speciale (Second Capitulary of Herstal), ed. H. Mordek, 'Karls des Großen zweites Kapitular von Herstal und die Hungersnot der Jahre 778/770', *Deutsches Archiv* 61 (2005), pp. 1–52, at pp. 44–52.

Cathwulf, *Epistola ad Karolum*, ed. E. Dümmler, MGH Epistolae IV (Berlin 1895), pp. 501–5.

Charlemagne, *Karoli ad Ghaerbaldum episcopum epistola*, ed. A. Boretius, MGH Cap. I, pp. 245–6.

Charlemagne, *Letter of Charlemagne to Fastrada*, ed. E. Dümmler, MGH Epistolae IV, pp. 528–9.

Chronicon Moissiacense, ed. G. H. Pertz, MGH SS 1 (Hanover 1826), pp. 280–313.

Collectio Dacheriana, ed. L d'Achery and L.-F.-J. De la Barre, *Spicilegium sive collectio veterum aliquot scriptorum qui in Galliae bibliothecis delituerant* (Paris 1723), pp. 509–64.

Collectio Hibernensis, ed. H. Wasserschleben, *Die irische Kanonensammlung* (2nd edn Leipzig 1885; reprint Aalen 1966).

Collectio Vetus Gallica, ed. H. Mordek, *Kirchenrecht und Reform im Frankenreich. Die Collectio Vetus Gallica, die älteste systematische Kanonessammlung des fränkischen Gallien. Studien und Edition*, Beiträge zur Geschichte und Quellenkunde des Mittelalters 1 (Berlin / New York 1975), pp. 341–617.

Columbanus, *Epistolae*, ed. G. Walker, *Sancti Columbani Opera*, Scriptores Latini Hiberniae 2 (Dublin 1970), pp. 1–59.

Regula Coenobialis, ed. Walker, *Sancti Columbani Opera*, pp. 142–69.

Concilium Germanicum (742/3), ed. R. Rau, *Briefe des Bonifatius. Willibalds Leben des Bonifatius. Nebst einigen zeitgenössischen Dokumenten*, Ausgewählte Quellen zur deutschen Geschichte des Mittelalters. Freiherr vom Stein-Gedächtnisausgabe, vol. IVb (Darmstadt 1968), pp. 376–81.

Concordia Episcoporum (813), ed. A. Werminghoff, MGH Conc. II,1 pp. 297–301.

Council of Agde, ed. C. Munier, *Concilia Galliae A. 314 – A. 506*. CC SL 148 (Turnhout 1963), pp. 189–228.

Council of Ancyra (314), ed. C. H. Turner, *Ecclesiae occidentalis monumenta iuris antiquissima canonum et conciliorum graecorum interpretationes Latinae*, vol. II,1 (Oxford 1907), pp. 3–141.

Council of Arles (813), ed. A. Werminghoff, MGH Conc. II,1 (Hanover / Leipzig 1906), pp. 248–53.

Council of Chalon (647–53), ed. C. De Clercq, *Concilia Galliae A.511–A.695*, CC SL 148A (Turnhout 1963), pp. 302–10.

Council of Chalon (813), ed. A. Werminghoff, MGH Conc. II,1 (Hanover / Leipzig 1906), pp. 273–85.

Council of Cloveshoe, ed. A. Haddan and W. Stubbs, *Councils and Ecclesiastical Documents Relating to Great Britain and Ireland*, vol. III (Oxford 1871; repr. 1964), pp. 362–76.

Council of Mâcon (585), ed. C. De Clercq, *Concilia Galliae A.511–A.695*, CC SL
148A (Turnhout 1963), pp. 237–50.
Council of Mainz (813), ed. A. Werminghoff, MGH Conc. II,1 (Hanover /
Leipzig 1906), pp. 258–73.
Council of Mainz (852), ed. W. Hartmann, MGH Conc. 3 (Hanover 1984),
pp. 235–52.
Council of Orléans (511), ed. de Clercq, *Concilia Galliae*, pp. 3–19.
Council of Orléans (538), ed. de Clercq, *Concilia Galliae*, pp. 113–30.
Council of Paris (829), ed. A. Werminghoff, MGH Conc. II,2 (Hanover / Leipzig
1908), pp. 605–80.
Council of Reims (813), ed. A. Werminghoff, MGH Conc. II,1 (Hanover /
Leipzig 1906), pp. 253–8.
Council of Soissons (744), ed. R. Rau, *Briefe des Bonifatius. Willibalds Leben
des Bonifatius. Nebst einigen zeitgenössischen Dokumenten*, Ausgewählte
Quellen zur deutschen Geschichte des Mittelalters. Freiherr vom
Stein-Gedächtnisausgabe, vol. IVb (Darmstadt 1968), pp. 384–9.
Council of Toledo (589), ed. J. Vives, *Concilios Visigóticos e Hispano-Romanos*
(Barcelona / Madrid 1963), pp. 107–45.
Council of Tours (461), ed. Munier, *Concilia Galliae*, pp. 142–9.
Council of Tours (813), ed. A. Werminghoff, MGH Concilia II,1,
pp. 286–93.
Council of Vannes (465), ed. Munier, *Concilia Galliae*, pp. 150–8.
Fourth Lateran Council, ed. A. García y García, *Constitutiones Concilii quarti
Lateranensis una cum Commentariis glossatorum*, Monumenta Iuris Canonici,
Series A: Corpus Glossatorum 2 (Vatican 1981), pp. 41–118.
Ebo of Reims, *Letter to Halitgar*, ed. E. Dümmler, MGH Epp. V (Berlin 1899),
pp. 616–17.
Ekkehard IV of St Gallen, *Casus Sancti Galli*, ed. H. Haefele, AQ X (Darmstadt
1980).
*Episcoporum de poenitentia, quam Hludowicus imperator professus est,
relatio Compendiensis*, ed. A. Boretius and V. Krause, MGH Capit. II,
pp. 51–5.
Eusebius, *Historia Ecclesiastica*, ed. E. Schwartz, T. Mommsen and
F. Winkelmann, *Eusebius Werke: Die Kirchengeschichte* 2.1. Die Griechischen
christlichen Schriftsteller der ersten Jahrhunderte, NF 6.2 (Berlin 1999,
reprint of the 1st edition).
Evagrius of Pontus, *The Praktikos*, ed. A. Guillaumont and C. Guillaumont,
Évagre le Pontique, Traité pratique ou Le moine (SC 170–1) (Paris 1971).
Excerpts of a book of David, ed. Bieler, *Irish Penitentials*, pp. 70–3.
Faustus of Riez, Epistola 5 ad Paulinum, ed. A. Engelbrecht, *Fausti Reiensis Opera
praeter sermones Pseudo-Eusebianos, accedunt Ruricii epistulae*, CSEL 21
(Prague / Vienna / Leipzig 1891).
Formulae Salicae Merkelianae, ed. K. Zeumer, MGH Formulae (Hanover 1886),
pp. 239–63.
Fulk of Reims, *Letter to Alfred*, ed. D. Whitelock, M. Brett and C. Brooke,
Councils and Synods with Other Documents Relating to the English Church,
vol. I,1 (Oxford 1981), pp. 6–12.

Gelasian Sacramentary of St. Gall, ed. C. Mohlberg, *Das fränkische Sacramentarium Gelasianum in alamannischer Überlieferung (codex Sangall. No. 348)* (3rd edn Münster 1971).

Gratian, *Decretum,* ed. E. Friedberg, *Corpus iuris canonici I: Decretum magistri Gratiani* (Leipzig 1879).

Gregory the Great, *Dialogi,* ed. A. de Vogüé, *Dialogues.* SC 251, 260 and 265 (Paris 1978–80).

Gregory of Tours, *Historiae,* ed. B. Krusch and W. Levison, MGH SS rer. mer. I,1 (Hanover 1956).

  Liber vitae patrum, ed. B. Krusch, MGH SS rer. mer. I,2 (Hanover 1885), pp. 211–94.

Gregory VII, *Registrum,* ed. E. Caspar, *Das Register Gregors VII,* MGH Epistolae selectae 2 (Berlin 1920).

Haito of Basel, *Capitula Episcoporum,* ed. P. Brommer, MGH Cap. Ep. I (Hanover 1984) pp. 203–19.

Héloise, Letter 1, ed. J. Monfrin, *Historia Calamitatum* (Paris 1978, 4th edn), pp. 111–17.

Historia Silense, ed. J. Pérez de Urbel and A. González Ruiz-Zorilla (Madrid 1959).

Homo quidam, ed. P. Michaud-Quantin, 'Un manuel de confession archaïque dans le manuscrit Avranches 136', *Sacris Erudiri* 17 (1966), pp. 5–54.

Hrabanus Maurus, *Paenitentiale ad Otgarium,* PL 112, cols. 1397–424.

  Paenitentiale ad Heribaldum, PL 110, cols. 467–94.

Hugh of Cluny, *Epistola* VIII, PL 159, cols. 930–2.

Isidore of Seville, *Etymologiae,* ed. W. Lindsay, *Isidori Hispalensis Episcopi Etymologiarum sive Originum Libri XX* (Oxford 1911).

Ivo of Chartres, Prologue to his *Decretum,* ed. B. Brasington, *Ways of Mercy. The Prologue of Ivo of Chartres. Edition and Analysis* (Münster 2004).

Jerome, *Epistola* 77, ed. I. Hilberg, *Sancti Eusebii Hieronymi epistula. Pars II: epistulae LXXI–CXX,* CSEL 55 (Vienna / Leipzig 1912).

John Cassian, *Collationes,* ed. M. Petschenig, CSEL 13 (Vienna 2004).

  Institutiones, ed. J.-C. Guy, *Jean Cassien, Institutions cénobitiques,* SC 109 (Paris 1965).

Julianus Pomerius, *De vita contemplativa,* PL 59, cols. 415–520.

Lampert of Hersfeld, *Annales,* ed. O. Holder-Egger, AQ 13 (4th edn, Darmstadt 2011).

Leo I, *Tractatus septem et nonaginta,* ed. A. Chavasse, *Sancti Leonis Magni Pontificis Tractatus,* CC SL 138A (Turnhout 1973).

Lex Frisionum, ed. H. Siems, *Studien zur Lex Frisionum* (Ebelsbach 1980), supplement.

Monastery of Tallaght, ed. E. Gwynn and W. J. Purton, 'The Monastery of Tallaght', *Proceedings of the Royal Irish Academy* 29 C (1911), pp. 115–80.

Nicholas I (pope), *Epistola* 99, ed. E. Perels, MGH Epp. VI (Berlin 1925), pp. 568–600.

  Letter Confirming the Decisions of a Council Held in Mainz (861–863), ed. W. Hartmann, MGH Conc. 4 (Hanover 1998), pp. 127–31.

Origen, *Homélies sur le Lévitique*, ed. M. Borret, SC 286–7 (Paris 1981).

Paenitentiale Ambrosianum, ed. L. Körntgen, *Studien zu den Quellen der frühmittelalterlichen Bußbücher*, Quellen und Forschungen zum Recht im Mittelalter 7 (Sigmaringen 1993), pp. 257–70.

Paenitentiale Bigotianum, ed. Bieler, *Irish Penitentials*, pp. 198–239.

Paenitentiale Bobbiense, ed. Kottje, *Paenitentialia minora*, pp. 66–71.

Paenitentiale Burgundense, ed. Kottje, *Paenitentialia minora*, pp. 61–5.

Paenitentiale Cantabrigiense, ed. K. Delen, A. Gaastra, M. Saan and B. Schaap, 'The *Paenitentiale Cantabrigiense*. A witness of the Carolingian contribution to the tenth-century reforms in England', *Sacris Erudiri* 41 (2002), pp. 341–73.

Paenitentiale Columbani, ed. Bieler, *Irish Penitentials*, pp. 96–107.

Paenitentiale Cordubense, ed. F. Bezler, *Paenitentialia Hispaniae*, CC SL 156A (Turnhout 1998), pp. 43–69.

Paenitentiale Cummeani, ed. Bieler, *Irish Penitentials*, pp. 108–35.

Paenitentiale Excarpsus Cummeani, ed. H. J. Schmitz, *Die Bussbücher und das kanonische Bussverfahren: Nach handschriftlichen Quellen dargestellt* (Düsseldorf 1898), pp. 597–644.

Paenitentiale Floriacense, ed. Kottje, *Paenitentialia minora*, pp. 95–103.

Paenitentiale Halitgarii Cameracensis, PL 105, cols. 651–710.

Paenitentiale Halitgarii Cameracensis, bk. III–VI, ed. Schmitz, *Die Bussbücher und das kanonische Bussverfahren*, pp. 252–300.

Paenitentiale Hubertense, ed. Kottje, *Paenitentialia minora*, pp. 105–15.

Paenitentiale Merseburgense A, ed. Kottje, *Paenitentialia minora*, pp. 123–69.

Paenitentiale Oxoniense I, ed. Kottje, *Paenitentialia minora*, pp. 87–93.

Paenitentiale Oxoniense II, ed. Kottje, *Paenitentialia minora*, pp. 179–205.

Paenitentiale Parisiense simplex, ed. Kottje, *Paenitentialia minora*, pp. 73–79.

Paenitentiale Pseudo-Egberti, ed. H. Wasserschleben, *Die Bussordnungen der abendländischen Kirche* (Halle 1851), pp. 231–47.

Paenitentiale Pseudo-Gregorii (III), ed. F. Kerff, 'Das Paenitentiale Pseudo-Gregorii. Eine kritische Edition', in H. Mordek (ed.), *Aus Archiven und Bibliotheken. Festschrift für Raymund Kottje zum 65. Geburtstag* (Frankfurt a.M. / Bern / etc. / 1992), pp. 161–88.

Paenitentiale Pseudo-Theodori, ed. C. van Rhijn, *Paenitentiale Pseudo-Theodori*. CC SL 156 B (Turnhout 2009).

Paenitentiale Remense, ed. F. B. Asbach, 'Das Poenitentiale Remense und der sogen. Excarpsus Cummeani: Überlieferung, Quellen und Entwicklung zweier kontinentaler Bußbücher aus der 1. Hälfte des 8. Jahrhunderts' (Dissertation Regensburg, 1975), supplement, pp. 1–77.

Paenitentiale Sangallense simplex, ed. Kottje, *Paenitentialia minora*, pp. 117–21.

Paenitentiale Silense, ed. F. Bezler, *Paenitentialia Hispaniae*, CC SL 156A (Turnhout 1998), pp. 15–42.

Paenitentiale Sletstatense, ed. Kottje, *Paenitentialia minora*, pp. 81–5.

Paenitentiale Theodori, Canones Basilienses (Ba), ed. Asbach, 'Das Poenitentiale Remense', supplement, pp. 79–89.

Paenitentiale Theodori, Canones Cottoniani (Co), ed. Finsterwalder, *Die Canones Theodori Cantuariensis*, pp. 271–84.

Paenitentiale Theodori, Canones Gregorii (G), ed. Finsterwalder, *Die Canones Theodori Cantuariensis*, pp. 253–70.

Paenitentiale Theodori, Capitula Dacheriana (D), ed. Finsterwalder, *Die Canones Theodori Cantuariensis*, pp. 239–52.

Paenitentiale Theodori, Discipulus Umbrensium (U), ed. P. W. Finsterwalder, *Die Canones Theodori Cantuariensis*, pp. 285–334.

Paenitentiale Vallicellianum I, ed. H. J. Schmitz, *Die Bussbücher und die Bussdisciplin der Kirche. Nach handschriftlichen Quellen dargestellt* (Mainz 1883), pp. 227–342

Paenitentiale Vigilanum, ed. F. Bezler, *Paenitentialia Hispaniae*, CC SL 156A (Turnhout 1998), pp. 1–13.

Paenitentiale Vindobonense C, ed. R. Meens, '"Aliud benitenciale". The ninth-century *Paenitentiale Vindobonense C*', *Mediaeval Studies* 66 (2004), pp. 21–6.

Paenitentiale Vinniani, ed. Bieler, *Irish Penitentials*, pp. 74–95.

Old Gelasian Sacramentary, ed. L. Mohlberg, L. Eizenhöfer and P. Siffrin, *Liber Sacramentorum Romanae ecclesiae ordinis anni circuli (Sacramentarium Gelasianum)*, Rerum Ecclesiasticarum Documenta. Series Maior 4 (Rome 1960).

Old Irish Penitential, ed. D. A. Binchy, 'The Old Irish Penitential', in Bieler, *Irish Penitentials*, pp. 258–74.

Paschasius Radbertus, *Epitaphium Arsenii*, ed. E. Dümmler, *Abhandlungen der kaiserlichen Akademie der Wissenschaften zu Berlin, phil.-hist. Klasse* (Berlin 1900), pp. 1–98.

Patrick, *Letter to Coroticus*, ed. and transl. D. R. Howlett, *The Book of Letters of Saint Patrick the Bishop* (Dublin 1994).

Paul the Deacon, *Historia Langobardorum*, ed. L. Bethman and G. Waitz, MGH SS rer. Lang. et Ital. I (Hanover 1878), pp. 12–187.

Paulinus, *Vita Ambrosii*, ed. M. Pellegrino (Rome 1961).

Peter Abelard, *Scito te ipsum*, ed. D. Luscombe, *Peter Abelard's 'Ethics'*. Oxford Medieval Texts (Oxford 1971).

Possidius, *Vita Augustini*, ed. W. Geerlings (Paderborn /Munich / etc 2005).

Preface of Gildas on Penance, ed. Bieler, *Irish Penitentials*, pp. 60–5.

Prosper Tiro, *Epitoma Chronicon*, ed. T. Mommsen, MGH AA 9 (Berlin 1892), pp. 341–486.

Pseudo-Cyprian, *De duodecim abusivis*, ed. S. Hellmann, 'Pseudo-Cyprianus: *De XII abusivis saeculi*', *Texte und Untersuchungen zur Geschichte der altchristlichen Literatur* 34 (1909), pp. 1–61.

Rather of Verona, *Epistola 25*, ed. F. Weigle, *Die Briefe des Bischofs Rather von Verona*, MGH, Briefe der deutschen Kaiserzeit I (Weimar 1949), pp. 133–7.

Regino of Prüm *Chronicle*, ed. R. Rau, *Quellen zur karolingischen Reichsgeschichte III*, AQ 7 (4th edn, Darmstadt 2002). [English translation by S. MacLean, *History and Politics in Late Carolingian and Ottonian Europe. The Chronicle of Regino of Prüm and Adalbert of Magdeburg* (Manchester / New York 2009)].

Libri duo de synodalibus causis et disciplinis ecclesiasticis, ed. H. Wasserschleben, *Reginonis libri duo de synodalibus causis et disciplinis ecclesiasticis* (Leipzig 1840).

Regula Benedicti, ed. A. De Vogüé and J. Neufville, *La Règle de Saint Benoît*, SC 181–2 (Paris 1972).

Riculf of Mainz, *Epistola ad Eginonem*, ed. A. Boretius, MGH Cap. I, p. 249.

Roman Germanic Pontifical, ed. C. Vogel and R. Elze, *Le Pontifical Romano-Germanique du dixième siècle*, 3 vols., Studi e Testi 226, 227 and 269 (Vatican City 1963–72).

Rule of the Céli Dé, ed. W. Reeves, 'On the Céli Dé', *Transactions of the Royal Irish Academy* 24 (1873), pp. 205–15.

Ruotger of Trier, *Capitula Episcoporum*, ed. P. Brommer, MGH Cap. Ep. 1 (Hanover 1984), pp. 57–70.

Sacramentary of Angoulême, ed. P. Saint-Roch, *Liber Sacramentorum Engolismensis. Manuscrit B.N. Lat. 816. Le Sacramentaire Gélasien d'Angoulême*, CC SL 159 C (Turnhout 1987).

Sacramentary of Autun, ed. O. Heiming, *Liber Sacramentorum Augustodunensis*, CC SL 159 B (Turnhout 1984).

Sacramentary of Gellone, ed. A. Dumas, *Liber Sacramentorum Gellonensis*, CC SL 159A (Turnhout 1981).

Sidonius Apollinaris, Ep. V.14, ed. W. B. Anderson, *Sidonius Apollinaris. Poems and Letters*, vol. II (Cambridge MA and London 1965), pp. 216–18.

Sozomenos, *Historia Ecclesiastica*, ed. and tr. G. C. Hansen, Fontes Christiani 73/3 (Turnhout 2004).

Statuta Ecclesiae Antiqua, ed. C. Munier, *Les 'Statuta ecclesiae antiqua': édition, études critiques* (Paris 1960).

Synod of North Britain, ed. Bieler, pp. 66–7.

Synod of the Grove of Victory, ed. Bieler, pp. 68–9.

Synodus I S. Patricii (First Synod of St. Patrick), ed. Bieler, *Irish Penitentials*, pp. 54–9.

Tertullian, *De paenitentia*, ed. C. Munier, *Tertullien, La pénitence. Introduction, texte critique, traduction et commentaire*, Sources Chrétiennes 316 (Paris 1984).

Theodoretus, *Historia Ecclesiastica*, ed. L. Parmentier e.a., SC 501 and 530 (Paris 2006 and 2009).

Theodulph of Orléans, *Capitula Episcoporum I*, ed. P. Brommer, MGH Cap.Ep. I (Hanover 1984), pp. 73–142.

Thietmar of Merseburg, *Chronicle*, ed. W. Trillmich, *Thietmar von Merseburg, Chronik*, Ausgewählte Quellen zur deutschen Geschichte des Mittelalters 9 (Darmstadt 1985) [translated in D. Warner, *Ottonian Germany. The 'Chronicon' of Thietmar of Merseburg* (Manchester 2001)].

Thomas of Chobham, *Summa Confessorum*, ed. F. Broomfield, Analecta Mediaevalia Namurcensia 25 (Louvain / Paris 1968).

Visio Baronti, c. 12, ed. W. Levison, MGH SS rer. mer. V, pp. 368–94.

Visio Fursei, ed. C. Carozzi, *Le voyage de l'âme dans l'au-delà d'après la littérature latine (Ve–XIIIe siècle)* (Rome 1994), pp. 677–92.

Vita Bertilae abbatissae Calensis, ed. W. Levison, MGH SS rer. mer. VI (Hanover / Leipzig 1913), pp. 95–109.

Vita Brigitae, ed. and tr. Donncha Ó hAodha (Dublin 1978).

Vita Caesarii, ed. G. Morin, *Sancti Caesarii episcopi Arelatensis Opera Omnia nunc primum in unum collecta*, vol. II (Maredsous 1942) [translated in: Caesarius of Arles, *Life, Testament, Letters*, translated by W. E. Klingshirn, Translated Texts for Historians 19 (Liverpool 1994)].

Vita Columbae, ed. A. O. and M. A. Anderson, *Adomnán's 'Life of Columba'* (Oxford 1991).

Vita Columbani abbatis discipulorumque eius, ed. B. Krusch, MGH SS rer. mer. IV, pp. 61–152.

Vita Fursei, ed. B. Krusch in MGH SS rer. mer. IV (Hanover / Leipzig 1902), pp. 423–51.

Vita sancti Oudalrici episcopi Augustani auctore Gerhardo, ed. G. Waitz, in: *Lebensbeschreibungen einiger Bischöfe des 10.-12. Jahrhunderts*, tr. Hatto Kallfelz, AQ XII (2nd edn, Darmstadt 1986), pp. 35–167.

Vita Sigiramni, ed. Krusch, MGH SS rer. mer. IV, pp. 603–25.

Vita Theudarii, ed. B. Krusch, MGH SS rer. mer. III (Hanover 1896), pp. 525–30.

Vita Liudgeri, ed. W. Diekamp, *Die Geschichtsquellen des Bistums Münster* 4 (Münster 1881), pp. 1–53.

Willibald, *Vita Bonifatii*, V, ed. R. Rau, *Briefe des Bonifatius*, pp. 451–525.

Bibliography

Airlie, S., 'Private bodies and the body politic in the divorce case of Lothar II',
Past and Present 161 (1998), pp. 3–38.

Althoff, G., *Verwandte, Freunde und Getreue. Zum politischen Stellenwert der
Gruppenbindungen im früheren Mittelalter* (Darmstadt 1990).

Spielregeln der Politik im Mittelalter. Kommunikation in Frieden und Fehde
(Darmstadt 1997).

'Das Privileg der deditio. Formen gütlicher Konfliktbeendung in der
mittelalterlichen Adelsgesellschaft', in Althoff, *Spielregeln der Politik*,
pp. 99–125.

'Empörung, Tränen, Zerknirschung. Emotionen in der öffentlichen
Kommunikation des Mittelalters', in Althoff, *Spielregeln der Politik*,
pp. 258–81.

'Königsherrschaft und Konfliktführung im 10. und 11. Jahrhundert', in
Althoff, *Spielregeln der Politik*, pp. 21–56.

Die Macht der Rituale. Symbolik und Herrschaft im Mittelalter (Darmstadt 2003).

Heinrich IV (Darmstadt 2006).

Ambrose, S., 'The codicology and palaeography of London, BL, Royal 5 E. XIII
and its abridgment of the *Collectio Canonum Hibernensis*', *Codices Manuscripti*
54/55 (2006), pp. 1–26.

Andrade, J., 'Textos penitenciales y penitencia en el Noroeste de la peninsula
Ibérica', in M. W. Herren, C. J. McDonough and R. Arthur (eds.), *Latin
Culture in the Eleventh Century. Proceedings of the Third International Conference
on Medieval Latin Studies. Cambridge, September 9–12–1998* (Turnhout 2002),
pp. 29–38.

Angenendt, A., 'Die irische Peregrinatio und ihre Auswirkungen auf dem
Kontinent vor dem Jahre 800', in H. Löwe (ed.), *Die Iren und Europa im
früheren Mittelalter* (Stuttgart 1982), vol. I, pp. 52–79.

Das Frühmittelalter. Die abendländische Christenheit von 400 bis 900 (Stuttgart /
Berlin / Cologne 1990).

'"Er war der Erste...". Willibrords historische Stellung', in P. Bange and
A. Weiler (eds.), *Willibrord, zijn wereld en zijn werk. Voordrachten gehouden
tijdens het Willibrordcongres Nijmegen, 28–30 september 1989*, Middeleeuwse
Studies 6 (Nijmegen 1990), pp. 13–34.

Geschichte der Religiosität im Mittelalter (Darmstadt 1997).

Grundformen der Frömmigkeit im Mittelalter (Munich 2004).

Angenendt, A., Braucks, T. and Busch. R., 'Gezählte Frömmigkeit', *Frühmittelalterliche Studien* 29 (1995), pp. 1–71.

Anton, H. H., *Fürstenspiegel und Herrscherethos in der Karolingerzeit*, Bonner historische Forschungen 32 (Bonn 1968).

'Königsvorstellungen bei Iren und Franken im Vergleich', in F.-R. Erkens, *Das frühmittelalterliche Königtum. Ideelle und religiöse Grundlagen*, Ergänzungsbände zum Reallexikon der Germanischen Altertumskunde 49 (Berlin / New York 2005), pp. 270–330.

Asbach, F. B., 'Das Poenitentiale Remense und der sogen. Excarpsus Cummeani: Überlieferung, Quellen und Entwicklung zweier kontinentaler Bußbücher aus der 1. Hälfte des 8. Jahrhunderts' (Dissertation, Regensburg, 1975).

Austin, G., 'Jurisprudence in the service of pastoral care. The *Decretum* of Burchard of Worms', *Speculum* 79 (2004), pp. 929–59.

Shaping Church Law Around the Year 1000. The Decretum of Burchard of Worms (Farnham 2009).

'Authority and the canons in Burchard's *Decretum* and Ivo's *Decretum*, in M. Brett and K. Cushing (eds.), *Readers, Texts and Compilers in the Earlier Middle Ages. Studies in Medieval Canon Law in Honour of Linda Fowler-Magerl* (Farnham 2009), pp. 35–58.

Bachrach, D. S., 'Confession in the Regnum Francorum (742–900)', *Journal of Ecclesiastical History* 54 (2003), pp. 3–22.

Religion and the Conduct of War c. 300 – c. 1215 (Woodbridge 2003).

Bailey, L., '"Our own most severe judges": The power of penance in the Eusebius Gallicanus sermons', in A. Cain and N. Lenski (eds.), *The Power of Religion in Late Antiquity* (Farnham 2009), pp. 201–11.

Baldwin, J., *Masters, Princes and Merchants. The Social Views of Peter the Chanter & His Circle*, 2 vols. (Princeton 1970).

Barrow, J., 'Demonstrative behaviour and political communication in later Anglo-Saxon England', *Anglo-Saxon England* 36 (2007), pp. 127–50.

Bartlett, R., *The Making of Europe. Conquest, Colonization and Cultural Change 950–1350* (Harmondsworth 1994).

Becher, M., '*Cum lacrimis et gemitu*. Vom Weinen der Sieger und der Besiegten im frühen und hohen Mittelalter', in G. Althoff (ed.), *Formen und Funktionen öffentlicher Kommunikation im Mittelalter*, Vorträge und Forschungen. Konstanzer Arbeitskreis für Mittelalterliche Geschichte 51 (Stuttgart 2001), pp. 25–52.

Beck, H., *The Pastoral Care of Souls in South-East France During the Sixth Century* (Rome 1950).

Bedingfield, M., 'Public penance in Anglo-Saxon England', *Anglo-Saxon England* 31 (2002), pp. 223–55.

Benson, R. L. and Constable, G. (eds.), *Renaissance and Renewal in the Twelfth Century* (Oxford 1982).

Bezler, F., 'Chronologie relative des Pénitentiels d'Albelda et de Silos', *Sacris Erudiri* 23 (1991), pp. 163–9.

Les Pénitentiels Espagnols. Contribution à l'étude de la civilisation de l'Espagne chrétienne du haut Moyen Âge, Spanische Forschungen der Görresgesellschaft, 2. Reihe, Bd. 30 (Münster 1994).

Bieler, L., 'The Irish Penitentials: their religious and social background', in *Studia Patristica VIII. Papers presented to the Fourth International Conference on Patristic Studies held at Christ Church, Oxford 1963* (Berlin 1966), pp. 329–39.

Bijsterveld, A., 'The medieval gift as agent of social bonding and power', in Bijsterveld, *Do ut des. Gift Giving, 'Memoria', and Conflict Management in the Medieval Low Countries* (Hilversum 2007), pp. 17–50.

Bischoff, B., *Lorsch im Spiegel seiner Handschriften*, Münchener Beiträge zur Mediävistik und Renaissance-Forschung (Munich 1974).

Bischoff, B. and Lapidge, M., *Biblical Commentaries from the Canterbury School of Theodore and Hadrian* (Cambridge 1994).

Bishko, C., 'The liturgical context of Ferdinand I's last days', *Hispania Sacra. Revista de Historia Eclesiástica* 17 (1964), pp. 47–59 [reprinted in C. J. Bishko, *Spanish and Portuguese Monastic History 600–1300*, Variorum Reprints (London 1984), no. 7].

Bisson, T., *The Crisis of the Twelfth Century. Power, Lordship, and the Origins of European Government* (Princeton / Oxford 2009).

Bitel, L., 'Women's monastic enclosures in early Ireland: a study of female spirituality and male monastic mentalities', *Journal of Medieval History* 12 (1986), pp. 15–36.

Isle of the Saints. Monastic Settlement and Christian Community in Early Ireland (Ithaca and London 1990).

Blair, J., *The Church in Anglo-Saxon Society* (Oxford 2005).

Blair, J. and Sharpe, R. (eds.), *Pastoral Care Before the Parish* (Leicester, London etc. 1992).

Blöcker, M., 'Wetterzauber: Zu einem Glaubenskomplex des frühen Mittelalters', *Francia* 9 (1981), pp. 117–31.

Blomme, R., *La doctrine du péché dans les écoles théologiques de la première moitié du XII siècle* (Louvain 1958).

Bonnassie, P., 'Consommation d'aliments immondes et cannibalisme de survie dans l'occident du Haut Moyen Age', *Annales ESC* 44 (1989), pp. 1035–56.

Booker, C., *Past Convictions. The Penance of Louis the Pious and the Decline of the Carolingians* (Philadelphia 2009).

Bossy, J. (ed.), *Disputes and Settlements. Law and Human Relations in the West* (Cambridge 1983).

Bouhot, J.-P., 'Les pénitentiels attribués à Bède le Vénérable et à Egbert d'York', *Revue d'histoire des textes* 16 (1986), pp. 141–69.

Bowes, K., *Private Worship, Public Values, and Religious Change in Late Antiquity* (Cambridge 2008).

Boylan, A., 'The library at Santo Domingo de Silos and its catalogues (XIth–XVIIIth centuries)', *Revue Mabillon* 64 (1992), pp. 59–102.

Boyle, L., 'Summae Confessorum', in *Les genres littéraires dans les sources théologiques et philosophiques médiévales: définition, critique et exploitation: Actes du Colloque International de Louvain-la-Neuve, 25–27 mai 1981* (Louvain-la-Neuve 1982), pp. 227–37.

'The Fourth Lateran Council and manuals of popular theology', in T. J. Heffernan (ed.), *The Popular Literature of Medieval England* (Knoxville TN 1985), pp. 30–43.

Brakke, D., 'The problematization of nocturnal emissions in early Christian Syria, Egypt, and Gaul', *Journal of Early Christian Studies* 3 (1995), pp. 419–60.

Breatnach, L., *A Companion to the Corpus Iuris Hibernici*, Early Irish Law Series 5 (Dublin 2005).

Breen, A., 'The date, provenance and authorship of the pseudo-Patrician canonical materials', *ZRG Kan.* 81 (1995), pp. 83–129.

'*De XII Abusivis*: text and transmission', in P. Ní Chatháin and M. Richter (eds.), *Ireland and Europe in the Early Middle Ages. Texts and Transmission / Irland und Europa im früheren Mittelalter. Texte und Überlieferung* (Dublin 2002), pp. 78–94.

Brett, M., 'Finding the law: the sources of canonical authority before Gratian', in P. Andersen, M. Münster-Swendsen and H. Vogt (eds.), *Law before Gratian: Law in Western Europe, c. 500–1100. Proceedings of the Third Carlsberg Academy Conference on Legal History* (Copenhagen 2007), pp. 51–72.

Brommer, P., '*Capitula Episcoporum*'. *Die bischöflichen Kapitularien des 9. und 10. Jahrhunderts*, Typologie des sources 43 (Turnhout 1985).

Brown, P., 'The rise and function of the Holy Man in Late Antiquity', *Journal of Roman Studies* 61 (1971), pp. 80–101.

'Society and the supernatural: a medieval change', *Daedalus* 104 (1975), pp. 133–51 (reprinted in Brown, *Society and the Holy*, pp. 302–32).

The Cult of Saints. Its Rise and Function in Latin Christianity (Chicago 1981).

Society and the Holy in Late Antiquity (Berkeley / Los Angeles / Oxford 1982).

Power and Persuasion in Late Antiquity. Towards a Christian Empire (Madison WI / London 1992).

'The rise and function of the Holy Man in Late Antiquity, 1971–1997', *Journal of Early Christian Studies* 6 (1998), pp. 353–76.

The Rise of Western Christendom. Triumph and Diversity, A.D. 200–1000 (2nd edn, Oxford 2003).

Brundage, J., 'Prostitution, miscegenation and sexual purity in the First Crusade', in P. Edbury (ed.), *Crusade and Settlement* (Cardiff 1985), pp. 57–65.

Law, Sex, and Christian Society in Medieval Europe (Chicago / London 1987).

'The rise of professional canonists and the development of the Ius Commune', *ZRG Kan.* 81 (1995), pp. 26–63.

'Legal learning and the professionalization of canon law', in H. Vogt (ed.), *Law and Learning in the Middle Ages. Proceedings of the Second Carlsberg Academy Conference on Medieval Legal History 2005* (Copenhagen 2006), pp. 5–27.

'The teaching of canon law in the schools', in W. Hartmann and K. Pennington (eds.), *The History of Medieval Canon Law in the Classical Period. From Gratian to the Decretals of Pope Gregory IX* (Washington DC 2008), pp. 98–120.

Buc, P., *The Dangers of Ritual. Between Early Medieval Texts and Social Scientific Theory* (Princeton 2001).

Buck, T. M., *Admonitio und Praedicatio. Zur religions-pastoralen Dimension von Kapitularien und kapitulariennahen Texten (507–814)* (Frankfurt 1997).

Bull, M., *Knightly Piety and the Lay Response to the First Crusade. The Limousin and Gascony, c. 970–c. 1130* (Oxford 1993).

Bullough, D., 'The career of Columbanus', in M. Lapidge (ed.), *Columbanus. Studies on the Latin Writings* (Woodbridge 1997), pp. 1–28.

'The Carolingian liturgical experience', in R. Swanson (ed.), *Continuity and Change in Christian Worship*, Studies in Church History 35 (Woodbridge 1999), pp. 29–64.

Alcuin: Achievement and Reputation. Being Part of the Ford Lectures Delivered in Oxford in Hilary Term 1980 (Leiden / Boston 2004).

Busch, J., *Vom Amtswalten zum Königsdienst. Beobachtungen zur 'Staatssprache' des Frühmittelalters am Beispiel des Wortes 'administratio'*, MGH Studien und Texte 42 (Hanover 2007), pp. 42–57.

Cameron, M., 'Abelard (and Héloise?) on intention', *American Catholic Philosophical Quarterly* 81 (2007), pp. 323–38.

Carozzi, C., *Le voyage de l'âme dans l'au-delà d'après la littérature latine (Ve–XIIIe siècle)* (Rome 1994).

Carr, E., 'Penance among the Armenians: notes on the history of its practice and its theology', *Studia Liturgica* 11 (1976), pp. 65–100.

Cerquiglini, B., *Éloge de la variante. Histoire critique de la philologie* (Paris 1989).

Chadwick, O., 'Gregory of Tours and Gregory the Great', *Journal of Theological Studies* 50 (1949), pp. 38–49.

Charles-Edwards, T., 'The social background to Irish *peregrinatio*', *Celtica* 11 (1976), pp. 43–59.

'The pastoral role of the church in the early Irish laws', in J. Blair and R. Sharpe (eds.), *Pastoral Care Before the Parish* (Leicester / London etc. 1992), pp. 63–80.

'The penitential of Theodore and the Iudicia Theodori', in M. Lapidge, (ed.), *Archbishop Theodore. Commemorative Studies on his Life and Influence* (Cambridge 1995), pp. 141–74.

'The penitential of Columbanus', in M. Lapidge (ed.), *Columbanus*, pp. 217–39.

Early Christian Ireland (Cambridge 2000).

Cheyette, F. L., 'Suum cuique tribuere', *French Historical Studies* 6 (1970), pp. 287–99.

Chiffoleau, J., *La comptabilité de l'au-delà: les hommes, la mort et la religion dans la région d'Avignon à la fin du moyen âge* (Rome 1980).

Ciccarese, M. P., 'Le visioni di S. Fursa', *Romanobarbarica: Contributi allo studio dei rapporti culturali tra mondo latino e mondo barbarico* 8 (1984/1985), pp. 231–303.

Clanchy, M., *Abelard. A Medieval Life* (Oxford 1997).

Clark, F., *The 'Gregorian' Dialogues and the Origins of Benedictine Monasticism* (Leiden 2003).

Clarke, H. B. and Brennan, M., (eds.), *Columbanus and Merovingian Monasticism* (Oxford 1981).

Collins, R., 'Continuity and loss in medieval Spanish culture: the evidence of MS, Silos, Archivo Monástico 4', in R. Collins and A. Goodman (eds.), *Medieval Spain. Culture, Conflict, and Coexistence. Studies in Honour of Angus MacKay* (Basingstoke / New York 2002), pp. 1–22.

Constable, G., 'Medieval charters as sources for the history of the crusades', in P. Edbury (ed.), *Crusade and Settlement. Papers Read at the First Conference of the Society for the Study of the Crusades and the Latin East Presented to R. C. Smail* (Cardiff 1985), pp. 73–89.

The Reformation of the Twelfth Century (Cambridge 1996).

Contreni, J., 'The Carolingian Renaissance: education and literary culture', in R. McKitterick (ed.), *The New Cambridge Medieval History*, vol. II, pp. 709–57.

Cooper, K. and Gregory, J., (eds.), *Retribution, Repentance, and Reconciliation*, Studies in Church History 40 (Woodbridge 2004).

Corradini, R., Diesenberger, M. and Niederkorn-Bruck, M. (eds.), *Zwischen Niederschrift und Wiederschrift. Hagiographie und Historiographie im Spannungsfeld von Kompendienüberlieferung und Editionstechnik*, Forschungen zur Geschichte des Mittelalters 18 (Vienna 2010).

Costambeys, M., 'An aristocratic community on the northern Frankish frontier 690–726', *Early Medieval Europe* 3 (1994), pp. 39–62.

Couser, J., 'Inventing paganism in eighth-century Bavaria', *Early Medieval Europe* 18 (2010), pp. 26–42.

Cowdrey, H., *The Cluniacs and the Gregorian Reform* (Oxford 1970).

The Age of Abbot Desiderius. Montecassino, the Papacy, and the Normans in the Eleventh and Early Twelfth Centuries (Oxford 1983).

'The spirituality of Gregory VII', in J. Hogg (ed.), *The Mystical Tradition and the Carthusians* (Salzburg 1995), vol. I, pp. 1–22 [reprinted in H. Cowdrey, *Popes and Church Reform in the Eleventh Century* (Aldershot 2000)].

Cubitt, C., *Anglo-Saxon Church Councils c. 650–c.850* (London / New York 1995).

'Bishops, priests and penance in late Anglo-Saxon England', *Early Medieval Europe* 14 (2006), pp. 41–63.

Cusack, C., *Conversion among the Germanic Peoples* (London / New York 1998).

Cushing, K., *Papacy and Law in the Gregorian Revolution. The Canonistic Work of Anselm of Lucca* (Oxford 1998).

'Anselm of Lucca and Burchard of Worms: re-thinking the sources of Anselm 11, *De Penitentia*', in K. Cushing and R. Gyug (eds.), *Ritual, Text and Law. Studies in Medieval Canon Law and Liturgy Presented to Roger E. Reynolds* (Aldershot 2004), pp. 225–39.

Dahlhaus-Berg, E., *Nova antiquitas et antiqua novitas. Typologische Exegese und isidorianisches Geschichtsbild bei Theodulf von Orléans*, Kölner Historische Abhandlungen 23 (Cologne / Vienna 1975).

Dam, R. van, *Saints and Their Miracles in Late Antique Gaul* (Princeton 1993).

Dassmann, E., *Ambrosius von Mailand. Leben und Werk* (Stuttgart 2004).

Davies, W. and Fouracre, P. (eds.), *The Settlement of Disputes in Early Medieval Europe* (Cambridge 1986).

Davis, A., *The Holy Bureaucrat. Eudes Rigaud and Religious Reform in Thirteenth-Century Normandy* (Ithaca / London 2006).

Delen, K, Gaastra, A., Saan, M. and Schaap, B., 'The *Paenitentiale Cantabrigiense*. A witness of the Carolingian contribution to the tenth-century reforms in England', *Sacris Erudiri* 41 (2002), pp. 341–73.

Delumeau, J., *Le catholicisme entre Luther et Voltaire* (Paris 1979).

Devroey, J.-P., *Le polyptyque et les listes de cens de l'abbaye de Saint-Remi de Reims (IXe-XIe siècles)*, Travaux de l'Académie Nationale de Reims 163 (Reims 1984).

Diaz y Diaz, M., 'El escriptorio de Silos', *Revista de Musicologia* 15 (1992), pp. 389–401.

Diem, A., 'Virtues and vices in early texts on pastoral care', *Franciscan Studies* 62 (2004), pp. 193–223.

Das monastische Experiment. Die Rolle der Keuschheit bei der Entstehung des westlichen Klosterwesens, Vita Regularis. Ordnungen und Deutungen religiösen Lebens im Mittelalter 24 (Münster 2005).

'Monks, kings, and the transformation of sanctity: Jonas of Bobbio and the end of the holy man', *Speculum* 82 (2007), pp. 521–59.

Dierkens, A., *Abbayes et chapitres entre Sambre et Meuse (VIIe – IXe Siècles)* (Sigmaringen 1985).

'Prolégomènes à une histoire des relations culturelles entre les îles britanniques et le continent pendant le Haut Moyen Age. La diffusion du monachisme dit colombanien ou iro-franc dans quelques monastères de la région parisienne au VIIe siècle et la politique religieuse de la reine Bathilde', in H. Atsma (ed.), *La Neustrie. Les pays au nord de la Loire de 650 à 850*, 2 vols., Beihefte der Francia 16 (Sigmaringen 1989), vol. II, pp. 371–94.

Dumville, D., 'Gildas and Uinniau', in M. Lapidge and D. Dumville (eds.), *Gildas. New Approaches* (Woodbridge 1984), pp. 207–14.

Dunn, M., 'Gregory the Great, the Vision of Fursey and the origins of purgatory', *Peritia* 14 (2000), pp. 238–54.

The Emergence of Monasticism. From the Desert Fathers to the Early Middle Ages (Oxford 2003).

The Christianization of the Anglo-Saxons c. 597–c. 700. Discourses of Life, Death and Afterlife (London 2009).

Dutton, P., 'Thunder and hail over the Carolingian countryside', in P. Dutton, *Charlemagne's Mustache and Other Cultural Clusters of a Dark Age* (New York 2004), pp. 169–88.

(ed.), *Carolingian Civilization. A Reader* (Peterborough, Ontario 1993).

Eberhardt, O., *Via Regia. Der Fürstenspiegel Smaragds von St Mihiel und seine literarische Gattung*, Münstersche Mittelalter-Schriften 28 (München 1977).

Egmond, W. van, 'Radbod van de Friezen, een aristocraat in de periferie', *Millennium* 19 (2005), pp. 24–44.

Etchingham, C., *Church Organisation in Ireland A.D. 650–1000* (Maynooth 1999).

Faris, M. J., *The Bishops' Synod ('The First Synod of St. Patrick'). A Symposium with Text, Translation and Commentary* (Liverpool 1976).

Faulhaber, C., *Medieval Manuscripts in the Library of the Hispanic Society of America* (New York 1983).

Finsterwalder, P. W., *Die Canones Theodori Cantuariensis und ihre Überlieferungsformen*, Untersuchungen zu den Bußbüchern des 7., 8. und 9. Jahrhunderts 1 (Weimar 1929).

Firey, A., 'Ghostly recensions in early medieval canon law: the problem of the *Collectio Dacheriana* and its shades', *Tijdschrift voor Rechtsgeschiedenis* 68 (2000), pp. 63–82.

A Contrite Heart. Prosecution and Redemption in the Carolingian Empire (Leiden / Boston 2009).

Fischer, A., *Karl Martell. Der Beginn der karolingischen Herrschaft* (Stuttgart 2012).

Flandrin, J.-L., *Un temps pour embrasser. Aux origines de la morale sexuelle occidentale (VI–XI siècle)* (Paris 1983).

Flechner, R., 'The making of the Canons of Theodore', *Peritia* 17–18 (2003–4), pp. 121–43.

Fletcher, R., *The Conversion of Europe. From Paganism to Christianity, 371–1386 AD* (London 1997).

Flint, V., *The Rise of Magic in Early Medieval Europe* (Oxford 1991).

Follet, W., 'Cassian, contemplation, and medieval Irish hagiography', in G. R. Wieland, C. Ruff and R. G. Arthur (eds.), *Insignis Sophiae Arcator. Essays in Honour of Michael W. Herren on his 65th Birthday* (Turnhout 2006), pp. 87–105.

Céli Dé in Ireland. Monastic Writing and Identity in the Early Middle Ages, Studies in Celtic History 23 (Woodbridge 2006).

Fouracre, P., *The Age of Charles Martel* (Harlow 2000).

Fournier, P., 'Études sur les pénitentiels', *Revue d'histoire et de littérature religieuses* 6 (1901), pp. 289–317, 7 (1902), pp. 59–70 and 121–7, 8 (1903), pp. 528–553 and 9 (1904), pp. 97–103 [reprinted in P. Fournier, *Mélanges de droit canonique* (Aalen 1983)].

'Un tournant de l'histoire du droit 1060–1140', *Nouvelle revue historique de droit français et étranger* 41 (1917), pp. 129–80 [reprinted in Fournier, *Mélanges de droit canonique*, (Aalen 1983), vol. II, pp. 373–424].

Fowler-Magerl, L., *Clavis canonum. Selected Canon Law Collections Before 1140. Access with Data Processing*, MGH Hilfsmittel 21 (Hanover 2005).

Frantzen, A., *The Literature of Penance in Anglo-Saxon England* (New Brunswick, 1983).

'The penitentials attributed to Bede', *Speculum* 58 (1983), pp. 573–97.

Fried, J., 'Der Pakt von Canossa. Schritte zur Wirklichkeit durch Erinnerungsanalyse', in W. Hartmann and K. Herbers (eds.), *Die Faszination der Papstgeschichte. Neue Zugänge zum frühen und hohen Mittelalter* (Cologne / Weimar / Vienna 2008), pp. 133–97.

Gaastra, A., 'Penance and the law: the penitential canons of the *Collection in Nine Books*', *Early Medieval Europe* 14 (2006), pp. 85–102.

'Between liturgy and canon law. A study of books of confession and penance in eleventh- and twelfth-century Italy' (Dissertation, University of Utrecht, 2007).

Gameson, R., 'The origin of the Exeter Book of Old English poetry', *Anglo-Saxon England* 25 (1995), pp. 135–85.

Ganz, D., *Corbie in the Carolingian Renaissance* (Sigmaringen 1990).

'Book production in the Carolingian empire and the spread of Caroline minuscule', in R. McKitterick (ed.), *The New Cambridge Medieval History*, vol. II (Cambridge 1995), pp. 786–808.

Garnier, C. and Kamp, H. (eds.), *Spielregeln der Mächtigen. Mittelalterliche Politik zwischen Gewohnheit und Konvention* (Darmstadt 2010).

Garrison, M., 'Letters to a king and biblical exempla: the examples of Cathuulf and Clemens', *Early Medieval Europe* 7 (1998), pp. 305–28.

Gaudemet, J., 'Le débat sur la confession dans la Distinction I du "De penitentia" (Décret de Gratien C.33, q.3)', *ZRG KA* 71 (1985), pp. 52–75.

Gerriets, M., 'Theft, penitentials, and the compilation of the early Irish laws', *Celtica* 22 (1991), pp. 18–32.

Glatthaar, M., *Bonifatius und das Sakrileg. Zur politischen Dimension eines Rechtsbegriffs*, Freiburger Beiträge zur mittelalterlichen Geschichte 17 (Frankfurt a.M. etc. 2004).

Gneuss, H., *Handlist of Anglo-Saxon Manuscripts. A List of Manuscripts and Manuscript Fragments Written or Owned in England up to 1100*, Medieval and Renaissance Texts and Studies 241 (Tempe AZ 2001).

Godding, R., *Prêtres en Gaule mérovingienne*, Subsidia hagiographica 82 (Brussels 2001).

Godman, P. and Collins, R. (eds.), *Charlemagne's Heir. New Perspectives on the Reign of Louis the Pious (814–840)* (Oxford 1990).

Göller, E., 'Studien über das gallische Bußwesen zur Zeit des Cäsarius von Arles und Gregors des Grossen', *Archiv für katholisches Kirchenrecht* 109 (1929), pp. 3–126.

Goering, J., 'The internal forum and the literature of penance and confession', in Hartmann and Pennington, *History of Medieval Canon Law in the Classical Period*, pp. 379–428.

Goering, J. and Mantello, F., 'The early penitential writings of Robert Grosseteste', *Recherches de Théologie Ancienne et Médiévale* 54 (1987), pp. 52–112.

Goetz, H.-W., 'Die Chronik Thietmars von Merseburg als Ego-Dokument. Ein Bischof mit gespaltenem Selbstverständnis', in R. McKitterick, I. van Renswoude and M. Gillis (eds.), *Ego Trouble. Authors and Their Identities in the Early Middle Ages*, Forschungen zur Geschichte des Mittelalters 15 (Vienna 2010), pp. 259–70.

Goez, W., 'Canossa als deditio?', in M. Thumser (ed.), *Studien zur Geschichte des Mittelalters. Jürgen Petersohn zum 65. Geburtstag* (Stuttgart 2000), pp. 92–9.

Gorman, M., 'Theodore of Canterbury, Hadrian of Nisida and Michael Lapidge', *Scriptorium* 50 (1996), pp. 184–92.

Gurevich, A., *Medieval Popular Culture. Problems of Belief and Perception* (Cambridge 1988).

Gyug, R., 'The list of authorities in the illustrations of the Collection in Five Books (Ms. Vat. lat. 1339)', in K. Cushing and R. Gyug (eds.), *Ritual, Text and Law. Studies in Medieval Canon Law and Liturgy Presented to Roger E. Reynolds* (London 2004), pp. 241–54.

Hägele, G., *Das Paenitentiale Vallicellianum I. Ein oberitalienischer Zweig der frühmittelalterlichen kontinentalen Bußbücher. Überlieferung, Verbreitung und Quellen*, Quellen und Forschungen zum Recht im Mittelalter 3 (Sigmaringen 1984).

Hägermann, D., *Karl der Große. Herrscher des Abendlandes: Biographie* (3rd edn, Berlin 2006), pp. 609–13.

Haggenmüller, R., *Die Überlieferung der Beda und Egbert zugeschriebenen Bußbücher* (Frankfurt a.M. / Bern / etc.1991).

'Frühmittelalterliche Bußbücher – Paenitentialien – und das Kloster Lorsch', *Geschichtsblätter Kreis Bergstraße* 25 (1992), pp. 125–54.

'Zur Rezeption der Beda und Egbert zugeschriebenen Bußbücher', in
H. Mordek (ed.), *Aus Archiven und Bibliotheken. Festschrift für Raymund
Kottje zum 65. Geburtstag* (Frankfurt a.M. / Bern / etc. 1992), pp. 149–59.

'Die Überlieferung Ps.-Beda *De Remediis Peccatorum* in der Würzburger Hs.
M.p.j.q. 2. Ein weiteres Zeugnis der Vorstufe des *Paenitentiale Additivum
Ps.-Beda-Egberti', Bulletin of Medieval Canon Law N.S.* 23 (1999), pp. 66–76.

Hamilton, S. *The Practice of Penance, 900–1050* (Woodbridge 2001).

'The unique favour of penance: the Church and the people c. 800 – c. 1100', in
P. Linehan and J. Nelson (eds.), *The Medieval World* (London / New York
2001), pp. 229–45.

'Penance in the age of the Gregorian Reform', in K. Cooper and J. Gregory
(eds.), *Retribution, Repentance, and Reconciliation,* Studies in Church History
40 (Woodbridge 2004), pp. 47–73.

'The Rituale: the evolution of a new liturgical book', in R. Swanson (ed.),
The Church and the Book, Studies in Church History 38 (Woodbridge 2004),
pp. 74–86.

'Rites for public penance in late Anglo-Saxon England', in H. Gittos and
M. B. Bedingfield (eds.), *The Liturgy of the Late Anglo-Saxon Church,* Henry
Bradshaw Society Subsidia 5 (London 2005), pp. 65–103.

'*Absoluimus uos uice beati petri apostolorum principis*: episcopal authority and the
reconciliation of excommunicants in England and Francia c. 900–1150', in
P. Fouracre and D. Ganz (eds.), *Frankland. The Franks and the World of the
Early Middle Ages. Essays in Honour of Dame Jinty Nelson* (Manchester 2008),
pp. 209–41.

Hammer, C., 'Country churches. Clerical inventories and the Carolingian
renaissance in Bavaria', *Church History* 49 (1980), pp. 5–19.

Harmening, D., *Superstitio. Ueberlieferungs- und theoriegeschichtliche
Untersuchungen zur kirchlich-theologischen Aberglaubensliteratur des Mittelalters*
(Berlin 1979).

Hartmann, W., 'Neue Texte zur bischöflichen Reformgesetzgebung aus den
Jahren 829–31. Vier Diözesansynoden Halitgars von Cambrai', *Deutsches
Archiv* 35 (1979), pp. 368–94.

Die Synoden der Karolingerzeit im Frankenreich und in Italien,
Konziliengeschichte, Reihe A: Darstellungen (Paderborn / Munich / Vienna /
Zürich 1989).

'Probleme des geistlichen Gerichts im 10. und 11. Jahrhunderts: Bischöfe und
Synoden als Richter im ostfränkisch-deutschen Reich', in *La Giustizia
nell'alto medioevo (secoli IX–XI),* Settimana di Studio 44 (Spoleto 1997),
pp. 631–72.

'Die Capita incerta im Sendhandbuch Reginos von Prüm', in O. Münsch and
T. Zotz (eds.), *Scientia veritatis. Festschrift für Hubert Mordek zum 65.
Geburtstag* (Ostfildern 2004), pp. 207–26.

'Zu Effektivität und Aktualität von Reginos Sendhandbuch', in W. P. Müller and
M. E. Sommar (eds.), *Medieval Church Law and the Origins of the Western Legal
Tradition. A Tribute to Kenneth Pennington* (Washington 2006), pp. 33–49.

*Kirche und Kirchenrecht um 900. Die Bedeutung de spätkarolingischen Zeit für
Tradition und Innovation im kirchlichen Recht,* Schriften der MGH 58
(Hanover 2008).

Hartmann, W. and Pennington, K. (eds.), *The History of Medieval Canon Law in the Classical Period. From Gratian to the Decretals of Pope Gregory IX* (Washington 2008).

Hase, A., *Mittelalterliche Bücherverzeichnisse aus Kloster Lorsch. Einleitung, Edition und Kommentar* (Wiesbaden 2002).

Haskins, C. H., *The Renaissance of the Twelfth Century* (Cambridge MA 1927).

Heidecker, K., *The Divorce of Lothar II. Christian Marriage and Political Power in the Carolingian World* (Ithaca 2010).

Heinzelmann, M., *Bischofsherrschaft in Gallien. Zur Kontinuität römischer Führungsschichten vom 4. bis zum 7. Jahrhundert. Soziale, prosopographische und bildungsgeschichtliche Aspekte* (Munich 1976).

  Gregor von Tours (538–594). 'Zehn Bücher Geschichte'. Historiographie und Gesellschaftskonzept im 6. Jahrhundert (Darmstadt 1994).

Heiser, L., *Die Responsa ad consulta Bulgarorum des Papstes Nikolaus (858–867)* (Trier 1979).

Hen, Y., *Culture and Religion in Merovingian Gaul A.D. 481–751* (Leiden / New York / Cologne 1995).

  'The structure and aims of the *Visio Baronti*', *Journal of Theological Studies*, NS 47 (1996), pp. 477–97.

  'The liturgy of St Willibrord', *Anglo-Saxon England* 26 (1997), pp. 41–60.

  'Knowledge of canon law among rural priests: the evidence of two Carolingian manuscripts from around 800', *Journal of Theological Studies* NS 50 (1999), pp. 117–34.

  The Royal Patronage of Liturgy in Frankish Gaul. To the Death of Charles the Bald (877), Henry Bradshaw Society. Subsidia 3 (London 2001).

  'Rome, Anglo-Saxon England and the formation of the Frankish liturgy', *Revue Bénédictine* 112 (2002), pp. 301–22.

Hen, Y. and Meens, R. (eds.), *The Bobbio Missal. Liturgy and Religious Culture in Merovingian Gaul*, Cambridge Studies in Palaeography and Codicology 11 (Cambridge 2004).

Herren, M. W., 'Gildas and early British monasticism', in A. Bammesberger and A. Wollmann (eds.), *Britain 400–600: Language and History* (Heidelberg 1990), pp. 65–78.

Heyworth, M., 'The 'Late Old English Handbook for the use of a Confessor': Authorship and connections', *Notes and Queries* 54 (2007), pp. 218–22.

Hill, J., 'The *Litaniae maiores* and *minores* in Rome, Francia and Anglo-Saxon England', *Early Medieval Europe* 9 (2000), pp. 211–46.

  'Archbishop Wulfstan: Reformer?', in Townend (ed.), *Wulfstan, Archbishop of York*, pp. 309–24.

Hitchcock, R., *Mozarabs in Medieval and Early Modern Spain. Identities and Influences* (Aldershot 2008).

Hoffmann, H. and Pokorny, R., *Das Dekret des Bischofs Burchard von Worms. Textstufen – Frühe Verbreitung – Vorlagen*, MGH Hilfsmittel 12 (Munich 1991).

Hood, A. B., 'Lighten our darkness – Biblical style in early medieval Britain and Ireland', *Early Medieval Europe* 8 (1999), pp. 283–96.

Howlett, D., *The Celtic Latin Tradition of Biblical Style* (Dublin 1995).

  'A response to "Lighten our Darkness"', *Early Medieval Europe* 9 (2000), pp. 85–92.

Hughes, K., *Early Christian Ireland. Introduction to the Sources* (Ithaca 1972).

Huisman, G., *Catalogus van de middeleeuwse handschriften in de Universiteitsbibliotheek Nijmegen* (Leuven 1997).

Humfress, C., 'Bishops and law courts in Late Antiquity: how (not) to make sense of the legal evidence', *Journal of Early Christian Studies* 19 (2011), pp. 375–400.

Humphries, M., 'Italy, A.D. 425–605', in A. Cameron, B. Ward-Perkins and M. Whitby (eds.), *The Cambridge Ancient History*, vol. xiv: *Late Antiquity: Empire and Successors, A.D. 425–600* (Cambridge 2000), pp. 525–51.

Hyams, P., *Rancor and Reconciliation in Medieval England* (Ithaca / London 2003).

Innes, M., *Introduction to Early Medieval Western Europe, 300–900. The Sword, the Plough and the Book* (London / New York 2007).

'"Immune from heresy": defining the boundaries of Carolingian Christianity', in P. Fouracre and D. Ganz (eds.), *Frankland. The Franks and the World of the Early Middle Ages. Essays in Honour of Dame Jinty Nelson* (Manchester 2008), pp. 101–25.

Jones, C., 'Wulfstan's liturgical interests', in Townend (ed.), *Wulfstan. Archbishop of York*, pp. 325–52.

Jong, M. de, 'Power and humility in Carolingian society: the public penance of Louis the Pious', *Early Medieval Europe* 1 (1992), pp. 29–52.

In Samuel's Image. Child Oblation in the Early Medieval West (Leiden / New York / Cologne 1996).

'What was public about public penance? *Paenitentia publica* and justice in the Carolingian world', in *La Giustizia nell'alto medioevo II (secoli IX–XI)*, Settimane di Studio 44 (Spoleto 1997), pp. 863–904.

'Pollution, penance and sanctity: Ekkehard's *Life* of Iso of St Gall', in J. Hill and M. Swann (eds.), *The Community, the Family, and the Saint. Patterns of Power in Early Medieval Europe* (Turnhout 1998), pp. 145–58.

'Transformations of penance', in F. Theuws and J. L. Nelson (eds.), *Rituals of Power. From Late Antiquity to the Early Middle Ages* (Leiden / Boston / Cologne 2000), pp. 185–224.

'Monastic prisoner or opting out? Political coercion and honour in the Frankish kingdoms', in M. de Jong, F. Theuws and C. van Rhijn (eds.), *Topographies of Power in the Early Middle Ages*, Transformation of the Roman World 6 (Leiden 2001), pp. 291–328.

'Sacrum palatium et ecclesia. L'autorité religieuse royale sous les Carolingiens (790–840)', *Annales HSS* 58 (2003), pp. 1243–69.

'Bonifatius: een Angelsaksische priester-monnik en het Frankische hof', *Millennium* 19 (2005), pp. 5–23.

'Charlemagne's Church', in J. Story (ed.), *Charlemagne. Empire and Society* (Manchester 2005), pp. 103–35.

The Penitential State. Authority and Atonement in the Age of Louis the Pious, 814–840 (Cambridge 2009).

Jordan, W., *Europe in the High Middle Ages* (London 2001).

Jungmann, J. A., *Die lateinischen Bussriten in ihrer geschichtlichen Entwicklung* (Innsbruck 1932).

Kaiser, R., *Bischofsherrschaft zwischen Königtum und Fürstenmacht. Studien zur bischöflichen Stadtherrschaft im westfränkisch-französischen Reich im frühen und hohen Mittelalter* (Bonn 1981).

Kaiser, W., 'Zur Rekonstruktion einer vornehmlich Bußrechtlichen Handschrift aus Bobbio (Hs. Vat. lat. 5751 ff. 1–54v + Hs. Mailand, Bibl. Ambr. G. 58 sup. ff. 41r–64v)', *ZRG Kan. Abt.* 86 (2000), pp. 538–53.

Keefe, S., *Water and the Word. Baptism and the Education of the Clergy in the Carolingian Empire* (Notre Dame 2002).

Kelly, F., *A Guide to Early Irish Law*, Early Irish Law series 3 (Dublin 1991).

Kenney, J. F., *The Sources for the Early History of Ireland: Ecclesiastical. An Introduction and Guide* (Blackrock 1993, 1st edition New York 1929).

Ker, N., *Catalogue of Manuscripts Containing Anglo-Saxon* (Oxford 1957).

Kerff, F., *Der Quadripartitus. Ein Handbuch der karolingischen Kirchenreform. Überlieferung, Quellen und Rezeption*, Quellen und Forschungen zum Recht im Mittelalter 1 (Sigmaringen 1982).

'Das Paenitentiale Pseudo-Gregorii III. Ein Zeugnis karolingischer Reformbestrebungen', *ZRG Kan Abt.* 69 (1983), pp. 46–63.

'Das sogenannte Paenitentiale Fulberti. Überlieferung, Verfasserfrage, Edition', *ZRG Kan. Abt.* 73 (1987), pp. 1–40.

'Mittelalterliche Quellen und mittelalterliche Wirklichkeit. Zu den Konsequenzen einer jüngst erschienenen Edition für unser Bild kirchlicher Reformbemühungen', *Rheinische Vierteljahrsblätter* 51 (1987), pp. 275–86.

'Libri paenitentiales und kirchliche Strafgerichtsbarkeit bis zum *Decretum Gratiani*. Ein Diskussionsvorschlag', *Zeitschrift der Savigny-Stiftung für Rechtsgeschichte, Kan. Abt.* 75 (1989), pp. 23–57.

'Das Paenitentiale Pseudo-Gregorii. Eine kritische Edition', in H. Mordek (ed.), *Aus Archiven und Bibliotheken. Festschrift für Raymund Kottje zum 65. Geburtstag* (Frankfurt a.M. / Bern / etc., 1992), pp. 161–88.

Kéry, L., *Canonical Collections of the Early Middle Ages (ca. 400–1140). A Bibliographical Guide to the Manuscripts and Literature* (Washington DC 1999).

Klingshirn, W., *Caesarius of Arles. The Making of a Christian Community in Late Antique Gaul* (Cambridge 1994).

Koeniger, A., *Die Sendgerichte in Deutschland* (Munich 1907).

Kolb, F., 'Der Bußakt von Mailand: Zum Verhältnis von Staat und Kirche in der Spätantike, in H. Boockmann, K. Jürgensen and G. Stoltenberg (eds.), *Geschichte und Gegenwart. Festschrift für Karl Dietrich Erdmann* (Neumünster 1980), pp. 41–74.

Körntgen, L., 'Ein italienisches Bußbuch und seine fränkische Quellen. Das anonyme Paenitentiale der Handschrift Vatikan, Arch. S. Pietro H 58', in Mordek (ed.), *Aus Archiven und Bibliotheken*, pp. 189–205.

Studien zu den Quellen der frühmittelalterlichen Bußbücher, Quellen und Forschungen zum Recht im Mittelalter 7 (Sigmaringen 1993).

'Der *Excarpsus Cummeani*, ein Bußbuch aus Corbie', in O. Münsch and T. Zotz (eds.), *Scientia veritatis. Festschrift für Hubert Mordek zum 65. Geburtstag* (Ostfildern 2004), pp. 59–75.

'Canon law and the practice of penance: Burchard of Worms's penitential',
   Early Medieval Europe 14 (2006), pp. 103–17.
'Kanonisches recht und Busspraxis. Zu Kontext und Funktion des
   Paenitentiale Excarpsus Cummeani', in W. P. Müller and M. E. Sommar
   (eds.), *Medieval Church Law and the Origins of the Western Legal Tradition.
   A Tribute to Kenneth Pennington* (Washington 2006), pp. 17–32.
'Bußbuch und Bußpraxis in der zweiten Hälfte des 9. Jahrhunderts', in W.
   Hartmann (ed.), *Recht und Gericht in Kirche und Welt um 900*, Schriften des
   Historischen Kollegs, Kolloquien 69 (Munich 2007), pp. 197–215.
Kottje, R., 'Einheit und Vielfalt des kirchlichen Lebens in der Karolingerzeit',
   Zeitschrift für Kirchengeschichte 76 (1965), pp. 323–42.
*Die Bussbücher Halitgars von Cambrai und des Hrabanus Maurus. Ihre
   Überlieferung und ihre Quellen*, Beiträge zur Geschichte und Quellenkunde
   des Mittelalters 8 (Berlin / New York 1980).
'Überlieferung und Rezeption der irischen Bußbücher auf dem Kontinent',
   in H. Löwe (ed.), *Die Iren und Europa im früheren Mittelalter* (Stuttgart 1982),
   vol. I, pp. 511–24.
'Paenitentiale Theodori', in *Handwörterbuch zur deutschen Rechtsgeschichte* 3
   (Berlin 1984), cols. 1413–16.
'Busspraxis und Bussritus', in *Segni e riti nella chiesa altomedievale occidentale*,
   Settimane di studio 33 (Spoleto 1987) pp. 369–95.
'"Buße oder Strafe?". Zur "Iustitia" in den "Libri Paenitentiales"', in *La
   Giustizia nell'alto medioevo (secoli V–VIII)*, Settimane di Studio 42
   (Spoleto 1995), pp. 443–74.
'Das älteste Zeugnis für das Paenitentiale Cummeani', *Deutsches Archiv* 61
   (2005), pp. 585–9.
'Ein Fragment des "Paenitentiale" Halitgars von Cambrai aus einem Frühdruck
   der "Institutionen" Justinians', *Sacris Erudiri* 44 (2005), pp. 241–6.
'Tötung im Krieg als rechtliches und moralisches Problem im früheren und
   hohen Mittelalter', in H. Hecker, *Krieg in Mittelalter und Renaissance*
   (Düsseldorf 2005), pp. 17–39.
Koziol, G., *Begging Pardon and Favor. Ritual and Political Order in Early Medieval
   France* (Ithaca / London 1992).
Künzel, R., 'Paganisme, syncrétisme et culture religieuse populaire au Haut
   Moyen Age', *Annales ESC* 47 (1992), pp. 1055–69.
*Beelden en zelfbeelden van middeleeuwse mensen. Historisch-antropologische studies
   over groepsculturen in de Nederlanden, 7e–13e eeuw* (Nijmegen 1997).
Kuttner, S., 'The father of the science of canon law', *Jurist* 1 (1941), pp. 2–19.
Laistner, M. L. W., 'Was Bede the author of a penitential?', in Laistner, *The
   Intellectual Heritage of the Early Middle Ages. Selected Essays*, ed. C. G. Starr,
   New York 1983 (1957), pp. 165–77 [originally published in: *Harvard
   Theological Review* 31 (1938), pp. 263–74].
Lake, S., 'Knowledge of the writings of John Cassian in early Anglo-Saxon
   England', *Anglo-Saxon England* 32 (2003), pp. 27–41.
Landau, P., 'Gratian and the Decretum Gratiani', in W. Hartmann and K.
   Pennington (eds.), *The History of Medieval Canon Law in the Classical Period.
   From Gratian to the Decretals of Pope Gregory IX* (Washington DC 2008),
   pp. 22–54.

Lapidge. M., 'The career of Archbishop Theodore', in Lapidge, *Archbishop Theodore*, pp. 1–29.

The Anglo-Saxon Library (Oxford 2006).

Lapidge, M., (ed.), *Archbishop Theodore. Commemorative Studies on his Life and Influence* (Cambridge 1995).

Columbanus. Studies on the Latin Writings (Woodbridge 1997).

Lapidge, M. and Sharpe, R., *A Bibliography of Celtic Latin Literature, 400–1200* (Dublin 1985).

Larson, A., 'The evolution of Gratian's *Tractatus de penitentia*', *Bulletin of Medieval Canon Law* n.s. 26 (2004–6), pp. 59–123.

'Gratian's *Tractatus de penitentia*: a textual study and intellectual history' (PhD thesis submitted at the Catholic University of America, at Washington DC 2010).

Lea, H. C., *A History of Auricular Confession and Indulgences in the Latin Church*, 2 vols. (Philadelphia 1896).

Le Goff, J., *La naissance du purgatoire* (Paris 1981).

Leonardi, C., 'Intellectual life', in T. Reuter (ed.), *The New Cambridge Medieval History*, vol. III: *c. 900 – c. 1024* (Cambridge 1999), pp. 186–211.

Leyser, C., 'Masculinity in flux: nocturnal emission and the limits of celibacy in the early Middle Ages', in D. Hadley (ed.), *Masculinity in Medieval Europe* (London / New York 1999), pp. 103–20.

Leyser, H., 'Clerical purity and the reordered world', in M. Rubin and W. Simons (eds.), *The Cambridge History of Christianity*, vol IV: *Christianity in Western Europe c. 1100–1500* (Cambridge 2009), pp. 11–21.

Löfstedt, B., 'Sprachliches zu den spanischen Bussbüchern', *Archivum Latinitatis Medii Aevi. Bulletin du Cange* 60 (2002), pp. 261–2.

Louth, A., 'Unity and diversity in the church of the fourth century', in R. Swanson (ed.), *Unity and Diversity in the Church*, Studies in Church History 32 (Oxford 1995), pp. 1–17.

Löwe, H., 'Salzburg als Zentrum literarischen Schaffens im 8. Jahrhundert', in Löwe, *Religiosität und Bildung im frühen Mittelalter. Ausgewählte Aufsätze*, ed. T. Struve (Weimar 1994), pp. 1–45 [originally published in: *Mitteilungen der Gesellschaft für Salzburger Landeskunde* 115 (1975)].

Luscombe, D., *The School of Peter Abelard. The Influence of Abelard's Thought in the Early Scholastic Period* (Cambridge 1970).

'The school of Peter Abelard revisited', *Vivarium* 30 (1992), pp. 127–38.

Lutterbach, H., 'Intentions- oder Tathaftung? Zum Bußverständnis in den frühmittelalterlichen Bußbüchern', *Frühmittelalterliche Studien* 29 (1995), pp. 120–43.

'Die Speisegesetzgebung in den mittelalterlichen Bußbüchern (600–1200). Religionsgeschichtliche Perspektiven', *Archiv für Kulturgeschichte* 80 (1998), pp. 1–37.

Sexualität im Mittelalter. Eine Kulturstudie anhand von Bußbüchern des 6. bis 12. Jahrhundert, Beihefte zum Archiv für Kulturgeschichte 43 (Cologne / Weimar / Vienna 1999).

'Die mittelalterlichen Bußbücher – Trägermedien von Einfachreligiosität?', *Zeitschrift für Kirchengeschichte* 114 (2003), pp. 227–44.

Maassen, F., *Geschichte der Quellen und der Literatur des canonischen Rechts im Abendlande*, (Graz 1870; reprint Graz 1956).

MacDonald, A., 'Adomnán's *Vita Columbae* and the early churches of Tiree', in J. Wooding (ed.), *Adomnán of Iona. Theologian, Lawmaker, Peacemaker* (Dublin 2010), pp. 219–36.

Mahadevan, L., 'Überlieferung und Verbreitung des Bussbuchs "Capitula Iudiciorum"', *ZRG Kan. Abt.* 72 (1986), pp. 17–75.

Mansfield, M., *The Humiliation of Sinners. Public Penance in Thirteenth Century France* (Ithaca / London 1995).

Marenbon, J., *The Philosophy of Peter Abelard* (Cambridge 1997).

Markus, R. A., *Gregory the Great and his World* (Cambridge 1997).

Martel, G. de, 'Les textes pénitentiels du ms. Lisbonne 232', *Sacris Erudiri* 27 (1984), pp. 443–60.

Martin Duque, A., 'Sancho III el Mayor de Navarra, entre la leyenda y la historia', in *Ante el milenario del reinado de Sancho el Mayor. Un rey Navarro para España y Europa*, XXX Semana de Estudios Medievales, Estella (Pamplona 2004), pp. 19–42.

McCormick, M., 'The liturgy of war in the early Middle Ages: Crisis, litanies, and the Carolingian monarchy', *Viator* 15 (1984), pp. 1–24.

Eternal Victory. Triumphal Rulership in Late Antiquity and the Early Medieval West (Cambridge 1986).

McKitterick, R., 'Unity and diversity in the Carolingian Church', in R. Swanson (ed.), *Unity and Diversity in the Church*, Studies in Church History 32 (Oxford 1996), pp. 59–82.

History and Memory in the Carolingian World (Cambridge 2004).

'Kingship and the writing of history', in McKitterick, *History and Memory in the Carolingian World* (Cambridge 2004), pp. 133–55.

'The scripts of the Bobbio Missal', in Hen and Meens (eds.), *The Bobbio Missal*, pp. 19–52.

Charlemagne. The Formation of a European Identity (Cambridge 2008).

'The scripts of the Prague Sacramentary, Prague Archivo O 83', *Early Medieval Europe* 20 (2012), pp. 407–27.

(ed.), *The New Cambridge Medieval History*, vol. II: *c. 700–c. 900* (Cambridge 1995).

McLynn, N., *Ambrose of Milan. Church and Court in a Christian Capital* (Berkeley / Los Angeles / London 1994).

McNeill, J. T. and Gamer, H., *Medieval Handbooks of Penance. A Translation of the Principal 'Libri Poenitentiale' and Selections from Related Documents* (New York 1938, repr. 1990).

Meeder, S., 'Boniface and the Irish heresy of Clemens', *Church History* 80 (2011), pp. 251–80.

Meens, R., 'Het heilige bezoedeld. Opvattingen over het heilige en het onreine in de vroegmiddeleeuwse religieuze mentaliteit', in P. Bange and A. Weiler (eds.), *Willibrord, zijn wereld en zijn werk. Voordrachten gehouden tijdens het Willibrordcongres Nijmegen, 28–30 september 1989*, Middeleeuwse Studies 6 (Nijmegen 1990), pp. 237–55.

'The Penitential of Finnian and the textual witness of the Paenitentiale Vindobonense B', *Mediaeval Studies* 55 (1993), pp. 243–55.

'Willibrords boeteboek?', *Tijdschrift voor Geschiedenis* 106 (1993), pp. 163–78.

'A background to Augustine's mission to Anglo-Saxon England', *Anglo-Saxon England* 22 (1994), pp. 5–17.

'Children and confession in the early Middle Ages', in D. Wood (ed.), *The Church and Childhood*, Studies in Church History 31 (Oxford 1994), pp. 53–65.

Het tripartite boeteboek. Overlevering en betekenis van vroegmiddeleeuwse biechtvoorschriften (met editie en vertaling van vier tripartita), Middeleeuwse Studies en Bronnen 41 (Hilversum 1994).

'Pollution in the early Middle Ages: the case of the food regulations in penitentials', *Early Medieval Europe* 4 (1995), pp. 3–19.

'Kanonisches Recht in Salzburg am Ende des 8. Jahrhunderts. Das Zeugnis des *Paenitentiale Vindobonense B*', *Zeitschrift der Savigny-Stiftung für Rechtsgeschichte Kanonistische Abteilung* 82 (1996), pp. 13–34.

'Ritual purity and the influence of Gregory the Great in the early Middle Ages', in R. Swanson (ed.), *Unity and Diversity in the Church*, Studies in Church History 32 (Oxford 1996), pp. 31–43.

'The frequency and nature of early medieval penance', in P. Biller and A. J. Minnis, (eds.), *Handling Sin: Confession in the Middle Ages*, York Studies in Medieval Theology 2 (Woodbridge 1998), pp. 35–61.

'Politics, mirrors of princes and the Bible: sins, kings and the well-being of the realm', *Early Medieval Europe* 7 (1998), pp. 345–57.

'Questioning ritual purity. The influence of Gregory the Great's answers to Augustine's queries about childbirth, menstruation and sexuality', in R. Gameson (ed.), *St. Augustine and the Conversion of England* (Stroud 1999), pp. 174–86.

'Christentum und Heidentum aus der Sicht Willibrords? Überlegungen zum *Paenitentiale Oxoniense II*', in M. Polfer (ed.), *L'évangélisation des régions entre Meuse et Moselle et la fondation de l'abbaye d'Echternach (Ve–IXe siècle). Actes des 10es Journées Lotharingiennes*, Publications de la Section Historique de l'Institut G.-D. de Luxembourg 117 (Luxemburg 2000), pp. 415–28.

'The oldest Manuscript witness of the *Collectio canonum Hibernensis*', *Peritia* 14 (2000), pp. 1–19.

'The uses of the Old Testament in early medieval canon law', in Y. Hen and M. Innes (eds.), *The Uses of the Past in Early Medieval Europe* (Cambridge 2000), pp. 67–77.

'Reforming the clergy: a context for the use of the Bobbio penitential', in Hen and Meens (eds.), *The Bobbio Missal*, pp. 154–67.

'"Aliud benitenciale": The ninth-century *Paenitentiale Vindobonense C*', *Mediaeval Studies* 66 (2004), pp. 1–26.

'Het christendom van Willibrord en Bonifatius', *Trajecta* 15 (2006), pp. 342–58.

'Penitentials and the practice of penance in the tenth and eleventh centuries', *Early Medieval Europe* (2006), pp. 7–21.

'The sanctity of the basilica of St. Martin. Gregory of Tours and the practice of sanctuary in the Merovingian period', in R. Corradini, R. Meens, C. Pössel and P. Shaw (eds.), *Texts and Identities in the Early Middle Ages*, Forschungen zur Geschichte des Mittelalters 12 (Vienna 2006), pp. 277–87.

'Aspekte der Christianisierung des Volkes', in F. J. Felten, J. Jarnut and L. von Padberg (eds.), *Bonifatius. Leben und Nachwirken (754–2004)* (Wiesbaden 2007), pp. 211–29.

'Die Bußbücher und das Recht im 9. und 10. Jahrhundert. Kontinuität und Wandel', in W. Hartmann (ed.), *Recht und Gericht in Kirche und Welt um 900* (Munich 2007), pp. 217–33.

'Kirchliche Buße und Konfliktbewältigung. Thietmar von Merseburg näher betrachtet', *Frühmittelalterliche Studien* 41 (2007), pp. 317–30.

'Sanctuary, penance and dispute settlement under Charlemagne. The conflict between Alcuin and Theodulf of Orléans over a sinful cleric', *Speculum* 82 (2007), pp. 277–300.

'The historiography of early medieval penance', in A. Firey (ed.), *The New History of Penance* (Leiden 2008), pp. 73–95.

'Thunder over Lyon. Agobard, the *tempestarii* and Christianity', in C. Steel, J. Marenbon and W. Verbeke (eds.), *Paganism in the Middle Ages*, Mediaevalia Lovaniensia Studia 42 (Leuven 2013).

Meijns, B., 'Within were fightings, within were fears. Pope Gregory VII, the canons regular of Watten and the reform of the Church in the diocese of Thérouanne (*c.* 1075–*c.* 1100)', in P. Andersen, M. Münster-Swendsen and H. Voght (eds.), *Law and Power in the Middle Ages. Proceedings of the fourth Carlsberg Academy Conference on Medieval Legal History* (Copenhagen 2008), pp. 73–96.

Mews, C., *Abelard and Heloise* (Oxford 2005).

Meyvaert, P., 'The authentic *Dialogues* of Gregory the Great', *Sacris Erudiri* 43 (2004), pp. 55–129.

Moore, R., *The First European Revolution, c. 970–1215* (Oxford 2000).

Moorhead, J., *Ambrose. Church and Society in the Late Roman World* (Harlow 1999).

Mordek, H., *Kirchenrecht und Reform im Frankenreich. Die Collectio Vetus Gallica, die älteste systematische Kanonessammlung des fränkischen Gallien. Studien und Edition*, Beiträge zur Geschichte und Quellenkunde des Mittelalters 1 (Berlin / New York 1975).

Bibliotheca capitularium regum Francorum manuscripta. Überlieferung und Traditionszusammenhang der fränkischen Herrschererlasse, MGH Hilfsmittel 15 (Munich 1995).

Moreton, B., *The Eighth-Century Gelasian Sacramentary. A Study in Tradition* (Oxford 1976).

Morey, A., *Bartholomew of Exeter, Bishop and Canonist. A Study in the Twelfth Century* (Cambridge 1937).

Morris, C., *The Discovery of the Individual 1050–1200* (New York 1972).

Mostert, M., 'What happened to literacy in the Middle Ages? Scriptural evidence for the history of the western literate mentality', *Tijdschrift voor Geschiedenis* 108 (1995), pp. 323–5.

754, Bonifatius bij Dokkum vermoord (Hilversum 1999).

Murray, A., 'Confession before 1215', *Transactions of the Royal Historical Society*, 6th series, 3 (1993), pp. 51–81.

Muschiol, G., *Famula Dei. Zur Liturgie in merowingischen Frauenklöstern* (Münster 1994).

'Men, women and liturgical practice in the early medieval West', in L. Brubaker and J. Smith (eds.), *Gender in the Early Medieval World. East and West, 300–900* (Cambridge 2004), pp. 198–216.

Muzzarelli, M. G. (ed.), *Una componente della mentalità occidentale: penitenziali nell'alto medio evo*, Il mondo medievale. Studi di storia e storiografia 9 (Bologna 1980).

Nathan, G., 'Rogation ceremonies in Late Antique Gaul', *Classica et Medievalia* 21 (1998), pp. 276–303.

Nees, L., 'The illustrated manuscript of the *Visio Baronti* [*Revelatio Baronti*] in St Petersburg (Russian National Library, cod. lat. Oct. v.I.5)', in C. Cubitt, *Court Culture in the Early Middle Ages. The Proceedings of the First Alcuin Conference* (Turnhout 2003), pp. 91–126.

Nelson, J., 'Women at the court of Charlemagne. A case of monstrous regiment?', in J. Parsons (ed.), *Medieval Queenship* (New York 1993), pp. 43–62 and 203–6.

'"... sicut olim gens Francorum ...": Fulk's letter to Alfred revisited', in J. Roberts, J. Nelson and M. Godden (eds.), *Alfred the Wise. Studies in Honour of Janet Bately on the Occasion of her Sixty-fifth Birthday* (Cambridge 1997), pp. 135–44.

Neumann, F., *Öffentliche Sünder in der Kirche des späten Mittelalters. Verfahren – Sanktionen – Rituale* (Cologne / Weimar / Vienna 2008)

Noble, T., 'Louis the Pious and his piety reconsidered', *Revue Belge de philologie et d'histoire* 58 (1980), pp. 297–316.

'The Christian church as an institution', in T. F. X. Noble and J. M. H. Smith (eds.), *The Cambridge History of Christianity*, vol. III: *Early Medieval Christianities c. 600 – c. 1100* (Cambridge 2008), pp. 249–74.

Nodes, D., '*De subitanea paenitentia* in letters of Faustus of Riez and Avitus of Vienne', *Recherches de théologie ancienne et médiévale* 55 (1988), pp. 30–40.

Nonn, U., 'Castitas et vitae et fidei et doctrinae – Bonifatius und die Reformkonzilien', in F. J. Felten, J. Jarnut and L. von Padberg (eds.), *Bonifatius. Leben und Nachwirken (754–2004)* (Wiesbaden 2007), pp. 271–80.

Noonan, J. T., 'Gratian slept here: the changing identity of the father of the systematic study of canon law', *Traditio* 35 (1979), pp. 145–72.

Ó Corráin, D. 'Irish Vernacular Law and the Old Testament', in P. Ní Chatháin and M. Richter (eds.), *Irland und die Christenheit / Ireland and Christendom* (Stuttgart 1987), pp. 284–307.

'Women in early Irish society', in M. McCurtain and D. Ó Corráin (eds.), *Women in Irish Society. The Historical Dimension* (Dublin 1987), pp. 1–13.

Ó Corráin, D., Breatnach, L. and Breen, A., 'The laws of the Irish', *Peritia* 3 (1984), pp. 382–438.

Ó Cróinín, D., *Early Medieval Ireland 400–1200* (London / New York 1995).

Ó Cróinín, D. and Walsh, M., *Cummian's Letter 'De Controversia Paschali' and the 'De Ratione Computandi'* (Toronto 1988).

Ohst, M., *Pflichtbeichte. Untersuchungen zum Bußwesen im Hohen und Späten Mittelalter* (Tübingen 1995).

Ó Riain, P., 'Finnian or Winniau?', in P. Ní Chatháin, M. Richter (eds.), *Ireland and Europe. The Early Church / Irland und Europa. Die Kirche im Frühmittelalter* (Stuttgart 1984), pp. 52–7.

'Finnio and Winniau: a return to the subject', in J. Carey, J. T. Koch and P.-Y. Lambert (eds.), *Ildánach ildírech. A Festschrift for Proinsias Mac Cana* (Aberystwyth 1999), pp. 187–202.

Padberg, L. von, *Bonifatius. Missionar und Reformer* (Munich 2003).

Palazzo, E., *Le Moyen Age. Des origines au XIIIe siècle*, Histoire des livres liturgiques (Paris 1993).

Les sacramentaires de Fulda. Étude sur l'iconographie et la liturgie à l'époque ottonienne, Liturgiewissenschaftliche Quellen und Forschungen 77 (Münster 1994).

Palmer, J., 'Defining paganism in the Carolingian world', *Early Medieval Europe* 15 (2007), pp. 402–25.

Paxton, F., *Christianizing Death. The Creation of a Ritual Process in Early Medieval Europe* (Ithaca / London 1990).

Payer, P., *Sex and the Penitentials. The Development of a Sexual Code, 550–1150* (Toronto 1984).

'The humanism of the penitentials and the continuity of the penitential tradition', *Mediaeval Studies* 46 (1984), pp. 340–54.

'The origins and development of the later *canones penitentiales*', *Mediaeval Studies* 61 (1999), pp. 81–105.

Sex and the New Medieval Literature of Confession, 1150–1300 (Toronto 2009).

Peyroux, C., 'The leper's kiss', in S. Farmer and B. H. Rosenwein (eds.), *Monks & Nuns, Saints and Outcasts. Religion in Medieval Society* (Ithaca / London 2000), pp. 172–88.

Pohl, W., 'Introduction: Ego trouble?', in R. Corradini, M. Gillis, R. McKitterick and I. van Renswoude (eds.), *Ego Trouble. Authors and their Identities in the Early Middle Ages*, Forschungen zur Geschichte des Mittelalters 15 (Vienna 2010), pp. 9–21.

Pokorny, R., 'Exkurs II: Ist Theodulf II tatsächlich ein Kaiptular Theodulfs von Orléans?', in R. Pokorny (ed.), *Capitula Episcoporum* IV, MGH Cap. Ep. IV (Hanover 2005), pp. 96–100.

Pontal, O., *Histoire des conciles mérovingiens* (Paris 1989).

Poschmann, B., *Die abendländische Kirchenbusse im Ausgang des christlichen Altertums* (Munich 1928).

Die abendländische Kirchenbusse im frühen Mittelalter, Breslauer Studien zur historischen Theologie 16 (Breslau 1930).

Buße und letzte Ölung, Handbuch der Dogmengeschichte 4.3 (Freiburg im Breisgau 1951) [tr. as *Penance and the Anointing of the Sick* (New York 1964)].

Price, R., 'Informal penance in early medieval Christendom', in Cooper and Gregory (eds.), *Retribution, Repentance*, pp. 29–39.

Pricoco, R., 'Dialogi: autenticità', in G. Cremascoli and A. Degl'Innocenti (eds.), *Enciclopedia Gregoriana. La vita, l'opera e la fortuna di Gregorio Magno* (Florence 2008), pp. 88–9.

Prinz, F., 'Die bischöfliche Stadtherrschaft im Frankenreich vom 5. bis zum 7. Jahrhundert', *Historische Zeitschrift* 217 (1974), pp. 1–35.

Frühes Mönchtum im Frankenreich. Kultur und Gesellschaft in Gallien, den Rheinlanden und Bayern am Beispiel der monastischen Entwicklung (4. bis 8. Jahrhundert) (2nd edn, Darmstadt 1988).

Rapp, C., *Holy Bishops in Late Antiquity. The Nature of Christian Leadership in an Age of Transition* (Berkeley / Los Angeles / London 2005).

Rasmussen, N. K., *Les pontificaux du haut Moyen Age. Genèse du livre de l'évêque. Texte mise au point par Marcel Haverals*, Spicilegium Sacrum Lovaniense. Études et documents 49 (Leuven 1998).

Reuter, T., '"Kirchenreform" und "Kirchenpolitik" im Zeitalter Karl Martells: Begriffe und Wirklichkeit', in J. Jarnut, U. Nonn and M. Richter (eds.), *Karl Martell in seiner Zeit* (Sigmaringen 1994), pp. 35–59.

Medieval Polities and Modern Mentalities, ed. J. Nelson (Cambridge 2006).

'Contextualising Canossa: excommunication, penance, surrender, reconciliation', in Reuter, *Medieval Polities and Modern Mentalities*, pp. 147–66.

'Peace-breaking, feud, rebellion, resistance: violence and peace in the politics of the Salian era', in Reuter, *Medieval Polities and Modern Mentalities*, pp. 355–87,

Reynolds, R., 'Rites and signs of conciliar decisions in the early Middle Ages', in *Segni e riti nella chiesa altomedievale occidentale*, Settimane di Studio 33 (Spoleto 1987), pp. 225–44.

'The South-Italian canon law *Collection in Five Books* and its derivatives: new evidence on its origins, diffusion and use', *Mediaeval Studies* 52 (1990), pp. 278–95.

'A Visigothic-script folio of a Carolingian collection of canon law', *Mediaeval Studies* 58 (1996), pp. 321–5.

'The transmission of the *Hibernensis* in Italy: tenth to twelfth century', *Peritia* 14 (2000), pp. 20–50.

'Penitentials in south and central Italian canon law manuscripts of the tenth and eleventh centuries', *Early Medieval Europe* 14 (2006), pp. 65–84.

Rhijn, C. van, 'Priests and the Carolingian Reforms: the bottlenecks of local *correctio*', in Corradini, Meens, Pössel and Shaw (eds.), *Texts and Identities in the Early Middle Ages*, pp. 219–37.

Shepherds of the Lord. Priests and Episcopal Statutes in the Carolingian Period (Turnhout 2007).

Rhijn, C. van, and Saan, M., 'Correcting sinners, correcting texts: a context for the *Paenitentiale pseudo-Theodori*', *Early Medieval Europe* 14 (2006), pp. 23–40.

Richter, M., *Ireland and Her Neighbours in the Seventh Century* (Dublin 1999).

Rio, A., *Legal Practice and the Written Word in the Early Middle Ages. Frankish Formulae, c. 500–1000* (Cambridge 2009).

Robinson, I., *Henry IV of Germany 1056–1106* (Cambridge 1999).

Rohr, C., 'Hagiographie als historische Quelle: Ereignisgeschichte und Wunderberichte', *MIÖG* 103 (1995), pp. 229–64.

Rolker, C., 'The earliest work of Ivo of Chartres: the case of Ivo's Eucharist florilegium and the canon law collections attributed to him', *ZRG Kan.* 93 (2007), pp. 109–27.

'The collection in seventy-four titles', in M. Brett and K. Cushing (eds.), *Readers, Texts and Compilers in the Earlier Middle Ages. Studies in Medieval Canon Law in Honour of Linda Fowler-Magerl* (Farnham 2009), pp. 59–72.

Canon Law and the Letters of Ivo of Chartres (Cambridge 2010).

Rosenwein, B., *To be the Neighbor of St. Peter. The Social Meaning of Cluny's Property, 909–1049* (Ithaca 1989).

Emotional Communities in the Early Middle Ages (Ithaca and London 2006).

Rusche, P., 'St Augustine's Abbey and the tradition of penance in early tenth-century England', *Anglia* 120 (2002), pp. 159–83.

Russell, J. C. *The Germanization of Early Medieval Christianity. A Sociohistorical Approach to Religious Transformation* (Oxford / New York 1994).

Saint-Roch, P., *La pénitence dans les conciles et les lettres des papes des origines à la mort de Grégoire le Grand* (Vatican City 1991).

Salmon, P., 'Un "Libellus Officialis" du XIe siècle', *Revue Bénédictine* 87 (1977), pp. 257–88.

Schäferdiek, K., 'Kilian von Würzburg: Gestalt und Gestaltung eines Heiligen', in H. Keller and N. Staubach (eds.), *Iconologia Sacra: Mythos, Bildkunst und Dichtung in der Religions- und Sozialgeschichte Alteuropas. Festschrift für Karl Hauck zum 75. Geburtstag*, Arbeiten zur Frühmittelalterforschung 23 (Berlin 1994), pp. 313–40.

Scheibelreiter, G., 'Ein Gallorömer in Flandern: Eligius von Noyon', in W. Pohl (ed.), *Die Suche nach den Ursprüngen. Von der Bedeutung des frühen Mittelalters* (Vienna 2004), pp. 117–28.

Schieffer, R., 'Von Mailand nach Canossa. Ein Beitrag zur Geschichte der christlichen Herrscherbuße von Theodosius d. Gr. bis zu Heinrich IV', *Deutsches Archiv* 28 (1972), pp. 333–70.

'"Redeamus ad fontem". Rom als Hort authentischer Überlieferung im frühen Mittelalter', in A. Angenendt and R. Schieffer, *Roma: Caput et Fons* (Opladen 1989), pp. 45–70.

'Zur Entstehung des Sendgerichts im 9. Jahrhundert', in W. P. Müller and M. E. Sommar (eds.), *Medieval Church Law and the Origins of the Western Legal Tradition. A Tribute to Kenneth Pennington* (Washington DC 2006), pp. 50–6.

Schieffer, T., *Winfrid-Bonifatius und die christliche Grundlegung Europas* (Darmstadt 1980).

Schmitz, G., 'Schuld und Strafe. Eine unbekannte Stellungnahme des Rathramnus von Corbie zur Kindestötung', *Deutsches Archiv* 38 (1982), pp. 363–87.

'Die Reformkonzilien von 813 und die Sammlung des Benedictus Levita', *Deutsches Archiv* 56 (2000), pp. 1–31.

Schmitz, H. J., *Die Bussbücher und die Bussdisciplin der Kirche. Nach handschriftlichen Quellen dargestellt* (Mainz 1883) [reprint Graz 1958].

Die Bussbücher und das kanonische Bussverfahren (Düsseldorf 1898) [reprint: Graz 1958)].

Sharpe, R., 'Hiberno-Latin *laicus*, Irish *láech* and the devil's men', *Ériu* 30 (1979), pp. 75–92.

'Some problems concerning the organization of the Church in early medieval Ireland', *Peritia* 3 (1984), pp. 230–70.

Siems, H., *Studien zur Lex Frisionum* (Ebelsbach 1980).
  '*In ordine posuimus*: Begrifflichkeit und Rechtsanwendung in Reginos
  Sendhandbuch', in W. Hartmann (ed.), *Recht und Gericht in Kirche und
  Welt um 900*, Schriften des Historischen Kollegs. Kolloquien 69
  (Munich 2007), pp. 67–90.
Smith, J., *Europe after Rome. A New Cultural History* (Oxford 2005).
Smyth, A., 'The effect of the Scandinavian raiders on the English and Irish
  churches: a preliminary reassessment', in B. Smith, *Britain and Ireland
  900–1300. Insular Reponses to Medieval European Change* (Cambridge 1999),
  pp. 1–38.
Somerville, R. and Brasington, B., *Prefaces to Canon Law Books in
  Latin Christianity. Selected Translations, 500–1245* (New Haven / London
  1998).
Southern, R., *The Making of the Middle Ages* (New Haven 1953).
  Scholastic Humanism and the Unification of Europe, vol. I: *Foundations*
  (Oxford 1995).
Stacey, R. Chapman, *Dark Speech. The Performance of Law in Early Ireland*
  (Philadelphia 2007).
Stancliffe, C., 'The thirteen sermons attributed to Columbanus and the question
  of authorship', in Lapidge (ed.), *Columbanus*, pp. 93–202.
  'Christianity amongst the Britons, Dalriadan Irish and Picts', in P. Fouracre
  (ed.), *The New Cambridge Medieval History* (Cambridge 2005), vol. I,
  pp. 426–61.
Staubach, N., *Das Herrscherbild Karls des Kahlen* (Münster 1981).
Stevenson, J. B., 'The monastic rules of Columbanus', in Lapidge (ed.),
  Columbanus, pp. 203–16.
Story, J., 'Cathwulf, kingship, and the royal abbey of Saint-Denis', *Speculum* 74
  (1999), pp. 1–21.
Taliadoros, J., 'Bartholomew of Exeter's penitential: some original observations
  on his personal dicta', in P. Erdö and S. A. Szuromi (eds.), *Proceedings of the
  Thirteenth International Congress of Medieval Canon Law: Esztergom, 3–8
  August 2008* (Vatican City 2010), pp. 457–76.
Teetaert, A., *La confession aux laïcs dans l'Église latine depuis le VIIIe jusqu'au XIVe
  siècle* (Paris / Louvain 1926).
Townend, M. (ed.), *Wulfstan, Archbishop of York. The Proceedings of the Second
  Alcuin Conference* (Turnhout 2004).
Trevett, C., '"I have heard from some teachers": the second-century struggle
  for forgiveness and reconciliation', in Cooper and Gregory (eds.),
  Retribution, Repentance, pp. 5–28.
Tyerman, C., *God's War. A New History of the Crusades* (Cambridge MA 2006).
Ubl, K., *Inzestverbot und Gesetzgebung. Die Konstruktion eines Verbrechens
  (300–1100)* (Berlin / New York 2008).
Uhalde, K., *Expectations of Justice in the Age of Augustine* (Philadelphia 2007).
Vanderputten, S., 'Canterbury and Flanders in the late tenth century',
  Anglo-Saxon England 35 (2006), pp. 219–44.
Vauchez, A., 'The Church and the laity', in D. Abulafia (ed.), *The New
  Cambridge Medieval History*, vol. V: *c. 1198 – c. 1300* (Cambridge 2008),
  pp. 182–203.

Vogel, C., *La discipline pénitentielle en Gaule des origines à la fin du VIIe siècle* (Paris 1952).

'Les rites de la pénitence publique aux Xe et XIe siècle', in P. Gallais and Y.-J. Riou (eds.), *Mélanges René Crozet* (Poitiers 1966), vol. I, pp. 137–44.

Le pécheur et la pénitence au Moyen Age. Textes choisis, traduits et présentés par Cyrille Vogel (Paris 1969).

Les 'Libri Paenitentiales', Typologie des sources du Moyen Âge occidental 27 (Turnhout 1978).

Medieval Liturgy. An Introduction to the Sources (Washington 1986).

Vogüé, A. de, 'Is Gregory the Great the author of the "Dialogues"?', *American Benedictine Review* 56 (2005), pp. 309–14.

Wagner, S. Morgyn, 'Ritual purity and the Céli Dé. Sin, theology and practice in the eighth and ninth centuries' (PhD thesis, University of Edinburgh 2005).

Wallace-Hadrill, J. M., *Bede's Ecclesiastical History of the English People. A Historical Commentary* (Oxford 1988).

Wasserschleben, H., *Die Bussordnungen der abendländischen Kirche* (Halle 1851).

Weaver, R., *Divine Grace and Human Agency. A Study of the Semi-Pelagian Controversy* (Macon GA 1996).

Weiler, A., *Willibrords Missie. Christendom en cultuur in de zevende en achtste eeuw* (Hilversum 1989).

Weinfurter, S., *Canossa. De Entzauberung der Welt* (Munich 2006).

Wemple, S., 'The canonical resources of Atto of Vercelli (926–960)', *Traditio* 26 (1970), pp. 335–50.

White, S. D., 'From peace to power: the study of disputes in medieval France', in E. Cohen and M. de Jong (eds.), *Medieval Transformations. Texts, Power, and Gifts in Context* (Leiden / Boston / Cologne 2001). pp. 203–18.

Wickham, C., *The Inheritance of Rome. A History of Europe from 400 to 1000* (London 2009).

Wilmart, A., 'Notice du Missel de Bobbio', in A. Wilmart, E. A. Lowe and H. A. Wilson (eds.), *The Bobbio Missal. Notes and Studies*, Henry Bradshaw Society 61 (London 1924), pp. 38–9 [reprinted in 1991 in one volume with E. A. Lowe (ed.), *The Bobbio Missal. A Gallican Mass-book (Ms. Paris. Lat. 13246)*, Henry Bradshaw Society 58].

Winroth, A., *The Making of Gratian's 'Decretum'* (Cambridge 2000).

Wolfram, H., 'Virgil als Abt und Bischof von Salzburg', in H. Dopsch and R. Juffinger (eds.), *Virgil von Salzburg. Missionar und Gelehrter* (Salzburg 1985), pp. 342–56.

Wood, I., 'Administration, law and culture in Merovingian Gaul', in R. McKitterick (ed.), *The Uses of Literacy in Early Medieval Europe* (Cambridge 1990), pp. 63–81.

The Merovingian Kingdoms 450–751 (London / New York 1994).

The Missionary Life. Saints and the Evangelization of Europe, 400–1050 (Harlow 2001).

'Liturgy in the Rhône valley and the Bobbio Missal', in Hen and Meens (eds.), *The Bobbio Missal*, pp. 206–18.

Wormald, P., 'Archbishop Wulfstan and the holiness of society', in Wormald, *Legal Culture in the Early Medieval West. Law as Text, Image and Experience* (London / Rio Grande 1999), pp. 225–51.

The Making of English Law. King Alfred to the Twelfth Century, vol. I: *Legislation and its Limits* (Oxford 1999).

'Archbishop Wulfstan: eleventh-century state builder', in A. Townend (ed.), *Wulfstan, Archbishop of York*, pp. 9–27.

Wright, R., 'In what language are the glosses of San Millán and Silos?', in Wright, *A Sociophilological Study of Late Latin*, Utrecht Studies in Medieval Literacy 10 (Turnhout 2002), pp. 232–42.

Yorke, B., *The Conversion of Britain. Religion, Politics and Society in Britain c. 600–800* (Harlow 2006).

Zechiel-Eckes, K., *Florus von Lyon als Kirchenpolitiker und Publizist. Studien zur Persönlichkeit eines karolingischen 'Intellektuellen' am Beispiel der Auseinandersetzung mit Amalarius (835–838) und des Prädestinationsstreits* (Stuttgart 1999).

'Zur kirchlichen Rechtspraxis im späteren 8. Jahrhundert. Die Zwei-Bücher Sammlung der Kölner Dom-Handschrift 210 (fol. 122–151)', in H. Finger (ed.), *Mittelalterliche Handschriften der Kölner Dombibliothek: Zweites Symposium der Diözesan- und Dombibliothek Köln zu den Dom-Manuskripten (1. bis 2. Dezember 2006)* (Cologne 2008), pp. 187–229.

General index

Aachen 117, 182
Abelard 191, 199, 201–3, 209, 213,
  222–3
  Scito te ipsum 191, 200–1, 203, 213
Achéry, Jean-Luc d' 91
Ad aquas Salvias, monastery 89
Adalhard of Corbie 126
Adhémar of Le Puy 187
Admonitio Generalis 113, 124
Adomnán 66, 69, 88
adultery 50
Aelfric of Eynsham 163
Aethelred II, King 161
Agilulf, king of the Lombards 53
Agobard of Lyon 1, 119, 127–8
Agrestius 54, 73
Áid the Black 66
Aidan 88
Alaric II, Visigothic king 27
Alcobaça, monastery 172
Alcuin 107, 116, 124
Aldebert 108
Alfred the Great 158, 163, 221
Ambrose 21–5, 126
Anatolia 25
Annals of Fulda 126
Annals of St Bertin 126
Annegray 52
Ansegisus 115, 144
Anselm of Laon 197, 199, 201
Anselm of Lucca 149, 192, 195
Antioch 89, 187
Arles 31, 116
Armenia 25
Arn of Salzburg 88
Artchain on Tiree, monastery 66
Ash Wednesday 29, 79, 152, 154–6, 174
Astronomer, the 126–7, 129
Attigny 126
Atto of Vercelli 173–4, 179, 188
audientia episcopalis 19
Augsburg 144, 182

Augustine of Canterbury 7, 84
Augustine of Hippo 19–20, 25
Aunacharius of Auxerre 71, 76–7
Auxerre 38
Auxilius 44
Avars 125
Avitus of Vienne 28, 31

Balthild, Queen 79
Bangor, monastery 52
Barontus 85–6
Bartholomew of Exeter 204, 206–11, 222
  Contra fatalitatis errorem 207
  handbook for confessors 205–9
Basil the Great 25, 93
Bathsheba 22
Battle of the Lech 182
Beatus of Liebana 169
Bede 88, 90, 96, 113, 135, 138, 142, 208,
  210
Benedict of Aniane 54
Benevento 176
Beonanus 83
Bernar, priest 188
Bernhard of Italy 126
Bernhard of Saxony 181
Bertila of Chelles 79
bestiality 18, 42, 50, 56
Bischoff, Bernhard 8
Blickling Homilies 163
Bobbio 53, 82, 172
Bobbio Missal 78
Boleslav Chrobry, King 180, 185–6
Bologna 196–7, 204
Boniface 87, 107–10, 113, 218
Bonizo of Sutri 149
booklist 99, 114, 163
Bourges 85
Brittany 160
Brown, Peter 83
Bulgarians 174, 185
Bulgarus 197

Burchard of Worms 148, 154, 179, 189, 191, 195, 197, 206, 220, 222
Burgundofara 80
Butherich 21

Caesarius of Arles 26–9, 32–4, 36
caliphate of Cordoba 170
canon law collections
  Burchard of Worms
    Decretum 148, 150, 154, 161, 172, 176–7, 191–2, 195, 205, 208, 210
    Collectio 77 capitulorum 144
    Collectio Anselmo dedicata 173
    Collectio Dacheriana 119, 121, 130–1, 135, 138
    Collectio Dionysiana 19
    Collectio Dionysiana aucta 173
    Collectio Dionysio-Hadriana 114, 124, 131, 133
    Collectio Herovalliana 137
    Collectio Hibernensis 44, 49, 58, 60–1, 64, 91, 96, 108, 124, 177
    Collectio Hispana 133, 165, 167, 170
    Collectio Vetus Gallica 32, 71, 77, 92, 96, 108, 110
    Collection in Five Books 176–7, 179, 192–3
    Collection in Nine Books 176–7, 179, 192
  Cresconius
    Concordia canonum 137
  Gratian
    Decretum 196, 205, 208, 222
  Gregory IX
    Liber Extra 212
  Ivo of Chartres
    Decretum 194–5, 205, 207, 222
    Panormia 194–5, 205, 222
  Statuta Ecclesiae Antiqua 32
canon lawyers 198
Canones Hibernenses 63
Canossa 182–3, 186
Canterbury 100, 205
Capetians 149, 221
Carolingian empire 122, 127
Carolingian reform councils (813), (828) 115, 117–18, 120, 122, 127, 130, 133, 219
Carolingian Reforms 102, 114, 132, 158, 160
Carolingian Renaissance 114
Carolingians 102, 106, 111, 113–14, 138, 156, 218
Cassian, John 39, 46, 58, 61
Castile 167, 171

Catalonia 171
Cathwulf 123–4
Céli Dé 62–3
Chagnoald of Laon 80
Chalon 81
Charlemagne 114–15, 117–18, 123–5, 182, 219
Charles Martel 106
Chartres 209
Chelles 29, 79
Chiffoleau, Jacques 186
Chilperic 74
Chiusi 197
Chlothar II, King 82
Christ Church Abbey, Canterbury 160, 164
Church of the Twelve Apostles, Rome 175
Cilicia 89
Clemens 108
Clermont 31, 187
Clovis II, King 82
Cluny 185
Cnobheresburg 82
Cnut, King 161
Codex Theodosianus 116
Cologne 156, 182
Colonatus 87
Colum Cille *see* Columba
Columba 64–5, 67, 69
Columbanian monasticism 54, 72–4, 77, 79–80
Columbanus 36, 45, 47, 52, 54–7, 65, 69–72, 75, 77–8, 81, 83–4, 93, 102, 106, 109, 172, 217
  Instructiones 54
  Regula Coenobialis 54–5, 72
  Regula Monachorum 53
Concordia Episcoporum 117
confession to God alone 122
Constans II, Emperor, 90
Constantinople 18, 89
Corbie, monastery 82, 92, 108
Cordoba 167
Cornwall 40
Coroticus 38
Corrector sive Medicus see canon law collections: Burchard of Worms: *Decretum*
council
  Fourth Lateran Council (1215) 214, 224
council of Agde (506) 27
council of Agde (508) 32
council of Ancyra (314) 18, 42, 76, 137
council of Arles (813) 115, 118, 120
council of Auxerre (585–92) 71, 76

council of Chalon-sur-Saône (603/4) 53, 73
council of Chalon-sur-Saône (647–53) 80–1
council of Chalon-sur-Saône (813) 115, 117–18, 120–1, 219
council of Cloveshoe (747) 105
council of Coyonza (1055) 171
council of Hertford (673) 91
council of Mâcon (581/3) 71
council of Mâcon (585) 71, 74, 77
council of Mainz (813) 115, 122
council of Mainz (847) 133
council of Mainz (852) 152
council of Neocaesarea (314/15) 137
council of Nicaea (325) 25, 76, 137
council of Orléans (511) 31
council of Orléans (538) 27
council of Paris (829) 101, 130–1, 220
council of Reims (813) 120, 122
council of Rome (721) 108
council of Rome (1080) 186
council of Soissons (744) 107
council of Soissons (853) 133
council of Toledo (589) 164
council of Tours (813) 115
Cresconius 137
Cummean 57, 61, 69, 178, 192

David of Menevia 40
David, King 22
De arreis 63
De duodecim abusivis saeculi 61
deditio 10, 180–1, 183, 222
Deusdedit, archbishop 90
dietary rules 63, 95
Dionysius Exiguus 19
dispute settlement 10–11, 45, 50–1, 64, 66, 75, 106, 126, 129, 217, 222
Domingo, abbot 169
Donatus of Besançon 80

Easter 153
Eberulf, royal treasurer 74
Ebo of Reims 128, 130, 132–3, 135, 220
Edessa 89
Egbert of York 96, 113, 135, 138, 218
Egino of Konstanz 125
Ekkehard IV of St Gall 152
Eligius of Noyon 80, 84
Eoda 92
episcopal statutes 110, 141, 143, 160, 173
episcopal visitations 142, 145, 151

Erchinoald, mayor of the palace 82
ethics 203
Eucharist 59, 104, 110, 118, 153, 184, 186, 210, 214, 224
Eudes Rigaud 145
Eusebius Gallicanus 25
Eusebius of Caesarea 22
Evagrius of Pontus 46
Excerpts of a Book of David 40, 42
excommunication 44, 46, 106, 118, 184, 186, 208
Exeter 160, 164
exile 56
exorcism 34

Fabiola 20
Farfa 177, 179
Fastrada 125
Faustus of Riez 28, 39
Ferdinand I, King 170–1, 185, 221
Field of Lies, battle of 127
Findchán 66
Finnian 45, 55, 57, 60, 63, 69, 93
Finnian of Clonard 47
Finnian of Moville 47
First Crusade 187–8, 222
First Synod of St. Patrick 39, 44, 63
Florus of Lyon 119
Fontaines 52, 71
Fontanelle, monastery 115
forum externum 199
forum internum 199
Fournier, Paul 37
Frantzen, Allen 158, 163
Frisia 103
Fructuosus of Braga 167
Fulbert of Chartres 195
Fulda, monastery 132, 156, 179
Fulk of Reims 159
Fursa 82–4, 86

Galicia 168
Gallus of Clermont 31
Gaul 14, 25, 27–31, 34, 38, 45, 52, 71–2, 78, 82, 84, 216
Gennadius of Marseille 32
Gerhard, biographer of Ulrich of Augsburg 143
Germanus of Auxerre 38
Germanus of Capua 35
Giebichenstein 181
gift-giving 106
Gilbert de la Porrée 209
Gildas 41, 45, 47, 58
Gottschalk of Freising 181

Gozbert, duke 87
Gratian 149, 196–8, 206, 209–10, 222
   Tractatus de penitentia 198
Gregorian Reform 192–3
Gregory of Nazianze 93
Gregory of Tours 12, 34, 74
Gregory the Great 7, 12, 14, 35–6, 53, 61,
   84–5, 97, 131, 171
   Dialogues 35
Grimbald of St Bertin 159
Grimo of Corbie 108
Guntram 71, 74, 102

Hadrian, monk 90, 195
Haggenmüller, Reinhold 97, 113
Haito of Basel 206
Halitgar of Cambrai 130, 134–5, 137,
   141–2, 220
Hartmann, Wilfried 131
Hatto of Mainz 141
healing rituals 34
Héloise 200–1
Henry II, King 185, 205
Henry IV, King 182–4
Henry of Schweinfurt, margrave 180–1
Heraclius, Emperor 89
Heribald of Auxerre 133
Heribert of Cologne 182
Hessen, 107
Hiberno-Frankish monasticism 77
Hippo 15, 20, 24–5
Historia Silense 185
Holy Ghost, sins against 208
holy men 33, 50, 73, 106
homosexuality 50, 56
Hrabanus Maurus 132, 134, 141, 220
Hugh, abbot of Cluny 185

incarceration 107
incest 42
infanticide 104, 202
Iona 64–7, 69, 86, 88
Iserninus 44
Isidore of Seville 61
Iso of St Gall 152–3
Italy 112, 156
Ivo of Chartres 149, 194, 206, 222
   Prologue 194–5, 197

Jerome 20
Jerusalem 187
Jews 168
John of God 212, 223
Jonas of Bobbio 36, 52, 70, 72–4
Jonas of Orléans 130

Jouarre 29, 79
Julianus Pomerius 25, 131

Khan Boris 185
Kilian of Würzburg 87
Konstanz 216

Lagny, monastery 82–3
Lampert of Hersfeld 184
Laon 197, 199
Lawrence, papal candidate 35
Lea, Henry Charles 5
Lent 127, 146–7, 154
León 167, 170–1, 185, 221
Lex Alamanorum 144
Lex Baiuvariorum 144
Lex Frisionum 104
Lex Romana Visigothorum 116
Librán 65–6
Liège 173
Life of Brigit 68
Life of Columba 68
Life of Columbanus 70, 75
Life of Liudger 104
Life of Louis 126
Life of Ulrich of Augsburg 143, 145–6
Lindisfarne 88
Longoretus, monastery 85
Lorsch, monastery 97, 113
Lothar I 127, 129
Lothar II, Emperor 175
Louis (the German) 127
Louis the Pious 125, 128, 130, 132, 219
Luxeuil 52, 55, 71, 75, 80
Lyon 33, 119, 121

Mael Ruain 62
magister Serlo 208
Mainz 110, 116, 133, 136, 154, 156, 218
Mamertus of Vienne 14, 30
manaig, monastic tenants 48–9
Mansfield, Mary 216
marriage 8, 48, 65, 68, 105, 175
martyrs 33
Matilda of Tuscany 183
Maundy Thursday 23, 29, 79, 93, 148,
   154–5, 174, 182, 216
Mead, Margaret 3
Meaux 79
Meldanus 83
Merseburg 182
Middle Rhine region 157
Milan 21–5
Mirrors of Princes 124
missi dominici 142

Montanists *see* New Prophecy
Montecassino 176–7, 179, 189, 221
Mozarabic community 168
Mozarabs 221
Muslims 168

Nantes 142
Navarra 171
New Prophecy 16
Nineveh 13
Northumbria 103

Old Testament 51
ordo paenitentium 20
Origen 15, 61
Otgar of Mainz 133
Otto II, Emperor 182
Otto III, Emperor 176, 182
Otto the Great 182
Ottonians 149, 156, 180–1, 185, 220, 222
Ovid 209

Paenitentiale Sangermanense see penitentials:
    Paenitentiale Cantabrigiense
Palladius 37
Paraclete, monastic community 200
Paris 79, 204, 209
parochial system 146
Parsiphae 209
Paschasius, Roman deacon 35
Passio of Kilian 87
Patrick 38, 44, 68
Paul the Deacon 96
    History of the Lombards 96
Paulinus of Milan 23
Pelagianism 38
Pelagius 35, 39
penance
    corporal punishment 54, 107
    deathbed penance 27–8, 33
    episcopal control 138, 179, 189, 220
    fasting 20, 27, 30, 36, 41–2, 44–5, 55,
        188, 219
    frequency 139, 146, 165, 210
    liturgy 79, 118, 139, 146, 152–8, 160,
        164, 207
        Northern-French rite 157
    penitential stages 25
    pilgrimage 187
    private 156, 216
        concept 11
    public 10, 26, 33, 55, 94, 115, 118, 120,
        122, 126–8, 147, 152, 154, 164, 169,
        182–3, 207, 215, 219
    ritual 10

royal 127–8, 181, 219, 222
secret 118, 152
sincerity 186
violence 187
penitential garb *see* sackcloth
penitential handbooks 143
    criticism of 101, 115, 130, 135, 137
penitential holy war 187
penitential pilgrimage 121
penitentials
    Excarpsus Cummeani 82, 88, 108, 110–12,
        136, 165, 167, 170–1, 178, 218,
        221
    Handbook 163
    Homo quidam 204, 209–10, 222
    Hrabanus Maurus 134, 137
        Paenitentiale ad Heribaldum 133, 144
        Paenitentiale ad Otgarium 132
    Old English Introduction 162
    Old English Penitential 162
    Old Irish Penitential 62, 65, 69
    *Paenitentiale Albeldense see Paenitentiale
        Vigilanum*
    Paenitentiale Ambrosianum 45, 49–51,
        58
    Paenitentiale Bigotianum 61, 69
    Paenitentiale Bobbiense 76, 78
    Paenitentiale Burgundense 76, 78
    Paenitentiale Cantabrigiense 161
    Paenitentiale Capitula Iudiciorum 112,
        173, 176, 179, 192
    Paenitentiale Casinense 176
    Paenitentiale Cordubense 221
    Paenitentiale Floriacense 76
    Paenitentiale Hubertense 76
    Paenitentiale in duobus libris 112, 176
    Paenitentiale Lucense 176
    Paenitentiale Merseburgense A 112, 136,
        172
    Paenitentiale mixtum pseudo-Bedae-Egberti
        138
    Paenitentiale Oxoniense I 76
    Paenitentiale Oxoniense II 103, 105–6,
        109, 112, 201–2
    Paenitentiale Parisiense simplex 76
    Paenitentiale Pseudo-Bedae 138, 140, 142,
        195, 210
    Paenitentiale Pseudo-Bedae-Egberti 162,
        173, 176
    *Paenitentiale Pseudo-Bedae-Egberti
        additivum* 160
    Paenitentiale Pseudo-Bedae-Egberti mixtum
        142, 144
    Paenitentiale Pseudo-Egberti 96–7, 100–1,
        134, 140, 160, 218

Paenitentiale Pseudo-Romanum 131, 142, 195, 210
Paenitentiale Pseudo-Theodori 136, 162, 178
Paenitentiale Remense 118, 167, 170–1, 179, 221
Paenitentiale Sangallense tripartitum 111–12
Paenitentiale Silense 169, 221
Paenitentiale Vallicellianum C. 6 176
Paenitentiale Vallicellianum E. 62 176
Paenitentiale Vallicellianum I 136, 172–4
Paenitentiale Vaticanum 175–6
Paenitentiale Vigilanum 165, 167, 170, 179, 221
Paenitentiale Vindobonense C 138
penitential attributed to Fulbert of Chartres 195
penitential of Columbanus 55, 72
penitential of Cummean 57, 59, 70, 83–4, 88, 93, 101, 109, 111
penitential of Finnian 47–8, 58–9, 65, 83, 88
penitential of Halitgar 131–2, 134, 136–8, 144, 150, 159, 162, 173–4, 178
penitential of Pseudo-Gregory III 135, 171
penitential of Theodore 88, 99, 106, 108–9, 111, 134, 136, 142, 159, 161–2, 172, 195, 210
    Canones Cottoniani 91
    Canones Gregorii 91, 172, 176
    Capitula Dacheriana 91, 162
    Capitula Dacheriana (D) 91
    Discipulus Umbrensium 58, 91, 93–4, 162
    Quadripartitus 134, 137, 160
    scrift boc 162
simple Frankish penitential 111
peregrinatio 52, 70
perjury 65
Peronna Scottorum 82–4
Peter the Lombard 205
    Sententiae 205, 208
Philip I, King 185
Philip the Arab 22
Pippin II, mayor of the palace 102
Pippinids 106
polygamy 168
Pontificale Romano-Germanicum 154–5
Pope Alexander III 205
Pope Celestine I 37
Pope Gelasius II 12
Pope Gregory VII 182–4, 186–7
Pope Gregory IX 212
Pope Innocent III 214

Pope Leo I 37
Pope Leo IX 187
Pope Martin I 89
Pope Nicholas I 174
Pope Sergius 104
Pope Symmachus 35
Pope Urban II 187–8, 194, 222
Pope Vitalian 90, 195
Poschmann, Bernhard 5, 15
Possidius 19
Prague 181
Preface of Gildas on Penance 40–2, 44, 63
Prosper of Aquitaine 37
Prüm 141
Pseudo-Cyprian
    De XII abusivis saeculi 124
purgatorial fire 35, 84

Radbod, King 103
Raphael, archangel 85
Rath Melsigi, monastery 103
Rather of Verona 173–4
Rathlin 65
Rathramnus of Corbie 201
reconciliation 34
reconciliation of penitents 80, 93, 154
Regino of Prüm 135, 141, 143, 146, 150, 154, 185, 189, 208, 214, 220, 223
    Two books on synodal investigations and ecclesiastical instruction 141–3, 145, 147, 151, 161, 179
Reims 116, 133–4, 136
Rhine-Main area 113
Riculf of Mainz 125
Robert Grosseteste 212
Robert of Flamborough 208
Rogations 14, 30
Roman law 197
Rome 20, 89, 175–6, 182
Rosenwein, Barbara 57
Rouen 142
Royal Frankish Annals 126
Rule of Benedict 39, 61, 114
Rule of Fructuosus of Braga 167

sackcloth 16, 147, 153, 181, 184–5
sacramentary
    eighth-century Gelasian sacramentaries 30
    Fulda sacramentary 156
    Gregorianum-Hadrianum 114, 156
    Old Gelasian Sacramentary 29–30, 79, 118, 127
sacraments 207
Salians 149, 222

Salzburg 87, 100, 112, 156
San Millán de la Cogolla, monastery
    170–1, 179
Sancho III of Navarra, King 167
sanctuary 50
Santo Domingo of Silos, monastery 169,
    179
Schmitz, Herman Joseph 37
secrecy in confessing 95
Ségéne of Iona 57
Septimania 171
Sergius, patriarch 89
sermons 163
sexuality 42
simple Frankish penitentials 76
sin
    ontological status 199
sinful thoughts 26, 40, 42, 47, 56
Soissons 74, 128–9
Sozomenos 18, 20
Spoleto 176
St Apollinare, Rome 175
St Augustine's Abbey, Canterbury 159–60,
    164
St Cuthbert 89
St Cyran 86
St Eustratius 175
St Eutizio 177
St Gall 153
St. Martin in Albelda, monastery 165
St Martin in Tours, monastery 116
St Medard 74
St Patrick 178, 192
St Peter 85
St Peter in Salzburg, monastery 87
St Peter's, Rome 175
Stilicho 23
superstitio 33, 106
Synod of North Britain 40
Synod of the Grove of Victory 40–1

Tagino of Magdeburg 181
Tarsus 89
tempestarii 1
Tertullian 16–17
The First Synod of St. Patrick 44
Theodore of Canterbury 7, 58, 61, 89–90,
    93–4, 96–7, 100, 109, 135, 138, 158,
    178, 192, 195, 208, 210, 217
Theodoretus 23
Theodosius, Emperor 21–4, 126, 129

Theodulf of Orléans 116, 122
theology 199
Theuderic, King 74
Theudorius of Arles 81
Thietmar of Merseburg 180–2,
    185, 188
Thomas Becket 205
Thomas of Chobham 204
Thuringia 87, 107
Tiree 65–6, 69
Totnanus 87
Tours 74, 116
Trevett, monastery of 65
Tribur 184
Trier 156
triumphal rulership 125

Ulrich of Augsburg 143, 182
Umbria 175–6
unfree 105
Uriah 22

Vercelli 172–4
Vercelli Homilies 163
vernacular 162
Verona 173
Vienne 31, 33
Vigilanus, scribe 165
Viking invasions 158
Virgil of Salzburg 87
Visio Baronti 85
visions of the afterlife 35, 83, 85
Vita Bonifatii 107
Vita Fursei 83, 85
Vogel, Cyrille 15

Wales 40
Wamba, King 126
Wigheard 90
Wilfrid, bishop 90
William of Champeaux 199, 201
William of St-Thierry 203
Willibald 107
Willibrord 87, 102, 104, 106, 113, 201,
    218
Winroth, Anders 196
Wulfstan of York 161, 163, 167, 179, 189,
    221, 223
    commonplace books 161
    Sermo Lupi ad Anglos 161
Würzburg 87

Manuscript index

Albi, Bibliothèque municipale, 38 (59) 232
Albi, Bibliothèque municipale, 38 bis (61) 232
Antwerpen, Museum Plantin-Moretus/ Prentenkabinet, M 82 (66) 135
Arezzo, Biblioteca Consorziale, Ms. 312 234
Aschaffenburg, Stiftsbibliothek, Ms. Perg. 37 229
Avignon, Bibliothèque municipale, Cod. 175 229
Avranches, Bibliothèque municipale, 136 211

Bamberg, Staatliche Bibliothek, Ms. Can.2 (A.I.35) 234
Bamberg, Staatsbibliothek, Cod. Lit. 55 155
Barcelona, Biblioteca de la Universidad, Ms. 228 137, 234
Basel, Universitätsbibliothek, Fragm. N I 4 229
Berlin, Staatsbibliothek Preußischer Kulturbesitz, Hamilton 132 (H) 227
Berlin, Staatsbibliothek Preußischer Kulturbesitz, Hamilton 290 234
Berlin, Staatsbibliothek Preußischer Kulturbesitz, Phillipps 1667 229
Brussels, Koninklijke Bibliotheek, 10127–44 76, 82, 227
Brussels, Koninklijke Bibliotheek, 10034–7 234

Cambrai, Bibliothèque municipale 625 (567) 61
Cambridge, Corpus Christi College, 190 136, 162
Cambridge, Corpus Christi College, 265 97, 231, 234
Cambridge, Corpus Christi College, 279 44
Cambridge, Corpus Christi College, 320 227

Châlons-en-Champagne, Bibliothèque municipale, Ms. 32 233–4
Cologne, Dombibliothek, 91 227, 229
Cologne, Dombibliothek, 117 (Darmst. 2116) 234
Cologne, Dombibliothek, 118 134, 233
Cologne, Dombibliothek, 120 134
Cologne, Dombibliothek, 210 91, 227
Copenhagen, Kongelige Bibliotek, Ny. Kgl. S. 58 8° 229
Cordoba, Biblioteca del Cabildo, Cod. 1 167

Darmstadt, Hessische Landes- und Hochschulbibliothek, Hs. 895 Fragm. 103
Darmstadt, Hessische Landesbibliothek, Hs. 895 Fragm. 229
Düsseldorf, Universitätsbibliothek, B. 113 133, 233

Einsiedeln, Stiftsbibliothek, Cod. 281 (886) 234
Einsiedeln, Stiftsbibliothek, Cod. 326 229
El Escorial, Real Biblioteca de San Lorenzo, d.I.1 (Codex Aemilianensis) 165
El Escorial, Real Biblioteca de San Lorenzo, d.I.2 (Codex Vigilanus sive Albeldensis) 165
El Escorial, Real Biblioteca de San Lorenzo, L III 8 232
Eton, College Library, Bp 5.16 227

Florence, Biblioteca Medicea Laurenziana, Ashburnham 1814 137, 234

Gent, Bibliotheek der Rijksuniversiteit, Ms. 506 136, 234

Heiligenkreuz, Stiftsbibliothek, Ms. 217 134, 233–4

Karlsruhe, Badische Landesbibliothek,
   Aug. CCLV 232
Karlsruhe, Badische Landesbibliothek,
   Aug. IC 229
Kassel, Landesbibliothek und Murhardsche
   Bibliothek der Stadt Kassel, Theol.
   Q 24 232
Koblenz, Landeshauptarchiv, Best. 701
   Nr.759,7 234
Kynžvart, Zámecká Knihovna, 20 K 20
   112, 134, 226, 234

Leiden, Bibliotheek der Rijksuniversiteit,
   Cod. Vulc. 108 nr. 12 229
London, British Library, Add. 8873 226
London, British Library, Add. 11695 169
London, British Library, Add. 16413 112,
   173, 226–7
London, British Library, Add. 19725 232
London, British Library, Add. 30853 169
London, British Library, Royal 5 E. VIII
   205
London, British Library, Royal 5 E. XII 232
London, British Library, Royal 5 E. XIII
   160

Madrid, Biblioteca Nacional, 10008 172
Madrid, Biblioteca Nacional, Vitr. 5.5 172
Mainz, Stadtbibliothek, lat. 76 203
Marburg, Hessisches Staatsarchiv, Hr 4,7
   60
Merseburg, Dombibliothek, Ms. 103 172,
   226, 232
Milan, Biblioteca Ambrosiana, Ms. G. 58
   sup. 232
Milan, Biblioteca Ambrosiana, Ms. I 145
   inf. 137
Milan, Biblioteca Ambrosiana, Ms. L 28
   sup. 234
Milan, Biblioteca Ambrosiana, Ms. Trotti
   440 234
Monte Cassino, Archivio dell'Abbazia,
   Cod. 372 226
Monte Cassino, Archivio dell'Abbazia,
   Cod. 541 (ext. 541) 135
Monte Cassino, Archivio dell'Abbazia, 554
   (ext. 541) 120
Monte Cassino, Archivio dell'Abbazia,
   Cod. 557 bis 0 234
Montpellier, Bibliothèque
   Interuniversitaire, Médecine 304 235
Montpellier, Bibliothèque Interuniversitaire,
   Médecine H 137 136
Montpellier, Bibliothèque Interuniversitaire,
   Médecine H 387 231

Munich, Bayerische Staatsbibliothek,
   Clm 3851 134, 233, 235
Munich, Bayerische Staatsbibliothek,
   Clm 3852 226
Munich, Bayerische Staatsbibliothek,
   Clm 3853 134, 144, 233, 235
Munich, Bayerische Staatsbibliothek,
   Clm 3909 134, 235
Munich, Bayerische Staatsbibliothek,
   Clm 6241 226
Munich, Bayerische Staatsbibliothek,
   Clm 6243 229
Munich, Bayerische Staatsbibliothek,
   Clm 6245 226
Munich, Bayerisch Staatsbibliothek,
   Clm 6311 232
Munich, Bayerische Staatsbibliothek,
   Clm 6333 112
Munich, Bayerische Staatsbibliothek,
   Clm 12673 232, 235
Munich, Bayerische Staatsbibliothek,
   Clm 12888 60
Munich, Bayerische Staatsbibliothek,
   Clm 14160 203
Munich, Bayerische Staatsbibliothek,
   Clm 14531 233
Munich, Bayerische Staatsbibliothek,
   Clm 14532 138, 235
Munich, Bayerische Staatsbibliothek,
   Clm 14789 226
Munich, Bayerische Staatsbibliothek,
   Clm 17068 233, 235
Munich, Bayerische Staatsbibliothek,
   Clm 17195 235
Munich, Bayerische Staatsbibliothek,
   Clm 18597 203
Munich, Bayerische Staatsbibliothek,
   Clm 22288 97, 227, 229, 231
Munich, Bayerische Staatsbibliothek,
   Clm 28363 203
Munich, Bayerische Staatsbibliothek,
   Clm 29505/1 229
Münster, Staatsarchiv, VII 5201 233, 235

New York, Library of the Hispanic Society
   of America, HC 380/819 171, 230
Nijmegen, Universiteitsbibliotheek Ms. 185
   148
Novara, Biblioteca Capitolare, 18 (LXXI)
   235

Orléans, Bibliothèque municipale 229, 149
Orléans, Bibliothèque municipale, Ms. 216
   (188) 235
Oxford, Baillol College, Ms. 296 203

Oxford, Bodleian Library, Barlow 37 97, 231
Oxford, Bodleian Library, Bodl. 311 60, 76, 103, 160, 226
Oxford, Bodleian Library, Bodl. 516 (2570), 235
Oxford, Bodleian Library, Bodl. 572 110, 230
Oxford, Bodleian Library, Bodl. 718 97, 135, 160, 231
Oxford, Bodleian Library, Junius 121 162
Oxford, Bodleian Library, Laud, Misc. 263 230
Oxford, Bodleian Library, Laud Misc. 482 162
Oxford, Bodleian Library, Ms. Can.Patr. lat. 49 235

Paris, Bibliothèque Nationale de France, lat. 614 a 235
Paris, Bibliothèque Nationale de France, lat. 1603 227
Paris, Bibliothèque Nationale de France, lat. 2077 235
Paris, Bibliothèque Nationale de France, lat. 2123 226
Paris, Bibliothèque Nationale de France, lat. 2296 230
Paris, Bibliothèque Nationale de France, lat. 2341 120, 232, 235
Paris, Bibliothèque Nationale de France, lat. 2373 235
Paris, Bibliothèque Nationale de France, lat. 2843 235
Paris, Bibliothèque Nationale de France, lat. 2998 232, 235
Paris, Bibliothèque Nationale de France, lat. 2999 235
Paris, Bibliothèque Nationale de France, lat. 3182 47, 61
Paris, Bibliothèque Nationale de France, lat. 3842A 227
Paris, Bibliothèque Nationale de France, lat. 3846 227
Paris, Bibliothèque Nationale de France, lat. 3848 B 226
Paris, Bibliothèque Nationale de France, lat. 3878 134, 233, 235
Paris, Bibliothèque Nationale de France, lat. 4283 148
Paris, Bibliothèque Nationale de France, lat. 7193 76, 79, 82
Paris, Bibliothèque Nationale de France, lat. 8508 235

Paris, Bibliothèque Nationale de France, lat. 10588 230
Paris, Bibliothèque Nationale de France, lat. 12021 47
Paris, Bibliothèque Nationale de France, lat. 12315 235
Paris, Bibliothèque Nationale de France, lat. 12444 91, 227
Paris, Bibliothèque Nationale de France, lat. 12445 227
Paris, Bibliothèque Nationale de France, lat. 13246 76, 82
Paris, Bibliothèque Nationale de France, lat. 13452 227
Paris, Bibliothèque Nationale de France, lat. 1454 227
Paris, Bibliothèque Nationale de France, lat. 1455 227
Paris, Bibliothèque Nationale de France, lat. 14993 137
Paris, Bibliothèque Nationale de France, lat. 18220 235
Paris, Bibliothèque Nationale de France, Ms. lat. 13582 211
Paris, Bibliothèque Nationale de France, nouv. acq. lat. 281 112, 173, 226
Prague, Knihovna pražké kapituly, O. LXXXIII 226
Prague, Státni Knihova, Tepla 1 232

Rome, Biblioteca Vallicelliana, E 15 137
Rome, Biblioteca Vallicelliana, F 54 137
Rome, Biblioteca Vallicelliana, T. XVIII 235

Salzburg, Stiftsbibliothek St Peter, Ms. a IX 32 134
Sélestat, Bibliothèque Humaniste, 132 97, 110, 230–1
St Gall, Stiftsbibliothek, Cod. 150 47, 112, 227
St Gall, Stiftsbibliothek, Cod. 184 236
St Gall, Stiftsbibliothek, Cod. 277 236
St Gall, Stiftsbibliothek, Cod. 550 230
St Gall, Stiftsbibliothek, Cod. 570 236
St Gall, Stiftsbibliothek, Cod. 675, 230
St Gall, Stiftsbibliothek, Cod. 676 134, 236
St Gall, Stiftsbibliothek, Cod. 677 97, 231
St Gall, Stiftsbibliothek, Cod. 679 236
St Gall, Stiftsbibliothek, Cod. 682 232
St Petersburg, Publicnaja Biblioteka im. M. E. Saltykova –Ščedrina, Cod. Q. v. I. nr. 34 (Corbie 230) 236
Stuttgart, Württembergische Landesbibliothek, Cod. fragm. 100 A 103

Stuttgart, Württembergische
  Landesbibliothek, Cod. HB VI 107
  134, 227, 236
Stuttgart, Württembergische
  Landesbibliothek, HB VI 109 227
Stuttgart, Württembergische
  Landesbibliothek, HB VI 112 228
Stuttgart, Württembergische
  Landesbibliothek, HB VI 113 230
Stuttgart, Württembergische
  Landesbibliothek, Cod. HB VII 62 135

Trier, Stadtbibliothek, Ms. 1084/115 135
Troyes, Bibliothèque municipale, Ms. 1349
  236
Troyes, Bibliothèque municipale, Ms. 1386
  148
Troyes, Bibliothèque municipale, Ms. 1979
  236
Turin, Biblioteca Nazionale, G. V. 38 55
Turin, Biblioteca Nazionale, G. VII. 16 55

Uppsala, Universitätsbibliothek, Ms. C 60
  208

Vatican, Arch. S. Pietro, H 58 236
Vatican, Biblioteca Apostolica Vaticana,
  Barb. lat. 477 233
Vatican, Biblioteca Apostolica Vaticana,
  Ottob. lat. 3295 133, 236
Vatican, Biblioteca Apostolica Vaticana,
  Pal. lat. 294 97, 231–2
Vatican, Biblioteca Apostolica Vaticana,
  Pal. lat. 485 60, 97, 228, 230–2
Vatican, Biblioteca Apostolica Vaticana,
  Pal. lat. 554 97, 228, 231
Vatican, Biblioteca Apostolica Vaticana,
  Pal. lat. 585 148
Vatican, Biblioteca Apostolica Vaticana,
  Pal. lat. 586 148
Vatican, Biblioteca Apostolica Vaticana,
  Reg. lat. 191 236
Vatican, Biblioteca Apostolica Vaticana,
  Reg. lat. 207 236
Vatican, Biblioteca Apostolica Vaticana,
  Reg. lat. 215 236
Vatican, Biblioteca Apostolica Vaticana,
  Reg. lat. 263 236
Vatican, Biblioteca Apostolica Vaticana,
  Reg. lat. 316 79
Vatican, Biblioteca Apostolica Vaticana,
  Reg. lat. 407 236
Vatican, Biblioteca Apostolica Vaticana,
  Vat. lat. 152 205

Vatican, Biblioteca Apostolica Vaticana,
  Vat. lat. 1339 192
Vatican, Biblioteca Apostolica Vaticana,
  Vat. lat. 1347 135
Vatican, Biblioteca Apostolica Vaticana,
  Vat. lat. 1352 135
Vatican, Biblioteca Apostolica Vaticana,
  Vat. lat. 5751 112, 173, 236
Vendôme, Bibliothèque Municipale,
  Ms. 55 135
Vercelli, Biblioteca Capitolare CXLIII
  (159) 137, 173, 236
Vercelli, Biblioteca Capitolare, CLXXIX
  (152) 137
Vercelli, Biblioteca Capitolare, Ms. CCIII
  (32) 112, 173, 236
Verdun, Bibliothèque municipale, 69 232
Verona, Biblioteca Capitolare, Ms. LXIII
  (61) 233, 236
Vesoul, Bibliothèque municipale, Ms. 79
  (73) 230, 233
Vienna, Österreichische Nationalbibliothek,
  lat. 956 (Theol.320) 236
Vienna, Österreichische Nationalbibliothek,
  lat. 2171 230, 232
Vienna, Österreichische Nationalbibliothek,
  lat. 2195 228, 230
Vienna, Österreichische Nationalbibiothek,
  lat. 2223 97, 112, 228, 231
Vienna, Österreichische Nationalbibliothek,
  lat. 2225 230
Vienna, Österreichische Nationalbibliothek,
  lat. 2231 120
Vienna, Österreichische Nationalbibliothek,
  2233 47

Wolfenbüttel, Herzog August Bibliothek,
  656 (Helmsted.) 133, 237
Wolfenbüttel, Herzog August Bibliothek,
  Cod. Guelf. 141 Helmstadt 155
Würzburg, Priesterseminar, Ms. Membr. 1
  237
Würzburg, Universitätsbibliothek, M. p. th.
  q. 32 228
Würzburg, Universitätsbibliothek,
  M.p.j.q. 2 232

Zürich, Zentralbibliothek, Ms. Car. C 123
  134, 237
Zürich, Zentralbibliothek, Ms. Car. C 176
  138, 231, 237
Zürich, Zentralbibliothek, Ms. Rh. 102
  237
Zurich, Zentralbibliothek, Rh. XXX 230